# Mac OS® X Snow Leopard™

on Demand

## Steve Johnson

**Perspection, Inc.**

Que Publishing, 800 East 96th Street, Indianapolis, IN 46240 USA

# Mac OS® X Snow Leopard™ On Demand

Library of Congress Cataloging-in-Publication Data is on file

ISBN-10: 0-7897-3985-2
ISBN-13: 978-0-7897-3985-8

Printed and bound in the United States of America
First Printing: September 2009
12 11 10 09       4 3 2 1

Que Publishing offers excellent discounts on this book when ordered in quantity for bulk purchases or special sales.

For information, please contact: U.S. Corporate and Government Sales

   1-800-382-3419 or corpsales@pearsontechgroup.com

For sales outside the U.S., please contact: International Sales

   1-317-428-3341 or International@pearsontechgroup.com

**Publisher**
Paul Boger

**Associate Publisher**
Greg Wiegand

**Acquisitions Editor**
Laura Norman

**Managing Editor**
Steve Johnson

**Author**
Steve Johnson

**Technical Editor**
Beth Teyler

**Page Layout**
James Teyler

**Interior Designers**
Steve Johnson
Marian Hartsough

**Photographs**
Tracy Teyler

**Indexer**
Katherine Stimson

**Proofreader**
Beth Teyler

**Team Coordinator**
Cindy Teeters

# Acknowledgements

a

## Perspection, Inc.

*Mac OS X Snow Leopard On Demand* has been created by the professional trainers and writers at Perspection, Inc. to the standards you've come to expect from Que publishing. Together, we are pleased to present this training book.

Perspection, Inc. is a software training company committed to providing information and training to help people use software more effectively in order to communicate, make decisions, and solve problems. Perspection writes and produces software training books, and develops multimedia and Web-based training. Since 1991, we have written more than 100 computer books, with several bestsellers to our credit, and sold over 5 million books.

This book incorporates Perspection's training expertise to ensure that you'll receive the maximum return on your time. You'll focus on the tasks and skills that increase productivity while working at your own pace and convenience.

We invite you to visit the Perspection Web site at:

*www.perspection.com*

## Acknowledgements

The task of creating any book requires the talents of many hard-working people pulling together to meet impossible deadlines and untold stresses. We'd like to thank the outstanding team responsible for making this book possible: the writer, Steve Johnson; the technical editor, Beth Teyler; the production editor, James Teyler; proofer reader, Beth Teyler; and the indexer, Katherine Stimson. We'd also like to thank Alan Greth for his contributions to the book.

At Que publishing, we'd like to thank Greg Wicgand and Laura Norman for the opportunity to undertake this project, Cindy Teeters for administrative support, and Sandra Schroeder for your production expertise and support.

*Perspection*

## About The Author

**Steve Johnson** has written more than 50 books on a variety of computer software, including Adobe Photoshop CS4 and CS3, Adobe Flash CS4 and CS3, Dreamweaver CS4 and CS3, Adobe InDesign CS4, Adobe Illustrator CS4, Microsoft Office 2007 and 2003, Microsoft Windows Vista and XP, Microsoft Expression 2, Microsoft Office 2008 for the Macintosh, and Apple Mac OS X Leopard. In 1991, after working for Apple Computer and Microsoft, Steve founded Perspection, Inc., which writes and produces software training. When he is not staying up late writing, he enjoys playing golf, gardening, and spending time with his wife, Holly, and three children, JP, Brett, and Hannah. Steve and his family live in Pleasanton, California, but can also be found visiting family all over the western United States.

# We Want To Hear From You!

As the reader of this book, *you* are our most important critic and commentator. We value your opinion and want to know what we're doing right, what we could do better, what areas you'd like to see us publish in, and any other words of wisdom you're willing to pass our way.

As an associate publisher for Que, I welcome your comments. You can email or write me directly to let me know what you did or didn't like about this book—as well as what we can do to make our books better.

Please note that I cannot help you with technical problems related to the topic of this book. We do have a User Services group, however, where I will forward specific technical questions related to the book.

When you write, please be sure to include this book's title and author as well as your name, email address, and phone number. I will carefully review your comments and share them with the author and editors who worked on the book.

Email:   feedback@quepublishing.com

Mail:    Greg Wiegand
         Que Publishing
         800 East 96th Street
         Indianapolis, IN 46240 USA

For more information about this book or another Que title, visit our Web site at *informit.com/register*. Type the ISBN (excluding hyphens) or the title of a book in the Search field to find the page you're looking for.

# Contents

C

**6  Using Mac OS X Applications                  129**

# Introduction

Welcome to *Mac OS X Snow Leopard On Demand*, a visual quick reference book that shows you how to work efficiently with Apple Mac OS X Snow Leopard. This book provides complete coverage of basic to advanced Mac OS X skills.

## How This Book Works

You don't have to read this book in any particular order. We've designed the book so that you can jump in, get the information you need, and jump out. However, the book does follow a logical progression from simple tasks to more complex ones. Each task is presented on no more than two facing pages, which lets you focus on a single task without having to turn the page. To find the information that you need, just look up the task in the table of contents or index, and turn to the page listed. Read the task introduction, follow the step-by-step instructions in the left column along with screen illustrations in the right column, and you're done.

## What's New

If you're searching for what's new in Mac OS X Snow Leopard, just look for the icon: **New!**. The new icon appears in the table of contents and throughout this book so you can quickly and easily identify a new or improved feature in Snow Leopard. A complete description of each new feature appears in the New Features guide in the back of this book.

## Keyboard Shortcuts

Most menu commands have a keyboard equivalent, such as ⌘+P, as a quicker alternative to using the mouse. A complete list of keyboard shortcuts is available on the Web at *www.perspection.com*.

## How You'll Learn

**How This Book Works**

**What's New**

**Keyboard Shortcuts**

**Step-by-Step Instructions**

**Real World Examples**

**Workshop**

**Get More on the Web**

## Step-by-Step Instructions

This book provides concise step-by-step instructions that show you "how" to accomplish a task. Each set of instructions includes illustrations that directly correspond to the easy-to-read steps. Also included in the text are time-savers, tables, and sidebars to help you work more efficiently or to teach you more in-depth information. A "Did You Know?" provides tips and techniques to help you work smarter, while a "See Also" leads you to other parts of the book containing related information about the task.

**Easy-to-follow introductions** focus on a single concept.

**Illustrations** match the numbered steps.

**Numbered steps** guide you through each task.

**See Also** points you to related information in the book.

**Did You Know?** alerts you to tips, techniques and related information.

## Real World Examples

This book uses real world examples files to give you a context in which to use the task. By using the example files, you won't waste time looking for or creating sample files. You get a start file and a result file, so you can compare your work. Not every topic needs an example file, such as changing options, so we provide a complete list of the example files used through out the book. The example files that you need for project tasks along with a complete file list are available on the Web at *www.perspection.com*.

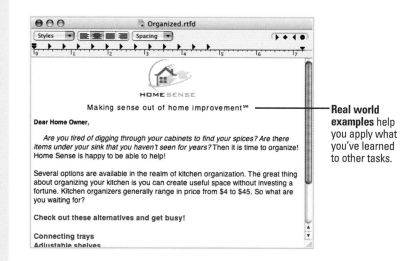

**Real world examples** help you apply what you've learned to other tasks.

# Workshops

This book shows you how to put together the individual step-by-step tasks into in-depth projects with the Workshop. You start each project with a sample file, work through the steps, and then compare your results with project results file at the end. The Workshop projects and associated files are available on the Web at www.perspection.com.

# Get More on the Web

In addition to the information in this book, you can also get more information on the Web to help you get up to speed faster with Mac OS X. Some of the information includes:

## Transition Helpers

◆ **Only New Features.** Download and print the new feature tasks as a quick and easy guide.

## Productivity Tools

◆ **Keyboard Shortcuts.** Download a list of keyboard shortcuts to learn faster ways to get the job done.

The **Workshops** walks you through in-depth projects to help you put the Mac OS X Snow Leopard to work.

**Additional content** is available on the Web.

## More Content

- ◆ **Photographs.** Download photographs and other graphics to use in your documents.

- ◆ **More Content.** Download new content developed after publication, such as a chapter on *Using Basic Unix Commands*.

You can access these additional resources on the Web at *www.perspection.com.*

Download and use **Photographs** to help you add impact to your documents.

# Getting Started with Mac OS X Snow Leopard

1

## Introduction

Mac OS X Snow Leopard is an **operating system (OS)**, a computer program that controls the basic operation of your Macintosh computer and the programs you run. A **program**, also known as an application, is task-oriented software you use to accomplish a specific task, such as word processing, managing files on your computer, or performing calculations.

The **Finder** is part of the Mac OS and starts when you turn on your computer. The Finder displays a menu bar and desktop on your screen that you can use to work with windows, icons, and files. A **window** can contain the contents of a file and the application in which it was created, icons (picture representations of an application or a file), or other usable data. This use of windows and icons is called a **graphical user interface** (**GUI**, pronounced "gooey"), meaning that you ("user") interact ("interface") with the computer through the use of graphics: icons and other meaningful words, symbols, and windows. A **file** is a collection of information (such as a letter or list of addresses) that has a unique name, distinguishing it from other files. You can use the Finder to open, copy, delete, list, and organize your computer files.

When you turn on your Macintosh computer, the Finder might ask you to log in. Your Macintosh is built to share with other people and work with other computers. If you are sharing your computer with others or accessing other computers over a network, you need to log in (type a user name and password) and log out to switch users or access information. When you're done working on your computer, you should put it to sleep for short periods or shut it down for longer stints.

# Starting Mac OS X

Mac OS X automatically starts when you turn on your computer. When you first start Mac OS X, you see the desktop screen, or a Login window depending on your installation. The Mac OS X desktop screen indicates you are using a stand-alone computer (you're the only person using the computer), while the Login window identifies you're on a shared computer. After you click or type your user name in the Login window, and then possibly type a password, you'll see the Mac OS X desktop.

## Start Mac OS X Using a Stand Alone Computer

 Turn on your computer, and then wait while Mac OS X loads.

The Mac OS X Snow Leopard desktop screen appears.

### Did You Know?

***The Login window doesn't always appear.*** If Mac OS X is set up to log in automatically, you don't normally see the Login window. However, if you select the Log Out command from the Apple menu, you do see the Login window. If you see the Login window, click Restart to log in again automatically.

### See Also

*See "Adding a User Account" on page 388 for information on creating a user account.*

*See "Activating the Login Window" on page 387 for information on changing log in options.*

Desktop          Your system's hard drive

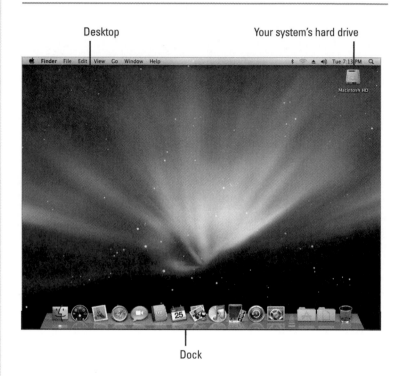

Dock

## For Your Information

### Creating a Shared Computer

During the Mac OS X Snow Leopard installation process, you create a user account for the computer administrator and possibility other accounts for each person who uses your computer. An administrator account can create other user accounts, install software, and change computer settings. When you create accounts for more than one account, your computer changes from a stand-alone computer to a shared computer. Each user maintains separate files, a home folder, and preferences without affecting other users.

## Start Mac OS X Using a Shared Computer

① Turn on your computer and wait while Mac OS X loads.

The Login window opens.

② Click or type your user name.

③ Type your password. Be sure to use the correct capitalization.

④ Click **Log In**.

**TROUBLE?** *If you forget your password, your third attempt to type the password correctly displays your password hint, and a Reset button, where you can use the administrator's master password to create a new password.*

### Did You Know?

***The password is case-sensitive.*** Macintosh makes a distinction between uppercase and lowercase letters. Your password should be at least seven characters long, the optimal length for encryption, which is the process of logically scrambling data to keep a password secure.

***You can set up your computer to automatically log in (by pass the Login window).*** Click the Apple menu, click System Preferences, click Accounts, and then select the administrator account. Next, click Login Options, select the Automatically Login pop-up, and then click an account. Type a password, and then click OK.

***You can sleep, restart, and shut down from the Login window.*** In the Login window, click Sleep, Restart, or Shut Down, and then click the appropriate button or wait 60 seconds.

Login window

# Exploring the Finder and Desktop

When you first start Mac OS X Snow Leopard, you see the Finder desktop with a new transparent look and feel, or a log in screen (a way to identify yourself on the computer), depending on your installation. The desktop is an on-screen version of an actual desk, containing windows, icons, files, and applications. You can use the desktop to access, store, organize, modify, share, and explore information (such as a letter or a list of addresses), whether it resides on your computer, a network, or the Internet. The desktop contains icons that represent volumes (such as your Hard Disk to store data), applications, documents, folders, and the Trash. If you upgraded your computer to Mac OS X from a previous version, your desktop might contain many different icons. These icons can also appear a number of different ways depending on your view. When you open an icon, a window or application appears, displaying its contents or an application work environment. The bar at the bottom

Menu bar

Menu status area

Finder window

Background picture on the desktop

Dock

of the desktop is called the **Dock** (if it's hidden, point to the bottom of the screen to display it); it allows you to start applications and switch among currently running ones. At the top of the screen is a menu bar, which contain commands you use to perform tasks and customize your environment. At the right end of the menu bar is the menu status area, which displays the time, date, current user, and application related icons—including Spotlight, AirPort, Volume, Eject, and Bluetooth to name

a few. Your list of icons may differ depending on the applications you have installed. The new Mac OS X Snow Leopard dynamic user interface includes a transparent look and feel with design themes and a reflective floor for the Dock. A **design theme** is a professionally designed look and feel that coordinates all aspects of the user interface, including the desktop, menus, and windows.

Fast user switching

Desktop icons

Open application window

Application windows

Application commands

Open Application icon in the Dock

# Using the Mouse

A **mouse** is a handheld input device you roll across a flat surface (such as a desk or a mouse pad) to position the **mouse pointer**, the small symbol that indicates the pointer's relative position on the desktop. When you move the mouse, the mouse pointer on the screen moves in the same direction. The shape of the mouse pointer changes to indicate different activities. However, the pointer usually looks like an arrow pointer in the Finder. Once you move the mouse pointer (the arrow's tip) to a desired position on the screen, you use the mouse button to tell your computer what you want it to do. Macintosh computers typically come with a mouse that contains a single button. However, you can use a mouse with two buttons (left and right), trackball device, or writing tablet to perform the same function. For a two button mouse, such as the Apple Mighty Mouse, the left button performs the same function as the single button.

Dragging

Mouse pointer

Clicking

## Basic Mouse Techniques

| Task | What to do |
| --- | --- |
| Pointing | Move the mouse to position it over an item. |
| Clicking | Press and release the mouse button. |
| Double-clicking | Press and release the mouse button twice quickly. |
| Dragging | Point to an item, press and hold the mouse button, move the mouse to a new location, and then release the mouse button. |
| Pressing | Press and hold the mouse button. |

# Working with Menus, Toolbars, and Panes

A **menu** is a list of commands that you use to accomplish certain tasks, such as when you use the View menu to open the Customize Toolbar dialog. A **command** is a directive that provides access to an application's features. Each application has its own set of menus, which are on the menu bar along the top of the application window. The menu bar organizes commands into groups of related operations. Each group is listed under the name of the menu, such as File or Help. To access the commands in a menu, you click the name of the menu, and then click the command name. If a menu command is gray, the option is not available at this time; availability depends on what is selected. If a command on a menu includes a keyboard reference, known as a **keyboard shortcut**, such as ⌘+1 for the As Icons command, you can perform the action by pressing and holding the first key, and

then pressing the second key to perform the command quickly. When a menu command is followed by an ellipse (...), a dialog appears when you select it. On a menu, a **check mark** identifies a currently selected feature, meaning that the feature is enabled, or turned on. To disable, or turn off the feature, you click the command again to remove the check mark, or you can select another command (within the menu section, separated by gray lines) in its place. You can also carry out some of the most frequently used commands on a menu by clicking a button on a toolbar. A **toolbar** contains buttons that are convenient shortcuts for menu commands and navigation. A **pane** is a frame within a window, such as a Sidebar, where you can quickly access navigation controls. You can use menus, toolbar buttons, and commands in a pane to change how a window's contents appear.

# Using Menus for Quick Results

The Finder uses several different types of menus to help you use the commands you need to get the results you want. The Finder uses four types of menus: pull-down, submenu, pop-up, and contextual. The **pull down** menu appears on the menu bar when you click a menu name or status icon in the menu status area. A **submenu** appears when you point to a menu with a triangle. A **pop-up** menu appears in a window or dialog when you click the double arrow. A **contextual** menu appears when you hold down the Control key while you click an item, such as an icon, text, or graphic. A contextual menu displays a list of commands related to the selected item, like the Action pop-up menu. When you click a menu name, the menu stays open. If you don't want to select a menu command, you can click outside the menu or press the Esc key to close it.

## Use a Pull Down Menu

1. Point to the name or menu status icon on the menu bar, and then click to open the menu.

2. Point to the menu option you want.

3. If a submenu opens, point to the menu option you want.

4. Click to select the command.

### Did You Know?

*You can rearrange menu status icons on the menu bar.* Press and hold ⌘, and then drag the icon to reposition it.

## Use a Contextual Menu

1. Point to the item on which you want to act upon.

2. Press and hold down the Control key, and then click to display a contextual menu.

   If you are using a mouse with two buttons, right-click the item.

3. Select the command you want.

Pull down menu    Menu status icons

Submenu   3

# Choosing Dialog Options

The Finder and Mac OS X applications use dialogs to carry out options, provide alert messages, and gather information. A **dialog** is a window that opens when the Finder or an application wants to alert you of an event, or you select a menu command or button followed by an ellipsis. In a dialog, you acknowledge an alert message or select various options, and then provide information for completing the command.

## Choose Dialog Options

All dialogs contain the same types of options, including the following:

◆ **Tabs.** Click a tab to display its options. Each tab groups a related set of options.

◆ **Option buttons.** Click an option button to select it. You can usually select only one in a group.

◆ **Check box.** Click the box to turn on or off the option. A checked box means the option is selected; a cleared box means it's not.

◆ **Pop-up menu.** Click the arrow to display a list of commands or options, and then click the one you want.

◆ **Entry field.** Click in the field, and then type the requested information.

◆ **Up and down arrows.** Click the up or down arrow to increase or decrease the number, or type a number in the field.

◆ **Scroll bar.** Drag a slider control to change screen position.

◆ **Preview area.** Many dialogs show an image that reflects the options you select.

◆ **Slider.** Drag a slider control to change a screen position.

◆ **Push button.** Click a button to perform an action or command. A button name followed by an ellipsis (...) opens another dialog.

Option button    Pop-up menu

Check box

Entry field

Push buttons

Help button    Opens a different dialog

## For Your Information

### Navigating and Working in a Dialog

Rather than clicking to move around a dialog, you can press the Tab key to move from one field to the next. You can also use Shift+Tab to move backward. When a field appears with a dark border around it, the text you type appears in the active field. The default button is the one that appears highlighted. You can press the Return key to perform the default button. If you decide not to use options you set in a dialog, you can press the Esc key to perform the Cancel button and disregard the options. Before you can use the keyboard shortcuts, you need to turn on the option. Click the Apple menu, click Preferences, and then click the Keyboard icon. Click the Keyboard Shortcuts tab, select the Turn On Full Keyboard Access check box, and then click the Close button.

# Working with Icons

Mac OS X uses various icons to graphically represent different items on the desktop, in the Dock, or in a window. The icons represent applications, documents, folders, volumes, and the Trash. **Application icons** are programs you use to create documents. **Document icons** are files you create with applications. **Folder icons** are a storage area for files. **Volume icons** are storage devices, such as hard disks, removable disks, network disks, Internet computers, CDs, DVDs, and iPods. The **Trash icon** (located in the Dock) appears in three different ways: empty, full, and ejecting removable media. On the desktop or within a window, you can select and deselect one or more icons to perform tasks, such as opening, launching, copying, and moving. When you select an icon, the icon graphic and its name become highlighted. Within a Finder window, icons appear in different ways, depending on the window view you select.

## Select Icons

◆ **Select an icon.** Click the icon you want to select.

◆ **Select multiple icons by clicking.** Click the first icon you want to select, hold down ⌘, and then click the other icons you want to select within the same window.

> **TIMESAVER** *Click the first icon, press the Shift key, and then click the last one to select every icon in between.*

◆ **Select multiple icons by dragging.** Position the mouse pointer to the left of the first icon you want to select, drag diagonally across the adjacent icons you want to select, and then release the mouse button.

A shaded box appears as you drag to indicate the selection area.

◆ **Select all icons.** Click the Edit menu, and then click Select All.

> **TIMESAVER** *Press ⌘+A to select all icons.*

Start dragging here

Selection rectangle

Select multiple icons by dragging

Select multiple icons by clicking

10

## Deselect Icons

◆ **Deselect all icons.** Click a blank area in the window or on the desktop.

◆ **Deselect an icon in a multiple selection.** Press and hold down ⌘, and then click the icon you want to deselect, while keeping the others selected.

Deselect all icons

## Move or Copy Icons

① To move multiple icons, select the ones you want to move; to copy an icon, hold down the Option key.

② Point to the icons, and then drag them to the new location.

As you drag, a shaded image of the icon moves along with the mouse pointer.

**TROUBLE?** *Press the Esc key to cancel the move or copy.*

③ Release the mouse button and the Option key, if necessary.

**TIMESAVER** *Press ⌘+X to move or press ⌘+C to copy selected icons; and then press ⌘+V to paste them.*

Move icons

---

### Did You Know?

***You can change the icon view size.*** In as Icons view, drag the Zoom control on the Status bar (**New!**).

---

### For Your Information

#### Viewing Content in Icons

When you display a multi-page document or a QuickTime movie file in Icon view, you can thumb through the document or watch the movie (**New!**). When you point to a multi-page document, such as a PDF, or a QuickTime move (.MOV), the thumbnail displays Previous and Next buttons or Play/Pause button, which you can click to view or play it as a thumbnail preview. The icon preview is also available in the Preview pane in Column and Cover Flow views (**New!**).

# Viewing Windows

A window displays icons and other information in the Finder, and documents in an application. One of the powerful things about the Mac OS X is that you can open more than one window or application at once. You can identify a window by its name on the title bar at the top of the window. Before you can work with a window, you need to activate it first. The active window is the one in front with the available buttons (red, yellow, and green) in the upper-left corner. When you're done using a window, you can quickly close it to reduce the clutter on the desktop.

## Parts of a Window

Windows in Mac OS X consist of the following parts:

◆ **Close button.** Closes the window.

◆ **Minimize button.** Shrinks the window to an icon in the Dock.

◆ **Zoom button.** Toggles the window size between full and a custom size.

◆ **Title bar.** Displays the name of the window.

◆ **Toolbar Control button.** Toggles the toolbar on and off.

◆ **Toolbar.** Displays buttons and controls for commonly used window commands.

◆ **Size control.** Allows you to set a custom window size.

◆ **Zoom control (New!).** Allows you to set a view percentage in as Icons view.

◆ **Status bar.** Displays information about selected items.

◆ **Sidebar.** Displays commonly used volumes and folders.

◆ **Column heading.** Displays the names of columns and sorts them (in list view only).

◆ **Search box.** Allows you to find files based on the name.

◆ **Scroll bar.** Displays the content of the window.

## Open and Close a Window

◆ **Open a Finder window.** Double-click a volume or folder icon.

◆ **Open a new Finder window.** Click the File menu, and then click New Finder Window.

◆ **Close a window.** Click the red button to close the window, or hold down the Option key, and then click the red button to close all windows.

> **TIMESAVER** *If you see a dot in the center of the Close button, you need to save your changes.*

Click to close window          Double-click to open Finder window

New Finder window

## Activate a Window

◆ **Activate a window.** Click anywhere on the window, or click the Window menu, and then click the window name.

◆ **Activate and bring all Finder windows to front**. Click the Window menu, and then click Bring All To Front. All open Finder windows that are not minimized are moved in front of application windows.

◆ **Activate and bring a specific application window to the front.** Display the Dock, press (click and hold) an application icon to display a menu, and then select the window you want to make active.

Active window

# Managing Windows

When you open multiple windows, your desktop can get cluttered with many open windows for the various applications you are using. To organize your desktop, you may need to move it to a different location or change the size of a window. Each window has resize buttons in the upper-left corner to minimize or zoom a window, and a size control in the lower right-corner that you can use to resize the window to a custom size. An icon appears in the Dock for each minimized window, which you can use to quickly switch between windows or redisplay it. You can also press and hold the Finder icon to use Exposé (**New!**) or Control-click it to switch between open windows.

## Switch Among Open Windows

① Display the Dock, if hidden.

② Press (click and hold) activate Exposé or Control-click the Finder or an application icon to display a menu.

③ Click the window you want from the menu.

### See Also

*See "Customizing Exposé" on page 92 for information on temporarily showing and hiding all windows.*

## Move a Window

① Point to the window's title bar.

② Drag the window to a new location, and then release the mouse button.

**TIMESAVER** *Hold down the A key while you drag the title bar of an inactive window to move it without making it active.*

## Use Buttons to Resize a Window

All windows contain the same sizing buttons:

◆ **Minimize button (active window).** Click the yellow button to shrink a window as an icon in the Dock, or double-click the title bar.

**TIMESAVER** *Press ⌘+M to minimize the active window.*

◆ **Minimize button (all windows).** Hold down the Option key, and then click the yellow button or double-click the title bar to minimize all windows.

◆ **Redisplay minimized window.** Click the window's icon in the Dock or click the Window menu, and then click the window's name.

◆ **Zoom button.** Click the green button to toggle between the smallest possible size that fits on your screen, and the size you set with the size control.

Minimize button
Zoom button

Minimized window

## Use the Mouse to Resize a Window

1 Move the mouse over the size control in the lower-right corner of the window.

2 Drag the size control until the window is the size you want.

# Using the Sidebar

The Sidebar is a panel which appears in the left column of Finder windows, that you can use to quickly access commonly used locations on your computer. The panel appears with multiple sections, including Devices, Shared, Places, and Search For. The Devices section contains items for volumes attached to your computer, including your hard disk. The Shared section contains shared and networked computers. The Places section contains items for folders, including your home folder (labeled with your name), Desktop, Applications, and Documents. The Search For section contains items for Smart folders. You can use the Sidebar to move and copy documents to disks and folders on or connected to your computer, eject removable disks, and burn a CD or DVD.

## Use the Sidebar

◆ **Display icons.** Click icons in the Sidebar to display contents.

◆ **Move or copy icons.** Drag the folder or document icons from the Contents pane to the Sidebar icon in order to move or copy them.

◆ **Add a file, folder or application.** Drag its icon to the Places area.

◆ **Remove icon.** Drag its icon out of the Sidebar.

◆ **Change column width.** Position the mouse pointer over the divider, and then drag to change the width.

◆ **Hide or show sidebar and toolbar.** Click the oval button in the upper-right corner of the window.

◆ **Hide or show sidebar.** Click the **View** menu, then click **Hide Sidebar** or **Show Sidebar** (**New!**).

◆ **Eject a disk.** Click the **Eject** button next to any removable disk.

◆ **Burn a CD.** Insert a blank CD or DVD, drag files and folders to it, and then click the **Burn** button (looks like a beach ball).

## See Also

*See "Customizing the Sidebar" on page 86 for information on using Finder preferences to customize the Sidebar.*

Eject button

Sidebar          Drag here to change width.

# Using Toolbars

The toolbar, in a Finder window, provides easy access to commonly used window commands. You can use the Toolbar Control button three different ways: to hide the toolbar and sidebar, to display more information in the window, or to show the toolbar to display tools and navigational controls. When you hide the toolbar, the Finder also hides the Sidebar panel and window borders, and moves the status bar to display under the title bar.

## Parts of a Toolbar

Toolbars in the Finder consist of the following parts:

◆ **Back and Forward buttons.** Displays the content from the previous or next window.

◆ **View buttons.** Displays the window in different views.

◆ **Quick Look button.** Displays an expanded slide show view for selected items.

◆ **Action pop-up menu.** Displays commands for working with a window or selected items.

◆ **Search box.** Allows you to search for a file by name.

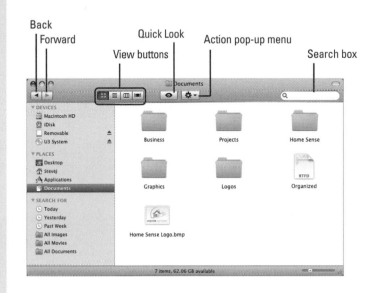

## Show or Hide the Toolbar and Sidebar

① Click the **Toolbar Control** button in the upper-right corner of the window to toggle between them.

> **TIMESAVER** *Hold down the* ⌘ *key while you repeatedly click the Toolbar Control button to display various toolbar styles.*

If a double arrow appears at the right side of the toolbar, the window is too small to show all the icons. You can either resize the window, or click the double arrow, and then select a toolbar item.

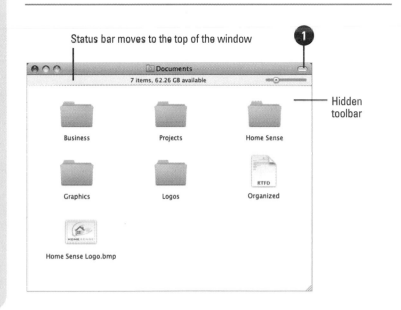

# Displaying and Using the Dock

The Dock is a bar at the bottom of the screen that you can use to open frequently used applications and utilities, system preferences, Web sites and the Trash, as well as redisplay minimized applications and Finder windows. If you don't see the Dock at the bottom of your screen, then its automatically hidden. You can change an option in the Dock pane of System Preferences to always display the Dock. The Dock has two sides with a divider line separating the two. The left side is for applications and the right side is for everything else: stacks, files, documents, folders, and disks. When you point to an icon, its name appears above it. Document and folder icons in the Dock actually display an image of the contents to make it a little easier to distinguish between them. When you click an icon, it launches or opens it. When you launch an application, it's icon appears in the Dock with a shinny image below it. When you press and hold an icon, a list of commands appears on a menu or in Exposé (**New!**). When you quit an application or window not permanently placed in the Dock, its icon is removed from the Dock. In addition to the predefined icons in the Dock, you can also quickly and permanently add your own icons in the Dock.

## Display and Use the Dock

- **Display a hidden Dock.** Move the mouse pointer to the bottom or side of the screen.

- **Open, launch or redisplay a minimized item.** Click its icon.

- **Choose commands for an item.** Press and hold or Control-click the icon in the Dock, and then click a command.

- **Choose commands for an open item.** Press and hold (activates Exposé (**New!**)) or Control-click the open icon in the Dock, and then click a command.

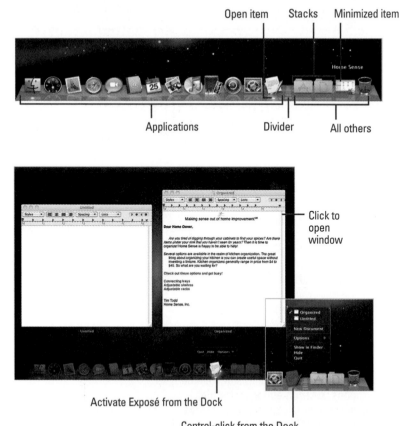

Open item   Stacks   Minimized item

Applications          Divider      All others

Click to open window

Activate Exposé from the Dock

Control-click from the Dock

## Did You Know?

*You can turn Dock hiding off and on.* Click the Apple menu, point to Dock, and then click Turn Hiding Off or Turn Hiding On.

*You can quickly switch between applications in the Dock.* Hold down ⌘, and then repeatedly press the Tab key. Release the keys to switch.

# Displaying and Using Stacks on the Dock

Folders in the Dock are called **stacks**. You can use stacks to reduce clutter and quickly access folders of documents, applications, and other folders. When you click a stack in the Dock, it springs open to display an arc or a grid of icons for the items in the stack. You can scroll through stacks, open folders, and navigate back (**New!**). The Dock comes with two stacks, the Applications (**New!**) and Downloads folders, which stores OS X applications and downloaded items from the Internet. You can create more stacks by dragging the folder you want to the Dock and modify stacks by Control-clicking it in the Dock.

## Work with Stacks on the Dock

◆ **Display a stack.** Click a folder in the Dock.

◆ **Open the stack folder.** Control-click the folder in the Dock, and then click **Show in Finder** or **Open "name"**.

◆ **Open an item in a stack folder.** Click the folder in the Dock, and then click the item. If you click a folder in Grid view, you can click the return path icon in the upper left of the stack to return (**New!**).

◆ **Add a stack to the Dock.** Drag the folder to the Dock.

◆ **Remove a stack from the Dock.** Control-click the folder in the Dock, and then click **Remove from Dock**.

◆ **Change the stack display.** Control-click the folder in the Dock, and then click **Automatic**, **List** (**New!**), **Grid**, or **Fan**. Automatic displays in a fan or grid depending on available space.

◆ **Change stack icon in the Dock.** Control-click the folder or stack in the Dock, and then click **Folder** or **Stack** (**New!**).

◆ **Sort items in a stack.** Control-click the folder in the Dock, and then select the sort type (under Sort by) you want.

Fan stack for Documents folder

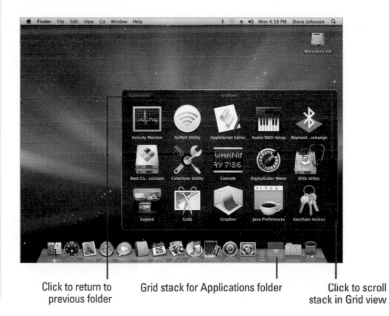

Click to return to previous folder  Grid stack for Applications folder  Click to scroll stack in Grid view

# Exposing Windows

When you have multiple windows and applications open at the same time, the screen can get cluttered and make it difficult to work. Exposé lets you quickly move (temporarily) windows out of the way to make it easier to work with windows to find, move, or copy files. You can quickly hide all the open windows to see your desktop, or show all open windows or all open windows in the current application at the same time. When you press any of the Exposé keys quickly, the windows (hidden or shown) stay active using Exposé until you press the key again. However, if you press and hold the keys to use Exposé, the windows return to normal when you release the keys. When you're using Exposé, you can point to a window to see its name and hold the pointer over it or click the window to bring it to the front.

## Use Exposé

◆ **Show all open windows at once.** Press the F9 key. When you're done, press the F9 key again.

   For temporary use, hold down the F9 key, and then release.

◆ **Show all open windows in the current application.** Press the F10 key. When you're done, press the F10 key again.

   For temporary use, hold down the F10 key, and then release.

◆ **Hide all open windows (show desktop).** Press the F11 key. When you're done, press the F11 key again. .

   For temporary use, hold down the F11 key, and then release.

◆ **Display a window name.** Exposé (F9) all open windows, and then point to a window.

◆ **Activate a window.** Exposé (F9) all open windows, and then click or hold your pointer over a window to bring it to the front and release Exposé.

◆ **Activate an application window from the Dock.** Press and hold an open application icon in the Dock (**New!**). Press Tab to move to the next application.

Shows all open windows at once

Display a window name

Click to open window

Click to select an option

Activate Exposé from the Dock

# Grouping Windows into Spaces

With Spaces, you can group and arrange windows to reduce desktop clutter and organize materials into unique spaces. You can organize home, work, or other projects into different spaces. You can quickly view and select the space you want or toggle between them. Each space displays only the windows for that space. You can spread out your work in different spaces by assigning an application to a space from its icon in the Dock (**New!**). Spaces also works well with Exposé to make working with different projects easier. The first time you start Spaces, you need to setup your spaces in Exposé & Spaces preferences, where you can also change keyboard shortcuts and display a Spaces menu in the menu bar.

## Group Windows into Spaces

◆ **Switch Spaces.** Click the **Spaces** icon in the Dock or press the F8 key, and then click the space you want. If a setup dialog box appears, click **Set Up Spaces**.

   See "Setting Up and Customizing Spaces" on page 93.

◆ **View a space.** Press the Control key and the number key for the space you want, or press the arrow keys to scroll the spaces.

◆ **View all windows in all spaces.** Press F8 to view all your spaces, and then press F9 to see all your windows within each space. This uses Spaces and Exposé.

◆ **Arrange spaces.** Press the F8 key to view all your spaces, and then drag the spaces.

◆ **Move a window between spaces.** Press the F8 key to view all your spaces, and then drag the window to the new space.

   Drag the window to the edge of your screen and pause for a moment, then the window is switched to the new space.

   Move the point over the window, and hold down the mouse button while pressing the Control key and an arrow or number key.

View spaces

Move between spaces

# Switching Users

Many users can use the same computer. Their individual Mac OS X accounts allow them to keep their files completely private and to customize the operating system with their own preferences. Mac OS X manages these separate accounts by giving each user a unique user name and password. When a user selects an account and types a password (if necessary), Mac OS X starts with that user's configuration settings and network permissions. When you want to change users, you can logout, which closes all running applications, saves your settings, and signs you off the computer. Or, switch users, which quickly switches between users without having to logout, close applications, and save your current settings. With fast user switching, the name of the current user appears in the status menu area, where you can quickly switch to a new user. If you leave your computer unattended for any period of time, you can set additional security logout options to protect your information.

## Fast User Switching

1. Click the *user name* in the upper-right corner of the menu bar.

2. Click the user account to which you want to switch.

   The name grayed out is the current user, and an orange check mark next to a name indicates that another is logged in.

   If required, a Login window opens, requesting a password.

3. If necessary, type your password.

4. Click **Log In**.

   The computer switches to the new user's desktop (like a box switching sides), which includes the user's home folder, mail, and personal settings.

### See Also

*See "Setting Fast User Switching" on page 396 for information on enabling Fast User Switching.*

Another user logged in ①

Current user

## Logout of Your Computer

1. Click the **Apple** menu, and then click **Log Out** *user name*.

   **TIMESAVER** *Press Shift+⌘+Q to log off. If you press the Option key while you select the Log Out menu command, Mac OS X skips the confirmation dialog.*

2. Click **Log Out** or wait 60 seconds to close all your applications, save your settings, and sign yourself off the computer.

   A Login window appears, displaying user accounts.

3. Click your name.

4. If required, type your password, and then click **Log In**.

Counts down from 60 seconds until automatic log out.

## Set Logout Security Options

1. Click the **System Preferences** icon in the Dock, and then click the **Security** icon.

2. Click the **General** tab.

3. Select or clear the **Require password X after sleep or screen saver begins** check box, and then specify a time delay before the password is required (**New!**).

4. Select or clear the **Log out after X minutes of inactivity** check box, and then enter the number of minutes you want.

   **IMPORTANT** *If any dialogs for unsaved documents or open applications appear, your computer will not log you out.*

5. Click the **Close** button.

# Sleeping, Restarting, and Shutting Down

When you finish working on your computer, you can put your computer to sleep for a little while or shut it down for longer periods of inactivity. Sleeping causes your computer screen to go blank and halt the spinning of your hard disk. Shutting down your computer causes Mac OS X to properly save and close all open files, close all open windows, quit all running applications, and finally, turn off the Macintosh itself. If you turn off the computer by pushing the power switch while Mac OS X or other applications are running, you could lose important data and cause system problems; shutting down correctly avoids these potential problems. Snow Leopard provides faster shut down and wake-up (**New!**).

## Sleep, Restart, or Shut Down

When you're done working on your computer, do one of the following:

◆ Sleep. Click the **Apple** menu, and then click **Sleep**.

   IMPORTANT *When your computer is inactive for 20 minutes (the default), Mac OS X automatically puts your computer to sleep.*

   To wake up your computer, click the mouse button or press any keyboard key.

◆ Restart. Click the **Apple** menu, and then click **Restart**. Click the Restart button or wait 60 seconds.

◆ Shut Down. Click the **Apple** menu, and then click **Shut Down**. Click the Shut Down button or wait 60 seconds.

   If other users are logged in, type the administrator name and password, and then click **Shut Down**.

   IMPORTANT *If you press the Option key while you select the Restart or Shut Down command, Mac OS X skips the dialog.*

   IMPORTANT *If your computer has a power key, you can press it to display a dialog with Sleep, Restart, and Shut Down buttons.*

| | |
|---|---|
| About This Mac | |
| Software Update… | |
| Mac OS X Software… | |
| System Preferences… | |
| Dock | ▶ |
| Recent Items | ▶ |
| Force Quit… | ⌥⌘⌫ |
| Sleep | ⌥⌘⏏ |
| Restart… | |
| Shut Down… | |
| Log Out Steve Johnson… | ⇧⌘Q |

Sleep, Restart, and Shut Down commands

There are currently logged in users who may lose unsaved changes if you shut down this computer.

Restarting or shutting down the computer will quit applications in other sessions where documents have not been saved. The data will be lost. Enter an administrator's name and password and click Shut Down, or choose Cancel to dismiss.

Name:
Password:

Switch User…          Cancel     Shut Down

Dialog appears if others are logged in.

## Understanding Your Options

| Option | When to use it |
|---|---|
| Sleep | When you want to stop working for a little while, save computer memory, and conserve power (ideal for saving battery life in a Mac portable computer). |
| Shut Down | When you finish working on your Macintosh and you want to turn off the power to the computer. |
| Restart | When you have problems and want to reset your computer (clear computer memory and reload system files). |

# Managing Files and Folders

## Introduction

File management involves organizing and keeping track of files and folders. It helps you stay organized so information is easy to locate and use. A **folder** is a container for storing applications and files, similar to a folder in a file cabinet. As with a file cabinet, working with poorly managed files is like looking for a needle in a haystack—it's frustrating and time-consuming to search through irrelevant, misnamed, and out-of-date files to find the one you want.

Finder allows you to organize folders and files in a file hierarchy, imitating the way you store paper documents in real folders. Just as a file cabinet contains several folders, each containing related documents with dividers grouping related folders together, so the Finder file hierarchy allows you to organize your files in folders, and then place folders in other folders. At the top of each hierarchy is the name of the hard drive or main folder. This drive or folder contains several files and folders, and each folder contains related files and folders.

Using the file management tools, you save files in folders with appropriate names for easy identification, quickly and easily create new folders so you can reorganize information, delete files and folders that you no longer need, search for a file when you cannot remember where you stored it, create shortcuts to files and folders for quick and easy access, and compress files and folders to save space.

## What You'll Do

**Open and View Disks**

**View and Open Documents**

**Change the Window View**

**Arrange Files and Folders in Icon View**

**Work with Files and Folders in List View and Column View**

**View Files with Cover Flow**

**View Files Using Quick Look**

**Go to Common or Recent Places**

**Organize Files and Folders by Color**

**Create and Rename Files and Folders**

**Copy and Move Files and Folders**

**Use Spring-Loaded Folders**

**Share Files or Folders with Others**

**Delete and Restore Files and Folders**

**Get and Set File Information**

**Create a CD or DVD Using the Finder**

**Mount and Eject Disks**

# Opening and Viewing Disks

The desktop is the starting point to access every disk, folder, and file on your computer. When Finder Preferences are appropriately set to display desktop icons, the desktop displays several types of local, removable, and network drives. Drives and folders are represented by icons on the desktop. Each icon graphic represents a different type of disk. Disks are devices that store information used by the computer. The disk with the Mac OS X installed on it is called the **startup disk**, which is typically the hard disk inside your computer. The files related to Mac OS X are stored in the **System folder** on your startup disk. You should not move this folder or make any changes to its contents. Additional Mac OS X related files are stored in the **Library folder**, which stores system and application preference settings and files. Also on your startup disk is an **Applications folder** that contains the complete collection of Mac OS X programs on your computer. You double-click a disk icon, such as your hard disk or a removable disk, on the desktop to open a Finder window, displaying the contents of the disk. Once you open more than one drive or folder, you can use buttons on the toolbar to help you move quickly between folders.

## Open and View Disks

1. If you want to view a disk, insert it in your drive.

   The removable disk appears on the desktop along with your other drivers, such as your hard disk or a network disk.

2. Double-click the drive icon on the desktop to open it.

3. Double-click a folder icon in the Finder window to open it.

   **TIMESAVER** *The top section of the Sidebar in the Finder window displays the same disk icons found on the desktop.*

4. Click the **Back** or **Forward** buttons on the toolbar to return or move to a previously visited window.

   **TIMESAVER** *Hold down A and click a window's title bar to display a folder hierarchy menu.*

5. When you're done, click the **Close** button.

Finder window

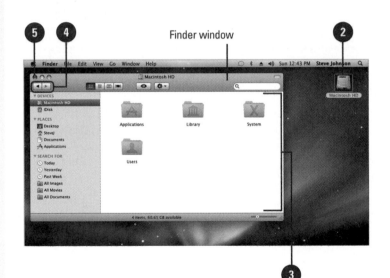

## Did You Know?

***You can display disk icons on the desktop.*** Click the Finder menu, click Preferences, click General, select the check boxes for the disk icons you want to show, and then click the Close button.

***You can display icons in the Sidebar.*** Click the Finder menu, click Preferences, click Sidebar, select the check boxes for the icons you want to show, and then click the Close button.

***You can open a disk or folder in a separate window.*** Click the Finder menu, click Preferences, click General, select the Always Open New Folders In A New Window check box, and then click the Close button.

***An uneven CD or DVD may have trouble loading.*** If your CD or DVD drive seems to make vibrating noises, the disc's weight might be uneven. Sometimes with older drives, the CD or DVD won't load. If it does load, you're fine.

## See Also

See "Changing the Window View" on page 30 for information on changing the display of a folder's contents.

See "Mounting and Ejecting Disks" on page 54 for information on using disks, CDs, and DVDs.

## Typical Disks on a Computer

| Icon | Type Description |
|---|---|
| | **Local**   A hard magnetic disk (or hard disk) located inside your computer on which you can store large amounts of data. The disk stores all the files on your computer. |
| | **External**   A hard magnetic disk (or hard disk) connected to your computer using a FireWire or USB plug. The disk provides extra storage. |
| | **Network**   A hard magnetic disk (or hard disk) connected to your computer over a network. The disk provides extra storage and file sharing. |
| | **iPod**   A portable hard magnetic disk that plays MP3 music and works with iTunes, which you can also use as a hard disk. The disk provides a compact, bootable hard drive. |
| | **Removable**   A soft removable magnetic disk on which you can store 1 GB or more of computer data. USB drives are standard on all computers. |
| | **Compact Disc-Read-Only Memory (CD-ROM )**   An optical disk on which you can read or copy up to 1 GB (typical size is 650, 700, or 740 MB) of data. The disc cannot be erased or burned with new data. |
| | **Compact Disc-Recordable (CD-R)**   A non-reusable disc on which you can burn up to 1 GB (typical size is 650, 700, or 740 MB) of data in multiple sessions. The disc can be burned again with new data until full, but cannot be erased. |
| | **Compact Disc-Rewritable (CD-RW)**   A reusable disc on which you can read, write, and erase data. Discs come in normal and high-speed formats (typical size is 650, 700, or 740 MB). |
| | **Digital Video Disc (DVD)**   A disc that holds a minimum of 4.7 GB, enough for a full-length movie. The disc cannot be erased or burned with additional data. |
| | **Digital Video Disc-Recordable (DVD-R)**   A non-reusable disc on which you can burn up to 4.7 GB of data in multiple sessions. The disc can be burned again with new data until full, but cannot be erased. |
| | **Digital Video Disc-Rewritable (DVD-RW)**   A reusable disc on which you can read, write, and erase data. The disc holds up to 4.7 GB on each side. |
| | **Flash**   A memory card the size of a large stamp that holds 128, 256, 512 MB, or greater. Flash drives connect directly into a USB plug and work on any Mac or Windows PC (no software required). |

# Viewing and Opening Documents

When you open a disk, the Finder window displays the contents of the disk, which includes files and folders containing information and software on your computer. Mac OS X creates a **Users folder** that contains a set of personal folders, known as the **Home folder**, for each user on a shared computer. The Home folder makes it easy to manage the personal and business files and folders you work with every day. The Home folder contains these folders: Desktop, Documents, Downloads, Library, Movies, Music, Pictures, Public, and Sites. Depending on your previous installation, devices installed, or other users, your personal folders might differ. You can quickly access your Home folder and many other personal folders from the Sidebar. In the Home folder, you can view file information, organize files and folders, and open files and folders. Once you open more than one folder, you can use buttons on the toolbar to help you move quickly between folders.

## View and Open Documents

1. Double-click the Hard Disk icon (the startup disk) on the desktop or in the Computer window.

2. In the bottom section of the Sidebar, select from the following:

   ◆ Desktop

   ◆ Home (the one with your name)

   ◆ Applications

   ◆ Documents

3. To open a folder, double-click it.

4. If available, drag the scroll box, or click the scroll arrows to view additional documents.

   **TIMESAVER** *Hold down A and click a window's title bar to display a folder.*

5. To open a document, double-click the file to open its associated application and the document.

6. When you're done, click the **Close** button.

## Did You Know?

*You can quickly open the Home folder from the desktop.* Press Shift+⌥⌘+H. You can also click the desktop background, and then press ⌥⌘+Up Arrow, which is the Enclosing Folder command on the Go menu. Since your Desktop folder is actually in your Home folder, using the command takes you back one folder level.

*Your Favorites folder still exists.* The Favorites folder from previous versions of the Mac OS is located in the Library folder of your Home folder. The Favorites folder contained links to your favorites files, folders, and Web sites in Microsoft Internet Explorer. If you want to use it, drag the Favorites folder to the Sidebar for quick and easy access.

## See Also

*See "Changing the Window View" on page 30 for information on changing the display of a folder's contents.*

## Folders in the Home Folder

| Folder | Type Description |
|---|---|
| Desktop | Each users desktop is mirrored in this folder to keep one separate and maintain the unique custom look and feel. |
| Documents | A folder designated to store your personal documents and folders. |
| Downloads | A folder designated to store your items downloaded from the Internet. |
| Library | Each user maintains a personal Library folder, like the main Library folder for Mac OS X, to store your preferences, which includes fonts, e-mail, Internet bookmarks, keyboard layouts, and so on. |
| Movies | A folder designated to store your movie files; programs, iMovie, use this folder. |
| Music | A folder designated to store your music files; programs, iTunes, use this folder. |
| Pictures | A folder designated to store your picture files; programs, iPhoto, use this folder. |
| Public | A folder where you can place documents and folders that you can share with other users on your computer or a network. |
| Sites | A folder where you can place Web pages that you can make available on the Internet, known as a **Web server.** |

## For Your Information

### Opening a Document with a Different Program

Most documents on your computer are associated with a specific application. For example, if you double-click a document whose file name ends with the three-letter extension ".txt," Mac OS X automatically opens the document with TextEdit, a word processing application. There are situations, though, when you need to open a document with a program other than the one Mac OS X chooses, or when you want to choose a different default program. For example, you might want to open a text document in Microsoft Word rather than TextEdit so that you can take advantage of advanced features. To do this, Control-click the document icon you want to open, point to Open With, and then click the application you want to use to open the document, or drag the file onto the application icon in the Dock.

# Changing the Window View

Mac OS X displays the contents of a drive or folder in different ways to help you find the information you're looking for about a file or folder. The available views include Icon, List, Column, and Cover Flow. You can change the window view from the View menu, or you can click the View buttons on the Finder window toolbar.

**Icon** view displays icons, sorted alphabetically in horizontal rows, with the name of the file or folder below each icon. You can also customize the display to include information about the file next to each icon, or a miniature representation of the file or folder. A picture file displays a thumbnail preview of the image. A multi-page document or a QuickTime movie file allows you to thumb through the document or watch the movie (**New!**). When you point to a multi-page document, such as a PDF, or a QuickTime move (.MOV), the thumbnail displays Previous and Next buttons or Play/Pause button, which you can click to view or play it as a thumbnail preview. The icon preview is also available in the

Preview pane in Column and Cover Flow views (**New!**). In Icon View, you can drag the Zoom control (**New!**) slider on the Status bar to adjust the view percentage.

**List** view displays small icons, sorted alphabetically in a single vertical column with the name of the file or folder and additional information, such as size and date, in columns to the right.

**Column** view displays icons, sorted alphabetically into vertical panes, or frames, which allows you to view information from two different locations. This arrangement enables you to view the file hierarchy of your computer and the contents of a folder simultaneously, making it easy to copy, move, delete, and rename files and folders.

**Cover Flow** displays a flip through screen with a large preview of a documents first page at the top and displays list view at the bottom. This enables you to page through multipage documents or play movies. You can also display search results in an easy-to-read format.

## Icon View

Point to icon to display buttons

Multi-page document    QuickTime movie

## Customize Views

Every window remembers its view settings independently. You might prefer to look at your Documents folder in List view, but your Applications folder in Column view.

However, you can set view specific options to permanently customize the way you view icons in each view. In Icon view, you can change icon size, show item information or icon preview, label position, arrangement, and background. In List and Cover Flow views, you can change file size, date, and status related information. In Column view, you can show icons and the preview column (summary information in the right column). See "Customizing Finder Window Views" on page 82 for more information about the specific options.

### List View

### Column View

### Cover Flow View

# Arranging Files and Folders in Icon View

When you select List view to display your files and folders, you can change the way individual files and folders are sorted by using the Arrange By menu options on the View menu. You can sort the files by name, date, size, file kind, or color label. You can also have Mac OS X help you clean up your windows by aligning icons to an invisible grid. Each window contains an invisible grid, which icons snap to when called to line up. The Arrange By menu options and the Clean Up command are only temporary until you make changes to the window. If you want Mac OS X to automatically keep icons arranged or cleaned up, you need to select appropriate options using the Show View Options command on the View menu.

## Arrange or Clean Up Items in Icon View

1. Display the desktop or open the folder you want to arrange.

2. Click the **Icon View** button on the toolbar.

3. To arrange icons, click the **View** menu, point to **Arrange By**, and then click the view you want to use:

   ◆ **Name**

   ◆ **Date Modified**

   ◆ **Date Created**

   ◆ **Size**

   ◆ **Kind**

   ◆ **Label**

   **TIMESAVER** *Click the Action button, point to Arrange By, and then click the view you want.*

4. To clean up icons, select the icons you want or deselect all, click the **View** menu, and then click **Clean Up** or **Clean Up Selection**.

### See Also

*See "Customizing Finder Window Views" on page 82 for information on setting options in Show View Options.*

Icons arranged by name

## Did You Know?

***You can override the grid settings as you drag.*** When the Snap To Grid setting is turned on (in Show View Options), pressing ⌘ lets you drag the icon freely; when the Snap To Grid setting is turned Off, pressing ⌘ snaps the icon to the grid. When you perform this operation, begin the drag before you press the ⌘ key.

## Options for Arranging Files and Folders

| Option | Arranges Files and Folders |
|---|---|
| Name | Alphabetically |
| Date Modified | Chronologically by their last modification date, with the latest modification date listed last. |
| Date Created | Chronologically by their creation date. |
| Size | By size, with the largest folder or file listed first. |
| Kind | By type, such as all documents created using the TextEdit program. |
| Label | By color label |
| Clean Up | Automatically in rows and columns by invisible grid points. |

## For Your Information

### Compressing Files and Folders to Save Space

You can compress files and folders into a single file using Stuffit compression software to decrease their size. Compressed folders are useful for reducing the file size of one or more large files, thus freeing disk space and reducing the time it takes to transfer files to another computer over the Internet or network. When a file is compressed, a copy is used in the compression, and the original remains intact. You can uncompress, or extract, a file from the compressed file and open it as you normally would. See "Compressing and Uncompressing Files and Folders" on page 435, and "Opening Compressed Files" on page 434 for more information about compressing and uncompressing files and folders.

# Working with Files and Folders in List View

You can display files and folders in a variety of different ways, depending on what you want to see and do. When you view files and folders in List view, a default list of file and folder information appears, which consists of Name, Date Modified, Size, and Kind. If the default list of file and folder details doesn't provide you with the information you need, you can add and remove any file and folder information using Show View Options. If you need to change the way Mac OS X sorts your files and folders, you can use the column header buttons. Clicking on one of the column header buttons (such as Name, Date Modified, Size, or Kind) in List view, sorts the files and folders by the type of information listed in the column. If the columns are not organized in the order you want, you can use the mouse to quickly rearrange columns. If you see an ellipsis in a column, it is too small to display all the information in it. You can drag the column divider to change column sizes all at once or individually.

## Show and Hide Folders in List View

1. Open the folder you want to view.

2. Click the **List View** button on the toolbar.

3. Click the triangle (pointing right) next to a folder in the list.

    **TIMESAVER** *Select the folder, and then press ⌘+Right Arrow.*

    The folder expands to display an indented list of folders and files from within the folder.

4. Click the triangle (pointing down) next to a folder in the list.

    **TIMESAVER** *Select the folder, and then press ⌘+Left Arrow.*

    The folder collapses.

Drag to change column width

## Did You Know?

*You can quickly show the full text with ellipsis.* Point to the icon's name without clicking for a moment to display a balloon. Hold down the Option key to display it immediately.

## Sort Files and Folders by Column in List View

1. Open the folder you want to view.

2. Click the **List View** button on the toolbar.

3. Click the column header name to sort the file and folder in ascending or descending order.

4. To reverse the column sort, click the column header name again.

### Did You Know?

*You can add and remove columns in List view.* Click the View menu, click Show View Options, select or clear the check boxes you want to add or remove, and then click the Close button.

## Rearrange and Widen Columns

1. Open the folder you want to view.

2. Click the **List View** button on the toolbar.

3. To rearrange columns, drag the column header to a new position.

4. To change the width of columns, drag the column divider.

The width of the column changes and all the columns to the right shift based on the change.

Indicates sort direction

# Viewing Files with Cover Flow

Just as you use Cover Flow to flip through album art in iTunes, now you can use it to flip through your files. Cover Flow displays a flip through screen with a large preview of a documents first page at the top and displays List view at the bottom. Cover Flow enables you to page through multipage documents or play movies. You can also display search results in an easy-to-read format. List view at the bottom of Cover Flow displays a default list of file and folder information, which consists of Name, Date Modified, Size, and Kind.

## View Files with Cover Flow

① Open the folder you want to view.

② Click the **Cover Flow** button on the toolbar.

③ Use either one of the following methods to display a file in Cover Flow.

◆ **Top pane.** Click the item, right and left arrows, or drag the slider to display the file you want.

◆ **Bottom pane.** Click the triangle (pointing right) next to a folder in the list to display an indented list of folders and files from within the folder, and then select the file you want to display.

Top pane

Bottom pane

### See Also

See "Working with Files and Folders in List View" on page 34 for information on using List view.

# Working with Files and Folders in Column View

Column view makes is easy to display several levels of folders in alphabetical order at the same time within the same window. Column view displays the window in panes, which allows you to view information from different locations making it easy to copy, move, delete, and rename files and folders. When you click a disk or folder in the first pane, the second pane shows a list of all the folders in it. Each time you click a folder in one pane, the pane to its right shows its contents. The other panes slide to the left, in some cases, out of view, which you can scroll back to display them. When you find and click the file you want, the next pane to the right, the **Preview column**, shows a file icon and information about it. If the file is a picture or PDF, the Finder displays the picture or PDF miniature. If the file is a sound or movie, you can play it in the Finder window.

## View Folders in Column View

1. Open the folder you want to view.

2. Click the **Column View** button on the toolbar.

3. Double-click the folder you want to open in a pane.

   The contents of the folder appears in the next pane to the right.

4. To resize a column, drag its right-side handle.

5. Click the file you want to view in the Preview column.

Preview column

## Did You Know?

*You can open new windows in Column view.* Click the Finder menu, click Preferences, click General, select the Open New Windows In Column View check box, and then click the Close button.

## Keyboard Options for Column View

| Option | Description |
| --- | --- |
| Left or Right Arrow | Jumps one pane to the left or right |
| Up or Down Arrow | Within a pane, moves up or down to select an item |

# Viewing Files Using Quick Look

Quick Look allows you to view the contents of a file or folder without opening it or starting an application. The content you see in Quick Look depends on the type of file you select in the Finder. If you select a single or multipage text document, you can read the text and scroll through it; if you select a video, you can play it; or if you select an image, a thumbnail preview appears. When you select more than one image or item, you can display a slide show and use arrow buttons to move from slide to slide.

## View Files Using Quick Look

1. Open the folder you want to view.

2. Select the one or more files or folder you want to view.

3. Click the **Quick Look** button on the toolbar.

   **TIMESAVER** *Press ⌘+Y to display Quick Look.*

4. If you selected more than one item or image, use the follow buttons to navigate through the items.

   ◆ **Previous and Next.** Navigate from slide to slide.

   ◆ **Play.** Display a slide show of the selected images or items.

   ◆ **Index.** Display a pictorial index of the selected images or items. Click an index item to display it.

5. To view the selected item in full screen, click the **Full Screen** button. To return to the previous view, click the **Exit Full Screen** button.

6. When you're done, click the **Close** button.

# Going to Common or Recent Places

Mac OS X keeps a list of your most recently used files, folders, and network computers. Instead of navigating through a long list of folders to open a recently used file, you can use the Recent Folders list to find it quickly. If you want to go to a common location, such as your computer, network connections, iDisk, Home folder, Applications folder, Documents folder (**New!**), Utilities folder, or one you specify, the Go menu makes it quick and easy. After you have opened several folders, you can use the secret folder hierarchy menu in a window's title bar to quickly go backwards through the chain of folders.

## Go Places

① Click the **Go** menu.

② Select any of the following:

◆ **Common locations.** Click the name of the place.

◆ **Recent folders.** Point to **Recent Folders**, and then click the name of the folder.

◆ **Specific folder.** Click **Go to Folder**, type a path location, and then click **Go**. You can use the tilde (~) to indicate the Home folder, "~/Documents/".

③ To go backwards through the folders, hold down ⌘, click the window's title bar, and then click a location from the folder hierarchy menu.

**TIMESAVER** Press ⌘+[ to go Back a folder; press ⌘+] to go Forward a folder.

④ When you're done, click the **Close** button.

### Did You Know?

*You can quickly open recent applications and documents.* Click the Apple menu, point to Recent Items, and then click the recently used application or document you want to open.

Common locations

Recent folders

Specific folder

# Organizing Files and Folders by Color

Giving an icon or folder a distinctive color can help you organize and find them later. Mac OS X provides seven different colors labels from which to select. The default color label names appear as Red, Orange, Yellow, Green Blue, Purple, and Gray, but you can customize them to suit your own needs and preferences, such as "Final," "In Progress," "Work," "Personal," and "Backup." When you change an icon's color, the icon and name take on the selected color shade. In List or Column view, the entire row takes on the color shade. In List view, you can sort files and folders quickly by color label. Sorting by color label also lets you create alphabetical groups within for color label in a single list. You can also use color labels with the Find command to search for files and folders with a particular color label.

## Color a File or Folder Icon

**1** Open the folder window with the file or folder icons you want to color.

**2** Select the icons you want to color.

**3** Click the **Action** button, and then click the color label you want.

> **TIMESAVER** *You can also use the File menu, or Control-click to access the color labels.*

**4** When you're done, click the **Close** button.

### Did You Know?

***You can quickly take off a color.*** Control-click the icon, and then click No Color (the x under Color Label).

### See Also

*See "Searching for Files Using the Find Window" on page 66 for information on searching for files and folders by color label.*

Select a color

Blue color for icons

## Sort a List View by Label

1. Open the folder window with the file or folder icons you want to sort by color.

2. Click the **List View** button.

3. Click the Label column heading.

   The files and folder are sorted by color. Within each color, the files and folder are sorted in alphabetical order.

4. When you're done, click the **Close** button.

### Did You Know?

*You need to display the label column before you can sort by color.* In List view, click the View menu, click Show View Options, select the Labels check box, and then click the Close button.

## Change Color Label Names

1. Click the **Finder** menu, and then click **Preferences**.

2. Click **Labels**.

3. Change the color names with ones that convey more meaning.

   When you go back to List view, instead of seeing the color names, you'll see your new names (such as Personal, Work, In Progress).

4. Click the **Close** button.

# Creating and Renaming Files and Folders

The keys to organizing files and folders effectively within a hierarchy are to store related items together and to name folders informatively. Creating a new folder can help you organize and keep track of files and other folders. In order to create a folder, you select the location where you want the new folder, create the folder, and then lastly, name the folder. You should name each folder meaningfully, so that just by reading the folder's name you know its contents. After you name a folder or file, you can rename it at any time.

## Create a Folder

1 Open the drive or folder where you want to create a folder.

2 Click the **File** menu, and then click **New Folder**.

> **TROUBLE?** If the New Folder command is grayed out, you don't have permission to create a folder in the folder. Click the File menu, and then click Get Info to change permissions.

3 With the new folder name selected, type a new name.

4 Press Return.

Untitled new folder

### Did You Know?

*File names can be up to 255 characters.* You can use spaces and underscores in names, but you can't use a colon (:). If you are going to use these files on a Windows PC, then don't use the following characters: * : < > | ? " \ or /. It's probably best to keep the name descriptive, but short. This allows you to view the file name in all view settings.

## Rename a File or Folder

1️⃣ Open the drive or folder with the file or folder you want to rename.

2️⃣ Click the file or folder to select it.

3️⃣ To erase the entire current name, press Return.

**TROUBLE?** *If you can't change the name of a file or folder, you may not have permission to make changes to the item. Click the File menu, and then click Get Info to change permissions.*

4️⃣ With the name selected, type a new name, or click to position the insertion point, and then edit the name.

**IMPORTANT** *If extensions are showing, changing the name doesn't change the extension as long as the extension stays the same. If you change the extension, the file type changes and you may not be able to open the file with the application in which it was created.*

5️⃣ Press Return.

The file may move to a location based on sort and view.

### See Also

*See "Showing or Hiding File Extensions" on page 81 for information on file extensions.*

## For Your Information

### Correcting Your Most Recent Action in the Finder

Everyone makes mistakes and changes their mind at some point, especially when you make changes in the Finder. You can instantly correct your most recent action by using the Undo command (⌘+Z) on the Edit menu. If you change your mind about undoing an action, you can just as easily use the Redo command (⌘+Y) to restore the action you reversed.

# Copying and Moving Files and Folders

Sometimes you'll need to move a file from one folder to another, or copy a file from one folder to another, leaving the file in the first location and placing a copy of it in the second. You can move or copy a file or folder using a variety of methods. If the file or folder and the location where you want to move it are visible in a window or on the desktop, you can simply drag the item from one location to the other. Moving a file or folder on the same disk relocates it, whereas dragging it from one disk to another copies it so that it appears in both locations. When the destination folder or drive is not visible, you can use the Cut (to move), Copy, and Paste commands on the Edit menu to move or copy the items.

## Copy or Move a File or Folder

1. Open the drive or folder containing the file or folder you want to copy or move.

2. Select the files or folders you want to copy.

3. Click the **Edit** menu, and then click **Cut** (to move) or **Copy**.

    **TIMESAVER** *Press* ⌘*+X to move or press* ⌘*+C to copy.*

4. Navigate to the drive or folder containing the folder where you want to copy or move the items.

5. Click the **Edit** menu, and then click **Paste**.

    **TIMESAVER** *Press* ⌘*+V to paste.*

    **TROUBLE?** *If you can't copy a file or folder, you may not have permission to make changes to the item. Click the File menu, and then click Get Info to change permissions.*

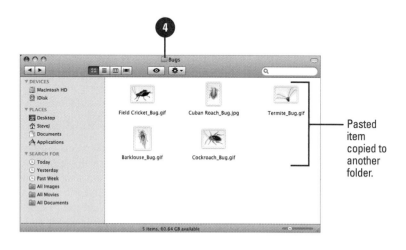

Pasted item copied to another folder.

## Copy or Move a File or Folder Using Drag and Drop

① Open the drive or folder containing the files and folders you want to move or copy.

② Drag the selection onto a folder, an icon in the Sidebar, or the desktop.

To copy files and folder, hold down the Option key while you drag.

**IMPORTANT** *If you pause for a few moments on the destination folder (when spring-loaded folders is turned on) the destination folder automatically opens.*

③ Release the items.

### Did You Know?

***You need certain permissions to move or copy a file.*** You need Read Only or Read & Write permissions to the item you want to move or copy. You need Read & Write Only access to the location where you want to place it.

### See Also

*See "Using Spring-Loaded Folders" on page 46 for information on copying and moving items using spring-loaded folders.*

## For Your Information

### Moving and Copying Items Using Exposé

Exposé can make it easier to move and copy files and folders using drag and drop. To move or copy items between open windows, start to drag the items (hold down the Option key to copy or hold down ⌘+Option to create an alias), press F9 (show all open windows) or F10 (show all open windows in the same application), point to the window where you want to move or copy the item, release F9 or F10, and then drag some more or release the items. A similar process works moving or copying items to the desktop using F11. The Exposé shortcut keys can be changed, so check System Preferences if they are not working properly.

# Using Spring-Loaded Folders

When you are moving or copying files and folders around, it can be tiresome to drag a selection to a folder, open the folder, and then continue to drag it to another folder. Spring-loaded folders allow you to drag a file or folder on top of another folder and it springs open to let you continue dragging the selection to another location in one continuous motion. When you drag a selection onto a folder (or even an icon in the Sidebar) and pause for a moment (with the mouse pressed), the window for the folder opens, so you can continue to drag to another folder as desired. You can use Finder Preferences to turn spring-loaded folders on and off, and set the delay setting for the amount of time you want to pause. If you set a long delay or turn off spring-loaded folders, you can press the Spacebar while you drag a selection to open the window immediately. The Spacebar method is useful because windows don't automatically open when you don't want them to, yet you still have the option to use spring-loaded folders when you need it.

## Use Spring-Loaded Folders

1. Open the drive or folder containing the files and folders you want to move or copy.

2. Drag the selection onto a folder or an icon in the Sidebar.

   To copy files and folders, hold down the Option key while you drag.

3. Press the Spacebar, or pause for a few moments.

   The folder window automatically opens centered on your cursor:

   ◆ **In Icon view**, the new window replaces the previous window.

   ◆ **In List view**, a new window opens.

   ◆ **In Column view**, a new column opens, displaying the new folder's contents.

Drag continues in spring-loaded folder.

# Sharing Files or Folders with Others

Mac OS X maintains a set of personal folders and options for everyone on your computer to make sure the contents remain private, unless you decide to share the contents with others. If you want the other users on your computer, or those connected to your computer over a network to have access to files, you can place those files in the Shared folder that each user can access. The Shared folder is located in the Users folder. It is set up with Read & Write permissions so that all users can open the files in this folder and copy files to the folder. If you want to share files with a specific user on your computer, you can use their Public folder. A Public folder is set up with Read Only permissions that allow others to see and copy its contents, but not change it. Each Public folder is located in the users' Home folder and also contains a Drop Box folder, which is set up with tighter permissions so other people can copy files to a Drop Box, but they cannot see its contents.

## Share Files in the Shared Folder or a Public Folder

1. Open the drive or folder containing the files or folders you want to share.

2. Select the files or folders you want to share.

3. Click the **Edit** menu, and then click **Copy**.

4. Click the **Hard Disk** icon in the Sidebar.

5. Double-click the **Users** folder.

6. Open the folder you want to use to share files:

   ◆ **Shared folder**. Double-click the Shared folder.

   ◆ **Public folder**. Double-click the user name, and then double-click the Public folder.

7. Click the **Edit** menu, and then click **Paste**.

8. To use the Drop Box folder in a Public folder, drag the files and folder onto the Drop Box folder.

Public folder resides in each users folder.

## Deleting and Restoring Files and Folders

When you organize the contents of a folder, disk, or the desktop, you might find files and folders that you no longer need. You can delete these items or remove them from the disk. If you delete a file or folder from the desktop or from the hard disk, it goes into the Trash. The **Trash**, located on the right side of the Dock, is a temporary storage area for deleted files. The Trash stores all the items you delete from your hard disk so that if you accidentally delete an item, you can remove it from the Trash to restore it. You can use the Put Back command (**New!**) to restore a deleted item to it's original folder. Be aware that if you delete a file from a removable disk, it is permanently deleted, not stored in the Trash. The files in the Trash do occupy room on your computer, so you need to empty it to free up space.

### Delete Files and Folders

① Select the files and folders you want to delete.

> **TROUBLE?** *If an item is locked, you can't put it in the Trash. Click the File menu, and then click Get Info to unlock it.*

② Drag the selection to the Trash in the Dock.

> **TIMESAVER** *Press ⌘+Delete key to delete selected items.*

③ Click the **Finder** menu, and then click **Empty Trash**.

> **TIMESAVER** *Click the Trash icon in the Dock, and then click Empty Trash, or press Shift+⌘ +Option+Delete to empty the trash and skip the warning dialog.*

④ Click **OK** to confirm the deletion.

Are you sure you want to remove the items in the Trash permanently?

You cannot undo this action.

Cancel    OK

## Restore Files and Folders

① In the Dock, click the **Trash** icon.

② Select the item or items you want to restore.

③ Click the **File** menu, and then click **Put Back (New!)** or drag the items back to your **Home** folder or any other location.

④ When you're done, click the **Close** button for the Trash window.

### Did You Know?

*You can undo a deletion.* If you accidentally delete a file, click the Edit menu, and then click Undo Delete. Mac OS X remembers your last three actions.

*You can still recover deleted files after you empty the Trash in some cases.* If you install special data recovery software, you still may be able to recover deleted files.

*You can turn off the empty Trash warning.* Click the Finder menu, click Preferences, click Advanced, clear the Show Warning Before Emptying The Trash check box, and then click the Close button.

### For Your Information

## Deleting Files Securely and Forever

If you are selling or giving away your computer, you can securely delete files and folders from your hard disk without any possibility of recovery. Drag the files and folders you want securely deleted into the Trash, click the Finder menu, click Secure Empty Trash, and then click OK to confirm the deletion. Files securely deleted are completely overwritten by meaningless data, which may take a few moments or minutes to complete depending on the size of the files.

# Getting and Setting File Information

You can get information about a hard disk, removable disk, network disk, application, folder, or file using the Info window. The Info window displays information about the kind, size, location, date created, and date modified. If you select a disk, the Info window also includes information about format, capacity, available space, and used space. In addition to displaying information, you can also use the Info window to add Spotlight text to enhance searches, create a stationery file, lock an item, change a files name and extension, determine which application to open a file with, change its ownership and permissions, and write a comment. When you set a file as stationery, the file opens as an untitled copy of the original, so the original file doesn't get changed. If you want to see information for different items without having to close the Info window, you can use Show Inspector to keep the Info window open while you select different items.

## Display Info Window

1. Select the files, disks, folders, applications, or alias; don't select anything to get desktop info.

2. Use one of the following methods:

   ◆ **Separate window for each item**. Click the **File** menu, and then click **Get Info**.

      A separate Info window appears for each selected item. This is useful for comparing settings and information.

   ◆ **Single window for all items**. Hold down the Option key, click the **File** menu, and then click **Show Inspector**.

      A single Info window appears, displaying statistics (by type and size) about the selected items and options common to all the selected items. This is useful for setting the same option for a lot of items, such as locking or unlocking files.

3. Click the expand button (triangle) to display category options, or the collapse button (down arrow) to hide them.

4. When you're done, click the **Close** button.

Add text for use in Spotlight searches.

Separate window for each item.

Expanded pane

Single window for multiple items.

Collapsed pane

50

## Set Info Window Options

1. Select the files, disks, folders, or applications you want to set.

2. Click the expand button (triangle) for the category in which you want to change options.

3. Change the options you want:

   ◆ **Comments**. Add your own comments, which you can display in List view and use in Spotlight searches.

   ◆ **General**. View information about the selected items; create a Stationery Pad (a file opens as untitled); and lock or unlock a file.

   ◆ **Name & Extension**. Read and edit item name and extension; and hide extensions.

   ◆ **Content Index**. Index a disk or folder for better search results.

   ◆ **Memory**. Set memory options for Classic applications only.

   ◆ **Open With**. Specify which application opens when you double-click an icon.

   ◆ **Preview**. Display magnified picture thumbnails or play sounds and movies.

   ◆ **Languages**. Add or remove languages for an application.

4. When you're done, click the **Close** button.

## See Also

See "Setting File Access Permissions" on page 390 for information on setting file permissions and ownership.

Comments

General

Name & Extension

Open With

Languages

Sharing & Permissions

# Creating a CD or DVD Using the Finder

The low cost and large storage size of CDs or DVDs (getting cheaper), and the popularity of recording hardware make using CDs and DVDs an effective approach to some file management tasks. For example, CDs or DVDs are an effective way to back up information or transfer information to another computer without a network or to a Microsoft Windows computer. Before you can create a CD or DVD, you must have blank CDs or DVDs and a CD-RW or DVD-RW drive (also known as a writer or burner) installed on your computer. You can copy or write files and folders to either CD-Rs or DVD-Rs (recordable) or CD-RWs or DVD-RWs (rewritable). With recordables, you can write files and folders only once and read them many times, but you can't erase them. With rewritables, you can read, write, and erase files and folders many times, just like a removable disk. When you write to, or **burn**, a CD or DVD, Mac OS X needs disk space on your hard disk to temporarily store files during the process, so make sure you have free hard disk space available for the size of the CD or DVD. Do not copy more files and folders to the CD or DVD than it will hold; anything beyond the limit will not copy. When the burn is complete, you can use the CD or DVD on a Macintosh or Windows PC appropriately equipped. You can also use other Mac OS X applications with disc burning features, such as iTunes, iPhoto, iDVD, or Disk Utility, to create specialized CDs or DVDs.

## Prepare to Burn a CD or DVD

1. Insert a blank CD-R, CD-RW, DVD-R, or DVD-RW disc into your drive.

   If you insert a CD-RW disc that you previously recorded, the dialog doesn't appear; you need to erase the disc with Disk Utility before you can burn data on it again.

   **TROUBLE?** *If the dialog doesn't appear, click the Apple menu, click Preferences, click CDs & DVDs, select the options you want, and then click the Close button.*

2. Click the **Action** pop-up, and then click **Open Finder**.

3. Select or clear the **Make this action the default** check box.

4. Click **OK**.

   The blank disc appears on the desktop, where you can add and remove files and folders.

Click to ignore action.

Click to eject CD.

## Add and Remove Files and Folders to a CD or DVD

1. Open a Finder window.

2. Navigate to the files and folders you want to add to the CD or DVD disc.

3. Drag the files and folders to the CD or DVD disc in the Sidebar, and then organize them.

   **IMPORTANT** *If you're using these files on a Windows PC, make sure the file names don't include \ / : * ? " < > |, otherwise you can't open them.*

4. To remove files and folders, click the CD or DVD disc in the Sidebar, or double-click the disc on the desktop, and then drag out the items you don't want.

## Create a CD or DVD

1. If you want, rename the CD or DVD disc just like any other file.

2. Use any of the following methods to create a CD or DVD:

   ◆ **Drag to Trash.** When you drag a disk icon onto the **Trash** icon, it changes to a Burn icon.

   ◆ **Burn command.** Select the disk icon, click the **File** menu, and then click **Burn**.

   ◆ **Sidebar Burn button.** Click the Burn button in the Sidebar.

3. Type a name for the disc.

4. Click the **Burn Speed** pop-up, and then select a speed.

5. Select the Save **Burn Folder To** check box, and then type a name to create a burn folder.

6. Click **Burn**.

Burn command on File menu

Sidebar Burn button

Drag to Trash

CD to burn

# Mounting and Ejecting Disks

When you insert a disk (such as a removable, CD, or DVD), its icon appears, or **mounts**, in the Computer window, in the Sidebar, and on the desktop (unless you've changed Finder Preferences) for you to open and use. When you no longer need a disk, you eject, or dismount, it from the drive. Mac OS X provides several different ways to eject a disk: drag the disk icon to the Trash (only happens for disks; a little strange, but its old time Mac functionality), use the Eject menu, select the Eject command, use the Sidebar, or hold down the Eject key. You can also use these methods to remove, or **unmount**, a network or FireWire drive, an iPod, or a disk image from your desktop.

## Mount and Eject Disks

1. Insert the disk into the appropriate drive to mount the disk.

2. Use any of the following methods to eject a disk:

   ◆ **Drag to Trash.** When you drag a disk icon onto the **Trash** icon in the Dock, it changes to an Eject icon.

   ◆ **Eject command.** Select the disk icon, click the **File** menu, and then click **Eject**. You can also Control-click the disk icon, and then click **Eject**.

   ◆ **Eject menu.** Click the **Eject** menu, and then click **Eject** *"disc name"* or press F12.

   ◆ **Sidebar Eject button.** Click the **Eject** button in the Sidebar.

   ◆ **Eject key.** Press and hold down the Media Eject key in the upper-right corner of your keyboard (if available) for a moment, or press F12.

   **TROUBLE?** *If a CD or DVD doesn't eject, insert a straightened paper clip into the small hole on the front of the drive, or click the Apple menu, click Restart, and hold down the mouse button until it ejects before the restart.*

Eject menu

Eject button

# Finding What You Want with Spotlight

## Introduction

If you're looking for specific content on your computer or network and you don't know where to find it, you can use Spotlight to help you locate it. Spotlight not only searches the names of your files and folders, it also searches their content. In addition, Spotlight searches other information stored in files, known as **metadata**, which describes how and when and by whom a particular set of data was collected, or how the data is formatted. Examples of metadata include authors, page size, creation and modification dates, duration of music and movies, dimensions of graphics or PDF documents, exposure time of a camera lens for photographs, and names of layers in Photoshop.

Spotlight is conveniently located on the right side of the menu bar on your Mac screen. You can identify Spotlight by the blue icon with a magnifying glass. Spotlight performs a live search of your Home folder on your computer using the information you know. As you type in Spotlight, a menu appears displaying a list of everything Spotlight can find to match what you've typed so far. As you continue to type, the list changes. Spotlight searches for everything on your computer that matches what you've typed, which includes every file, folder, program, e-mail message, address book entry, calendar appointment, picture, movie, PDF document, music file, Web bookmark, Microsoft Office document, and System Preferences panel, and lists the 20 best matches divided into categories, which you can customize later.

When you start Snow Leopard for the first time, Spotlight automatically starts collecting search information about your Home folder, known as **indexing**. The indexing process initially takes about 15 to 30 minutes to perform (the Spotlight icon pulses) and then updates take place as needed. Indexing the information on your computer reduces the time it takes to perform a search.

## What You'll Do

**Find Information Using Spotlight**

**Find Information in the Spotlight Window**

**Filter Spotlight Results**

**Group and Sort Spotlight Results**

**Work with Spotlight Results**

**Set Spotlight Preferences**

**Search for Files Using the Find Window**

**Search for Hard to Find Information**

**Work with Find Window Results**

**Create and Use Smart Folders**

**Use Smart Folders in the Sidebar**

**Get Help While You Work**

**Get Help Using Spotlight**

# Finding Information Using Spotlight

If you're looking for specific content on your computer and you don't know where to find it, you can use Spotlight to help you find it. Even if you can only remember part of the content. Spotlight performs a live search of your Home folder on your computer using the information you know. As you type in Spotlight, a menu appears displaying a list of everything Spotlight can find to match what you've typed so far. As you continue to type, the list changes. If you type two words, Spotlight finds items that contain both words. Spotlight searches for everything on your computer that matches what you've typed, which includes every file, folder, program, e-mail message, address book entry, calendar appointment, to-do item, picture, movie, PDF document, music file, Web bookmark, Microsoft Office document, and System Preferences panel, and lists the 20 best matches divided into categories, which you can customize later. Spotlight not only searches the names of your files and folders, it also searches their content. You can search by typing phrases or metadata attributes, and using boolean operators.

## Find Information Using Spotlight

1. Click the **Spotlight** (magnifying-glass) icon on the right side of the menu bar.

    **TIMESAVER** *Press* ⌘+Space bar to open Spotlight.

2. In the Spotlight field, start to type what you want to find. To find a specific phrase, place quotes around it. For example, "Apple Computer."

    **IMPORTANT** *Spotlight only recognizes the beginnings of words.*

    As you type, a menu begins to display a list of everything Spotlight can find to match what you've typed so far. As you continue to type, the list changes.

3. To open an item on the menu, click the item or use the arrow keys to scroll down the list, and then press Return.

4. To clear or stop a search, click the **Close** button (x) in the Spotlight field.

## Find Information with Metadata Using Spotlight

**1** Click the **Spotlight** (magnifying-glass) icon on the right side of the menu bar.

**TIMESAVER** *Press* ⌘+Space bar to open Spotlight.

**2** In the Spotlight field, type *code:keyword*. Use quotation marks around text to search for an exact phrase.

Where the code is a category, such as *kind*, *date*, *modified*, or *author*, and keyword is a specific type of category.

Here are some examples:

◆ **kind:preference network** displays the network system preference on your computer.

◆ **kind:contact steve** displays all the contacts with the name steve on your computer.

◆ **kind:music by:"Bruce Springsteen"** displays all music by Bruce Springsteen.

◆ **date:today kind:email** displays all the email for today on your computer.

### Did You Know?

*You can quickly cancel a Spotlight search.* Press the Esc key to close the Spotlight menu and erase what you've typed. Now, you can type a new search. Press the Esc key again to cancel the entire search. To cancel the entire search in one step, press ⌘+Space bar again, ⌘+period, or ⌘+Esc.

### Find Code and Keywords

| Find | Code:Keyword |
|---|---|
| Program | kind:app, kind:application |
| Address book contact | kind:contact |
| Folder | kind:folder |
| Mail message | kind:email, kind:mail message |
| iCal appointment | kind:event |
| iCal task | kind:to do, kind:todo |
| Image, picture | kind:image |
| Movie | kind:movie |
| Music or Sound | kind:music, kind:audio |
| PDF file | kind:pdf |
| System Preference | kind:preference, kind:system preference |
| Safari bookmark | kind:bookmark |
| Font | kind:font |
| Presentation | kind:presentation |
| Week | date:this week, date:next week |
| Month | date:this month, date:next month |
| Year | date:this year, date:next year |
| Today | date:today |
| Tomorrow | date:tomorrow |
| Yesterday | date:yesterday |

### For Your Information

#### Using Boolean Operators to Help Your Search

If you can't find the information you are looking for using the Spotlight field or Search field, you can use boolean operators (AND, OR, NOT, and dash (-) for AND NOT to exclude items) to refine your help search. For example, typing **report AND proposal** finds both words, typing **report OR proposal** finds either *report* or *proposal*, while typing **report NOT proposal** finds *report*, but excludes *proposal*. If you type **report -proposal**, Spotlight finds *report* but not *proposal*. You can also use keywords in your search with boolean operators. For example, typing **kind:pdf report AND kind:presentation proposal**, finds PDF documents with *report* and presentation files with *proposal*.

# Finding Information in the Spotlight Window

If you can't find what you're looking for on the Spotlight menu with the 20 most likely matches, you can click the Show All command at the top of the Spotlight menu to open the Spotlight window and view the complete list of matches organized by category. The Show All command displays the results of your search by retrieving content on your entire computer that matches the criteria. The Search bar, located below the toolbar, indicates the search location and type, which is "This Mac" and "Contents" by default. You can search your entire computer (This Mac), your Home folder, or shared network computer by either the contents of a file or the file name.

## Open and View the Spotlight Window to Locate Information

1. Click the **Spotlight** (magnifying-glass) icon on the right side of the menu bar.

   **TIMESAVER** *Press* Option+⌘+Space bar to open Spotlight window directly.

2. In the Spotlight field, start to type what you want to find.

3. Click **Show All** on the Spotlight menu.

   The Spotlight window opens, displaying the results of your search by category.

   If a search is currently in progress, a sprocket icon whirls around in the upper-left corner of the window.

4. To narrow or change the search, type the text you want to find in the Search field.

5. To open an item, double-click the item or use the arrow keys to scroll down the list, and then press Return.

6. To clear or stop a search, click the **Close** button (x) in the Search field.

7. When you're done, click the **Close** button.

## Narrow Results in the Spotlight Window

1. Press Option+⌘+Space bar or click **Show All** on the Spotlight menu to open the Spotlight window.

   The Spotlight window opens, displaying the results of your search by category.

   If a search is currently in progress, a sprocket icon whirls around in the upper-left corner of the window.

2. In the Search bar, click the button with the search location you want:

   ◆ **Servers.** Searches the server disks connected to your computer.

   ◆ **Computer.** Searches all the disks on your computer.

   ◆ **Home.** Searches your Home folder.

   ◆ **Volume "Hard Disk"** or **Folder "Name."** Searches only the currently opened volume or folder.

   ◆ **Contents or File Name.** Searches file contents or file name.

3. To narrow or change the search, type the text you want to find in the Search field.

4. To open an item, double-click the item or use the arrow keys to scroll down the list, and then press Return.

5. To clear or stop a search, click the **Close** button (x) in the Search field.

6. When you're done, click the **Close** button.

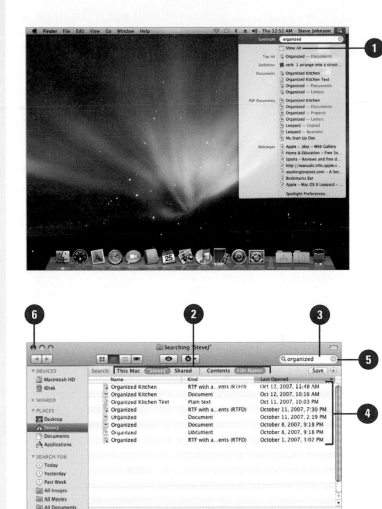

# Filtering Spotlight Results

If the list of Spotlight results is too long to find the results you want, you can revise your search text in the Search field or use the Search bar to filter, or narrow down, the list. The Search bar allows you to filter down the Spotlight results by location and type. The left side of the Search bar provides buttons to filter the search results by where the information is stored, such as This Mac (your entire computer), SteveJ (your Home folder), or Shared (your networked computers), if available. After you select where, you can select how. You can filter the result by whether the search criteria is in the content of a file or the file name of the results. If you want to further narrow down the Spotlight results, you can add other search criteria using file attributes.

## Filter Spotlight Results

1. Press Option+⌘+Space bar or click **Show All** on the Spotlight menu to open the Spotlight window, and then perform or narrow a search.

   The Spotlight window displays the results of your search by category.

2. In the Search bar, click the button with the search location you want:

   ◆ **Servers.** Searches the server disks connected to your computer.

   ◆ **Computer.** Searches all the disks on your computer.

   ◆ **Home.** Searches your Home folder.

   ◆ **Volume "Hard Disk"** or **Folder "Name."** Searches only the currently opened volume or folder.

   The Computer command displays or restores the full results list on all your drives in the Spotlight window.

3. In the Search bar, click **Contents** or **File Name** to specify how you want the results to appear.

4. When you're done, click the **Close** button.

Filtered results

## Change Spotlight Criteria in the Spotlight Window

**1** Press Option+⌃⌘+Space bar or click **Show All** on the Spotlight menu to open the Spotlight window.

The Spotlight window opens, displaying the results of your search by category.

If a search is currently in progress, a sprocket icon whirls around in the upper-left corner of the window.

**2** Click the **Action** button, and then click **Show Search Criteria**.

The Spotlight items option appears in the first Search pop-up, indicating Spotlight results in the window.

**3** Click the **Add** (+) button, and then specify the criteria you want.

**4** Click the first **Search** pop-up of the second criteria item, and then select or type the search criteria.

◆ Select **Other** on the pop-up to display a complete list of searchable attributes.

**5** Click the second **Search** pop-up of the second criteria item, and then select or type more specific search criteria.

**6** To remove search criteria, click the **Remove** (-) button.

**7** Click the **Action** button, and then click **Hide Search Criteria**.

**8** To clear or stop a search, click the **Close** button (x) in the Search field.

**9** When you're done, click the **Close** button.

Other available search criteria

# Grouping and Sorting Spotlight Results

After you perform a search using the Spotlight window, you can use the Keep Arranged By (**New!**) submenu on the Action menu or the column header button in List or Cover Flow view to group and sort the results of your search to make it easier to find what you're looking for. Clicking on one of the column header buttons (such as Name, Date Modified, Date Created, Last Opened, Size, Kind, or Label (**New!**)) in the search result window in either List or Cover Flow view, sorts the files and folders by the type of information listed in the column. If the columns are not organized in the order you want, you can use the mouse to quickly drag a column header to rearrange them.

## Group and Sort Spotlight Results

1. Press Option+⌘+Space bar or click **Show All** on the Spotlight menu to open the Spotlight window, and then perform or narrow a search.

   The Spotlight window displays the results of your search by category.

2. Click the **List View** or **Cover Flow** button on the toolbar to display the search results in list form.

3. Click a column header name to sort the file and folder in ascending or descending order:

   ◆ **Name.** List in alphabetical order by element name.

   ◆ **Date Modified.** List by the date you last modified it.

   ◆ **Date Created.** List by the date you created it.

   ◆ **Size.** List by size.

   ◆ **Kind.** List by kind of item, including applications, documents, or images.

   ◆ **Label.** List by color label.

4. To change the view options, click the **Action** button, click **Show View Options**, select options, and then click the **Close** button.

5. When you're done, click the **Close** button.

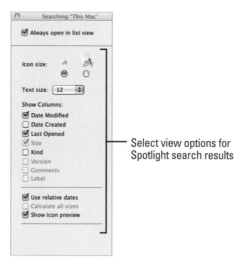

Select view options for Spotlight search results

# Working with Spotlight Results

After you perform a search using the Spotlight window, you can Control-click an item to display a shortcut menu and get more information about an item in the Spotlight results. When you Control-click an item, the shortcut menu allows you to open the item, get information about the item from the Get Info dialog box, locate the item in the Finder, display a slide show for graphic items, or create an e-mail with attachments using Mail.

## Work with Spotlight Results

1. Press Option+⌥⌘+Space bar or click **Show All** on the Spotlight menu to open the Spotlight window, and then perform or narrow a search.

   The Spotlight window displays the results of your search by category.

2. Option-click the item(s) you want, and then click the option you want:

   ◆ **Open.** Opens the selected item(s).

   ◆ **Open Enclosing Folder.** Displays the selected item(s) in a Finder window.

   ◆ **Get Info.** Opens the Get Info dialog box with basic file information for the selected item(s).

   ◆ **Quick Look.** View the contents of a file or folder without opening it.

   ◆ **Mail.** Point to **Open With** to open an e-mail message with the selected item(s) as attachments.

3. When you're done, click the **Close** button.

# Setting Spotlight Preferences

You can change Spotlight preferences to customize the way you use Spotlight. You can specify the categories, such as Applications, Documents, Folders, and so on, you want or don't want to include in a Spotlight search. In addition, you can change the order of the categories to prioritize the way the results appears. If you prefer different shortcut keys to display the Spotlight menu or open the Spotlight window, you can change them. When Spotlight performs a search, it looks every where on your computer (except for someone else's Home folder). If you want to keep certain disks, partitions, or folders private, you can add them to your privacy settings in Spotlight preferences. When you add an item to the privacy list, Spotlight removes them from the Spotlight index.

## Set Spotlight Search Results Preferences

1. Click the **System Preferences** icon in the Dock, and then click the **Spotlight** icon.

   **TIMESAVER** *Click Spotlight preferences at the bottom of the Spotlight menu (after you've started a search).*

2. Click the **Search Results** tab.

3. Select the check boxes you want to include in the search results or clear the check boxes you don't want to include in the search results.

4. To change the order to the search results categories, drag the categories to the location you want.

5. Click the **Close** button.

### Did You Know?

***You can use Spotlight everywhere (almost).*** The Spotlight Search field is also available in the Finder, Mail, System Preferences, and Open and Save dialogs to name a few.

---

## For Your Information

### Selecting the Default Search Location

You can specify the default search location for Spotlight (**New!**). Click the Finder menu, click Preferences, click Advanced, click the When performing a search pop-up, then click Search This Mac, Search the Current Folder, or Use the Previous Search Scope.

## Set Spotlight Privacy Preferences

1. Click the **System Preferences** icon in the Dock, and then click the **Spotlight** icon.

2. Click the **Privacy** tab.

3. Drag the items (disks, partitions, or folders) to the list of non-searchable items from the desktop, or click the **Add** (+) button, navigate to the item, and then click **Choose**.

4. To delete an item, click the item, and then press Delete or click the **Remove** (-) button.

5. Click the **Close** button.

## Set Keyboard Shortcuts for Spotlight

1. Click the **System Preferences** icon in the Dock, and then click the **Spotlight** icon.

2. Select the **Spotlight menu keyboard shortcut** check box, click the list arrow, and then select the shortcut you want.

3. Select the **Spotlight window keyboard shortcut** check box, click the list arrow, and then select the shortcut you want.

4. Click the **Close** button.

# Searching for Files Using the Find Window

Spotlight provides a quick and easy way to search for files, but if you need to perform a more specific search, the Find window can help you search for what you need. The Find window lets you specify where and how you want to search—Servers, Computer (everywhere), Home, or Shared, and Contents or File Name. You can also narrow your search by selecting or typing a specific list of criteria—such as name, location, size, kind, color label, extension, type, and by creation or last modification date—available in the Find window. For example, you can search for all graphic files with the *.jpg* extension you created last month that contain *web*. After you complete a search, a separate results window opens. Unlike the Spotlight, you can change the criteria and perform a new search, and then compare the results.

## Search for Files Using the Find Window

1. Open a Finder window, and then display a drive or folder if you want to narrow the search.

2. Click the **File** menu, and then click **Find**.

   **TIMESAVER** *Press* ⌘+F *to open the Find window.*

   ◆ You can also use the Search field located in every Finder window.

3. In the Search field, type the text in which you want to search.

4. Click the button with the search location you want:

   ◆ **Servers.** Searches the server disks connected to your computer.

   ◆ **Computer.** Searches all the disks on your computer.

   ◆ **Home.** Searches your Home folder.

   ◆ **Volume "Hard Disk"** or **Folder "Name."** Searches only the currently opened volume or folder.

   ◆ **Contents or File Name.** Searches criteria by file contents or file name.

**5** Click the first **Search** pop-up, and then select or type the search criteria; options vary depending on the criteria.

- ◆ **Kind**. Finds files that are or aren't a certain kind.

- ◆ **Last Opened**. Finds files that you last opened.

- ◆ **Last Modified**. Finds files according to the date modified.

- ◆ **Created**. Finds files according to the date created.

- ◆ **Keywords**. Finds files according to words and phrases.

- ◆ **Color Label**. Finds files according to label color.

- ◆ **Name**. Finds all or part of a file name (capitalization doesn't matter); select another option, such as Contains, Starts With, Ends With, or Is.

- ◆ **Contents**. Finds words inside your file; handy if you don't remember the name.

- ◆ **Size**. Finds files based on size, such as Equal to, Greater than, or Less than.

- ◆ **Other**. Finds files based on other attributes.

**6** Click the second **Search** pop-up, and then select or type more specific search criteria.

**7** To add search criteria, click the **Add** (+) button, and then specify the criteria you want.

**8** To remove search criteria, click the **Remove** (-) button.

The search results appear in the window.

**9** To pause or stop a search in progress, click the **X** button.

## For Your Information

### Setting a Search Location Preference

In the Finder Preferences dialog, you can specify a search location preference (**New!**). You can select any of the following options: Search This Mac, Search the Current Folder, or Use the Previous Search Scope. Click the Finder menu, click Preferences, click Advanced, click the When performing a search pop-up, and then select the option you want.

# Searching for Hard to Find Information

In addition to searching for typical information, such as name, location, size, or kind, you can also search for file specific metadata, such as visibility (visible files, not hidden one used by Mac OS X), duration, dimensions, pixel height and width, device make, and layers. There are over 115 different metadata search attributes from which to choose. For example, you can select search attributes to find visible files (not hidden ones used by Mac OS X), the duration of music and movies, the dimensions of graphics or PDF documents, the device used to acquire a document, and the names of layers in Photoshop.

## Search for Hard to Find Information

1. In the Finder, click the **File** menu, and then click **Find**.

   **TIMESAVER** *Press ⌘+F to open the Find window.*

   ◆ You can also use the Search field located in every Finder window.

2. In the Search field, type the text in which you want to search.

3. At the top of the window, click the button with the search location you want: **Servers**, **Computer**, **Home**, **Volume** or **Folder**, and **Contents** or **File Name**.

4. Click the first **Search** pop-up, and then click **Other**.

5. Select the search attribute you want to find.

6. Click **OK**.

# Working with Find Window Results

After you perform a search with the Find window, you can perform a variety of file management operations directly with the Find window results, which are similar to the ones you can perform in the Finder. For example, you can get file information, and move, copy, rename, or delete a file directly in the search results window. In addition, you can display the location of a file in the search results window, and then open its folder location or open the file.

## Work with Find Window Results

After you perform a search with the Find window, you can use the following options to work with the results:

◆ **Find the location of a file.** Click a file to display the location in the Path bar at bottom of the window.

◆ **Open the location of a file.** Click the **File** menu, and then click **Open Enclosed Folder**.

◆ **Open a file.** Double-click the file icon.

◆ **Move or delete a file.** Drag the file to a new location or the Trash.

◆ **Rename a file.** Click its name, select the text, and then type a new name.

◆ **Copy a file.** Use the **Copy** and **Paste** commands on the **Edit** menu.

◆ **Get file information.** Click the File menu, and then click **Get Info**. Add criteria to Spotlight Comments for use in Spotlight searches.

◆ **Sort the result by category.** Click the column header.

◆ **Start a new search.** Change the text in the Search field, or click the Close (x) button in the Search field and type a new search.

◆ **Close the search.** Click the **Close** button or press ⌘+W.

Double-click to open    Click column to sort

Path bar

Get info
spotlight comments

# Creating and Using Smart Folders

A Smart folder is a self-updating folder that performs a search based on the search criteria you set and save in the Search dialog box. You can create a Smart folder by specifying a search in the Search dialog box and then saving it as a saved search. For example, if you set up a search for *Last Opened* and *This week*, and saved it as a Smart folder. When you double-clicked the Smart folder, it opens displaying the files you're currently working on.

## Create and Use a Smart Folder

1. Click the **File** menu, and then click **New Smart Folder**.

2. Use the **Add** (+) button to specify the search criteria you want to save as a Smart folder.

3. Click the **Save** button.

4. Type a name for the Smart folder.

5. Specify the location where you want to save the Smart folder.

   The default location is the Saved Searches folder.

6. Select or clear the **Add To Sidebar** check box to either add or not add the Smart folder to the sidebar.

7. Click **Save**.

8. To use a Smart folder, click the Smart folder icon on the Sidebar, or navigate to the Saved Searches folder, and then double-click it.

   ◆ The Saved Searches folder is located in the Library folder, which is located in the Home folder.

## Did You Know?

*You can open a recent item.* Click the Apple menu, point to Recent Items, and then click the recently used document you want to open.

Smart folder

## Edit a Smart Folder

① Navigate to the Smart folder you want to edit; double-click the folder in the Smart folder to open it.

◆ The Smart folder is located in the Saved Searches folder in the Library folder, which is located in the Home folder.

◆ You can also use the Sidebar to select a Smart folder.

② Click the **Action** menu, and then click **Show Search Criteria**.

③ Change the search criteria you want to modify.

④ Click **Save**.

⑤ Click the **Action** menu, and then click **Hide Search Criteria**.

### Did You Know?

***You can save a copy of a Smart folder.*** If you have a Smart folder similar to the one you want to create, you can go to the Smart folder and then make a copy of the Smart folder you want. After you make a copy, open it and make the changes you want, and then click Save.

***You can delete a Smart folder.*** Open the Smart folder, and then drag the Smart folder you want to delete to the Trash icon.

***Where's the Smart folder?*** The Smart folder is located in the Saved Searches folder in the Library folder, which is located in the Home folder.

# Using Smart Folders in the Sidebar

The Sidebar appears in every Finder window. At the bottom of the Sidebar, the Search For section displays icons for Smart folders, which is a self-updating folder that performs a search based on the search criteria. The default Smart folder icons include Today, Yesterday, Past Week, All Images, All Movies, and All Documents. You can add your own Smart folders to the Sidebar or modify the ones already on the Sidebar.

## Use Smart Folders in the Sidebar

① Open a Finder window.

② Under the Search For heading in the Sidebar, click one of the following options:

- ◆ **Today.**

- ◆ **Yesterday.**

- ◆ **Past Week.**

- ◆ **All Images.**

- ◆ **All Movies.**

- ◆ **All Document.**

## Change the Search Criteria for a Smart Folder in the Sidebar

1. Open a Finder window.

2. Under the Search For heading in the Sidebar, click the Smart folder icon you want to view.

3. Click the **Action** menu, and then click **Show Search Criteria**.

4. Specify the search criteria you want to save for the Smart folder.

5. Click the **Save** button.

6. Click the **Action** menu, and then click **Hide Search Criteria**.

### Did You Know?

*You can add a Smart folder or other folder to the Sidebar.* Select the folder in a Finder window or desktop, click the File menu, and then click Add To Sidebar.

### See Also

*See "Creating and Using Smart Folders" on page 70 for information on adding a Smart folder to the Sidebar.*

# Getting Help While You Work

When you have a question about how to do something in Mac OS X, you can usually find the answer with several clicks of your mouse. Mac OS X Help is a resource of information to help you use Mac OS X. The Mac OS X Help is like an online book with a table of contents, complete with a search feature, and additional links to the Internet to make finding information a little bit easier. You can access help from the Help menu in the Finder as well as many other Mac OS X applications, such as Safari and iChat; you can even switch between the different help libraries using the Home button. If you see the Help button (question mark) in a window or dialog, you can click it to get feature related help. If you have an Internet connection, Help retrieves online updates to Mac OS X Help content as necessary. For additional help and support information, visit the Apple Computer Web site at *www.apple.com*.

## Browse for Help Information

1. In the Finder, or any other application, click the **Help** menu, and then click **Mac Help** or **Help <application name>**.

2. To select another Help, click and hold the **Home** button, and then click a help library.

3. Click a link in the Help window until you find the topic with the information you're looking for.

4. Use the Help toolbar to navigation help topics:

   ◆ Click the **Home** button to return to the first page of the help.

   ◆ Click the **Back** and **Forward** button to view previously viewed topics.

   ◆ Click the **Index** link to display an index like the back of this book. Click a letter to narrow the list, and then click the topic you want to display. Click the **Home** link to display the first page of the help.

5. Click the **Close** button to quit Help.

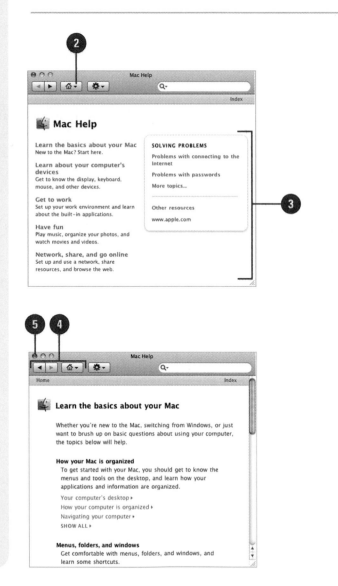

## Search for Help Information

1. In the Finder, or any other application, click the **Help** menu, and then click **Mac Help** or **Help <application name>**.

2. Click the magnifying glass in the Search field, and then click **Search Mac Help** or **Search All Help**.

3. Click in the Search field.

   **TIMESAVER** *Press the Tab key to quickly go to the Search field.*

4. Type the words you want to find in the help topics, and then press Return.

   A list of matches appears with a Relevance column ranking the results by percentage.

5. Double-click the topic you want to read in the search results list.

6. Use the navigation buttons (**Back** and **Forward**) on the Help toolbar to move between help topics.

7. Click the **Close** button to quit Help.

### Did You Know?

*You can start a new search in a new window.* Click the File menu, click New, and then perform a new search.

*You can print a help topic.* Display the help topic in the Help window, click the Action button on the Help toolbar, click Print, and then click Print again.

*You can change the size of Help text.* Click the Action button on the Help toolbar, click Make Text Smaller or Make Text Bigger.

# Getting Help Using Spotlight

In addition to using Spotlight to find files and other information on your computer, you can also use Spotlight to quickly find help information. When you click the Help menu, the Spotlight Search field appears at the top, where you can type the help information you want to find and display. You can access help from the Help menu in the Finder as well as many other Mac OS X applications, such as Safari and iChat. When you select a help topic from the Help menu, the Help window appears displaying the topic. If you want to display all the related help topics, click Show All Results. A complete search results appears, where you can double-click a topic to display it. If available, menu items appear on the Help menu, where you can select it to display an blue arrow pointing to the location of the menu.

## Get Help Using Spotlight

1. Click the **Help** menu.

2. In the Spotlight Search field, start to type what you want to find. To find a specific phrase, place quotes around it. For example, "Spotlight"

   As you type, a menu begins to display a list of everything Spotlight can find in Help to match what you've typed so far. As you continue to type, the list changes.

3. On the Help menu, select one of the following options:

   ◆ **Display a Help Topic.** Click the Help topic item or use the arrow keys to scroll down the list, and then press Return to open the Help window.

   ◆ **Show All Results.** Click **Show All Results** to display the search results for help topics, and then double-click the topic you want to open the Help window.

   ◆ **Display a Menu Item.** Point to the Menu item name to display a blue arrow pointing to the location of the menu item.

4. Click the **Close** button to quit Help.

Display menu item

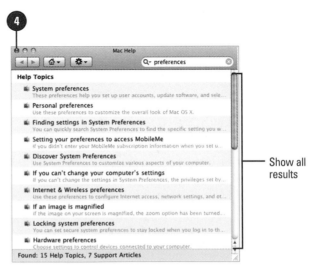

Show all results

# Customizing the Finder

## Introduction

Finder Preferences allow you to control how you interact with your desktop, windows, and icons. You can access Finder Preferences from the Finder menu. Finder Preferences are grouped into four main areas: General, Labels, Sidebar, and Advanced. The Finder Preferences window is a central location to set Finder related options. However, you can customize the Finder and the desktop in other places too.

In each of the Finder window views (Icon, List, and Column), you can set view specific options to customize the way you view icons. In addition to the predefined items in the Sidebar (the left pane in a Finder window), you can add your own items, including folders, documents, Web Internet Location files, to name a few. The Finder toolbar comes with a few standard buttons, and you can customize to add more. You can use the Customize Toolbar dialog to quickly drag button icons on and off the toolbar. You can set Dock preferences to adjust the Dock size and icon magnification (when you point to one), change the Dock position on the screen, apply a bounce effect to an icon when you launch an application, select a minimization special effect, and make it disappear when not in use.

To save some time, you can create shortcuts to the files, folders, or disks you use frequently, known as Aliases. An **alias** allows you to access the original folder or file from several different places. Exposé lets you quickly move windows out of the way temporarily to make it easier to work with windows in order to find, move, or copy files. If you have novice users who want to use your computer, you can set up a shared user account with Simple Finder, which is a simplified version of the Mac OS X Finder with fewer menus and icons. It's a great way for them to explore, yet keep your data safe.

## What You'll Do

**Understand Finder Preferences**

**Show Icons on the Desktop**

**Customize the Way Windows Open**

**Show or Hide File Extensions**

**Customize Finder Window Views**

**Customize the Toolbar**

**Customize the Sidebar**

**Customize the Dock**

**Create Aliases**

**Customize Exposé**

**Setup and Customize Spaces**

**Use Simple Finder**

# Understanding Finder Preferences

Finder Preferences allow you to control how you interact with your desktop, windows, and icons. Finder Preferences are grouped into four main areas: General, Labels, Sidebar, and Advanced. You can open Finder Preferences by selecting Preferences from the Finder menu.

The **General preferences pane** allows you to display icons for local and network disks on the desktop, select options for opening new Finder windows, and enable spring-loaded folders and windows. The **Labels pref-**

**erences pane** allows you to change the name of color labels for Finder items to more meaningful ones, such as work or project, which you can use as search criteria in the Find window. If you accidentally remove a Sidebar icon, you can use the **Sidebar preferences pane** to redisplay Finder specific icons, such as computer, hard disks, iDisk, network, desktop, and applications. The **Advanced preferences pane** provides options to show file extensions, a change file extension warning, an empty the Trash warning, empty the Trash securely, and where to perform a Spotlight search (**New!**).

## General

## Labels

## Sidebar

## Advanced

# Showing Icons on the Desktop

When you insert a removable disk, a CD, or DVD, or connect to a network server, an icon for the disk automatically appears on the desktop. Depending on your work style, you may or may not want icons to simply appear. You can use Finder Preferences to specify whether icons for hard and external disks, CDs, and network servers appear on your desktop. Having the icons on the desktop makes dragging them to the Eject icon in the Dock quick and easy, but the icons also add clutter to the desktop.

## Show Volume Icons on the Desktop

1 Click the **Finder** menu, and then click **Preferences**.

2 Click **General**.

3 Select or clear the checkmarks for the icons you want to show or hide on the desktop.

- ◆ Hard disks

- ◆ External disks

- ◆ CDs, DVDs and iPods

- ◆ Connected servers (computers attached to a network)

4 Click the **Close** button.

# Customizing the Way Windows Open

When you create a new Finder window, you can specify options to always open folders in a new window or use spring-loaded folders and windows. Spring-loaded folders allows you to drag a file or folder on top of another folder, and it springs open to let you continue dragging the selection to another location. Instead of starting and stopping when you move or copy items from one folder to another, you can drag items continuously from folder to folder.

## Customize the Way Finder Windows Open

1 Click the **Finder** menu, and then click **Preferences**.

2 Click **General**.

3 Click the **New Finder windows open** pop-up, and then select the window you want to open when you open a new Finder window.

4 Select or clear the **Always open folders in a new window** check box.

5 Select or clear the **Spring-loaded folders and windows** check box. If you select it, drag the slider to adjust the delay.

   **TIMESAVER** *When you drag an item to a folder with a spring-loaded folder, you can press the Spacebar to open the window immediately without the delay.*

6 Click the **Close** button.

80

# Showing or Hiding File Extensions

A **file extension** is a three-letter suffix at the end of a document's file name that identifies the file type. For Windows operating system users, a file extension determines which application can open a file; the Mac doesn't use it. You might never have seen a document's file extension because your system might be set up to hide it. The file extension for simple text files is ".txt" (pronounced "dot t-x-t"), and many graphic files have the extension ".bmp" or ".jpg". This means that the full name for a text file named Memo is Memo.txt. If you double-click a document whose file name ends with the three-letter extension ".txt," Finder automatically opens the document with TextEdit, a word processing application. If you plan to exchange files with the Windows operating system, then show the file extensions, so Windows recognizes them. As a precaution, you can also set an option to display a warning before allowing an file extension change.

## Show or Hide File Extensions

1. Click the **Finder** menu, and then click **Preferences**.

2. Click **Advanced**.

3. Select or clear the **Show all file extensions** check box.

4. Select or clear the **Show warning before changing an extension** check box.

5. Click the **Close** button.

# Customizing Finder Window Views

In each of the Finder window views (as Icons, as List, as Columns, and as Cover Flow, you can set view specific options to customize the way you view icons. For Icon, List, and Cover Flow views, you can select to apply your changes to the current window or to all Finder windows (a personal default). In Icon view, you can change icon size, label position, arrangement, and background. In List and Cover Flow views, you can change file size, date, and status related information. To make the display easier to view, you can display relative dates, such as "Today" and "Yesterday." In Column view, you can show icons and the preview column (summary information in the right column).

## Change Icon View Options

1. Open a Finder window.

2. Click the **View** menu, and then click **As Icons**.

3. Click the **View** menu, and then click **Show View Options**.

4. Drag the slider left or right to To change the icon size or the grid spacing.

5. To change the icon text size, click the pop-up, and then select a size.

6. Click the label position option (Bottom or Right) you want.

7. Select or clear the following check boxes:

   ◆ **Show item info**. Check to show item info under the icon name.

   ◆ **Show icon preview**. Check to show a preview in the icon.

   ◆ **Arranged by**. Select an arrange option from the pop-up.

8. Click the Background option you want, and any related settings.

9. Click **Use as Defaults** to apply view changes to all windows.

10. Select the **Always open in icon view** check box to apply view changes to the selected window.

11. Click the **Close** button.

## Change List View or Cover Flow Options

1. Open a Finder window.

2. Click the **View** menu, and then click **As List** or **Cover Flow**.

3. Click the **View** menu, and then click **Show View Options**.

4. Click an Icon size option.

5. To change the icon text size, click the pop-up, and then select a size.

6. Select or clear the check boxes with the information you want to display in list form.

7. Click **Use as Defaults** to apply view changes to all windows.

8. Select the **Always open in lists view** or **Always open in Cover Flow** check box to apply view changes to the selected window.

9. Click the **Close** button.

## Change Column View Options

1. Open a Finder window.

2. Click the **View** menu, and then click **As Columns**.

3. Click the **View** menu, and then click **Show View Options**.

4. Click the **Text size** pop-up, and then select a point size.

5. Select or clear the check boxes for **Show icons**, **Show icon preview**, and **Show preview column**, and select an **Arrange by** option.

6. Select the **Always open in column view** check box to apply view changes to the selected window.

7. Click the **Close** button.

# Customizing the Toolbar

The Finder toolbar comes with a few standard buttons, but you can add more. You can use the Customize Toolbar dialog to quickly drag button icons on and off. The buttons include Path (navigation pop-up), Eject, Burn, Customize, Separator (designates groups), Space (adds a gap), Flexible Space (adds a gap that expands), New Folder, Delete, Connect, Get Info, iDisk, Search, and Quick Look. If you want the simple look again, you can drag the Default Set of buttons onto the toolbar to reset it. In addition to the button icons in the dialog, you can also drag icons, such as favorite folders, disks, or applications, from the desktop or any Finder folder onto the toolbar. You can also use the A key to cycle through size combinations of large and small icons and text labels.

## Customize the Finder Toolbar

① Click the **View** menu, and then click **Customize Toolbar**.

② Click the **Show** pop-up, and then select a display option of **Icon Only**, **Icon & Text**, or **Text Only**.

**TIMESAVER** *Control-click the toolbar (without the dialog open), and then click a display option.*

③ Select or clear the **Use Small Size** check box.

④ To add icons to the toolbar, drag them into place from the gallery.

⑤ To remove icons, drag them up or down off the toolbar.

⑥ To rearrange icons, drag them horizontally on the toolbar.

⑦ To reset the toolbar, drag the default set of items onto the toolbar.

⑧ When you're finished, click **Done**.

## Did You Know?

***You can access buttons that don't fit on a narrow window.*** You can either resize the window, or click the double arrow, and then select a toolbar item.

## Add, Remove, or Rearrange Icons to the Toolbar

1. Display the icons you want to add to the Finder toolbar in the desktop or any folder window.

2. Drag icons from the desktop, or any folder window, directly onto the toolbar, and then pause before releasing the icon.

   **TROUBLE?** *If pausing doesn't work, use A while you drag.*

3. To remove an icon from the toolbar, hold down ⌘, and then drag the icon off the toolbar.

4. To rearrange an icon on the toolbar, hold down ⌘, and then drag the icon horizontally on the toolbar.

Icon added to toolbar

## Change Toolbar Styles

1. Hold down ⌘ while you repeatedly click the **Toolbar Control** button.

   Each time you click the button, a different toolbar style appears.

### Did You Know?

*You can change toolbar styles in some applications too.* You can also use ⌘ in Mac OS X applications, such as Mail, and many other applications.

Other toolbar styles

# Customizing the Sidebar

In addition to the predefined items in the Sidebar, you can add your own items, including folders, documents, and Web Internet Location files, to name a few. When you click a volume or folder in the Sidebar, the Finder displays its contents in the window. When you click an application, document, or Web Internet Location file, the item opens in its own application window. If you accidentally remove a Sidebar icon, you can't undo it, but you can redisplay Mac OS X specific items using Finder Preferences. Unfortunately, you have to recreate the ones you added.

## Customize the Sidebar

◆ **Add items.** Drag the items to the lower section of the Sidebar.

> **TIMESAVER** *Select an item, and then press* ⌘+T, *or use the Add To Sidebar command on the File menu.*

◆ **Remove items.** Drag the items outside of the Sidebar to detach them.

◆ **Rearrange items.** Drag the items up or down in the list.

◆ **Change the column width.** Position the mouse pointer over the divider between the Sidebar and the window contents, and then drag to change the width.

◆ **Hide and show the Sidebar.** Click the **Toolbar Control** button to hide and show the toolbar and Sidebar, or click the **View** menu, and then click **Hide Sidebar** or **Show Sidebar** (**New!**).

Add item to Sidebar

Drag to change column width

Double-click to hide or show Sidebar

Remove item from Sidebar

## Change Sidebar Preferences

1. Click the **Finder** menu, and then click **Preferences**.

2. Click **Sidebar**.

3. Select or clear the check boxes with the items you want or don't want to see in the Sidebar.

4. Click the **Close** button.

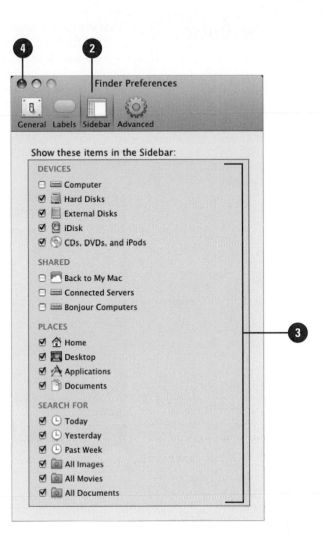

# Customizing the Dock

After you have worked with the Dock for a while, you probably want to customize it to better suit your needs. You can set Dock Preferences to adjust the Dock size and icon magnification when you point to one, change the Dock position on the screen, apply a bounce effect to an icon when you launch an application, select a minimization special effect, and even make it disappear when not in use.

## Customize the Dock

① Click the **Apple** menu, point to **Dock**, and then click **Dock Preferences**.

**TIMESAVER** *Control-click the divider in the Dock to quickly display the Dock submenu.*

② Select the Dock options you want:

◆ **Dock Size**. Drag slider to change the Dock size.

**TIMESAVER** *Position the pointer on the divider in the Dock, so it turns into a double-headed arrow, and then drag to size it.*

◆ **Magnification**. Check to enable it, and then drag the slider to magnify the icons when you point to them in the Dock.

◆ **Position on screen**. Click the Left, Bottom, or Right option.

◆ **Minimize using**. Click the pop-up, and then select an animation effect.

◆ **Minimize windows into application icon** (**New!**). Select to minimize windows into the application icon on the dock.

◆ **Animate opening applications**. Select to have the application icon bounce when you launch an application.

◆ **Automatically hide and show the Dock**. This changes when you select the Turn Hiding On menu command.

③ Click the **Close** button.

Magnifying icons

---

## For Your Information

### Displaying the Genie Effect

You can slow down the minimization of a window or application (a cool genie effect). Shift-click a window's Minimize button. The window collapses into the Dock about one-fifth the usual speed. You can also Shift-click the icon in the Dock to slowly unminimize the window. Unfortunately, you can't speed it up.

## Add, Remove, and Rearrange Items in the Dock

◆ **Add an item.** Drag an icon from a Finder window to the Dock, and then position application icons to the left of the divider line and all other icons to the right.

◆ **Add an open application item.** Open the application to display the icon in the Dock, press and hold (activates Exposé) or Control-click the application icon, point to **Options**, and then click **Keep In Dock**.

◆ **Open a document using an application item.** Drag the document icon to the application icon in the Dock.

◆ **Move an item.** Drag the icon to the position you want in the Dock.

◆ **Remove an item.** Drag an icon out of the Dock.

> **TROUBLE?** *If you delete an application or document from your computer with an icon in the Dock, the Dock icon changes to a question mark, which you can remove.*

◆ **Open a folder stack.** Click a folder icon to display the stack list, and then click an item.

◆ **Customize a folder stack.** Control-click a folder icon to display a shortcut menu, and then click an option.

Add an item

Add an open application

Open a document

Remove an item

Customize a folder stack

# Creating Aliases

It can take you a while to access a file or folder buried several levels down in a folder. To save some time, you can create shortcuts to the items you use frequently. **Aliases** are shortcuts that point to a folder or file. An alias allows you to access the original folder or file from several different places. When you create an alias to a folder or file, the icon includes a little arrow in the lower-left corner. You can't make an alias for an application. However, you can add an application into the Dock, which acts like an alias. When you double-click an alias icon, a folder opens with the contents of the original folder or a document opens using its associated application. If you delete an alias of a folder or file, the original folder or file is not deleted, just the alias.

## Create an Alias

1. Open the Finder window with the icon in which you want to create an alias.

2. Select the icon.

3. Click the **File** menu, and then click **Make Alias**.

   **TIMESAVER** *Hold down ⌘+Option, and then drag a file or folder to create an alias.*

   The alias icon appears in the Finder window.

4. If you want, rename the alias icon, and then press Return.

5. Drag the alias icon to the desktop or another folder.

## Did You Know?

*You can quickly find the original file or folder of an alias.* Select the alias file or folder, click the File menu, and then click Show Original. You can also press ⌘+R.

## Create an Alias with the Title Bar

1. Open the application and document in which you want to create an alias.

2. Position the mouse pointer on the icon next to the document title in the title bar.

3. Drag the icon to the desktop, or on a folder or disk.

### Did You Know?

*You can drag the Title bar icon onto an application Dock icon.* If you want to open a document created in one program (say TextEdit), and you want to open it up in another program (say Microsoft Word), you can drag the Title bar icon of a document in TextEdit to the Microsoft Word icon in the Dock to open it.

*You can drag an alias icon into the Dock.* Drag the alias icon into the Dock on the right side. When you release the mouse, the icon appears in the Dock.

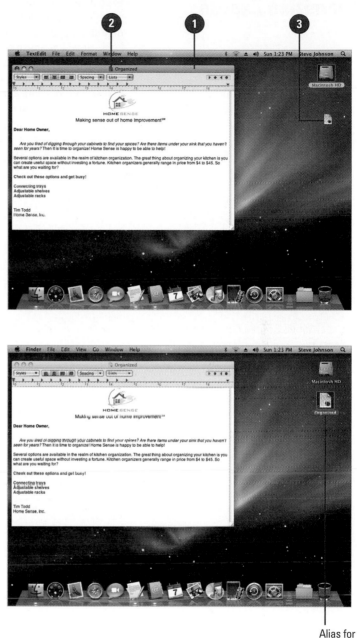

Alias for TextEdit document

# Customizing Exposé

Exposé lets you quickly move windows out of the way temporarily to make it easier to work with windows to find, move, or copy files. The default way to move windows with Exposé is to use keyboard function keys. However, these function keys might already be taken by other applications, or your computer. You can customize Exposé to move windows in three ways: screen corners, keyboard, and mouse. Using screen corners, you can trigger Exposé when you point to one of the screen corners, which you can customize to display different windows. Using the keyboard pop-ups, you can change the Exposé keyboard shortcuts. When you display the pop-ups, you can press other modifier keys, such as Shift, Option, Control, or ⌘ to create a new shortcut. If you have a mouse with two buttons, you can change options to trigger Exposé with your mouse.

## Customize Exposé

1. Click the **System Preferences** icon in the Dock, and then click the **Exposé & Spaces** icon.

2. Click the **Exposé** tab.

3. In the Active Screen Corners area, click the pop-ups for the corner you want to use, and then select an option:

   ◆ **All Windows**. Select to show all open windows at once.

   ◆ **Application Windows**. Select to show all open windows in the current application.

   ◆ **Desktop**. Select to hide all open windows and show desktop.

4. In the Keyboard area, click the pop-ups for each Exposé operation, press a keyboard modifier (Shift, Control, Option, or ⌘) if you want, and then select a shortcut key.

5. In the Mouse area, click the pop-ups for each Exposé operation, and then select a mouse button.

6. Click the **Close** button.

# Setting Up and Customizing Spaces

The first time you start Spaces, you need to setup your spaces in the Exposé & Spaces pane of System Preferences. With Spaces, you can group and arrange windows to reduce desktop clutter and organize materials into unique spaces. In the Exposé & Spaces preferences dialog box, you can enable Spaces, assign applications to every space or a specific one, change keyboard shortcuts to select and toggle between spaces, and display a Spaces menu in the menu bar.

## Set Up and Customize Spaces

1. Click the **System Preferences** icon in the Dock, and then click the **Exposé & Spaces** icon.

2. Click the **Spaces** tab.

3. Select the **Enable Spaces** check box.

4. Click the Rows and Columns **Plus** (+) or **Minus** (-) buttons to create the number of spaces you want.

5. To assign an application to a space, click the **Add** (+) button, select an application, and then click **Add**. Click the pop-up menu to the right, and then click **Every space** or **Space 1**, **Space 2**, etc.

   ◆ To remove an application, select the application, and then click the **Minus** (-) button.

6. In the Keyboard and Mouse Shortcuts area, click the pop-ups for each operation, and then select a keyboard key or option.

7. To switch between Spaces using a menu, select the **Show Spaces in menu bar** check box.

8. Select or clear the **When switching to an application, switch to a space with open windows for the application** check box (**New!**).

9. Click the **Close** button.

# Using Simple Finder

If you have novice users who want to use your computer, you should set up a user account with the Simple Finder in Parental Controls preferences. **Simple Finder** is a simplified version of the Mac OS X Finder with fewer menus and icons, and allows limited access to the items on your hard disk. The Dock contains only three folders: Documents, My Applications, and Shared. The Documents folder provides a place for users to save their documents, while the My Applications folder provides access to the applications you select for them in Parental Control preferences. If you want to share documents with them, they can access the items in the Shared folder.

## Set Up the Simple Finder

1. Click the **System Preferences** icon in the Dock, and then click the **Parental Controls** icon.

2. Click the user account for the person you want to set up the Simple Finder. If necessary, click the Lock icon and enter user name and password, first.

3. Click the **System** tab.

4. Select the **Use Simple Finder** check box.

5. Select or clear the **Only allow selected applications** check box.

6. Select or clear the applications you want to enable or disable for the account.

7. Select or clear the options you want to enable or disable for the account.

8. Click the **Close** button.

## Did You Know?

*You can get administrative access while logged in to Simple Finder.* Click the Finder menu, click Run Full Finder, and then type your name and password. When you're done, click the Finder menu, and then click Return To Simple Finder.

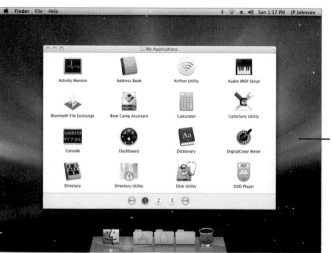

Simple Finder

# Setting System Preferences

## Introduction

System Preferences allows you to customize various parts of Mac OS X, such as the appearance of your desktop, your computers date and time, the way CDs and DVDs start up when you insert them, or use speech recognition to convert a spoken voice into commands or electronic text. For those of you with a Mac laptop, you can manage power usage for your computer. Universal Access preferences make it easier for a person with a disability, such as difficulty seeing or hearing or controlling a mouse, to use a computer. If you have an ink device attached to your computer, you can use Ink Preferences to improve the recognition of ink to text.

You can access System Preferences from the Dock or the Apple menu. Many applications also have their own preferences, which you can access from the application menu within the application. System Preferences are organized into categories by default. Each category contains a set of icons, which you can open to set customization options in preference panes for different aspects of the Macintosh operating system.

Some System Preference panes are locked for security reasons. If preference settings are all grayed out, the preference pane is locked to prevent non- administrators from making changes. Check the Lock icon at the bottom of System Preferences. If the Lock icon is locked, you need an administrator name and password to unlock it and make changes. If you log in as an administrator, the Lock icon is unlocked, unless you set a security option to have the preference panes stay locked. When you close the preference pane, it locks automatically.

## What You'll Do

**Understand System Preferences**

**View System Preferences**

**Lock and Unlock Preference Settings**

**Change Appearance Options**

**Set Up the Desktop**

**Set Up Screen Savers**

**Set the Date and Time**

**Change Language Options**

**Change Text Substitution Options**

**Save Energy and Manage Power**

**Select a Startup Disk**

**Change the Way a CD & DVD Starts**

**Control Sound**

**Recognize Your Speech**

**Let Mac Do the Talking**

**Set Universal Access Options**

**Explore and Use VoiceOver**

**Set Ink Preferences**

# Understanding System Preferences

System Preferences allow you to customize system wide settings for various aspects of Mac OS X and your computer. The System Preferences window is organized alphabetically or by categories: Personal, Hardware, Internet & Network, and System. Each category contains preference areas that you can change to customize the way Mac OS X works. Only an administrator can change system settings that affect everyone who uses the computer.

## Personal

**Appearance.** Change the look and feel of buttons, selected items, and scroll bars. See page 100.

**Desktop & Screen Saver.** Change the desktop background or select a visual screen effect to hide your desktop. See pages 102-103.

**Dock.** Change the location of the Dock, adjust the size of icons, set magnification, or hide the Dock. Sees page 88-89 in Chapter 4.

**Expose' & Spaces.** Set keyboard shortcuts or mouse positions to show or hide all your windows at one time, or create unique spaces for projects. See page 92-93 in Chapter 4.

**Language & Text.** Change your computer to read or write with other languages and substitute text. See pages 106-109.

**Security.** Protect your computer and the information on it, and adjust firewall settings to protect your computer from access over the Internet. See page 409 in Chapter 16.

**Spotlight.** Select the categories and priority order you want used in Spotlight searches. See pages 64-65 in Chapter 3.

## Hardware

**CDs & DVDs.** Set startup options when you insert a CD or DVD. See pages 113 and 316.

**Displays.** Set the screen size, resolution, color settings, and arrange multiple screens. See page 454-455 in Chapter 18.

**Energy Saver.** Set the computer to sleep and conserve power, and schedule automatic shutdown and startup. See page 110-111.

**Ink.** Set the computer to write text using a graphics tablet and stylus, recognize the ink, and turn it into words. (Available only if a graphics tablet or ink device is installed.) See page 128.

**Keyboard.** Change the speed of your keyboard, and customize universal keyboard shortcuts or application shortcuts. See page 453 in Chapter 18.

**Mouse.** Change the speed of your mouse, primary mouse button, or scroll wheel zoom. See pages 452 in Chapter 18.

**Print & Fax.** Add a printer, monitor print jobs, set up to receive faxes, and share printers and a fax modem with other users. See pages 198-199 in Chapter 8.

**Sound.** Change computer sound volume, effects, and sound input or output devices. See pages 114-115.

## Internet & Network

**MobileMe.** Create an online MobileMe account and set access options. See page 346 in Chapter 13.

**Network.** Create and manage network and Internet connection settings. See page 410 in Chapter 16.

**Bluetooth.** Control how to send and receive files between your computer and other Bluetooth devices. (Available if Bluetooth is enabled). See pages 413-415 in Chapter 16.

**Sharing.** Set services for Personal File Sharing, Personal Web Sharing, and Printer

Sharing; and share your Internet connection with others. See pages 404-407 in Chapter 16.

## System

**Accounts.** Set up accounts, access privileges, and log in and out settings to share your computer with others. See pages 387-388 in Chapter 15.

**Date & Time.** Set your computer's date, time, and time zone, or use a network time server. See pages 104-105.

**Parental Controls.** Set limits on computer use, including content, Mail & iChat, and time, and create logs. See pages 392-393 in Chapter 15.

**Software Update.** Set a schedule or options to check for updates automatically on the Internet. See pages 432-433 in Chapter 17.

**Speech.** Set the computer to speak the text on the screen or use spoken commands to control your computer. See pages 116-119.

**Startup Disk.** Select the disk or drive you want to use to start up your computer. See page 112.

**Time Machine.** Set options to back up everything on your computer. See page 477 in Chapter 20.

**Universal Access.** Set options for the visual or hearing impaired to make it easier to use the computer keyboard, mouse, and screen. See pages 120-127.

## Adding or Removing Third-Party System Preferences

In addition to the System Preferences included with Mac OS X, you can add other System Preferences developed by other companies, known as third-party system preferences. To install a third-party preference, download or drag the preference to your hard disk, double-click its icon, and then follow the on-screen instructions. To uninstall a third-party preference, use the method provided by the developer, or hold down the Control key, click the Preference icon in the System Preferences window, click Uninstall, and then follow the on-screen instructions.

Categories

# Viewing System Preferences

System Preferences are organized into categories by default. Each category contains a set of icons, which you can open to set customization options in preference panes for different aspects of the Macintosh operating system. You can also view the icons in the System Preferences window alphabetically, depending on your preference. Simply click a preference icon to open it, and then make the changes you want. The preferences take effect when you quit or close System Preferences.

## View System Preferences

1. Click the **Apple** menu, and then click **System Preferences** or click the **System Preferences** icon in the Dock.

2. To change preference organization, click the **View** menu, and then click **Organize By Categories** or **Organize Alphabetically**.

3. To open a preference, click the icon.

   TIMESAVER *Press the first letter of the preferences name to select the icon, and then press the Spacebar to open it.*

4. To switch to another preference, click the **View** menu, and then click the one you want to open.

   TIMESAVER *Click the Show All button on the toolbar to show all the preference icons.*

5. When you're done, click the **System Preferences** menu, and then click **Quit System Preferences**, or click the **Close** button.

## Did You Know?

*You can customize the System Preferences toolbar.* To add a button to the toolbar in System Preferences, drag an icon to the toolbar. To remove a button, drag it out of the toolbar.

# Locking and Unlocking Preference Settings

Some preference panes are locked for security reasons. If preference settings are all grayed out, the preference pane is locked to prevent non-administrators from making changes. Check the Lock icon at the bottom of System Preferences. If the Lock icon is locked, you need an administrator name and password to unlock it and make changes. If you log in as an administrator, the Lock icon is unlocked, unless you set a security option to have the preference panes stay locked. When you close the preference pane, it locks automatically.

## Unlock a Preference Pane

1. Click the **System Preferences** icon in the Dock.

2. Click the preference pane icon (such as Security) that you want to lock settings.

3. Click the **Lock** icon.

4. To unlock, type an administrator name and password.

5. Click **OK**.

6. Click the **Close** button.

## Set Preference Panes to Lock

1. Click the **System Preferences** icon in the Dock.

2. Click the **Security** icon, and then click the **General** tab.

3. If settings are grayed out, click the **Lock** icon, type an administrator name and password, and then click **OK**.

4. Select the **Require a password to unlock each secure system preference pane** check box.

5. Click the **Close** button.

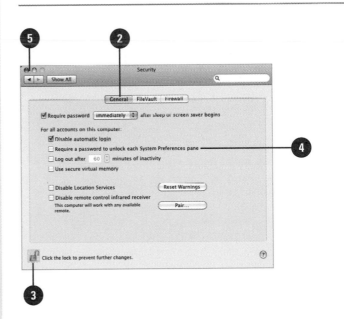

# Changing Appearance Options

The Appearance pane in System Preferences allows you to change the look and feel of Mac OS X in a few areas. You can change the color scheme for buttons, menus, and windows, and the highlight color for text and lists. Or if you're not comfortable using the scroll bars, you can change the way scroll bars work and the placement of the scroll arrows. If your text looks blurry or jagged, you can adjust the font smoothing, known as **anti-aliasing**, style to fix it (after you log out and back in). As you open files and applications, Mac OS X keeps a list in the Recent Items submenu in the Apple menu. In the Appearance pane, you can set the number of recent items that appear in the menu.

## Change the Appearance Color and Scroll Bars

1 Click the **System Preferences** icon in the Dock, and then click the **Appearance** icon.

2 Click the **Appearance** pop-up, and then select a color. If you select Other, the Color Picker palette appears so you can select a color.

3 Click the **Highlight Color** pop-up, and then select a color.

4 Click the **At top and bottom or together** option to set the placement of scroll arrows.

5 Click the **Jump to the next page** or **Jump to here** option to select an operation when you click in the scroll bar.

6 Select the **Use smooth scrolling** check box to avoid slight jumping when you click inside the scroll bar.

7 Select the **Double-click a window's title bar to minimize** check box to make it easier to minimize a window instead of using the small yellow Minimize button.

8 Click the **Close** button.

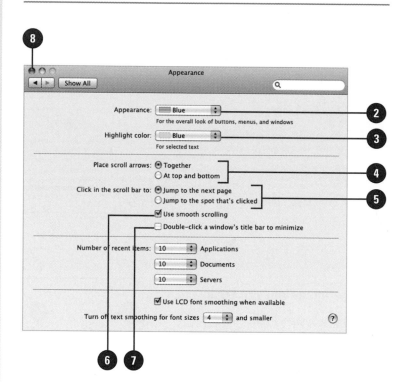

## Smooth Fonts

1. Click the **System Preferences** icon in the Dock, and then click the **Appearance** icon.

2. Select the **Use LCD font smoothing when available** check box to enable font smoothing, which reduces jagged edges for some fonts (**New!**).

3. Click the **Turn Off Text Smoothing For Font Sizes** pop-up, and then select a font size.

   All text in the font size or smaller is not smoothed, which makes it easier to read.

4. Click the **Close** button.

## Change Number of Recent Items

1. Click the **System Preferences** icon in the Dock, and then click the **Appearance** icon.

2. Click the pop-ups for the **Number of Recent Items**, and then select a number.

3. Click the **Close** button.

---

### Did You Know?

*You can clear the Recent Items sub-menu.* Click the Apple menu, point to Recent Items, and then click Clear Menu.

# Setting Up the Desktop

The desktop **background**, or wallpaper, is a picture that serves as your desktop's backdrop, the basic surface on which icons and windows appear. You can select a background picture from the ones provided with Mac OS X (which includes Apple Background, Nature, Abstract, or Solid Colors) or select one of your own in the Desktop & Screen Saver pane in System Preferences. You can select pictures in a variety of formats (such as JPEG, PICT, GIF, TIFF, PDF, or PSD) from your own Pictures folder, another folder you select, or even an iPhoto folder (Photo Library, Last Import, or iPhoto album), and then select options to display them on the screen. When you select a picture from a folder, you can display all the pictures at certain intervals in alphabetical or random order. In addition, you can turn on or off the translucent menu bar effect (**New!**).

## Select a Desktop Background

1 Click the **System Preferences** icon in the Dock, and then click the **Desktop & Screen Saver** icon.

2 Click the **Desktop** tab.

3 Click an image category folder in the left column.

4 Select a thumbnail.

5 If you want to use your own folder of pictures, click the **Add** (+) button, select the folder, and then click **Choose**.

◆ To remove one of your own added folders, select the folder, and then click the **Remove** (-) button.

6 To show all the pictures in a folder, select the **Change picture** check box, select an interval from the pop-up, and then select the **Random order** check box or clear it for random order.

7 Select the the **Translucent menu bar** check box (**New!**) to enable the menu effect or clear the check box disable it.

8 Click the **Close** button.

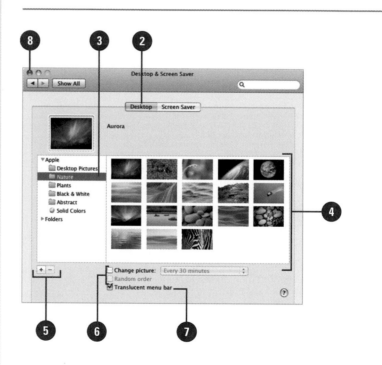

## For Your Information

### Using Quartz Extreme Enhanced Graphics

Mac OS X supports an accelerated graphics technology called **Quartz Extreme**. If you have a supported graphics card installed on your computer, you can take advantage of faster window resizing and scrolling, cross-fading when changing desktop pictures, and a cube-rotation animation when switching users. To find out if your computer supports Quartz Extreme, set your desktop to change background pictures every 5 seconds. If each background fades into the next, then you have it.

# Setting Up Screen Savers

In the past, you needed a screen saver (a continually moving display) to protect your monitor from screen burn in. Those days are gone with the emergence of new display technology. Screen savers are more for entertainment than anything else. When you leave your computer idle for a specified wait time, a screen saver displays a continuous scene, such as an aquarium, until you move your mouse to stop it. If a security option is set in the Security pane in System Preferences, your computer requires a password when you wake from a screen saver. You can select a screen saver from the ones provided with Mac OS X, or select a folder with pictures (all saved in the same format) or a published slideshow from a MobileMe account online or RSS feed, which gets downloaded to your computer.

## Set Up a Screen Saver

① Click the **System Preferences** icon in the Dock, and then click the **Desktop & Screen Saver** icon.

② Click the **Screen Saver** tab.

③ Select a screen saver, using any of the following methods:

◆ Click an Apple screen saver.

◆ Click **Pictures Folder**, and then select one, or click **Shuffle** to shuffle through screen saver pictures (**New!**).

◆ Select the **Use random screen saver** check box to use different screen savers each time.

◆ Select the **Show with clock** check box to show the clock.

④ Click **Options**, select the check boxes you want, and then click **OK**.

⑤ Drag the slider to determine when the screen saver starts.

⑥ To activate the screen saver with your mouse pointer, click **Hot Corners**, specify the options you want in the corner you want it.

⑦ Click **OK**.

⑧ Click the **Close** button.

Turns off screen saver

# Setting the Date and Time

The date and time you set on your computer is very important. When you save a file or send and receive an e-mail, your computer uses the date and time you set in the Date & Time preference pane. You can set the date and time manually, or if your computer is connected to the Internet, you can have a time server set it automatically. If you have an Internet connect, such as DSL or cable, use the time server, otherwise you should set it manually. To make sure your files and e-mail times are not off by a few hours, you need to set your time zone, either manually or automatically (**New!**). When you travel, Snow Leopard can automatically change your time zone using Wi-Fi (**New!**). You can also set the date and time to display as a digital (12:05 PM) or analog (round face with hands) clock in the menu bar, or have the computer speak, announcing the time at certain intervals.

## Set the Date and Time

1. Click the **System Preferences** icon in the Dock, and then click the **Date & Time** icon.

2. Click the **Date & Time** tab.

3. To set the time automatically over the Internet, select the **Set date & time automatically** check box, and then use the pop-up to select a time server.

4. To set the date and time manually, use any of the following methods:

   ◆ Select the individual date and time fields, and then enter a number, or use the up and down arrows.

   ◆ Click a date in the calendar and drag the hands on the clock.

5. Click the **Time Zone** tab.

   ◆ To automatically set the time zone, select the **Set time zone automatically using current location** check box (**New!**).

6. Click the part of the map closest to your location.

7. Click the **Closest City** pop-up, and then select the closest city to your location.

8. Click the **Close** button.

Select to automatically set the time zone to the current location

## Set Date and Time Options

1 Click the **System Preferences** icon in the Dock, and then click the **Date & Time** icon.

2 Click the **Clock** tab.

3 Select the **Show date and time in menu bar** check box.

4 Select the view as (**Digital** or **Analog**) option you want.

5 Select or clear the following check boxes:

◆ **Display the time with seconds**. Check to add seconds to the time (Menu bar).

◆ **Flash the time separators**. Check to show a blinking colon.

◆ **Use a 24-hour clock**. Check to show military time (18:00 instead of 6:00 PM).

◆ **Show AM/PM**. Check to show AM or PM.

◆ **Show the day of the week**. Check to show the day of the week (Menu bar).

◆ **Show the date**. Check to show the date (Menu bar) (**New!**).

6 To speak the time, select the **Announce the time** check box, click the pop-up, and then select an interval.

To change the computer voice, click **Customize Voice**.

7 Click the **Close** button.

Window view

### For Your Information

## Using the Menu Bar Clock

When you display the clock in the menu bar, the time appears in analog form or as a clock icon with the current time. If you want to know the date, click the clock. A menu drops down displaying the complete date. The menu also allows you to switch between digital and analog clock types and open the Date & Time pane in System Preferences.

# Changing Language Options

The Language & Text pane (**New!**) in System Preferences gives you options to use different languages for menus, dialogs, and the keyboard, as well as write text in other languages. The language you write can be different from the language for menus, dialogs, and the keyboard. The Language tab allows you to select a language that you use in application menus and dialogs, and write in an application. The Formats tab allows you to select international formats for dates, times, numbers, and measurement units. The Input Sources tab provides you with a list of languages that you can select a keyboard layout, which lets you type in other languages. If you're not familiar with the keyboard layout, you can use the Keyboard Viewer to show you what keys to press to display the keys you want in the input menu language. To make language selection easier, you can add the Input menu to the menu bar.

## Set Input Sources Options

1. Click the **System Preferences** icon in the Dock, and then click the **Language & Text** icon.

2. Click the **Input Sources** tab.

3. Select the check box next to the language(s) you want to use.

4. To see what the characters look like on your keyboard, select the **Keyboard Viewer** check box.

   The Keyboard Viewer is available on the menu bar in the Input Menu.

5. Click **Keyboard Shortcuts**, select the keyboard shortcut or text matching options you want, and then click **OK**.

6. Select an option to use the same or different input sources (**New!**).

7. To change input menu languages from the menu bar, select the **Show input menu in menu bar** check box.

8. Click the **Close** button.

   **TIMESAVER** Press ⌘+ Spacebar to switch between the two most recent keyboard layouts. Press Option+⌘+Spacebar to cycle down the list of keyboards.

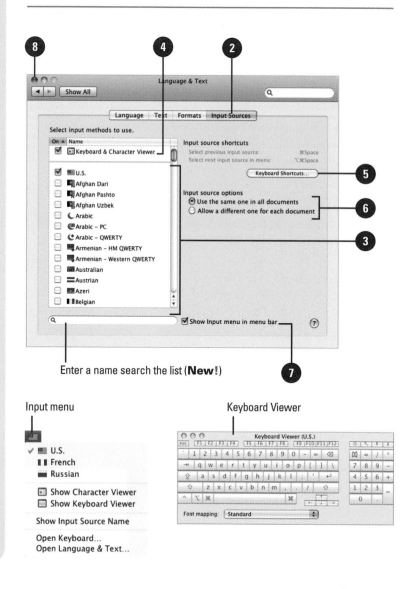

Enter a name search the list (**New!**)

Input menu

Keyboard Viewer

## Set International Date, Time, and Number Formats

1. Click the **System Preferences** icon in the Dock, and then click the **Language & Text** icon.

2. Click the **Formats** tab.

3. Click the **Region** pop-up, and then select a region. If necessary, select the **Show all regions** check box to display your region.

4. Click **Customize**, specify the formats you want for Dates, Times, and Numbers, and then click **OK**.

5. Select a **Currency** and **Measurements Units** from the pop-ups.

6. Click the **Close** button.

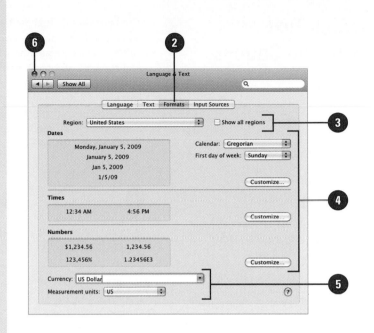

## Change Language Options for Menus and Dialogs

1. Click the **System Preferences** icon in the Dock, and then click the **Language & Text** icon.

2. Click the **Language** tab.

   A list of available languages on your computer appears.

3. To add or remove languages, click **Edit List**, select or clear the check boxes, and then click **OK**.

4. Drag the language you want to the top of the list.

   If an application can't support the first language, it tries to use the second one, and so on.

5. Click the **Close** button.

   Changes take place the next time you launch the Finder or an application.

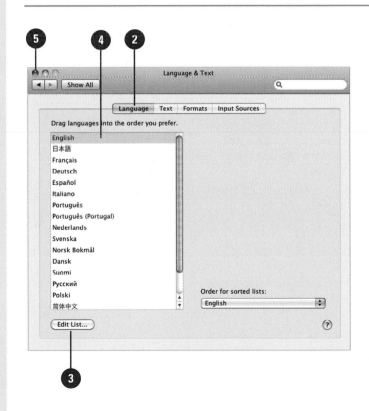

# Changing Text Substitution Options

The Language & Text pane (**New!**) in System Preferences gives you options to automatically correct common spelling errors and insert symbols as you type. Snow Leopard comes with a list of common text and symbol entries you can edit or remove. You can add words and phrases that you misspell, or add often-typed words and save time by just typing their initials. You can use text substitution to quickly insert symbols. For example, you can type (c) to insert ©. You can also set options to check spelling and select text by language, and automatically change double or single quotation marks.

## Set Symbol and Text Substitution Options

1. Click the **System Preferences** icon in the Dock, and then click the **Language & Text** icon.

2. Click the **Text** tab.

3. Select the check boxes you want to use for symbol and text substitution.

4. Select language and selection settings for the following options:

   ◆ **Spelling.** Allows you to check your spelling. Select **Automatic by Language** or a specific language.

   ◆ **Word Break.** Specifies how a word is highlighted when it's double-clicked. Select **Standard** or a specific language.

5. Select Smart Quote settings for the following options:

   ◆ **First.** Select a quote style when you type double quotation marks.

   ◆ **Second.** Select a quote style when you type single quotation marks.

6. To restore setting, click **Restore Defaults**.

7. Click the **Close** button.

## Add, Edit. or Remove a Text Substitution Entry

**1** Click the **System Preferences** icon in the Dock, and then click the **Language & Text** icon.

**2** Click the **Text** tab.

**3** Do one of the following:

◆ **Add.** Click the **Add** (+) button, type a misspelled word or an abbreviation, press Tab, type the replacement text, and then press Return.

◆ **Edit.** double-click an entry, make a change, and then press Return.

◆ **Remove.** Select an entry, click **Remove** (-) button.

**4** Click the **Close** button.

Add (+) and Remove (-) buttons

## Replace Text as You Type

◆ To correct spelling errors or insert symbols automatically, continue typing until text substitution makes the required correction.

See examples of text substitution in the following table.

### Examples of Text Substitution

| Type of Correction | If You Type | AutoCorrect Inserts |
|---|---|---|
| Common typos | can;t | can't |
| Common typos | windoes | windows |
| Superscript ordinals | 2nd | 2$^{nd}$ |
| Stacked fractions | 1/2 | ½ |
| Smart quotes | " " | " " |
| Em dashes | Madison--a small city in Wisconsin--is a nice place to live. | Madison—a small city in Wisconsin— is a nice place to live. |
| Symbols | (c) | © |
| Symbols | (r) | ® |

# Saving Energy and Managing Power

When you're not using your computer, you can save energy by putting it to sleep. When you put your computer to sleep, the power mode is set to low and the screen goes black to save energy. Your computer is still running, so it takes less time for it to wake up. You can use the Sleep command on the Apple menu to put your computer right to sleep, or you can put your computer and display to sleep automatically when it has been idle for a specific amount of time or when you schedule it at a regular time interval. You can also set the hard disk to sleep whenever possible to save more energy. If you have a Mac laptop, such as a MacBook, it automatically goes to sleep when you close the lid. You move your mouse or press a key to wake it up. If a security option is set in the Security pane in System Preferences, your computer requires a password when it wakes from a sleep. You can also schedule a computer restart or shutdown, at a regular time interval, or a restart after a power failure.

## Set Sleep Options

1. Click the **System Preferences** icon in the Dock, and then click the **Energy Saver** icon.

2. Drag the slider to set a time interval for Computer sleep and Display sleep.

   **IMPORTANT** *To prevent your computer from sleeping at any time, drag the sliders for Computer and Display sleep to Never.*

   **TROUBLE?** *If the sleep time is less than the screen saver time, then increase the sleep time or click Screen Saver to change its time.*

3. To conserve energy, select the **Put the hard disk(s) to sleep when possible** check box.

4. Click the **Close** button.

## Set a Sleep, Startup, or Shut Down Schedule

1. Click the **System Preferences** icon in the Dock, and then click the **Energy Saver** icon.

2. Click **Schedule**, and then click **Details**, if necessary.

3. Select or clear the **Start up or waker** check box. If so, select an interval from the pop-up, and then set a time.

4. Select or clear the bottom check box. If so, select an operation from the first pop-up menu, select an interval from the second pop-up, and then set a time.

5. Click **OK**, and then click the **Close** button.

## Set Wake and Power Failure Restart Options

1. Click the **System Preferences** icon in the Dock, and then click the **Energy Saver** icon.

2. Select or clear the **Wake for network access** check box.

3. Select or clear the **Allow power button to sleep the computer** check box.

4. Select or clear the **Start automatically after a power failure** check box.

5. Click the **Close** button.

# Selecting a Startup Disk

Instead of starting from your local hard disk, you can start your computer from a CD or DVD, a network volume, another disk or disk partition (a single hard disk separated into two distinct areas), or another operating system, such as Microsoft Windows XP, Vista, or 7. Starting your computer with Windows is useful when you want to use applications that are not compatible with Mac OS X. When you start your computer in Windows, you need to use the Startup Disk Control Panel in the Apple menu to switch back to your Mac OS X startup disk. If Windows is not available in the Startup Disk preference pane, you need to have an Intel-based Mac and use Boot Camp Assistant to set up your computer. You can also restart you computer in Target Disk Mode, which allows you to connect to another computer using a FireWire cable and use it as a hard disk.

## Select a Startup Disk

1. Click the **System Preferences** icon in the Dock, and then click the **Startup Disk** icon.

2. Click the icon of the system folder you want to use as the startup disk.

3. To restart your computer, click **Restart**.

   **TIMESAVER** *Hold down the Option key while you restart your computer, select a startup disk, and then click Restart.*

4. To restart your computer in order to connect to another computer using a FireWire cable, click **Target Disk Mode**, read the dialog for instructions, and then click **Restart**.

## See Also

*See Chapter 19,"Working with Mac OS X Along with Windows," on page 465 for information on starting your computer with Microsoft Windows XP, Vista, or 7.*

# Changing the Way a CD or DVD Starts

When you insert a CD or DVD into your computer, Mac OS X automatically performs an operation, such as opening iTunes and playing an audio CD. You can change what happens when you insert a CD or DVD in the CDs & DVDs preference pane in System Preferences. You can have Mac OS X open a dialog to ask you what to do, ignore it, run a script, or open an application, such as iTunes, iPhoto, iDVD, or Finder, to burn or play a disc. If you ignore a CD or DVD, the disc doesn't show up on the desktop or in a Finder window.

## Change CD or DVD Start Settings

1. Click the **System Preferences** icon in the Dock, and then click the **CDs & DVDs** icon.

2. Click the pop-ups for each type of CD or DVD, and then select a startup option:

   - **Ask what to do**. A dialog appears that asks you what to do with the disc.

   - **Open an application**. Select Open Finder, Open application name or click Open An Application to select one.

     Mac OS X automatically opens the application you select.

   - **Run Script**. Select and schedule a script to run.

   - **Ignore**. Nothing happens.

3. Click the **Close** button.

### Did You Know?

***You can change Finder preferences to show CDs or DVDs on the desktop.*** Click the Finder menu, click Preferences, click General, select the CDs, DVDs, and iPods check box, and then click the Close button.

# Controlling Sound

The Sound pane in System Preferences allows you to adjust input, output and alert volumes, change input and output sound devices, change alert sounds, and play Front Row, an entertainment system, and user interface sound effects, such as when you drag an icon to the Trash. You can use an input device, such as a microphone, to record your voice or give spoken commands on an output device, such as built-in or external speakers, to play music, words, and other sounds. If your computer has two stereo speakers, you can adjust the sound balance between them. If you don't want to hear sound from your speakers, you can turn on Mute, just like on your TV or stereo. If you use applications with volume controls, such as iTunes, the volume can only be equal to or less than the computer's output volume. To make volume control easier, you can add output volume to the menu bar.

## Change Sound Effects

1 Click the **System Preferences** icon in the Dock, and then click the **Sound** icon.

2 Click the **Sound Effects** tab.

3 To change an alert sound, click a sound from the list.

4 Drag the **Alert volume** slider to adjust the alert volume, which is relative to the output volume.

**TIMESAVER** *Hold down the Option key while you drag the main volume on the status menu bar to adjust the alert volume.*

5 To play Finder related sounds, select the **Play user interface sound effects** check box.

6 If you have volume keys on your keyboard, clear the **Play feedback when volume keys is changed** check box to disable the feedback option and use the volume keys.

7 To play sounds from Front Row, select the **Play Front Row sound effects** check box.

8 To change output volume from the menu bar, select the **Show volume in menu bar** check box.

9 Click the **Close** button.

Volume on menu bar

## Set Sound Output Options

1. Click the **System Preferences** icon in the Dock, and then click the **Sound** icon.

2. Click the **Output** tab.

3. Select a device for sound output.

   Options vary depending on the output sound device.

4. Drag the **Balance** slider to adjust the sound for the left and right speakers.

5. Drag the **Output volume** slider to increase or decrease the volume, or select the **Mute** check box to turn speaker sound off.

6. Click the **Close** button.

## Set Sound Input Options

1. Click the **System Preferences** icon in the Dock, and then click the **Sound** icon.

2. Click the **Input** tab.

3. Select a device for sound input.

   Options vary depending on the input sound device.

4. Drag the **Input volume** slider to increase or decrease the volume.

   The Input level meter displays the sound level coming from the selected sound device.

5. Click the **Close** button.

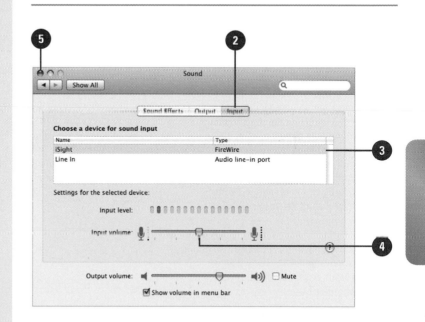

# Recognizing Your Speech

The Speech pane in System Preferences allows you to initialize and customize speech recognition on your computer. **Speech recognition** is the ability to convert a spoken voice into commands or electronic text. However, Apple's speech recognition only does half the job; it only executes commands listed in the Speakable Commands window, which you can add or remove in groups, such as menu bar commands. You need another program, such as iListen (*www.macspeech.com*) to convert voice to text. After you turn on speech recognition, the Feedback window (a small circle microphone) appears, displaying the Esc key in the middle. Press and hold or press the Esc key, which you can change, to turn listening on and off. Now you can speak your commands.

## Setup Listening Options

1. Click the **System Preferences** icon in the Dock, and then click the **Speech** icon.

2. Click the **Speech Recognition** tab, and then click the **Settings** tab.

3. Click the **Microphone** pop-up, and then select a microphone attached to your computer. Click **Calibrate** to improve recognition results, if necessary.

4. To change the listening key, click **Change Key**, enter a new key, and then click **OK**.

5. Click an option to listen while the listening key is pressed or while listening is turned on (by pressing the listening key).

   If you select the second option, you can type a name and use the **Name** pop-up to specify whether the name must be spoken before each command.

6. Select the **Speak command acknowledgement** check box to have your computer repeat the command it heard.

7. Click the **Play this sound pop-up** to select a sound to play when your computer recognizes a spoken command.

8. Click the **Close** button.

## Enable Speech Recognition and Select Commands

**1** Click the **System Preferences** icon in the Dock, and then click the **Speech** icon.

**2** Click the **Speech Recognition** tab.

**3** Click the **On** option to display the Feedback window. To remove the window later, click the **Off** option.

**4** Click the **Commands** tab.

**5** Select or clear the check boxes with the groups of commands you want to enable or disable. If available, click **Configure** to specify other options.

**6** Click a button or select the options you want:

  ◆ **Helpful Tips**. Click to display tips about speakable items.

  ◆ **Open Speakable Items Folder**. Click to open the Speakable Items folder.

**7** Click the **Close** button.

## Use Speech Recognition

**1** Hold down the listening key or press it to turn listening on.

**2** To display a list of commands, click the **Feedback window** triangle, and then click **Open Speech Commands Window**.

**3** Say the name if necessary, and then say a command.

Recognized commands appear above the Feedback window, while feedback appears below.

**4** Release or press the listening key to turn listening off.

Spoken command

Computer response

Commands you've spoken

Available commands to speak

# Letting Mac Do the Talking

Your Macintosh can speak to you as well as listen. Mac OS X can read aloud what appears on your screen, such as typed text, alert messages, window items, menus, and other interface items. It speaks using a synthesized voice, such as Pipe Organ, Cellos, or Junior. Some voices, such as Pipe Organ, are based on a song and sing the voice. Alex is a new synthesized English voice that uses advanced Apple synthesis to deliver a more natural speaking voice at a faster rate. You can use the Speech pane in System Preferences to select a default voice, set talking alert options for when alerts appear on the screen, and other spoken options for the user interface. Instead of just showing you, the Mac can tell you when an application needs your attention, such as when your printer is out of paper, or read buttons, icons, tabs, dialog options, and selected text in e-mails and documents when you point to it as well as read select text when you press a keyboard shortcut.

## Set the Default Speaking Voice

**1** Click the **System Preferences** icon in the Dock, and then click the **Speech** icon.

**2** Click the **Text to Speech** tab.

**3** Click the **System Voice** pop-up, and then select one of the voices from the list.

◆ Click **Show More Voices** at the bottom of the pop-up to display more voices from which to choose. Click **Show Fewer Voice** at the bottom of the pop-up to reduce the list.

The computer speaks so you can hear the voice, and a description of the voice appears on the right.

**4** To change the speed at which the voice speaks, drag the **Speaking Rate** slider.

**5** To hear the select speaking voice at the current rate, click **Play**.

**6** Click the **Close** button.

## Set Spoken User Interface Options

1. Click the **System Preferences** icon in the Dock, and then click the **Speech** icon.

2. Click the **Text to Speech** tab.

3. Select the **Announce when alerts are displayed** check box, click **Set Alert Options**, specify the following alert options, and then click **OK**.

   ◆ **Voice.** Reads the contents of an alert dialog. Use the pop-up to select an alert voice.

   ◆ **Phrase.** Speak a certain phrase when an alert appears. Use the pop-up to select a phrase.

   ◆ **Delay.** Drag to set the delay between the alert and the computer speaking.

   ◆ **Play.** Click to display a sample of the alert.

4. Select the other spoken items options you want:

   ◆ **Announce when an application requires your attention.** Check to verbally announce when an application needs your attention, such as your printer is out of paper.

   ◆ **Speak selected text when the key is pressed.** Check to read any text you select when you press a key combination. In the dialog, press a keyboard shortcut or stop speaking selected text, and then click **OK**.

5. Click the **Close** button.

# Setting Universal Access Options

Universal Access preferences make it easier for a person with a disability, such as difficulty seeing or hearing or controlling a mouse, to use a computer. You can set options to use VoiceOver so you can hear descriptions of screen items, have the screen flash when alert sounds occur, switch the screen to black and white for more visual contrast, zoom in on the screen to make images larger to see, use Sticky Keys or Slow Keys to help control the keyboard, and use Mouse Keys to make mouse functionality available on the numeric keypad.

## Set Seeing and Hearing Options

1. Click the **System Preferences** icon in the Dock, and then click the **Universal Access** icon.

2. Click the **Seeing** tab.

3. Click the VoiceOver **On** or **Off** option.

4. Click the Zoom **Screen**, **Window**, or **Off** option (**New!**).

   **TIMESAVER** *Press* ⌘+*Option +8 to turn zoom on or off.*

   ◆ Click **Options** to customize the way zoom works.

   **TIMESAVER** *Press* ⌘+*Option += (equal) to zoom in, or press* ⌘+*Option+- (minus) to zoom out.*

5. Click the **Black on White** or **White on Black** option.

   **TIMESAVER** *Press Shift+*⌘ *+Option+8 to switch to White-on-Black.*

6. Select or clear the **Use grayscale** check box.

7. Drag the slider to enhance the contrast as necessary.

8. Click the **Hearing** tab.

9. Select or clear the **Flash the screen when an alert sound occurs** check box.

10. Click the **Close** button.

## Set Keyboard Options

**1** Click the **System Preferences** icon in the Dock, and then click the **Universal Access** icon.

**2** Click the **Keyboard** tab.

**3** To press a group of modifier keys as a sequence, select the **On** option (Sticky Keys), select or clear the **Beep when a modifier key is set** check box, and then select or clear the **Display pressed keys on screen** check box. If so, white symbols appear when you press a modifier key.

**4** To make the keyboard respond more slowly, click the **On** option (Slow Keys), drag the **Acceptance delay** slider, and then select or clear the **Use click key sounds** check box.

**5** Click the **Close** button.

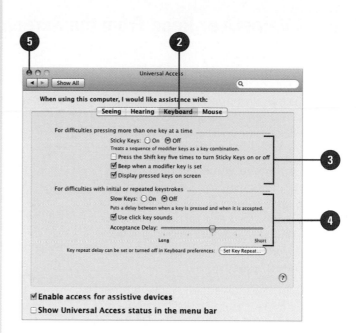

## Set Mouse Options

**1** Click the **System Preferences** icon in the Dock, and then click the **Universal Access** icon.

**2** Click the **Mouse** tab.

**3** Click the **On** option (Mouse Keys).

Press 5 on the numeric keypad to click an item on the screen. Press 0 to press and hold, and then press 5 again to release, press and hold.

**4** Set the slider options you want:

◆ **Initial Delay.** Sets how the pointer moves when you press a key.

◆ **Maximum Speed**. Sets the maximum pointer speed.

◆ **Cursor Size**. Sets the cursor size.

**5** Click the **Close** button.

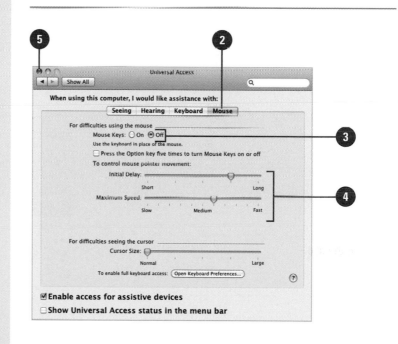

# Having VoiceOver Read From the Screen

VoiceOver is a screen reader utility for Mac OS X that speaks the text in documents and windows. When you open accessible applications in VoiceOver, the application automatically speak text. For example, iChat speaks new text messages as they arrive.

When you move around your screen or within documents using VoiceOver, a dark rectangle appears, known as the VoiceOver cursor, to indicate the screen focus area for what to speak. You can use your mouse and keyboard with VoiceOver to move and configure the VoiceOver cursor.

VoiceOver uses advanced Apple synthesis to deliver a more natural speaking voice at a faster rate. Mac OS X Leopard introduces a new synthesized English voice named Alex, which you can also customize to suit your needs.

VoiceOver also supports **Braille** (with greater display device support, including Bluetooth (**New!**)) and note-takers. If you have a supported Braille display connected to your computer, VoiceOver detects and configures it and can translate output into standard, Grade 2 contracted Braille for use in supported devices. A Braille display shows one line of screen content in a row of Braille cells.

## Getting Started with VoiceOver

Before you can use VoiceOver, you need to turn it on in the Universal Access pane of System Preferences or use the keyboard shortcut ⌘+F5. In addition to turning on VoiceOver, it's a good idea to use the VoiceOver utility to customize VoiceOver so it works the way you want. You can set options in the following areas: General, Verbosity, Speech, Navigation, Web, Sound, Visual, Commanders (**New!**), and Braille. If you have an MobileMe account, you can use VoiceOver syncing to automatically update your VoiceOver preferences on all your Macs.

## General

## Speech

## Working with VoiceOver

The easiest way to use VoiceOver is to use the VoiceOver keys, the Control and Option keys together. These are known as VO keys. When used together, the Control and Options keys allows you to control VoiceOver and move the VoiceOver cursor. However, it's easy to get lost. If you do get lost in VoiceOver and you're not sure where the focus is located, you can use the F1 through F6 keys with the VO keys to hear information about items where the VoiceOver cursor, keyboard, or mouse pointer is focused. If you are not sure what a key on the keyboard does in VoiceOver, you can use **keyboard help** to learn the names of the keys. After you start keyboard help, simply, press any key to hear its name. If you like to use the numeric pad on your extended keyboard, you can use **NumPad** and **Keyboard Commanders** (**New!**) to program the keys with VoiceOver commands. If you prefer using menus instead of VO keyboard shortcuts, you can use one of the VoiceOver menu's to get help with or exe-cute a command. The oversized white-on-black menu makes it easy to use.

In VoiceOver, you can navigate sequentially through a document or application or skip through by object. You can also create up to 10 **hot spots** to monitor an object or area in an accessible window and get notification when something changes. If you can't find what you're looking for, you can perform **smart searches** for objects and text in the current window.

When you're browsing the Web, VoiceOver can begin reading a Web page immediately when the page is loaded (**New!**) . It also allows you to intelligently navigate around Web pages, including tables, to important parts using Web spots (**New!**).

If you use a trackpad, you can control VoiceOver by touching the pad (**New!**). The surface of the trackpad acts as the active window with each corner representing absolute window coordinates. VoiceOver guides you through the process using voice commands.

## Braille

## Commanders

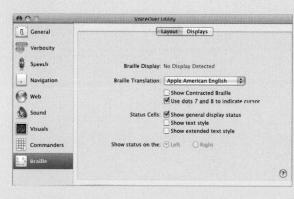

# Setting VoiceOver Preferences

Before you can use VoiceOver, you need to turn it on in the Universal Access pane of System Preferences. In addition to turning on VoiceOver, you can also open the VoiceOver utility, which you can use to set a variety of different options. You can set options in the following areas: General, Verbosity, Speech, Navigation, Web, Sound, Visual, NumPad, and Braille.

## Set VoiceOver Preferences

1. Click the **System Preferences** icon in the Dock, and then click the **Universal Access** icon.

2. Click the **Seeing** tab.

3. Click the VoiceOver **On** or **Off** option.

    **TIMESAVER** *Press* ⌘+F5 *to turn VoiceOver on and off.*

4. Click **Open VoiceOver Utility**.

    **TIMESAVER** *Double-click the VoiceOver Utility icon in the Utilities folder.*

5. Select a category on the left, and then select the options you want.

    ◆ **General.** Enter a login greeting and select a portable preference option.

    ◆ **Verbosity.** Specify text and announcement options. Also includes general and instructional hint options (**New!**).

    ◆ **Speech.** Specify voice and pronunciation options. You can mute speech or customize the voice rate, pitch, or volume.

    ◆ **Navigation.** Specify mouse and keyboard options. You can change VoiceOver cursor tracking options.

Verbosity Text options

- ◆ **Web.** Specify Web navigation options, either DOM (Document Object Model) or Group (such as paragraph to paragraph).

- ◆ **Sound.** Mute sounds and enable positional audio.

- ◆ **Visuals.** Specify VoiceOver cursor, Caption and Braille panel, and menu options.

- ◆ **Commanders.** Enable NumPad Commander and Keyboard Commander (**New!**), and customize commands.

- ◆ **Braille.** Specify display and input options.

6 Click the **Close** button.

Verbosity Announcements options

Navigation options

Visuals VoiceOver Cursor options

# Using VoiceOver Commands

The easiest way to use VoiceOver is to use the VoiceOver keys, the Control and Option keys together. These are known as VO keys. When used together, the Control and Option keys allows you to control VoiceOver and move the VoiceOver cursor. If you're not sure what a keyboard key does, you can enable keyboard help, where you can press any key to hear its name as well as the name of the VoiceOver command. In addition to the VO keys, you can also use the standard keyboard shortcuts that work within Mac OS X. You can quickly turn VoiceOver on and off using a keyboard shortcut, ⌘+F5. If your using a menu instead of a VO keyboard shortcut, you can use one of the VoiceOver menu's to get help with or execute a command. The over-sized white-on-black menu makes it easy to use. In VoiceOver, you can create up to 10 hot spots to monitor an object or area in an accessible window and get notification when something changes.

## Use VoiceOver Commands

1. To start or stop VoiceOver, press ⌘+F5.

2. Use the following keyboard shortcuts for help with VoiceOver.

   **IMPORTANT** *On a portable computer where function keys are used of other things, you need to press the Fn key first.*

   ◆ **VoiceOver menu.** VO+F7; use arrow keys to navigate

   ◆ **Item Chooser menu.** VO+I

   ◆ **Windows Chooser menu.** Lists all open windows: VO+F2 twice

   ◆ **Program Chooser menu.** Lists all open programs: VO+F1 twice.

   ◆ **VoiceOver Help.** VO+?; Help for an item: VO+H

   ◆ **Command menu.** Command menu for an item: VO+H+H

   ◆ **Select a menu.** Return

   ◆ **Stop an action or close a menu.** Esc

   ◆ **Keyboard help.** Hear key names on keyboard: VO+K

   ◆ **VoiceOver Utility.** VO+F8

VoiceOver Menu

---

## For Your Information

### VoiceOver Keyboard Commands

Using VoiceOver means learning a lot of keyboard commands. You can get a list of the VoiceOver keyboard shortcuts along with the Mac OS X keyboard shortcuts on the Web at *www.perspection.com*.

③ Use the following common commands for VoiceOver.

◆ **What's on the screen.** Under mouse: VO+F5; keyboard highlight: VO+F4; VoiceOver cursor box: VO+F3

◆ **Read everything.** VoiceOver cursor: VO+A; In window, Dock, or desktop, VO+Shift+W

◆ **Pause/resume speech.** Press and release Control; press again to resume. Repeat phrase: VO+Z

◆ **Show/Hide caption panel.** VO+Command+F10

◆ **Show/Hide Braille panel.** VO+Command+F9

◆ **NumPad Commander on/off.** VO+Clear

◆ **Navigation.** VO+arrow keys; visible area top or bottom: VO+Home or VO+End

◆ **Links on a Web page.** VO+U

◆ **Text in a document.** Read all text: VO+A; read sentence: VO+S; read line: VO+L

◆ **Search.** Find text: VO+F; find hyperlink: VO+Command+L; find graphic: VO+Command+G

④ Use the following commands to create and use hot spots.

◆ **Create Hot Spot.** Select item, and then press VO+Shift+ [number key]

◆ **Go to Hot Spot.** Press VO+ [number key]

◆ **Hear Hot Spot.** Press VO+ Command+[number key]

◆ **Watch for Hot Spot Changes.** Press VO+ Command+Shift+ [number key]

VoiceOver Navigation menu

VoiceOver Commands menu

# Setting Ink Preferences

If you have an ink device on your computer, you can use System Preferences to improve the recognition of ink to text. You can adjust Ink Preferences to your writing style, either widely or closely spaced, and to see how quickly your writing pen cursor changes back into a clicking device. You can improve recognition by adding words it may not know, such as names (like a custom dictionary for spell checking). As you write, Ink recognizes certain gestures or shapes, which get performed as commands, such as Undo, or pressed as keys, such as Delete or Space. The Gestures tab provides a list of gestures that you can turn on and off.

## Set Ink Preferences

1. Click the **System Preferences** icon in the Dock, and then click the **Ink** icon.

2. Click the **On** or **Off** option to turn handwriting recognition on or off.

3. Click the **Settings** tab.

4. Specify the options you want:

   ◆ **My handwriting style is**. Drag slider to set spacing.

   ◆ **Allow me to write anywhere**. Check to use Anywhere mode.

   ◆ **Language**. Click to select a ink writing language.

   ◆ **Ink pad font**. Click to select a default recognition font.

   ◆ **Show ink window**. Check to use Ink Pad mode.

   ◆ **Show ink in menu bar**. Check to add the Ink menu commands to the menu bar.

5. Click the **Gestures** tab.

6. Select or clear the check boxes to turn gesture actions on and off.

7. Click the **Word List** tab.

8. Use the buttons to add or change uncommon words you use.

9. Click the **Close** button.

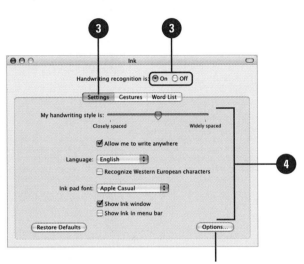

Click to adjust additional writing and mouse usage options.

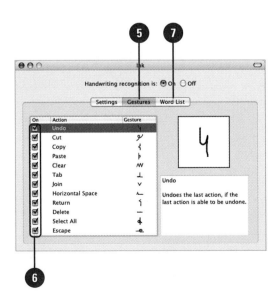

# Using Mac OS X Applications

## Introduction

Now that you know how to work with the graphical elements that make Mac OS X Snow Leopard work, you're ready to work with applications. An **application** is software you use to accomplish a specific task, such as word processing or managing files on your computer. Snow Leopard comes with several small applications and utilities that are extremely useful for completing basic tasks, such as creating a written document or performing basic calculations. Its suite of applications let you organize your workflow and create sticky notes. You can even edit and create digital media for use on the Internet, CD, or burn it onto a DVD. In addition, Snow Leopard makes setting up and communicating over the Internet easier than ever. And, if you happen to own an iSight (Macintosh Web camera), Snow Leopard helps you communicate with other iSight owners using audio and video. If you deal with a lot of fonts, Snow Leopard comes packaged with a font management system second to none. Snow Leopard's applications are powerful tools for organization, gaming, controlling digital media, and Internet communication, just to name a few.

## What You'll Do

**Use Mac OS X Applications**

**Launch and Quit Applications**

**Open Applications and Files**

**Work with File Extensions**

**Switch Between Applications**

**Use Mac OS X Applications**

**Create and Edit an Address Book**

**Manage an Address Book**

**Add an Image to an Address Book**

**Play Chess**

**Perform Calculations and Conversions**

**Capture Images with a Digital Camera**

**Capture Screen Shots with Grab**

**Preview Images and PDF's**

**Create Sticky Notes**

**Manage Fonts with Font Book**

**Activate, Deactivate, and Customize Fonts**

# Using Mac OS X Applications

Mac OS X comes with several accessories, built-in applications that, while not as feature-rich as many applications sold separately, are extremely useful for completing basic tasks. A frequently used list of Mac OS X applications is provided here. However, you can view a complete list of installed applications in the Applications folder on your hard disk drive. The Applications folder also contains a Utilities folder with additional applications you can use to perform specialized functions, which are detailed more in later chapters.

## Frequently Used Mac OS X Applications

| Program | Description |
| --- | --- |
| Address Book | Stores names, addresses, and other contact information |
| AppleScript | Automates tasks using a programming language |
| Automator | Automates tasks using workflows and no programming |
| Calculator | Performs arithmetic calculations |
| Dashboard | Provides a screen for mini-program called widgets |
| Dictionary | Provides an illustrated dictionary and thesaurus |
| Directory | Provides access to shared information about people, groups, location and resources. |
| DVD Player | Plays sound, music, and video |
| Font Book | Installs, previews, and manages fonts and font collections |
| Front Row | Provides an entertainment system to play music, movies, TV shows, and podcasts |
| iCal | Keeps track of calendar appointments |
| iChat | Sends and receives instant messages to online contacts |
| Image Capture | Transfers images from your camera to your computer |
| iSync | Compares information on your computer and devices and updates them to be the same |
| iTunes | Plays digital sound files |
| Mail | Provides e-mail, newsgroup, and directory services |
| Photo Booth | Takes pictures and adds visual effects |
| Preview | Views, rotates, resizes, crops, and converts image files |
| QuickTime Player | Plays and edits media located on your computer, a CD, or Internet |
| Safari | Displays Web (HTML) pages |
| Spaces | Organizes windows into groups, known as spaces, for individual projects |
| Stickies | Creates notes for reminders, lists, and messages |
| TextEdit | Creates, edits, and displays text, Rich Text Format, and Word documents |
| Time Machine | Backs up everything on your computer |

# Installing Other Applications

Mac OS X comes with a set of applications automatically loaded during the installation of the operating system, and appear on the hard drive within the Applications folder. All other third-party applications need to be installed separately. You can install a third-party application by inserting the software installation CD or DVD and following the instructions, or by downloading the software from the Web to your hard disk, uncompressing the file if necessary, starting the installer (typically in a disk image file, .dmg, which mounts as a disk icon), and following the instructions. In some cases, an installer application is not used to perform an installation. In that case, all you need to do is simply drag the software files to your hard disk, typically in the Applications folder. To uninstall an application, simply drag the icon (or its folder) to the Trash.

## Install Third-Party Applications Downloaded from the Internet

1 Download the software application from the Web.

The file typically appears on your desktop. If you use Safari to download your application file, it automatically uncompressed it into a disk image file (.dmg), so you don't have to.

Compressed files use these file extensions: **.sit** (standard Mac), **.zip** (standard Windows), **.tar** (tape archive Unix), **.gz** (standard Unix), **.tar.gz**, or **.tgz**

2 If the file is compressed, use the StuffIt Expander application (available at *www.download.com*) to uncompress the file.

3 Double-click the disk image file (**.dmg**).

A disk icon from the disk image mounts on your desktop.

4 Double-click the mounted disk icon to start the installer program, and then follow the instructions.

5 Drag the disk image file into the Trash to remove and eject it.

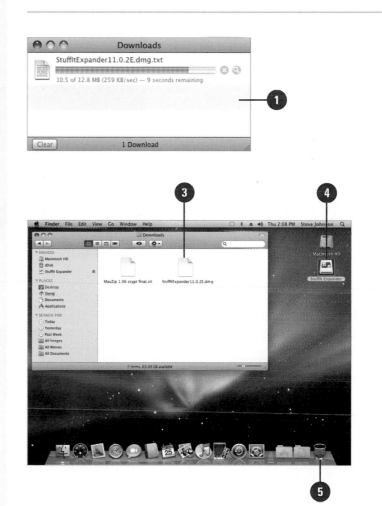

# Launching Applications

All Mac OS X applications are automatically loaded during the installation of the operating system, and appear on the hard drive within the Applications folder. All other third-party applications need to be installed separately. When you open the hard drive, you'll have the choice of viewing the file as icons, as file names (with information), or as file names in columns. Regardless of what view you choose to launch a Mac application, simply locate the desired application in the open window, and then double-click the application to load. If the application is in the Dock or in the Applications folder, you can click the icon in the Dock or click the Application folder icon in the Dock, and then click the application icon from the stack list (**New!**).

## Launch an Application from the Dock

1. Click the **Applications** folder in the Dock.

2. Click the icon you want from the stack list (**New!**).

3. To display additional applications, click the **Utilities** folder.

4. To return back to the Applications folder, click the **Return** button in the upper-left corner of the stack list.

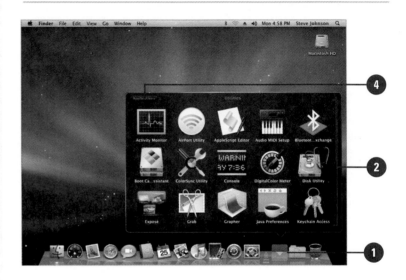

## Launch an Application from a Finder Window

1. Double-click the hard drive icon on your desktop.

2. To change views, click a view button, such as View By Columns.

3. Click the **Applications** folder or navigate to the application folder.

4. Double-click on the application name, or application icon, to launch.

Application details are displayed

# Opening Applications and Files

As you open applications and files, their names are kept in the Recent Items submenu in the Apple menu for easy access the next time you want to open a specific application or file. The Mac OS has always allowed you to double-click a document icon to launch the application used to create it and the document itself. If the Mac OS doesn't know what application created it (and gives you an error message), you can use drag and drop in the Dock to help you open the document. You can drag a document icon in the Dock on an application icon. If a document is stored in the Documents folder, you can click the Documents folder in the Dock and then click the document in the stack list to open it.

## Open Recently Used Applications and Files

① Click the **Apple** menu, and then point to **Recent Items**.

② Click the recent application or file under the **Applications** or **Documents** listing.

③ To clear the recent list, click the **Apple** menu, point to **Recent Items**, and then click **Clear Menu**.

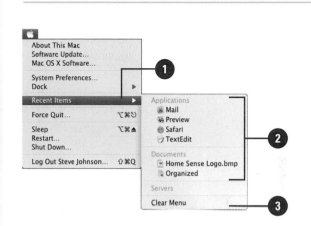

## Open Applications and Files

◆ Double-click the document icon.

◆ Drag the document icon to the application icon in the Dock, either the one that created the document or one that will accept it. If the application can possibly open it, the application icon becomes highlighted. Release the icon to open the application and the document.

**NOTE** *Hold down Option+⌘ while you drag a document icon into the Dock to force all applications to accept the icon. However, an error message may result.*

◆ Click the Documents folder in the Dock, and then click a document in the stack list.

Double-click to open          Blank icon; no association

Drag icon onto an accepting application icon to open    Documents folder

# Switching Between Applications

The Dock is initially located at the bottom of the desktop and is most often used to launch an application or switch from one application to another. When you launch an application, its icon appears in the Dock with a black arrow below it. If an application is not available in the Dock, you can hide any open applications to display the desktop, open your hard disk, and then launch the application you want. If you arrange open application windows so that they are visible, you can switch among them simply by clicking in the window in which you want to work.

## Hide and Show an Application

1.  Click the application menu.

    In this case, the Chess menu.

2.  Click **Hide *application name*** to hide the application.

    **TIMESAVER** *Press ⌘+H to hide the application.*

3.  Point to the bottom of the screen to display the Dock. You'll see the hidden application in the Dock.

4.  To show the application, click the application icon in the Dock.

## Hide Other Applications

1.  Click the application menu, and then click **Hide Others**.

    **TIMESAVER** *Press Option+ ⌘+H to hide all other applications.*

## Switch Between Applications

Mac OS X provides several ways to switch between applications:

◆ Click a visible window in the other application.

◆ Display the Dock, and then click an application icon to show (black triangle below icon) or launch the application.

◆ Press and hold down ⌘, and then repeatedly press the Tab key to highlight the Dock icon of an open application. (Use Shift+⌘+Tab to move backwards) Release both keys when you reach the one you want to open.

To leave without switching applications, press the Esc key.

**TIMESAVER** *Press ⌘+Tab once to open the application you used most recently. This is very useful when you are switching between two applications.*

◆ Press F11 (use Exposé) to hide all open windows, double-click the hard disk icon, open the Applications folder, and then double-click an application icon.

### Did You Know?

***You can quickly switch between windows within an application (including the Finder).*** Repeatedly press ⌘+~ (the Tilde key to the left of the number 1 key) to cycle through open windows in the application. Release both the keys to display the window you want.

Click menu to hide application    Click window to switch

Double-click to open and locate application to launch

Click icon in the Dock to switch

# Quitting Applications

When you're done working with an application, you should exit, or close it, to conserve your computer's resources. If an application stops responding while you work, Mac OS X provides you with the option to end the task. When you end a task, you'll probably lose any unsaved work in the problem application. If the problem persists, you might need to reinstall the application or contact product support to fix the problem.

## Quit an Application

① Click the application menu.

In this case, the Chess menu.

② Click **Quit** *application name.*

**TIMESAVER** *Press ⌘+Q to quit an application.*

③ If necessary, click **Save** to save your changes.

## Quit an Application That is Not Responding

① Click the **Apple** menu, and then click **Force Quit**.

**TIMESAVER** *Press ⌘+Option+Esc to force a quit.*

② Click the application name you want to force a quit.

③ Click **Force Quit**.

④ Click **Force Quit** again to confirm you want to force a quit.

⑤ Click the **Close** button.

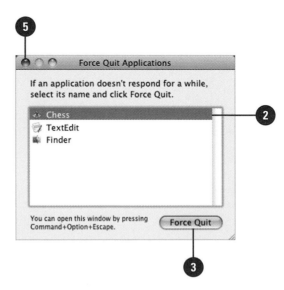

# Playing Chess

CHECKMATE, oh how I love to hear those words, or at least when I'm the one saying them. Computers aren't just for business proposals, worksheets, and documents. We all know that there are thousands of games available for computer systems, but one of the most challenging games in the world is available as soon as you load Mac OS X. Chess is available in the Applications folder and ready for you to play on your own screen. Chess gives you more options, and even makes it quite a challenge to those who have moved beyond the beginner stage.

## Play Chess

1. Click the **Applications** folder in the Dock, and then click the **Chess** icon.

2. Click and drag a piece. For example, the white Knight at G1 to F3.

3. Black responds with a move.

4. Click the **Moves** menu, and then click **Take Back Move**, **Show Hint**, or **Show Last Move**.

5. Click the **Chess** menu, and then click **Preferences**. Select from the following options:

   ◆ Click the **Board** pop-up to select a new playing surface.

   ◆ Click the **Pieces** pop-up to select different playing pieces.

   ◆ Select the check boxes for Speech to use voice recognition to call your moves.

   ◆ Drag the **Computer Plays** slider to increase or decrease the computer's playing skills.

   ◆ Select the **Show Move in Title** check box to display the current move in the Title bar.

6. Click the **Close** button.

7. Click the **Game** menu, and then select a game option, such as New Game or Save Game.

8. Quit Chess.

# Creating an Address Book

When you work with Address Book, you have the ability to create cards of information. Each card can hold all the information you want to keep on a contact, no matter how many phone numbers and e-mail addresses a particular friend, or company might have. In addition, you can add a picture with a drag and a drop. Address Book comes packaged with a bunch of features such as: label generation, change of address notification, synchronization with MobileMe, Google Contacts, or Yahoo Address Book, view iChat Buddy status, and even the ability to use speech recognition to look up and search the Address Book database. Creating an Address Book involves launching Address Book, and then working through the simple setup procedures.

## Create an Address Book

1. Click the **Applications** folder in the Dock, and then click the **Address Book** icon.

2. Click the **Add Group** (+) button to add a group.

3. Give the new group a descriptive name, and then press Return.

4. Click the **Add Name** (+) button to add a new card.

5. Type a Name, and then using the Tab key, type a Company Name (if necessary).

## Did You Know?

*You can share your address book online.* If you have an MobileMe account, you can share your address book online with contacts and synchronize across all your Macs. Click the Address Book menu, click Preferences, click Accounts, select the Synchronize with MobileMe check box, click MobileMe, click the Sync tab, select the Contacts check box in the list, then click the Close button. You can also set options to synchronize with Yahoo or Google. In addition, you can search for contacts and addresses on a Mac OS X, Microsoft Exchange 2007, or LDAP servers.

6　Click in the individual card fields to add information such as: Phone number, e-mail address, home address, Internet home page, and Instant Messaging user name (a MobileMe or AIM screen name).

If you enter an IM or AIM user name, you can view iChat Buddy status while browsing contacts in the Address Book.

7　If necessary, click the **Remove** button (-), located to the left of some of the data fields to remove that field.

8　Click in the **Note** field to add specific text notes.

9　If necessary, click on the **Field** pop-up to change the field name.

10　Repeat steps 4 thru 9 to add additional address cards.

11　Quit Address Book.

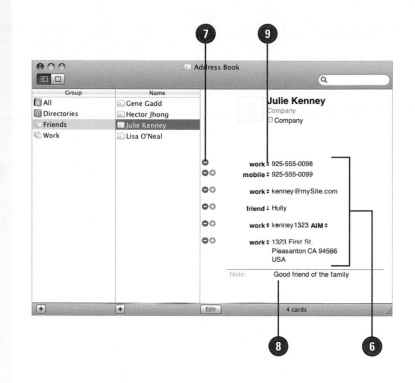

## Did You Know?

*You can archive your Address Book data.* If your Address Book data is important, you can back up the data in case of a catastrophic failure. Open the Address Book application, click the File menu, point to Export, and then click Address Book Archive. The file name comes with the date of the archive. All you have to do is select where you'd like to save the archive, and then click Save. To restore the data, click the File menu, point to Import, and then click Address Book Archive. Select the file with the correct date, and then click Open.

## For Your Information

### Importing Contacts into Address Book

Address Book creates and reads vCards, the standard method of exchanging data between applications. If you have vCards in another application, such as an e-mail application, you can import or export addresses with Address Book. To create a vCard, drag an address card out of the Address Book window. You can drag individual vCards in and out of the Address Book window. To import a set of vCards, click the File menu, point to Import, click vCards, select the file that contains the exported addresses, click Open, and then click OK (if you're updating contact information, click Review Duplicates to reconcile any conflicts). To see the last batch of addresses you added to Address Book, click Last Import in the Group column.

# Editing an Address Book

Once a contact is placed within the Address Book, it's a simple matter to edit or add information concerning a contact. The Address Book automatically saves the information as you change it, so there's no need to stop and save your work. Editing or updating an Address Book contact involves the same skills learned in creating a contact, with the exception that the information is already there, so all you need to do is edit, add, or delete the contact.

## Edit an Address Book

1. Click the **Applications** folder in the Dock, and then click the **Address Book** icon.

2. Select the Group that contains the contact or contacts you want to modify.

3. Select the Name from the available cards in the Group.

4. Click **Edit**.

   **IMPORTANT** *The Edit button is a toggle button, and once it's clicked, you'll be in edit mode for any selected name.*

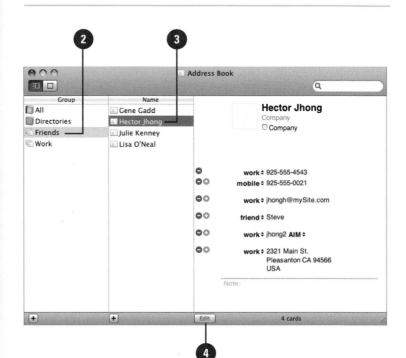

### Did You Know?

*The Address Book application remembers your location.* When you open the Address Book, it loads the Group that you had last used.

*You can move contacts in your Address Book.* Open the group, and then drag the contact from the open group to the new group.

5. Click in any of the fields to edit the existing information.

6. Click the **Remove** (-) button to remove a specific data piece.

7. Click the **Add** (+) button to add an additional data piece.

8. To remove a contact from the list, select a contact in the Name column, press the Delete key, and then confirm your delete.

9. Quit Address Book.

## Did You Know?

*You can undo mistakes in the Address Book.* If you accidentally delete a contact, don't worry, just click the Edit menu, and then click Undo Delete Record. The Address Book comes equipped with multiple undos.

*You can let the Address Book read a contact to you.* Control-click an item in the contact window, point to Speech, and then click Start Speaking. To end the audio, Control-click, point to Speech, and then click Stop Speaking.

*You can search for Address Book info in Google or Spotlight.* Control-click a searchable item (such as name or phone) in the contact window, and then click Search in Google or Search in Spotlight.

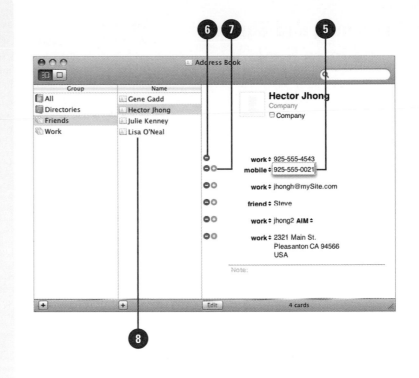

## For Your Information

### Printing from the Address Book

Address Book makes it easy to print a mailing list or print labels. The expanded Print dialog provides options to select a printing style and specify the specific fields from the Address Book you want to include in the printing. To print a mailing list or labels from Address Book, click the File menu, click Print, select a printer from the pop-up, select Lists or Mailing Labels from the Style pop-up, select a paper size from the pop-up, select an orientation, select or clear the attributes (fields) to display the information you want (such as phone, e-mail, address, Instant Messenger, photo, job title, etc.), select a font size from the pop-up, specify the number of copies, preview the results in the left pane, and then click Print.

# Managing and Sharing an Address Book

Any address book, even Snow Leopard's, can quickly become a confusing mess of unorganized data. Unlike paper address books, Snow Leopard's can create a very organized system… if you know what to do. For example, you could create logical groups, and then use obvious naming conventions for each contact. You can name your groups by family, school, work, community service, kids sports teams just to name a few. Address Book has many features that helps you manage your groups and the contacts you create, and then share them with others. You can even use the vCard format to exchange contact information between various programs or set up synchronization and sharing with MobileMe, Google Contacts, or Yahoo Address Book (**New!**).

## Manage an Address Book

1. Click the **Address Book** menu, and then click **Preferences**.

2. Click **General** to organize the viewable screen.

3. Make any of the following changes: Display Order, Sort By, Address Format, and Font Size.

4. Click **Accounts** to synchronize and share your Address Book.

5. Click the **Account information** tab to set options to use MobileMe, Yahoo!, or Google (**New!**).

6. Click the check box for the account you want, click the **MobileMe** or **Configure**, and then follow the step by step instructions to use MobileMe, Yahoo!, or Google.

7. Click the **Sharing** tab to set option to share your address book.

8. Select the **Share your Address Book** check box.

9. Click the **Add** (+) button, select the contacts with MobileMe accounts you want to have access.

10. Click **Send Invitation** to inform the contacts they have access.

**11** Click **Template** to organize the card data screen.

**12** Make any of the following changes: Work and Mobile phone numbers, Email and Homepage information, Names, and Work address.

**13** Click **Phone** to set the format for the phone number entry.

**14** Click the **Formats** pop-up, and then select a phone number format.

**15** Click **vCard** to set the preferences for vCards.

**16** Make any of the following changes: vCard Format, vCard 2.1 Encoding, Enable Private 'Me' Card, Export Notes in vCards, and Export Photos in vCards.

**17** Quit Address Book.

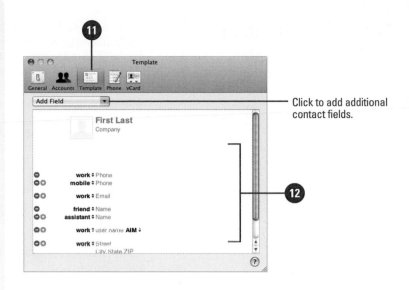

Click to add additional contact fields.

## Did You Know?

***You can notify contacts of changes to your address book information.*** Create a group of addresses, click the File menu, click Send Updates, select the group or groups you want to notify, type a subject and message, and then click Send.

***You can subscribe to an address book.*** Click the File menu, click Subscribe to Address Book, enter the MobileMe e-mail address of the user you want, and then click OK.

***You can exchange contacts in your Address Book with other Mac users.*** Select a contact, click the File menu, and then click Export vCard.

## For Your Information

### Using Directory to Share Information

Directory is an application, located in the Utilities folder, that allows you to share information about people, groups, locations, and resources within your organization. If you have access to your organization's directory server or Active Directory, you can configure Directory and authenticate your personal information using the Directory Utility in the Utilities folder. You can create shared contacts from your Address Book, use e-mail addresses to send e-mail using Mail, use names to chat in iChat, or load group Web services in Safari.

# Adding an Image to an Address Book

It's not unusual for an address book to grow quite large. Over time, you'll add more and more addresses and occasionally delete old ones, until you have dozens even hundreds of contacts listed in your address book. Sometimes, identification requires more than just a name or an address, so Apple gives you the ability to add an image to a contact. Maybe it's to help associate a face with a name, or just be reminded (visually) of a special someone—whatever the reason, adding an image is as simple as opening the file containing the image, and dragging it into the photo box for the selected contact.

## Add an Image to an Address Book

1. Click the **Applications** folder in the Dock, and then click the **Address Book** icon.

2. Select the Group which contains the contact.

3. Select the Name of the contact that you want to add the image to.

4. Drag the image into the active contact.

   Address Book opens an image placement dialog which lets you resize the image to fit in the allocated space.

5. Drag the slider left or right to resize the image.

6. Click **Set** to add the image to the contact.

7. Quit Address Book.

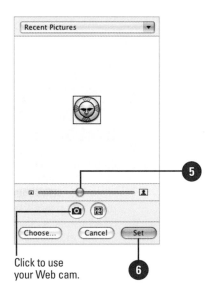

Click to use your Web cam.

## Did You Know?

**You can add instant pictures to an address contact.** Double-click the photo box, and then click the Take Video Snapshot button. If you have a Web cam attached to your computer, you can then take an instant snapshot based on anything the camera sees.

# Performing Graph Calculations

Grapher is an application, located in the Utilities folder, that allows you to graph mathematical functions and equations, so you can visualize what's happening. You can analyze equations and display algebraic relationships. With Grapher, you can create two- and three-dimensional graphs and format the results to get the visual display you want.

## Create a Graph with Grapher

1. Click the **Applications** folder in the Dock, click the **Utilities** folder, and then click the **Grapher** icon.

2. Click the **2D Graph** or **3D Graph** tab.

3. Select the type of graphic you want to create.

4. Click **Choose**.

5. Enter the expression in the entry field.

   **TIMESAVER** *To see an example, click the Examples menu, and then select an example.*

6. To format the graph text, layout, axes and frame, use the Format menu.

7. Click the **File** menu, and then click **Save As**.

8. Select the drive and folder in which you want to save the file.

9. Type a name for the file, and then click **Save**.

10. Quit Grapher.

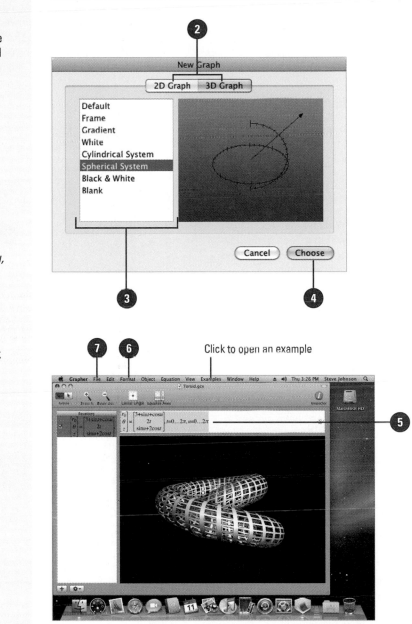

Click to open an example

# Performing Calculations and Conversions

Mac OS X comes with a great tool to help you perform common calculations and to do complex conversions. The Calculator application has been around for a long time, however, Mac OS X gave it a few powerful features, that just might make you want to reacquaint yourself with an old friend. If you're like most people, you probably have a dozen calculators laying about your home and office. If you're tired of all the mess, then take a look at the Mac's idea of a calculator. Not only does it help you add 2 + 2; it helps you convert miles into kilometers or the Euro dollar into American currency. The Calculator application gives you the ability to perform conversions on everything from currency to volume, from temperature to speed, and more.

## Work with the Calculator

1. Click the **Applications** folder in the Dock, and then click the **Calculator** icon.

2. Click the buttons on the calculator to perform standard calculations.

3. Click the **Window** menu, and then click **Show Paper Tape** to display a Paper Tape dialog, which shows all of your calculations.

4. Click **Clear** to clear the tape, or click **Recalculate Totals** to have the calculator refigure the total.

5. Click the **File** menu, and then click **Print Tape** to have a paper copy of your calculations.

6. Click the **View** menu, and then click **Scientific** to have access to a scientific calculator.

7. Quit Calculator.

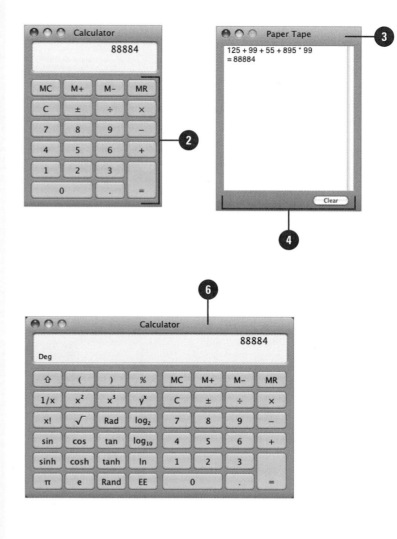

### Did You Know?

*You can use the keypad with the Calculator.* If you have a 10-keypad, instead of trying to click the calculator buttons, just use the keypad. The Calculator automatically reads the keypad objects, and display the results in the calculation window.

146

## Work with Conversions

1. Click the **Applications** folder in the Dock, and then click the **Calculator** icon.

2. Enter a value into the calculation window.

3. Click the **Convert** menu, and then click **Currency**.

4. Click the **Convert** pop-up, and then click **Currency**. If you need to change the convert type, click the Convert pop-up and make your change.

5. Click the **From** and **To** pop-ups to select currency countries.

6. If available, click **Update Currency Rates** to access the latest exchange rate (requires an Internet connection).

7. Click **OK**.

   The conversion results display in the calculation window.

8. Quit Calculator.

Conversion results

## Did You Know?

*You can save calculation results in memory.* Click the M+ (memory add) button to save a calculation result or to add a calculation result to the value residing in memory. At any time during the calculation, if you want to use that result, click the MR (Memory Recall) button and the number reappears. In addition, you can use the M- (memory subtract) to subtract a displayed result from the value in memory, or the MC (Memory Clear) button to clear out the memory.

# Capturing Images with a Digital Camera

Mac OS X has provided you a way to directly access your digital camera and organize your images and even sounds. Just plug in your digital camera or scanner directly, and import your pictures or sounds from any application that supports Services and Rich Text Format (most digital cameras and scanners). The Image Capture application lets you download all or selected contents from your digital camera, crop images to a variety of sizes, and even delete unwanted pictures from your camera. You can even use Image Capture to build a Web page, complete with individual thumbnails of your photos. Just click Build Web Page from the Automatic Task pop-up on the toolbar. Image Capture automatically generates the Web page and stores the images in the Pictures folder on your hard drive. In addition, you can use the images to create a slideshow or format them for printing.

## Capture Images with a Digital Camera

1. Plug a digital device into your computer.

2. If necessary, click the **Applications** folder in the Dock, and then click the **Image Capture** icon.

3. Click the **Download To** pop-up, and then select where to store the images.

4. Click the **Automatic Task** pop-up, and then select from the tasks.

5. Click **Options**, select from the available options, and then click **OK**.

6. Click **Download All** to move all the images from the digital device to the folder on your hard drive.

7. Click **Download Some**, and then select the images (hold down ⌘⌘ to select more than one).

8. Click **Rotate Left**, **Rotate Right**, or **Delete** buttons to adjust or delete.

9. Click **Download**.

10. Quit Image Capture.

Selected images to download

# Capturing Screen Shots with Grab

If there is something on your computer screen, such as an error dialog, window, or desktop, that you want to capture as a picture to show someone, you can use a built-in utility called Grab to get the job done. Grab is useful for taking pictures of different parts of the screen, like the ones in this book. This may not be a tool you'll use everyday (unless you are a computer trainer or book author), but it may come in handy one day.

## Capture Screen Shots with Grab

1. Display the screen you want to capture.

2. Open the **Applications** folder, open the **Utilities** folder, and then double-click the **Grab** icon.

3. Click the **Capture** menu, and then select the command with the method you want to use:

   ◆ **Selection**. Drag to select a capture area.

   ◆ **Window**. Click the **Choose Window** button, and then click a window.

   ◆ **Screen**. Click a screen.

   ◆ **Timed Screen**. Click the **Start Timer** button, display a screen, and then wait 10 seconds.

4. Click the **File** menu, and then click **Save As**.

5. Select the drive and folder in which you want to save the file.

6. Type a name for the file, and then click **Save**.

7. Quit Grab.

## Did You Know?

*You can show a pointer in a screen capture.* Click the Grab menu, click Preferences, click a pointer type or the blank one for no pointer, and then click the Close button.

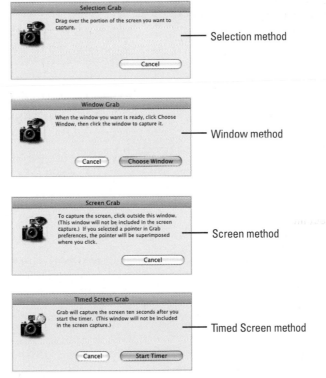

Selection method

Window method

Screen method

Timed Screen method

# Previewing Images and PDF's

Need a quick way to view images, or possibly a Portable Document File (PDF)? No problem, Snow Leopard's built-in PDF viewer, Preview, lets you quickly view graphics and PDF files with the click of a button. In fact, once you've opened a PDF document file, Preview lets you perform an improved indexed search (**New!**), select text (**New!**) and copy it to the clipboard, even view FAX documents using its built-in FAX support. The Preview application works to open any images or documents, which are not identified by another program, regardless of type. For example, double-clicking on a Photoshop document file (.psd) would open the image in Photoshop. However, if you double-click on a graphic file from your digital camera, chances are it would open in the Preview application. And the same would be true of a PDF document, if you owned Adobe Acrobat, or the Acrobat Reader application. When you open a PostScript or EPS (Encapsulated PostScript) file, Preview converts the file into the PDF format. You can open multiple PDFs in a single document window or import scan images in Preview (**New!**). You can also open and view multiple image files as a contact sheet (**New!**). If you want to adjust image size, you can use the Adjust Size command on the Tools menu for high-quality results (**New!**). If you want to add comments or annotations to a PDF, you can get easy access to the tools you need by using the Annotation toolbar (**New!**). If you want to see how images appear when printed, on the Web, or on a printing press, you can use Soft Proof with Profile to simulate the results (**New!**).

## Set Preview Preferences

1. Click the **Preview** icon in the Dock.

2. Click the **Preview** menu, and then click **Preferences**.

3. Click any of the following icons to set Preview preferences:

   - **General.** Sets options to open files in a single or separate windows.

   - **Images.** Sets options for scaling images.

   - **PDF.** Sets options to for scaling PDFs, opening and viewing documents, and annotations.

   - **Bookmarks.** Allows you to remove bookmarks.

4. Click the **Close** button.

PDF preferences

## Preview Images and PDF's

1. Click the **Preview** icon in the Dock.

2. Click the **File** menu, click **Open**, select one or more document or image files, and then click **Open**.

3. Click the **Sidebar** button to display it, if necessary.

4. To change the Sidebar display, click a view tools button:

   ◆ **Contact Sheet**. Displays full page of thumbnails.

   ◆ **Thumbnails**. Displays mini-images of the documents.

   ◆ **Table of Contents**. Displays document titles.

   ◆ **Annotations**. Displays a list of annotations.

5. To move between pages in a PDF document or another document, click the **Previous** or **Next** buttons or click an item in the Sidebar.

6. To increase or decrease the viewing size of the image, click the **Zoom In** or **Zoom Out** buttons.

7. To select a portion of a document or image, click a selection tool button (**Move**, **Text**, **Select**, or **Select arrow**), and then drag to select it.

   ◆ To copy the selection, click the **Edit** menu, and then click **Copy**.

8. To modify a selected image, click the **Tools** menu, and then click **Adjust Size** or **Adjust Color**.

9. To draw or add notes on the document, click the **Annotate** button to display the Annotation toolbar (**New!**), and then use the tools.

10. To print, display the document or select a portion of it, click the **File** menu, and then click **Print**.

11. Save the document, and then quit Preview.

Annotation toolbar

---

### For Your Information

### Using PDFs

The PDF (Portable Document File) format is the way to save and move documents between computers and operating systems. Do you need to send a document to several people, and you're not sure if they're using a Macintosh or Windows machine? Do you want the document to be viewed exactly as you created it? Then the PDF format is the way to go. Adobe's Portable Document File has literally swept the computer industry (Mac, Windows, and UNIX); allowing you to combine text and graphics into a format that can be viewed by literally anyone who has the Preview application (on Macintosh), or the Adobe Acrobat Reader application (available free from *www.adobe.com*). As a matter of fact, the Acrobat Reader is shipped with every computer, regardless of model or operating system.

# Creating Sticky Notes

The Sticky Notes application is not new to Snow Leopard, however it does give you the ability to tack notes onto your desktop; where they stay until removed. Just think, no longer do you need to worry about the sticky note on your monitor losing its "stick" and falling off. You can use your desktop the way Apple intended—to help with everyday life. Once you create a sticky note, you can change the color of the note, change the color and size of the text, or even have your sticky note talk to you by turning on the speech mode through the Edit menu.

## Create Sticky Notes

**1** Click the **Applications** folder in the Dock, and then click the **Stickies** icon.

When you first open the Stickies application, you'll see 3 pre-written stickies notes.

**2** Click the **File** menu, and then click **New Note**.

**3** Type the text into the note area.

**4** To increase or decrease the note size, drag the lower-right corner of the sticky note.

**5** Click the **Font** menu, and then select from the font options.

**6** Click the **Note** menu, and then select between **Floating Windows** or **Translucent Windows**.

**7** To change the color of the selected note, click the **Color** menu and make your change.

**8** Click the **File** menu to import or export notes, archive your notes, and to print or save your notes.

**9** Click the **Close** button to quit without saving.

**10** Quit Stickies.

---

**It's easy to customize your notes.**

Make your notes stand out and get noticed.

- Format text using different **fonts** and font sizes
- Add emphasis with **bold** and *italic* text styles or color.
- Include graphics ▢.

Stickies has lots of other great features, including a spell checker, import and export features, and other ways to arrange and customize your notes. Plus, you'll find a "Make New Sticky Note" service in many applications.

Look in Help to find out more abou[t]

**Make a note of it!**

Stickies lets you keep notes (like these) on your desktop. Use a Stickies note to jot down reminders, lists, or other information. You can also use notes to store frequently used text or graphics.

- To close this note, click the close button.

- To collapse this note, double click the title bar.

Your current notes appear when you open Stickies.

**1**

**9**

Make plans for the family vacation for this summer.

**3**

**4**

# Managing Fonts with Font Book

Most of us have fonts…a whole lot of fonts and Snow Leopard adds to it (**New!**): Hiragino Sans GB, Menlo, Chalkduster, and Heiti. Mac OS X organizes fonts into main folders: User and Computer. Fonts in the User folder reside in your Home folder for private use, while fonts in the Computer folder are available for all users. Besides these folders, you can also organize your fonts into specific user-defined folders, known as collections, and then activate those folders, or specific fonts within the folder without having to restart your application. In addition, Font Book gives you a window to view the font, and change its viewing size.

## Manage Fonts with Font Book

1. Click the **Applications** folder in the Dock, and then click the **Font Book** icon.

2. Click the **Add Collections** (+) button, type a name, and then press Return.

3. Click the **Add Fonts** (+) button.

4. Select the fonts you want to add to the New Collection (active folder).

5. Click **Open**.

6. Select a collection from the Collection column, and then click on a font to view a sample.

7. To increase or decrease the view of the font in the window, drag the view slider up or down.

8. To copy a font, click and drag a font from the Font window into another Collection.

9. If necessary, type search criteria to locate specific fonts.

10. To remove a font from a Collection (this does not delete the file from the hard drive), select a font, and then press the Delete key.

11. Quit Font Book.

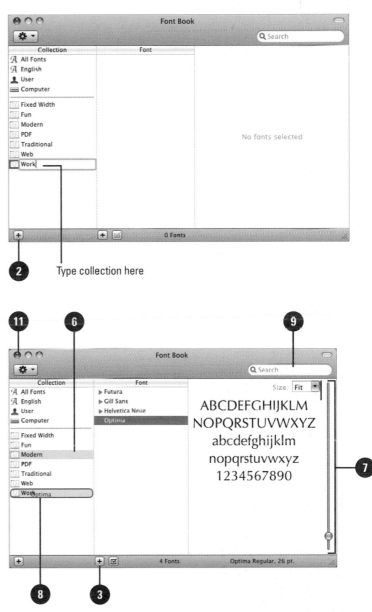

Type collection here

# Activating, Deactivating, and Customizing Fonts

Once you've created a series of font collections, it'll be necessary to instruct the Font Book application as to what fonts you want to use, and what fonts you want to turn off. It's important to understand that fonts consume memory on your computer. For example, if you have hundreds of fonts active (and that's not unusual), it takes more RAM memory to maintain those fonts; even if you're not using them. That's where font management comes into play. Using Font Book, you can decide what fonts you need, and what fonts can be retired, or disabled, for the remainder of the work session.

## Activate and Deactivate Fonts

1. Click the **Applications** folder in the Dock, and then click the **Font Book** icon.

2. To deactivate a collection or a font, select the collection or font, click **Disable**, and then click **Disable** to confirm.

   **IMPORTANT** *The Enable button is a toggle, when a font is active, it displays the word Disable, and when a font is disabled it displays the word Enable.*

3. To activate selected fonts, select one of more fonts from the Font column, and then click **Enable**.

   If a font is disabled, it says Off to the right of the font.

4. Quit Font Book.

### Did You Know?

***You can find duplicate fonts.*** If a dot appears next to a font family, it means you have a duplicate. You can correct the problem by disabling the one you don't want. Select the version you want, click the Edit menu, and then click Resolve Duplicates.

Disabled    Font window

2    Selected font

3

## Customize Fonts

1. Click the **Applications** folder in the Dock, and then click the **Font Book** icon.

2. Select the font you want to customize.

3. Click the **Preview** menu, and then click **Custom**.

4. Control-click your mouse in the font window, point to **Font**, and then select from the following customizing options:

   ◆ **Show Fonts**. Lets you adjust the font; including color, size and drop shadow.

   ◆ **Show Colors**. Lets you change the color of the selected font.

5. Make any changes to the font, and then close any open dialogs.

6. Quit Font Book.

### Did You Know?

*You can locate a font on your computer.* Select the font, click the File menu, and then click Reveal In Finder.

Text Strikethrough
Text color

Underline

Document color; opens Show Colors dialog

Drop Shadow features

Show Fonts dialog

Show Colors dialog

# Working with Dashboard

**Dashboard** is a Mac OS X screen that gives you quick access to widgets, such as news headlines and updates, slide shows, weather information, traffic maps, Internet radio streams, and slide shows of online photo albums. **Widgets** are mini-applications that can connect to Web services, such as an RSS feed (which automatically delivers Web content to your desktop), or integrate with many of your applications, such as viewing your calendar. You can customize Dashboard to suit the way you work by using the Widget bar. Mac OS X comes with a set of widgets to get you started. However, you can easily download more widgets online. You can quickly open Dashboard by pressing the F12 key. If you prefer a different shortcut key, you can select the one you want in the Exposé & Spaces pane of System Preferences.

## Work with Dashboard

◆ **Show or Hide Dashboard.** Press F12.

◆ **Open Widget Bar.** Click the **Open** (+) button in the lower-left corner of Dashboard or press ⌘+= (equal).

◆ **Close Widget Bar.** Click the **Close** (x) button or press ⌘+= (equal).

◆ **Scroll the Widget Bar.** Click the Left or Right Arrow buttons or press ⌘+Left Arrow or ⌘+Right Arrow.

◆ **Reload Current Widget.** Press ⌘+R.

### Did You Know?

*You can make widgets available to all users.* Move or copy the widget into the Widgets folder in the Library folder for your computer from the similar Library folder in your Home folder. All the Mac OS X pre-installed widgets are stored in the Widgets folder for your computer.

Dashboard widgets

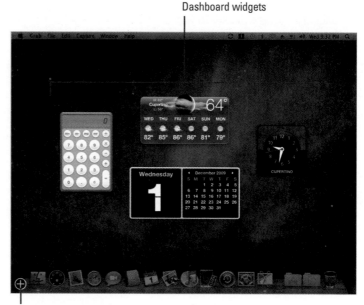

Click to open widget bar

## Change Dashboard Preferences

1. Click the **Apple** menu, and then click **System Preferences**.

2. Click the **Exposé & Spaces** icon.

3. Click the **Exposé** tab.

4. Click the **Hide and Show** pop-up, press a keyboard modifier (Shift, Control, Option, or ⌘) if you want, and then select the shortcut key you want.

   If you want to see more shortcut options, hold down the Shift, Control, Option, or Command keys, or a combination of the keys, while you view the pop-up menu.

5. If you have a Mighty Mouse or other multi-button mouse, you can use the other pop-up to set mouse button shortcuts.

   On the Mighty Mouse, Button 3 applies to the scroll-ball button and Button 4 applies to the pair of side buttons. You can use the scroll-ball button to open Dashboard.

6. Click the **Close** button.

---

## Did You Know?

*You can update all your Macs with widgets using .iMac.* With an .iMac account, you can use Dashboard syncing to automatically update all the widgets on all your Macs. Click the System Preferences icon on the Dock, click the .iMac icon, click the Sync tab, select the Synchronize With MobileMe check box, select the Dashboard Widgets check box, and then click the Close button.

# Using Dashboard Widgets

Dashboard comes with a wide variety of widgets pre-installed with Mac OS X Snow Leopard. Dashboard displays the Calculator, Weather, World Clock, and iCal widgets by default. However, you can add other pre-installed widgets to the Dashboard, which include Address Book, Business, Dictionary, ESPN, Flight Tracker, Google, iTunes, Movies, People, Ski Report, Stickies, Stocks, Tile Game, Translation, and Unit Converter. In fact, you can add more than one of the same widget, such as two World Clocks for two different times around the world. Some of the widgets are linked with applications and allow you to access information or functionality without opening the application. For example, the Weather widget displays Web-based content on the Dashboard without opening a Web browser.

## Show or Hide Widgets on the Dashboard

1. Press F12 to open Dashboard.

2. Click the **Open** (+) button in the lower left corner to display the Widget bar.

3. To hide a widget from the Dashboard, click the **Close** (x) button in the upper-left corner of the widget.

   **TROUBLE?** *If you don't see a Close button, press Option and move the pointer over the widget.*

4. To show a widget on the Dashboard, click the widget you want on the Widget bar.

5. To move a widget on the Dashboard, drag it to another location.

6. Click the **Close** (x) button in the Widget bar.

6. Toggles between (t) and (x).

## Use Pre-installed Widgets

◆ **Address Book.** Type a name, or click the arrow buttons.

◆ **Business.** Type a business name or category. Click the Info (i) button to change the local city.

◆ **Calculator.** Use the numeric pad or click buttons to enter numbers.

◆ **Dictionary.** Type a word to view a definition.

◆ **ESPN.** Click the Info (i) button to select a sport. Click New or Scores to change the display.

◆ **Flight Tracker.** Enter flight information, and then click Find Flights.

◆ **Google.** Type a word or phrase, and then press Return to display the Google search.

◆ **iCal.** Use the arrow buttons or arrow keys to move around the calendar. Click the today's date pane to expand/collapse it.

◆ **iTunes.** Use controls to use iTunes when it's open.

◆ **Movies.** Click the Info (i) button to enter your zip code to view theaters near you.

◆ **People.** Type first name, last name, and a city and state or zip code, and then press Return.

◆ **Ski Report.** Click the Info (i) button to type the name of a resort.

◆ **Stickies.** Type notes. Click the Info (i) button to change color and font.

◆ **Stocks.** Type a company. Click the Info (i) button to view a graph.

◆ **Tile Game.** Click a tile that borders the empty space to move it.

◆ **Translation.** Select a language, and then type the word or phrase.

◆ **Unit Converter.** Select a Convert category, select the unit converted and the unit converted to.

◆ **Weather.** Click the Info (i) button to check the weather forecast.

◆ **World Clock.** Click the Info (i) button to change the city.

Calculator    Weather    World Clock

iCal calender

Click to scroll through available widgets

Click to scroll through available widgets

# Adding and Removing Dashboard Widgets

Even though Mac OS X comes with a wide range of commonly used widgets, there is always room for more. Developers are continually creating new widgets, which you can download from the Internet and install onto your computer. If you no longer use a widget on the Dashboard, you can remove a pre-installed widget from the Widget bar or remove a widget you installed from your computer.

## Install a Dashboard Widget

1. Press F12 to open Dashboard.

2. Click the **Open** (+) button in the lower left corner to display the Widget bar.

3. Click **Manage Widgets**.

4. Click **More Widgets**.

5. Browse the widget Web site to find the widget you want to download and install.

6. Click the widget's Download button.

   The installer should automatically start. If it doesn't, double-click the downloaded file. If the file is compressed, you need to uncompress it first.

7. Click **Install**.

8. Click **Keep** to keep the widget or click **Delete** if you decide not to keep it.

9. Click the **Close** button.

## Remove a Dashboard Widget

① Press F12 to open Dashboard.

② Click the **Open** (+) button in the lower left corner to display the Widget bar.

③ Click **Manage Widgets**.

④ To remove (disable) a widget from the Widget bar, clear the check box next to the widget name you want to remove.

⑤ To remove a widget you installed, click the widget's **Remove** (-) button, and then click **OK.**

⑥ To close a widget from the screen and remain in the Widget bar, click the **Close** (x) button.

⑦ Click the **Close** button.

### Did You Know?

***You can customize a widget.*** When you point to a widget on the Dashboard and a small info (i) button appears, you can customize the widget. Click the small info (i) button to display the settings you can change. The available options vary depending on the widget.

***You can sort widgets on the Widget bar.*** Press F12, click the Open (+) button, click Manage Widgets, click the Sort pop-up, click Sort By Name or Sort By Date, and then click the Close button.

# Creating a Web Clip Dashboard Widget

You can also create your own widgets by using Web Clips or Dashcode. A Web Clip widget is a container for a Web page you can add to the Dashboard. When you open the Web Clip widget in Dashboard, the Web page associated with it opens. If you're a developer with a basic knowledge of HTML, JavaScript, and CSS, you can create your own Dashboard widget using Dashcode. Dashcode is out of the scope of this book. For more information on Dashcode, go to the Apple Developer Connection Web site.

## Create a Web Clip Dashboard Widget

1 Launch Safari, and then display the Web page you want to make into a Web Clip widget.

2 Click the **File** menu, and then click **Open in Dashboard**.

3 Move the page to highlight the area you want to use, and then click the mouse button.

4 To reposition the highlighted area, drag the area. To resize it, drag the circular handles on the edges of the box.

5 Click **Add**.

6 To customize the widget, point to it, click the small info (i) button, and then specify the options you want:

◆ **Edges.** Displays thumbnails of different edge styles. Click the style you want.

◆ **Only Play Audio in Dashboard.** Select or clear the check box to play or not play audio in Dashboard.

◆ **Edit.** Click to select a different highlighted area.

7 When you're finished, click **Done**.

# Working with Documents

## Introduction

Mac OS X comes with a word processing application, called TextEdit, you can use to create basic documents. TextEdit is designed especially for working with text, so it's a snap to create and edit letters, or any other word-based communication. TextEdit contains all the tools and features you need to produce interesting documents that say exactly what you mean, and have the look to match.

TextEdit is a versatile word-processing application. You can use TextEdit to view, create, and edit documents containing multi-lingual text, graphics, movies, and other document files. If you are working with HTML code (document as they appear in a Web browser), TextEdit makes the perfect editor. If you have speakers connected to your Macintosh, you can hear documents read aloud by your computer. When you're done working with a document, you can save it in multiple formats, such as plain text, Rich Text Format (RTF), Microsoft Word, and Portable Document File (PDF).

Tools, such as the Spelling Checker and Dictionary, help you present your thoughts accurately, clearly, and effectively. When your text is complete, you can quickly add formatting elements, such as bold type and special fonts, to make your documents look professional. Each document contains simple styles that have common design elements. Apply the existing styles for headings, titles, body text, and so forth. Then modify the styles, or create your own to better suit your needs. Make sure you get the look you want by adding emphasis using italics, boldface, and underline, changing text alignment, adjusting line and paragraph spacing, setting tabs and indents, creating bulleted or numbered lists, and adding tables. When you're done, your document is sure to demand attention and convey your message in its appearance.

## What You'll Do

**Create and Open a Document**

**Edit Text**

**Recognize Handwriting Ink**

**Make Corrections**

**Make Text Substitutions**

**Check Spelling and Grammar**

**Look Up Words with Dictionary**

**Find and Replace Text**

**Format Text**

**Display Rulers**

**Set Paragraph Tabs and Indents**

**Change Character Spacing**

**Change Line Spacing**

**Add Lists and Tables**

**Apply and Create a Style**

**Insert Special Characters**

**Add Pictures, Movies, or Files to a Document**

**Save and Close a Document**

**Set TextEdit Preferences**

# Creating and Opening a Document

A **document** is a file you create using a word processing program, such as a letter, memo, or resume. When you start TextEdit, a blank document appears in the work area, known as the document window. You can type information to create a new document and save the result in a file, or you can open an existing file (using the Sidebar and List or Column view) in various formats, and save the document with changes. You can also add pictures, movies, and files in your documents.

## Create a Document

1. Click the **Applications** folder in the Dock, and then click the **TextEdit** icon.

   If TextEdit is already open, click the **File** menu, and then click **New**.

2. To change the file format, click the **Format** menu, and then click **Make Plain Text** or **Make Rich Text**.

3. Type your text.

4. Press Return when you want to start a new paragraph.

5. When you're done, save and close the document.

Document window

### See Also

*See "Saving and Closing a Document" on page 190 for information on saving a document.*

*See "Setting Up Page Options" on page 204 for information on selecting paper size, orientation, and printer scaling and format.*

### Did You Know?

***You can set the file format for all new documents.*** Click the TextEdit menu, click Preferences, click the Plain Text or Rich Text option, and then click the Close button.

## For Your Information

### Understanding Document Formats

You can open and edit plain text, HTML (HyperText Markup Language, which displays Web pages in a browser), Rich Text Format (RTF), Rich Text Format Directory (RTFD), and Microsoft Word files in TextEdit. However, you can only save files in the plain text, RTF, and Word format. Plain text files use the file extension **.txt**, RTF files use **.rtf**, and Word files use **.doc**. If you add graphics to an RTF file, the file extension changes to **.rtfd**. The RTF and Word formats can include formatting, pictures, and other embedded files, while the plain text format can only include nonformatted text. In a plain text document, you cannot change preset tabs and font styles and colors are not saved. Since Microsoft Word is a full featured word processing application, not all Word features, such as tables, are supported in TextEdit.

## Open an Existing Document from Within an Application

① Click the **File** menu, and then click **Open**.

② Select the hard drive and the folder in which you want to open the file.

**TIMESAVER** *Click the Where pop-up to select from a list of recent places you already visited.*

③ Click the document you want to open.

④ If the document contains one or more languages, click the **Plain Text Encoding** pop-up, and then select **Unicode** (for multiple languages) or a specific language.

⑤ If you want to open a HTML document or create a plain text document, select the **Ignore rich text commands** check box.

⑥ Click **Open**.

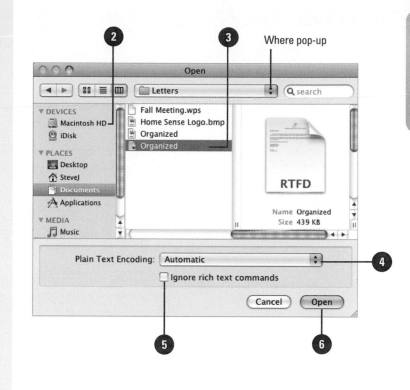

Where pop-up

## Open a Recent Document

① Click the **File** menu, and then point to **Open Recent**.

② Click the recently opened document you want to re-open.

### Did You Know?

*You can remove all recently used documents from the Open Recent submenu.* Click the File menu, point to Open Recent, and then click Clear Menu.

# Editing Text

One of the advantages of using a word processing program is that you can edit a document or change the contents without re-creating it. In the TextEdit work area, the mouse pointer changes to the I-beam pointer, which you can use to reposition the insertion point (called navigating) and insert, delete, or select text. Before you can edit text, you need to highlight, or select, the text you want to modify. Then you can delete, replace, move (cut), or copy text within one document or between documents even if they're different programs. When you cut or copy an item, it's placed on the Clipboard, which stores only a single piece of information at a time. You can also move or copy selected text without storing it on the Clipboard by using drag-and-drop editing.

## Select and Edit Text

1. Open a document, and then move the I-beam pointer to the left or right of the text you want to select.

2. Click, and then drag the pointer to highlight the text.

   **TIMESAVER** *Double-click a word to select it; triple-click a paragraph to select it.*

3. Perform one of the following editing commands:

   ◆ To replace text, type your text.

   ◆ To delete text, press the Delete key.

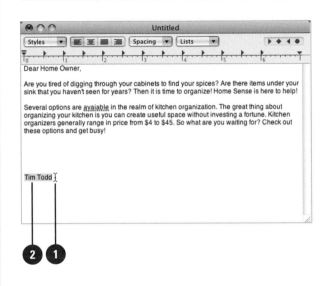

## Insert and Delete Text

1. Click in the document to place the insertion point where you want to make the change.

   ◆ To insert text, type your text.

   ◆ To delete text, press the Delete key.

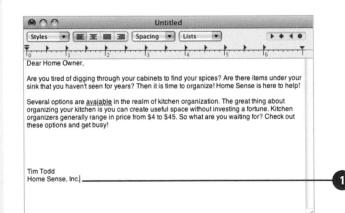

## Move or Copy Text

1. Select the text you want to move or copy.

2. Click the **Edit** menu, and then click **Cut** or **Copy**.

   **TIMESAVER** Press ⌘+X to cut or press ⌘+C to copy.

3. Click where you want to insert the text.

4. Click the **Edit** menu, and then click **Paste**.

   **TIMESAVER** Press ⌘+V to paste.

## Move or Copy Text Using Drag and Drop

1. Select the text you want to move or copy.

2. Point to the selected text, and then click and hold the mouse button.

   If you want to copy the text to a new location, also press and hold the Option key. A plus sign (+) appears in the pointer box, indicating that you are dragging a copy of the selected text.

3. Drag the selected text to the new location, and then release the mouse button (and the Option key, if necessary).

4. Click anywhere in the document to deselect the text.

# Recognizing Handwriting Ink

Although typing information into an document or e-mail through the keyboard is fast and efficient, you may find that you need to enter information in handwritten form, known as **ink**. Programs that accept ink, such as TextEdit or Mail, provide handwriting recognition to help you convert handwriting into text. Before you can insert handwritten text into a document, you need to have an ink device, or a handwriting tablet, such as Wacom, attached to and installed on your computer. With handwriting recognition turned on in the Ink pane in System Preferences, you can write in two ink modes: Anywhere or Ink pad. Anywhere mode is useful for writing in a word processing document. As you write in Anywhere mode, your ink strokes appear in a yellow lined translucent overlay. As the Mac recognizes the writing, it converts the ink to text, inserts it in the open document, and erases it from the overlay. When you need to use the mouse, you need to turn off Anywhere mode. Ink pad provides a floating window in which you can use the stylus to write ink and to perform commands as the mouse. Using ink can be tricky at first, but over time you'll get the hang of it.

## Insert Handwritten Text Anywhere into a Document

1. Open a program, such as TextEdit, that accepts ink.

2. Turn on handwriting recognition (Ink icon in System Preferences).

   The Ink toolbar appears.

3. Write your text in the yellow lined overlay. After recognition, the text that you write appears in the document.

4. To turn Anywhere mode off to use the mouse, click the **On/Off** button on the Ink toolbar.

5. When you're done, turn off handwriting recognition, and close any open documents.

### See Also

*See "Setting Ink Preferences" on page 128 for information on turning handwriting recognition on and off, as well as other options.*

Use buttons to perform keyboard shortcuts.

Shift key

Control key

Command key

Option key

Recognized text

Untitled

Hello

## Insert Handwritten Text Using the Ink Pad

① Open a program, such as TextEdit, that accepts ink.

② Turn on handwriting recognition (Ink icon in System Preferences).

The Ink toolbar appears.

③ Click the **Show Ink Pad** button on the Ink toolbar.

④ Click the **A** button to input text, or click the **Star** button to create a drawing.

⑤ Write your text or draw with the pen in the Ink Pad window.

**TROUBLE?** *If Ink makes a mistake, hold down the Option key, tap the word, and then select a transcription option.*

⑥ Use the Ink toolbar buttons (Command, Shift, Option, or Control) to perform keyboard shortcuts.

⑦ Click **Send** to have your text or drawing pasted into the open document behind it.

⑧ When you're done, turn off handwriting recognition, and close any open documents.

Ink drawing

Click to clear Ink pad.

### Did You Know?

***You can recognize gestures in Ink pad.***
As you write, Ink recognizes certain gestures, or shapes, which get performed as commands, such as Undo, or pressed as keys, such as Delete or Space. A list is available on the Gestures tab in the Ink pane in System Preferences.

---

## For Your Information

### Handwriting in Chinese

If you have a Multi-Touch trackpad on your Mac notebook, you can draw Chinese characters in your documents (**New!**). When you draw on the trackpad, the Chinese characters appear in an input window, which recommends closely matched characters and allows you to choose the one you want. The input window also provides suggestions for subsequent characters based on what you chose.

# Making Corrections

Everyone makes mistakes and changes their mind at some point, especially when creating or revising a document. With TextEdit you can instantly correct typing errors by pressing a key. You can also reverse more complicated actions, such as typing an entire word, formatting a paragraph, or creating a chart. If you need to undo several actions, you can use the Undo command multiple times. With the Undo command, if you change your mind, you can just as easily use the Redo command to restore the action you reversed.

## Undo or Redo an Action

◆ Click the **Edit** menu, and then click **Undo** to reverse your most recent action, such as typing a word or formatting a paragraph.

   **TIMESAVER** *Press ⌘+Z to undo.*

◆ Click the **Edit** menu, and then click **Redo** to restore the last action you reversed.

   **TIMESAVER** *Press ⌘+Shift+Z to redo your undo.*

   **NOTE** *The Undo and Redo commands may change based on the action that was last performed (such as typing or dragging).*

Click to undo
Click to redo

| Edit | |
| --- | --- |
| Undo Typing | ⌘Z |
| Redo Drag | ⇧⌘Z |
| Cut | ⌘X |
| Copy | ⌘C |
| Paste | ⌘V |
| Paste and Match Style | ⌥⇧⌘V |
| Delete | |
| Complete | ⌥⎋ |
| Select All | ⌘A |
| Insert | ▶ |
| Edit Link... | ⌘K |
| Find | ▶ |
| Spelling and Grammar | ▶ |
| Substitutions | ▶ |
| Transformations | ▶ |
| Speech | ▶ |
| Special Characters... | ⌥⌘T |

## Correct Typing Errors Using the Keyboard

| To Delete | Press |
| --- | --- |
| One character at a time to the left of the insertion point | Delete |
| One word at a time to the left of the insertion point | Option+Delete |
| Selected text | Delete |

# Making Text Substitutions

Text substitution (**New!**) allows you to correct words and phrases that you misspell or insert symbols. For example, you can type "teh" to change to "the" or type (c) to insert ©. You can add words, phrases, and symbols to the Symbol and Text Substitution list in Language & Text preferences. In TextEdit, you can use Smart Copy/Paste to adjust text formatting during a copy and paste, Smart Dashes to automatically replace a sequence of dashes to typographical dashes, Smart Quotes to replace quotes and apostrophes to typographical ones, and Smart Links to convert URLs into links. TextEdit also uses **data detectors** (**New!**) to analyze what you type to detect specialized text, such as dates and addresses, so you can take smart actions, such as create a contact, create an iCal event, or map an address depending on the type of information.

## Select Substitution Options

1. Click the **Edit** menu, point to **Substitutions**, and then select or deselect any of the following options:

   - **Show Substitutions.** Opens the Substitutions dialog where you can enable or disable text substitution options (*ones listed below*), open the Language & Text preferences dialog, or make text replacements.

   - **Smart Copy/Paste.** Adjusts the formatting for text when you copy and paste.

   - **Smart Quotes.** Replaces quotes and apostrophes to typographical ones.

   - **Smart Dashes.** Replaces a sequence of dashes to typographical dashes.

   - **Smart Links.** Converts URLs into links.

   - **Data Detectors.** Analyzes text, such as dates and addresses, in order to take smart actions.

   - **Text Replacement.** Replaces text using the list in Language & Text preferences.

Text substitution options in TextEdit

Text substitution options in Language & Text preferences in the Finder

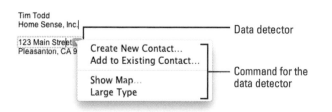

Data detector

Command for the data detector

# Checking Spelling and Grammar

As you type, a red wavy line appears under words not listed in TextEdit's dictionary (such as misspellings or names) or duplicated words (such as the the). You can correct these errors as well as grammatical problems as they arise or after you finish the entire document. For common spelling errors, such as "teh," TextEdit can automatically correct the mistake (**New!**) as you type. TextEdit uses symbol and text substitution options in Language & Text preferences (**New!**) to make the correction. Before you print your final document, use the Spell and Grammar Checker to ensure that your document is error-free.

## Correct Spelling and Grammar as You Type

1. Select the spelling and grammar commands to enable the options.

   ◆ **Check Spelling.** Click the **Edit** menu, point to **Spelling and Grammar**, and then click **Check Spelling While Type**.

   ◆ **Correct Spelling.** Click the **Edit** menu, point to **Spelling and Grammar**, and then click **Correct Spelling Automatically** (**New!**).

   ◆ **Check Grammar.** Click the **Edit** menu, point to **Spelling and Grammar**, and then click **Check Grammar With Spelling**.

2. Control-click a word with a red dotted underline.

3. Click a substitution, or click **Ignore Spelling** to skip any other instances of the word.

## Did You Know?

*You can add a familiar word to your dictionary.* Control-click the wavy line under the word in question, and then click Learn Spelling. The wavy line disappears and you've added the word or name to the dictionary.

Click to add a word or name to the dictionary.

## Correct Spelling and Grammar

1. Click at the beginning of the document or select the text you want to correct.

2. Click the **Edit** menu, point to **Spelling and Grammar**, and then click **Show Spelling and Grammar**.

   As it checks each sentence in the document or your selection, TextEdit selects misspelled words or problematic sentences and provides appropriate alternatives.

3. If necessary, click the **Language** pop-up, and then select a language.

4. To check grammar, select the **Check grammar** check box.

5. Select an option:

   ◆ Click a suggestion, and then click **Change** to make a substitution.

   ◆ If no suggestion is appropriate, click in the document and edit the text yourself. Click **Find Next** to continue.

   ◆ Click **Ignore** to skip the word.

   ◆ Click **Learn** to add the word to the dictionary.

   ◆ Click **Define** to look up the word in the dictionary.

   ◆ Click **Guess** to suggest possible corrections.

   The Spell Checker will beep when the process is done.

6. Click the **Close** button to return to the document.

Spelling and Grammar dialog

Suggestion window

# Looking Up Words with Dictionary

The Dictionary application, located in the Applications folder, gives you the ability to search for words and definitions as a stand-alone program or from any application, such as TextEdit. Within an application, you can view words in a Dictionary panel or open the Dictionary application. You can also use the Dictionary widget in Dashboard to look up and find the definitions you need. Dictionary provides several different sources for you to reference, including English and other language dictionaries, an Apple terms dictionary, a thesaurus (second edition) (**New!**), and Wikipedia, which is a free online encyclopedia. You can select which sources you want to use as well as set parental controls to limit access to some works for specific users.

## Look Up Words with Dictionary

1.  Start the Dictionary application as a stand-alone program or in another application:

    ◆ **Stand Alone.** Click the **Applications** folder in the Dock, and then click the **Dictionary** icon.

    ◆ **In an Application.** Hold down the Control key and click the word you want, click **Look Up in Dictionary** from the menu to display the word in the Dictionary application or panel.

    You can also point to the word you want, press Control+⌘+D to display the Dictionary panel. Click **More** to view the complete entry. Click the pop-up to change the source.

2.  Select the source you want to search: **All**, **Dictionary**, **Thesaurus**, **Apple**, **Wikipedia**, etc.

3.  Type a word or phrase, if necessary. Dictionary searches for matches as you type.

4.  Double-click the item you want to view.

5.  Click a link to find out about an item.

6.  Click the **Close** button.

Thesaurus for selected text

## Set Dictionary Preferences

1. Click the **Dictionary** menu, and then click **Preferences**.

2. Select or specify the various options you want to use:

   ◆ Sources. Select the check boxes for the dictionaries and thesaurus' you want to use, and then select the reference resource you want to set additional options.

   ◆ Pronunciation. If available, select the pronunciation option you want.

   ◆ Contextual Menu. Click the **Open Dictionary application** or **Open Dictionary panel** option.

   ◆ Font Size. Click the up and down arrows to set the font size.

3. Click the **Close** button.

4. Quit Dictionary.

### Did You Know?

*You can set parental controls for dictionary use.* As the administrator, click the System Preferences icon in the Dock, click the Parental Control icon, enter your administrator password, select the user you want to set limits, click Content, select the check box next to Dictionary, and then click the Close button.

*You can view recent dictionary searches.* To see previously viewed words, use the Back and Forward buttons. To skip to a specific word, hold down the Back or Forward buttons to see a menu of recent words, and then click the one you want.

### For Your Information

#### Speaking Text in a Document

TextEdit can speak all or part of the text in a document. To speak text in a document, deselect all text to speak the entire document or select the text you want to hear, click the Edit menu, point to Speech, and then click Start Speaking. To make the speaking stop, click the Edit menu, point to Speech, and then click Stop Speaking. The voice you hear is set in the Speech pane of System Preferences. To change the sound of the computer's voice, click the Apple menu, click System Preferences, click Speech, click the Default Voice tab, select a voice, and then click the Close button.

# Finding and Replacing Text

The Find and Replace commands make it easy to locate or replace specific text or formulas in a document. For example, you might want to find each reference to a individual or company name in a long report to verify that it's properly used. Or you might want to replace all references to a special character in your document with another one. If you only know part of a word you want to find, you can use the Contains pop-up to help you locate what you're looking for. If you are looking for a case sensitive text with upper and lower case characters, turn off the Ignore Case option. To make sure you check the entire document no matter where you start, turn on the Wrap Around option.

## Find Text

1. Click at the beginning of the document, or select the text you want to find.

2. Click the **Edit** menu, point to **Find**, and then click **Find**.

3. Type the text you want to find.

4. Click the **Contains** pop-up, and then select a search option: **Contains**, **Starts With**, or **Full Word**.

5. Select other options:

   ◆ **Ignore Case.** Check to ignore upper and lower case characters.

   ◆ **Wrap Around.** Check to wrap back to the beginning of the document.

6. Click **Next** until the text you want to find is highlighted.

   You can click **Next** repeatedly to locate each instance of the text.

7. If a message box appears when you reach the end of the document, click **OK**. Otherwise, the computer will beep when the Find is complete.

8. When you're done, click the **Close** button.

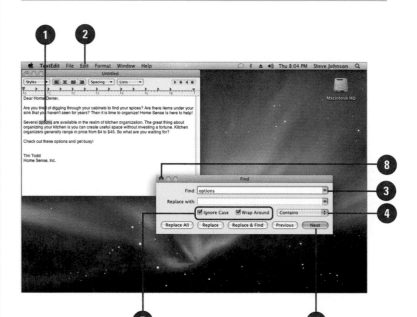

## Replace Text

① Click at the beginning of the document, or select the text you want to replace.

② Click the **Edit** menu, point to **Find**, and then click **Find**.

③ Type the text you want to find.

④ Type the text you want to replace.

⑤ Click the **Contains** pop-up, and then select a search option: **Contains**, **Starts With**, or **Full Word**.

⑥ Select or clear the **Ignore Case and Wrap Around** check boxes.

⑦ Click **Next** to begin the search and find the next instance of the search text.

⑧ Click one of the Replace buttons:

◆ **Replace All**. Click to substitute text throughout the entire document.

◆ **Replace**. Click to substitute the replacement text.

◆ **Replace & Find**. Click to substitute the replacement text and find the next instance.

You can click **Next** to locate the next instance of the search text without making a replacement.

⑨ If a message box appears when you reach the end of the document, click **OK**. Otherwise, the computer will beep when the process is done.

⑩ When you're done, click the **Close** button.

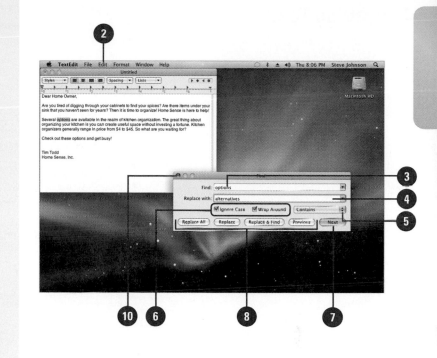

### For Your Information

## Using Bidirectional Text

If you use different languages in the same document, the mixing of the text can sometimes cause problems. For example, if you use one language, such as Hebrew or Arabic, written from right to left and another language, such as English, written from left to right, the flow of text between the to may not look right. With bidirectional text in Snow Leopard (**New!**), you can mix languages with the results you want. You can also use a split-cursor to help show you the right direction of the text at the boundary between right-to-left and left-to-right text. that shows the right direction.

# Formatting Text

When you are working with Rich Text Format (RTF) and Word Format documents, you can change the format or the appearance of text and graphics in a document so that the document is easier to read and more attractive. A quick and powerful way to add emphasis to parts of a document is to format text using bold, italics, underline, or color. For special emphasis, you can combine formats, such as bold and italics. In addition, you can change the font style and size. A **font** is a set of characters with the same typeface or design that you can increase or decrease in size, such as Arial or Times New Roman. Font size is measured in points; one point is 1/72 of an inch high.

## Format Text

**1** Select the text or click in the paragraph you want to format.

**2** Click an alignment button: **Left**, **Center**, **Justify**, and **Right**.

**3** Click the **Format** menu, and then point to **Font**.

**4** Select any of the formatting commands to open a dialog and style text:

◆ **Show Fonts**. Click to change multiple text formatting options at the same time.

◆ **Show Color**. Click to change text color.

**4** Select any of the formatting menu individual commands: Bold, Italic, Underline, Outline, Bigger (font size), or Smaller (font size).

**5** Click in the document to unselect the newly formatted text.

6 — Changed the selected text to italics.

Fonts dialog

Select options for font, typeface, and size.

Colors dialog

Select a text color

# Displaying Rulers

The TextEdit ruler does more than just measure. The horizontal ruler above the document shows the length of the typing line and lets you quickly adjust left and right margins, indents, and set tabs. You can hide the ruler to get more room for your document. When you press Return to start a new paragraph, TextEdit continues to use the same ruler settings. As you work with a document, ruler settings change. Instead of resetting ruler settings each time, you can copy and paste them.

## Show and Hide the Ruler

1 Click the **Format** menu, point to **Text**, and then click **Show Ruler**.

**TIMESAVER** Press ⌘+R to show or hide the ruler.

A check mark next to the command indicates the ruler is shown. A non check mark indicates the ruler is hidden.

## Copy and Paste the Ruler

1 Click in the line to place the insertion point or select the lines with the ruler settings you want to copy.

2 Click the **Format** menu, point to **Text**, and then click **Copy Ruler**.

**TIMESAVER** Press Control+ ⌘+Z to copy ruler.

3 Click in the line to place the insertion point or select the lines in which you want to paste the ruler.

4 Click the **Format** menu, point to **Text**, and then click **Paste Ruler**.

**TIMESAVER** Press Control+ ⌘+Z to paste ruler.

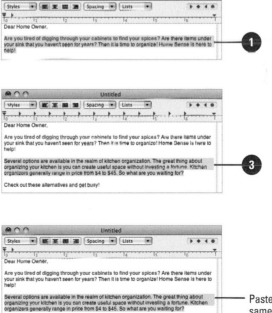

Pasted ruler, same as step 1.

# Setting Paragraph Tabs

Tabs set text or numerical data alignment in relation to the edges of a document. A **tab stop** is a predefined stopping point along the document's typing line. Default tab stops are set every half-inch on the ruler, but you can set multiple tabs per paragraph at any location. Each paragraph in a document contains its own set of tab stops. The default tab stops do not appear on the ruler, but the manual tab stops you set do appear. Once you place a tab stop, you can drag the tab stop to position it where you want. If you want to add or adjust tab stops in multiple paragraphs, simply select the paragraphs first.

## Create and Clear a Tab Stop

1. Select the text or click in the paragraph you want to format.

2. Drag a tab stop from the tab stop palette above the ruler or one already on the ruler where you want to set it.

3. To move a tab, drag the tab stop to position it where you want.

4. To clear a tab stop, drag it off the ruler.

### See Also

*See "Setting Up Page Options" on page 204 for information on changing the paper size.*

Tab stop palette

## Tab Stops

| Tab Stop | Name | Description |
|:---:|---|---|
| ▶ | Left tab stop | Aligns tab text to the left |
| ◆ | Center tab stop | Aligns tab text to the center |
| ◀ | Right tab stop | Aligns tab text to the right |
| ● | Decimal tab stop | Aligns numbers to the decimal point |

# Setting Paragraph Indents

When you indent a paragraph, you move its edge in from the left or right margin. You can indent the entire left or right edge of a paragraph or just the first line. The markers on the ruler control the indentation of the current paragraph. The ruler has three markers. The top rectangle, called the **paragraph indent marker**, controls where the first line of the paragraph begins. The bottom triangle, called the **left indent marker**, controls where the remaining lines of the paragraph begin. The triangle on the right side of the ruler, called the **right indent marker**, controls where the right edge of the paragraph ends.

## Change Paragraph Indents

Select the text or click in the paragraph you want to format.

◆ To change the left indent of the first line, drag the Paragraph Indent marker.

◆ To change the indent of the second and subsequent lines, drag the Left Indent marker (under the Paragraph Indent marker).

◆ To change the left indent for all lines, drag the Left Indent marker, and the Paragraph Indent marker to the same point.

◆ To change the right indent for all lines, drag the Right Indent marker.

As you drag a marker, the dotted guideline helps you position the indent accurately.

Paragraph Indent marker                    Right Indent marker

Left Indent marker

### Did You Know?

*You can set your text to be hyphenated.* Hyphenation prevents ugly gaps and short lines in text. Click the Format menu, and then click Allow Hyphenation. To turn hyphenation off, click the Format menu, and then click Disallow Hyphenation.

## For Your Information

### Changing Text Wrap

By default, TextEdit wraps lines of text based on the width of the window. If you change the width of the window, the lines of text get shorter or longer. If you widen the window, the text gets smaller. When you print the document, TextEdit reduces the font size of the text to match the printed document to what you see on the screen, which might not be the results you want to achieve. To avoid this, you can change the text to wrap to the paper size. TextEdit uses the paper size and orientation you set in Page Setup, to determine the point in which the text line wraps. To change text wrap, click the Format menu, and then click Wrap to Page or Wrap to Window. When you change the text wrap to Wrap To Page, a rectangle appears in the window indicating the margins of the document.

# Changing Character Spacing

Kerning is the amount of space between each character that you type. Sometimes the space between two characters is larger than others, which makes the word look uneven. You can expand or condense the spacing to create a special effect for a title, or re-align the baseline, which is the position of characters to the bottom edge of the text—this is helpful for positioning the copyright or trademark symbols.

## Change Character Spacing

1 Select the text you want to format.

2 Click the **Format** menu, point to **Font**, and then point to **Kern**.

3 Click any of the following options:

◆ **Use Default**. Uses default kerning.

◆ **Use None**. Removes kerning.

◆ **Tighten**. Moves the characters together slightly; you can repeat the command.

◆ **Loosen**. Moves the characters slightly apart; you can repeat the command.

## Change Character Baseline

1 Select the text you want to format.

2 Click the **Format** menu, point to **Font**, and then point to **Baseline**.

3 Click any of the following options:

◆ **Superscript**. Moves the text above the level of normal text.

◆ **Subscript**. Moves the text below the level of normal text.

◆ **Raise**. Moves the text up only a little bit; you can repeat the command.

◆ **Lower**. Moves the text down only a little bit; you can repeat the command.

# Changing Line Spacing

The lines in all TextEdit documents are single-spaced by default, which is appropriate for letters and most documents. But you can easily change your document line spacing to double or you can specify to allow extra space between every line. This is useful when you want to make notes on a printed document. Sometimes, you'll want to add space above and below certain paragraphs, for headlines, or indented quotations to help set off the text. To set specialized line spacing settings, use the Other command on the Spacing pop-up. You can select options for line height, inter-line spacing, and paragraph spacing. **Line height** is the distance from the top of a line to the top of the line below it; **inter-line spacing** is the distance from the bottom of a line to the top of the line below it; and **paragraph spacing** is the distance from the bottom of a paragraph to the top of the first line in the paragraph below it.

## Change Line Spacing

1. Select the text you want to change.

2. Click the **Spacing** pop-up on the ruler, and then select a spacing option:

   ◆ Click **Single** or **Double** to apply a single line space or double line spacing.

   ◆ Click **Other**, specify the exacting options you want, and then click **OK**.

### Did You Know?

***You can insert and remove a page break.*** Click the Format menu, and then click Wrap To Page (if necessary) so the page break can be visible. Click to place the insertion point where you want the page break, press Control+Q, and then press Control+L. To remove a page break, place the insertion point below the page break, and then press Delete.

Specify exacting line spacing options

# Adding Lists and Tables

The best way to draw attention to a list is to format the items with bullets or numbers. You can even create multi-level lists. For different emphasis, change any bullet or number style to one of TextEdit's many predefined formats. For example, switch round bullets to check boxes or Roman numerals to lowercase letters. You can also customize the list style or insert a picture as a bullet. If you move, insert, or delete items in a numbered list, TextEdit sequentially renumbers the list for you. A **table** neatly organizes information into rows and columns. The intersection of a column and row is called a **cell**. Enter text into cells just as you would anywhere else in TextEdit, except that pressing the Tab key moves you from one cell to the next. You can format a table just like you format any other text in TextEdit.

## Create a Numbered or Bulleted List

1. Select the text you want to change or click the place the insertion point where you want to start a list.

2. Click the **Lists** pop-up on the ruler, and then select the numbered or bulleted list option you want.

3. For a new list line, type a list item, and then press Return.

   ◆ To add to an existing list, place the insertion point at the end of the line, and then press Return.

4. To indent a list, place the insertion point at the beginning of the line, and then press Tab.

   ◆ To go back to the previous indent level, hold down the Shift key and press Return.

5. To finish a list, press Return twice.

## Add a Table

1. Place the insertion point where you want to insert a table.

2. Click the **Format** menu, and then click **Table**.

3. Type the number of rows and columns you want or use the arrow buttons.

4. Set any of the following table options:

   ◆ **Alignment**. Left, Center, Justified, Right, or Top, Baseline, Middle, or Bottom.

   ◆ **Cell Border**. Use the arrow button to set the pixel border.

   ◆ **Cell Background**. Click the pop-up to select **None** or **Color Fill**. Click the color box, click a color, and then click the **Close** button.

5. Click the **Close** button in the Table dialog box.

6. To adjust the height or width of a row or column, position the pointer over a cell border, and then drag the border.

### Did You Know?

***You can merge cells in a table.*** Select the cells you want to merge, click the Format menu, point to Text, click Table, click Merge Cells, and then click the Close button.

***You can create a table in a table.*** Select the cell you want to insert a table, click the Format menu, point to Text, click Table, click Nest Table, and then click the Close button.

# Applying and Creating a Style

When you want to apply multiple groupings of formatting, such as font type, size and color, use a style. A **style** is a collection of formatting settings saved within a document or favorites list that you can apply to text. TextEdit keeps track of all the styles in the current document. If you want to save a style for use in all documents, you can add it to a favorites list. TextEdit provides a few basic favorite styles. But you can add your own to create the exact look you want. If you need a quick way to apply a single instance of formatting, you can copy and paste it.

## Apply a Favorite Style

1. Select the text you want to apply a style.

2. Click the **Styles** pop-up on the Ruler.

3. Click the style you want to apply.

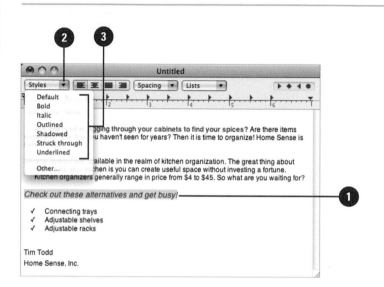

## Apply a Document Style

1. Select the text whose formatting you want to save as a style.

2. Click the **Format** menu, point to **Font**, and then click **Styles**.

3. If necessary, click the **Document Styles** option.

4. Click the arrow buttons to select the style you want to apply.

5. Click **Apply**, and then when you're done, click **Done**.

## Add a Style to Favorites

1. Select the text whose formatting you want to save as a style.

2. Click the **Format** menu, point to **Font**, and then click **Styles**.

3. Click **Add To Favorites**.

4. Type a name for the style.

5. Select or clear the check boxes to include the font or ruler as part of the style.

6. Click **Add**.

### Did You Know?

*You can remove a style favorite.* Click the Format menu, point to Font, click Styles, click the Favorite Styles option, click the pop-up, select the style favorite, and then click Remove From Favorites.

## Copy and Paste Formatting

1. Select the text in which you want to copy the formatting.

2. Click the **Format** menu, point to **Font**, and then click **Copy Style**.

   **TIMESAVER** *Press Option+⌥⌘+Z to copy ruler.*

3. Select the text to which you want to apply a style.

4. Click the **Format** menu, point to **Font**, and then click **Paste Style**.

# Inserting Special Characters

When you need to insert special characters such as ©, ™, or ® that don't appear on your keyboard, you can use a special accessory called Special Character to do the job. Special Character is available in Mac applications and displays all the characters that are available for each of the fonts on your computer.

## Insert a Special Character

1 Click in the text to place the insertion point where you want to insert a special character.

2 Click the **Edit** menu, and then click **Special Characters**.

3 Click the **View** pop-up, and then select a character set.

4 Click the **By Category** tab, and then select a category. To select from your favorites, click the **Favorites** tab, and then select a symbol.

5 Click the special character you want to insert.

6 Click **Insert**.

7 To add the character to a favorites list, click the **Action** button, and then click **Add To Favorites**.

8 Click the **Close** button.

## See Also

*See "Making Text Substitutions" on page 171 for information on quickly inserting symbols using text substitution while you type.*

Click a category

List of favorite special characters

# Adding Pictures, Movies, or Files to a Document

If you have a picture, movie, or another file, (such as another text file, spreadsheet, or PDF), you can place them within a TextEdit document. Before you can add a picture, movie, or files to a TextEdit document, the file needs to be converted to the Rich Text Format (RTF). Pictures and movies appear in the document as embedded graphics, while files appear as embedded icons. With embedding, a copy of the file becomes part of the TextEdit file. If you want to edit the embedded file, you make changes in the TextEdit file, and the original file remains intact. You can double-click the embedded graphics or icons to open and view the files.

## Add a Picture, Movie, or File to a Document

1. Click the **Format** menu, and then click **Make Rich Text**.

2. Switch to the Finder, and then open the folder containing the picture, movie, or file you want to add.

3. Display the picture, movie, or file icon in the Finder and the TextEdit document on the screen where you can view them both.

4. Drag the picture, movie, or file icon from the Finder to the document window where you want to place it.

   The image is placed in your document.

5. Close the Finder window.

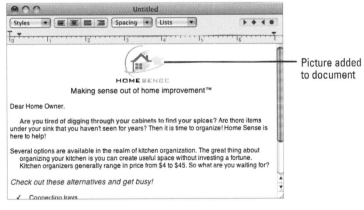

Picture added to document

# Saving and Closing a Document

Saving your files frequently ensures that you don't lose work during an unexpected power loss. The first time you save, specify a file name and folder in the Save As dialog. The next time you save, the program saves the file with the same name in the same folder. If you want to change a file's name or location, you can use the Save As dialog again to create a copy of the original file. The Save As dialog appears in a compact view (useful for saving in the same place) and an expanded view (useful for saving in a different location or creating a new folder). Expanded view includes the Sidebar, and List and Column view. To conserve your computer's resources, close any file you are not working on.

## Save a Document as Rich Text or Microsoft Word

1. For plain text only, click the **Format** menu, and then click **Make Rich Text**.

2. Click the **File** menu, and then click **Save As**.

3. Type a name for the file, or use the suggested name.

4. Select the hard drive and folder in which you want to save the file.

5. To change the format of a file, click the **File Format** pop-up, and then click **Rich Text Format (RTF)** or one of the Word formats.

6. Click **Save**.

Compact view

Click to expand dialog to show Sidebar and file list.

Did You Know?

*TextEdit can save documents as a PDF file* (**New!**). Click the File menu, click Save As PDF, type a name, navigate to a folder in which you want to save the file, and then click Save. *See "Previewing Images and PDF's" on page 151 for more information on working with PDF (Portable Document File) files.*

## For Your Information

### Protecting Documents

If you have content in your TextEdit document that you don't want users to change, you can make the document read-only. This is useful for documents, such as "read me" files, contracts, and any other document you want users to read, but not accidentally change. To prevent others from changing your TextEdit documents, click the Format menu, and then click Prevent Editing. To allow users to make changes to a read-only document, click the Format menu, and then click Allow Editing. Another way to protect a document is to lock it. When you lock a file, users can make changes to the file, but the application prevents them from saving it. To lock a file, select the files in the Finder, click the File menu, click Get Info, select the Locked check box, and then click the Close button.

## Save a Document as Plain Text

1. For plain text only, click the **Format** menu, and then click **Make Plain Text**.

2. Click the **File** menu, and then click **Save As**.

3. Type a name for the file, or use the suggested name.

4. Select the hard drive and folder in which you want to save the file.

5. Click the **Plain Text Encoding** pop-up, and then select an encoding format.

6. Click **Save**.

### Did You Know?

*You can revert to a previously saved document.* Before you save, click the File menu, and then click Revert To Saved.

## Close a Document

1. Click the **Close** button.

2. If necessary, click **Save** to save your changes.

   **TIMESAVER** *When a small dot appears in the Close button, it means the document needs to be saved.*

3. Quit TextEdit.

### See Also

*See Chapter 8, "Printing and Faxing" on page 195 for information on printing a document.*

Expanded view  ③  Click to collapse dialog.

Save As: Untitled

Where: Documents ← 4

Plain Text Encoding: Unicode (UTF-8) ← 5

☑ If no extension is provided, use ".txt".

Cancel   Save

6

# Using TextEdit for Web Design

You can use TextEdit to create and edit HTML code documents. You can open an existing HTML file or create a new one using plain text or RTF Rich Text Format. If you want to add graphics to your RTF document, you cannot save it as an HTML file. However, you can save it as a Web archive file. In addition, you can insert a link to an URL address into a document.

## Create Plain HTML Code Files

1. For plain text only, click the **Format** menu, and then click **Make Plain Text**.

2. Write the HTML code.

3. Click the **File** menu, and then click **Save As**.

4. Add the .html extension at the end of the file name.

5. Click **Save**.

6. Click **Use .html**.

### Did You Know?

*You can set preferences to save HTML files.* Click the TextEdit menu, click Preferences, click the Open and Save tab, select a document type, a setting for cascading style sheets (CSS), and an encoding. If you want to include code to preserve blank areas, select the Preserve White Space check box, and then click the Close button.

192

## Open an HTML Document

1. Click the **File** menu, and then click **Open**.

2. Select the hard drive and the folder in which you want to open the file.

3. Click the document you want to open.

4. Select the **Ignore rich text commands** check box.

5. Click **Open**.

## Add a Link

1. Select the text you want for the link.

2. Click the **Edit** menu, and then click **Add Link**.

3. Type or paste the URL link address in the Link Destination box.

4. Click **OK**.

### Did You Know?

*You can edit or remove a link.* To edit a link, select the link, click the Edit menu, click Edit Link, edit the link text, and then click OK. To remove a link, select the link, click the Edit menu, click Edit Link, and then click Remove Link.

# Setting TextEdit Preferences

TextEdit preferences help you configure some of the more common features of the program. You can set preferences for new documents, default fonts, rich text processing, default plain text encoding, editing, and saving. These preference areas allow you to turn features on and off as well as customize the way TextEdit works.

## Set General Preferences

1. Click the **TextEdit** menu, and then click **Preferences**.

2. Click the **New Document** tab.

3. Select or specify the various options you want to use:

   ◆ **Format.** Select options for document format and text wrapping.

   ◆ **Window Size.** Specify the width and height you want.

   ◆ **Font.** Click **Change** to select the default fonts you want.

   ◆ **Properties and Options.** Enter document properties and check or clear to enable or disable the editing options.

4. Click the **Open and Save** tab.

5. Select or specify the various options you want to use:

   ◆ **When Opening a File.** Check or clear to ignore or allow rich text commands.

   ◆ **When Saving a File.** Check or clear the options you want.

   ◆ **Autosaving.** Click the pop-up to select a auto saving interval.

   ◆ **Plain Text File Encoding.** Click the Open or Save pop-ups to select a text encoding default.

   ◆ **HTML Saving Options.** Click the pop-ups to select a default HTML type, styling, and encoding.

6. Click the **Close** button.

# Printing and Faxing

## Introduction

Let's face it, you work all day on a computer, but sooner or later, you're going to have to get your one-of-a-kind project, text document, or photograph off the computer. Computer data finds itself in the most unlikely places. For example, you could save a text document onto a CD or DVD, and then store the CD or DVD away; never to be seen again. Probably the most common place you find computer data is on paper. It might be nice to talk of a paperless society, however, most people prefer the satisfying feel of paper in their hands, as opposed to a cold computer monitor. That's where Mac OS X steps in and makes your life easy. Not only does Mac OS X give you all the standard ways to print to paper or fax, it also gives you hundreds of printer drives; supporting the vast majority of printers in the market. In addition, you can save paper by previewing your jobs—using Leopard's print preview feature—which shows you a color-accurate on-screen version of your print job.

If you fax documents, then Leopard is an operating system tailor-made expressly for your needs. Mac OS X integrates its faxing features with a state-of-the-art printing system. Just open the Print & Fax pane in System Preferences, and you can set up your computer to receive faxes. Then, when you go to print a document from virtually any application, you'll see a Fax button in the Print dialog. In addition, if you have a large print job that you would rather print after work, or a fax that has to be sent at a specific time; Mac OS X lets you schedule a time to print a document, or fax with the click of a button.

# Understanding Printers

Although there are many different kinds of printers, there are two main categories: ink-jet and laser. An **ink-jet printer** works by spraying ionized ink on a sheet of paper. Ink-jet printers are less expensive and considerably slower than laser printers, but they still produce a good quality output. A **laser printer** utilizes a laser beam to produce an image on a drum, which is rolled through a reservoir of toner and transferred to the paper through a combination of heat and pressure. Laser printers are faster and produce a higher quality output than ink-jets, but they are also more expensive. Ink-jet and laser printers are combined with other hardware devices, such as a copier and scanner, into a multi-function device. A **multi-function device** provides common device functionality at a lower cost than purchasing each device separately. Printers are classified by two main characteristics: resolution and speed. Printer resolution refers to the sharpness and clarity of a printed page. For printers, the resolution indicates the number of dots per inch (dpi). For example, a 300-dpi printer is one that is capable of printing 300 distinct dots in a line one-inch long, or 90,000 dots per square inch. The higher the dpi, the sharper the print quality. Printer speed is measured in pages per minute (ppm). The speed of printers varies widely. In general, ink-jet printers range from about 4 to 10 ppm, while laser printers range from about 10 to 30 ppm. The speed depends on the amount of printer memory (the more the better) and the page's contents: if there is just text or the page has only one color, the ppm is in the high range, but when a page contains graphics and/or has multiple colors, the ppm rate falls to the low range.

Ink-jet printer

Laser printer

Multi-function device

# Understanding Printer Drivers

Printer drivers are lines of code designed to help an operating system communicate with a specific printer. No two printer models are created equal: Some have two paper trays, while others have one; some are ink-jet, while others are laser; some are color and some black and white. Although there are generic printer drivers available, most printers have a driver program, designed specifically for that make and model. Mac OS X installs all of the printer drivers onto your hard drive when you run the Mac OS X installation program.

The drivers become available when you attach your printer and run the Printer Setup Utility. The good news is that with the release of Snow Leopard, the process of hooking up your printer, and being able to print, just became a lot easier. Mac OS X comes bundled with almost every conceivable printer driver; however, new printers and updates are being released all the time. When you plug in a new printer, Snow Leopard downloads the appropriate driver. Periodically, Snow Leopard checks to make sure it has the lastest driver using Software Update as needed (**New!**). It's always a good idea to keep the CD or DVD that came with your printer handy; it contains a driver for that particular model of printer. In addition, the Web sites for the printer companies such as *www.epson.com* or *www.hp.com*, contain the latest updates and patches for their printers. You can visit them to see if any updates are available.

Since you'll only need one or two printer drivers, you can delete the others. All those unused drivers take up over a gigabyte of space on your hard drive. Once you've installed the necessary printers, select the Library folder (located on the main hard drive), click Printers folder, and then delete the unused drivers. If necessary, you can always reinstall them from the OS X install disks.

# Adding or Removing a Printer

Setting up a printer use to be a difficult and time-consuming process. There were all kinds of questions to answer, driver files to find, and after all that time, you might still have problems. With Mac OS X, setting up a printer is easy. Adding a printer can be as simple as plugging it into your computer. In most cases that's all you need to do. Mac OS X automatically tries to autoconfigure almost any USB, FireWire, or Bluetooth connection. If you want to install a network printer, such as Bonjour, or your printer doesn't appear in the printer list, you can add it manually in the Print & Fax pane in System Preferences. If you no longer use a printer, you can quickly remove it while your in Print & Fax preferences.

## Add or Remove a Printer

1. To add a printer, follow the printer setup instructions to install any necessary software, and then connect it to your computer using a USB or FireWire connection.

   Mac OS X automatically tries to install the printer. In most cases, the printer is available in any Print dialog box.

   If the printer is not available, continue.

2. Click the **System Preferences** icon in the Dock, and then click the **Print & Fax** icon.

   The printer appears in the left column. If your printer doesn't appears in the list, follow the instructions to add a printer manually on the next page.

3. To remove a printer, select the printer you want to remove, click the **Remove** (-) button, and then click **OK**.

4. Click the **Close** button.

## Add a Printer Manually

1. Click the **System Preferences** icon in the Dock, and then click the **Print & Fax** icon.

2. Click the **Add** (+) button.

   **TIMESAVER** *In a Print dialog box, click the Printer pop-up, and then click Add Printer.*

3. Use the toolbar buttons to specify the information required to display (if necessary) and select the printer you want to add:

   ◆ **Default.** Displays available autoconfigured printers

   ◆ **Fax.** Displays available autoconfigured faxes.

   ◆ **IP.** Provides options to setup a network printer using an IP (Internet Protocol) address, such as 192.160.1.170.

     Also can provide options to setup special-case printers, such as Canon IJ Network, Epson FireWire or TCP/IP, or HP IP Printing.

   ◆ **Windows.** Displays network printers using Windows and an Ethernet connection.

4. Click **Add**, and then click **Continue**, if necessary.

5. Click the **Close** button in the Print & Fax Browser window.

6. Click the **Close** button.

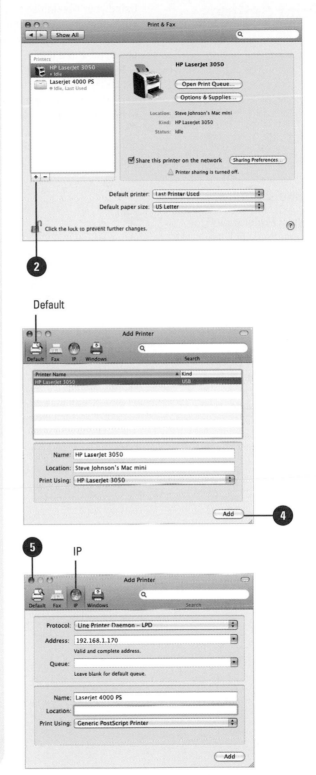

Default

IP

# Setting Print Settings

Using your Macintosh to print and fax is an obvious extension of the normal, everyday computing process. You write and create documents, and send them to paper; you take a photograph using a digital camera and send it to a photo-quality printer. You can use the Print & Fax pane in System Preferences to modify many of the aspects of printing. For example, you can set the default printer, the one that automatically appears when you want to print, and the default paper size. If you want to find out the available options for a specific printer, you can use Options and Supplies, where you can find printer information, change a printer name, select a different driver, and check out printer supplies available online, such as ink and toner.

## Set Default Printer Settings

1. Click the **System Preferences** icon in the Dock, and then click the **Print & Fax** icon.

2. Click the **Default Printer** pop-up, and then click **Last Printer Used** or select a default printer to appear first in the Print dialogs of all your applications.

3. Click the **Default Paper Size in Page Setup** pop-up, and then select a paper size to be used as a default in the Print dialogs of all your applications.

4. Click the **Close** button.

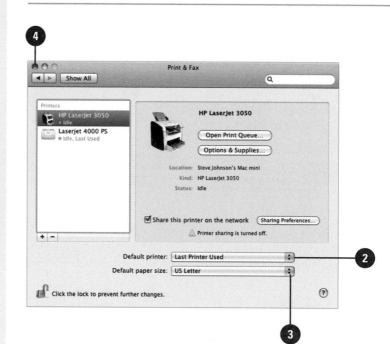

## Set Printer Specific Settings

1. Click the **System Preferences** icon in the Dock, and then click the **Print & Fax** icon.

2. Select the printer you want to change print settings.

3. Click **Options & Supplies**.

4. Click the tab for the area in which you want to change settings, such as General, Driver, or Supply Levels. The tabs vary depending on the printer.

   ◆ **General.** Displays printer information (queue and host name, and driver version). You can change the name and location of the printer.

   ◆ **Driver.** Allows you to select a different driver.

   ◆ **Supply Levels.** Allows you to access a Web site that lets you order more supplies, such as ink or toner. Click **Supplies** to open the Web site.

5. Click **OK**.

6. Click the **Close** button.

**4**

| General | Driver | Supply Levels |

Name: HP LaserJet 3050

Location: Steve Johnson's Mac mini

Queue Name: HP_LaserJet_3050

Driver Version: 5.3.0

URL: usb://Hewlett-Packard/HP%20LaserJet%203050?
serial=00CNBJ010249

Cancel    OK    **5**

---

## For Your Information

### Selecting a Printer's PPD File

A PostScript Printer Description (PPD) file specifies a printer's options and features. When you add a printer to your computer, Mac OS X selects a PPD for you. If you have another PPD for your printer (typically provided by the printer manufacturer), you can use it instead. Click the System Preferences icon in the Dock, click the Print & Fax icon, select your printer, click Options & Supplies, click the Driver tab, click the Print Using pop-up, click Other, select the PPD file you want, click OK or Open, and then click OK.

# Sharing a Printer

If you have a printer connected to your computer and your computer is connected to a network, you can share your printer with other network users. Before you can share a printer, you need to turn on printer sharing in the Sharing pane in System Preferences and then enable sharing for each printer in the Print & Fax pane. After you share a printer, other users—with Mac OS X, Mac OS 9, UNIX, or Windows computers—connected to your network can use your printer; you can also connect to other shared printers—including an AirPort base station—available on your network. For security purposes, if you want to share your printer with a Windows user via SMB/CIFS, you need to set Firewall options to allow all incoming connections on the Firewall tab of Security preferences. If a Windows user has Bonjour installed, the user can use the Bonjour wizard to connect to your printer on a Mac. After you share your printer, if a user connected to your network still cannot access your printer, you can provide them with your Mac IP address (available in Network preferences for the network connection, such as Built-in Ethernet) and queue name (available in Print & Fax preferences in Options & Supplies) to make the connection to the shared printer.

## Share a Printer

1. Click the **System Preferences** icon in the Dock, and then click the **Print & Fax** icon.

2. Select the printer you want to change print settings.

3. Select the **Share this printer on the network** check box.

4. If printer sharing is turned off, click **Sharing Preferences**, select the **Printer Sharing** check box, and then click the **Close** button.

    ◆ You can also click the **System Preferences** icon in the Dock, and then click the **Sharing** icon.

5. To share your printer with Windows users via SMB/CIFS, click **Show All**, click the **Security** icon, click **Firewall**, click **Start**, click **Advanced** (if you want to set other options), and then click the **Back** button.

6. Click the **Close** button.

Click to add a shared printer

## Access a Shared Printer

**1** Click the **System Preferences** icon in the Dock, and then click the **Print & Fax** icon.

**2** Click the **Add** (+) button.

**3** Use the toolbar buttons to specify the information required to display and select the printer you want:

◆ **IP.** Provides options to setup a network printer using an IP (Internet Protocol) address, such as 192.160.1.170.

Also can provide options to setup special-case printers, such as Canon IJ Network, Epson FireWire or TCP/IP, or HP IP Printing.

◆ **Windows.** Displays network printers using Windows and an Ethernet connection.

**4** Click **Add**.

**5** Click the **Close** button in the Print & Fax Browser window.

**6** Click the **Close** button.

---

**Add Printer**

| Default | Fax | IP | Windows | Q | Search |

| mshome | ► | admin | ► | HP LaserJet PS Admin |
| workgroup | ► | laptop2-pc | ► | |
| | | production1 | ► | |

Name: HP LaserJet PS Admin

Location:

Print Using: Generic PostScript Printer

Add

---

## For Your Information

### Using AirPort Base Station to Share a Printer

If you have an AirPort Extreme or AirPort Express base station, you can share a USB printer with other computers on your network. When you use an AirPort Express base station, you may not see error or status messages, such as *Out of Paper*. To use the AirPort base station, you need to follow setup instructions to install any software, connect the printer to your computer, print a test page, and then connect the printer to the AirPort base station. You can also print to shared Windows printers over a network or share your own printer with Windows users.

# Setting Up Page Options

With few exceptions, Macintosh applications give you the ability to print a document to paper. Programs such as: Microsoft Word, Corel WordPerfect; even TextEdit—Macintosh's proprietary word processing application—give you the option to print what you have committed to type. When you select the Print option (located under the File menu), you're instructing the application to use an output device (the printer) to place your words on paper. Since all printers have options, it's important to be able to set those options before printing. You might be using a specific size paper or printing orientation. For this operation, you'll use the Page Setup command, located within the File menu of most applications.

## Set Up Page Options

1. Open a document, such as a text document.

2. Click the **File** menu, and then click **Page Setup**.

3. Click the **Settings** pop-up, and then select from the following options:

   ◆ **Page Attributes**. This option lets you select a printer, specific paper size, orientation, and print scale.

   ◆ **Custom Paper Size**. Click **New** to create a customized paper size by entering height, width, and margin values into the appropriate input fields.

   ◆ **Document Specific Option**. This option gives you specific options for the current application.

   ◆ **Summary**. Click **Summary** to see an outline of your options.

   ◆ **Save As Default**. Click this option to save your current settings as default for future printing operations.

Settings: Page Attributes

Format for: Any Printer

Paper Size: US Letter
8.50 by 11.00 inches

Orientation:

Scale: 100 %

Cancel    OK

4. Click the **Format for** pop-up, and then select a printer from the available options.

5. Click the **Paper Size** pop-up, and then select a paper size from the available options.

6. Click the **Orientation** buttons, and then select from the following:

    ◆ **Portrait**

    ◆ **Landscape**

7. Enter in a printing scale percentage.

8. Click **OK**.

9. If necessary, save the file and close the application.

---

## Did You Know?

*You can send two different print jobs to two different printers.* Suppose you're printing a large job (50 pages), and you need another job (2 pages) printed right away. Just open the second job, click the File menu, and then click Print. Click the Printer pop-up, select another printer for the second job, and then click Print. Mac OS X processes both jobs on both printers at the same time.

---

| Settings: | Page Attributes |
| Format for: | Any Printer | ④ |
| Paper Size: | US Letter | ⑤ |
| | 8.50 by 11.00 inches | |
| Orientation: | ⬆👤  ⬆�êñ | ⑥ |
| Scale: | 100 % | |

(?)    ( Cancel )  ( OK )

⑦          ⑧

---

## For Your Information

### Using Page Setup

The Page Setup command changes the page properties within each application. Therefore, you can use the Page Setup command to generate individual defaults for each of your applications. To change the default settings for all applications at the same time, go to your Dock and click System Preferences, click Print & Fax, and then change the default paper size and printer in the pop-ups.

# Setting Basic Print Options

All applications that allow you to send a document to a printer, give you the ability to set up specific printing parameters. Some print options are generic, such as how many pages to print, and some are more specific, such as what paper tray to use (in a multi-tray printer). Regardless of the options, they're all located in one specific location, the Print command of the opened application. When you select the Print command, a dialog opens with all the options associated with the default printer; including the ability to change the default printer, and any other printing values.

## Set Basic Print Options

1. Open a document.

2. Click the **File** menu, and then click **Print**.

3. Click the **Printer** pop-up, and then select a printer from the available options.

4. Click the **Presets** pop-up, and then select a user-defined print setting.

5. Click the **Expand/Collapse** arrow, if necessary, to expand the Print dialog box.

6. Specify the following standard print options:

   ◆ **Preview Image.** Click the arrows below the preview image to view the document.

   ◆ **Copies.** Type the number of copies you want. Select or clear the **Collated** check box. Selected prints 1, 2, 3, 1, 2, 3. Cleared prints 1, 1, 2, 2, 3, 3.

   ◆ **Pages.** Click the **All** option or the **From** option, and then enter the print range you want.

   ◆ **Paper Size.** Select the paper size you want.

   ◆ **Orientation.** Select the portrait or landscape option you want.

7 Click the **Options** pop-up, and then select from the available options:

◆ **Application Specific Options.** If you're using Microsoft Word, this option lists specific options for that specific application.

◆ **Layout.** When printing large documents, allows you to select how many pages per sheet, the layout direction, border options, and two-sided printing.

◆ **Color Matching.** Gives you access to Macintosh's ColorSync management system, and the ability to apply the new Quartz Filters to the printed document.

◆ **Paper Handling.** Select to print in reverse order (page 1 prints last), whether to print all, odd, or even pages, and scale a document to fit the paper.

◆ **Paper Feed.** Select the paper tray for all pages or a different paper tray for the first and remaining pages.

◆ **Cover Page.** Lets you select options to print a cover page, such as standard, classified, unclassified, or confidential.

◆ **Scheduler.** Lets you schedule a time for printing the document.

◆ **Summary.** Shows a summary of all the printer options that have been selected.

**IMPORTANT** *The print settings on the Options pop-up vary depending on the selected printer.*

8 To save your print settings, click the **Presets** pop-up, click **Save As**, type a name, and then click **OK**.

9 Click **Print**.

# Previewing Documents

One of the most frustrating things is looking at a document on your monitor, clicking the Print command, and then deciding that what you see on the paper is not what you wanted. Unfortunately, a monitor is not a piece of paper, and the term What You See is What You Get (WYSIWYG), is a phrase that most computer users do not take very seriously. Once again, Macintosh comes to the rescue with a Preview utility that targets your default printer. If you see what you like, you can print a single copy directly from the Preview dialog, or you can close the preview, and then print using the standard Print option.

## Preview Documents

1. Open or create a document in an application.

2. Click the **File** menu, and then click **Print**.

3. Click the **Expand/Collapse** arrow, if necessary, to collapse the Print dialog box and display the Preview button.

4. Click **Preview**.

5. In Preview, select from the following options:

   ◆ **Next/Previous**. Click to move between pages.

   ◆ **Zoom In or Zoom Out**. Click to increase or decrease the viewing size of the image.

   ◆ **Move**. Click to move around the current page.

   ◆ **Text**. Click to select text on the current page.

   ◆ **Select**. Click to select a portion of the current page.

   ◆ **Annotate**. Click to display the Annotation toolbar (**New!**).

   ◆ **Sidebar**. Click to expand or collapse the thumbnail page view of the images.

6. Click **Cancel** to close or **Print** to print the document.

7. Quit Preview.

# Saving Documents as PDF Documents

The PDF (Portable Document File) format is undoubtedly the most successful multi-platform format ever created by any company. Designed by Adobe, it has become the standard for transferring text and graphics documents, spreadsheets; even creating interactive forms, that can be filled out by a visitor, and then sent back to the owner for processing. The reason for the success of the PDF format is Adobe's tight control over the Adobe Acrobat application (used to create PDF's), and the Acrobat Reader application (used by visitors to read PDF's). Once a PDF document is properly saved, it can be opened by virtually anyone that has Acrobat Reader, regardless of computer or operating system. And the good news is that the Reader application is a free download, just point your browser to *http://www.acrobat.com*, and then click Download Reader to obtain the latest version of the Acrobat Reader application, tailored for your specific operating system.

## Save Documents as a PDF

1. Open or create a document in an application.

2. Click the **File** menu, and then click **Print**.

3. Click **PDF**, and then select the type of PDF you want to create:

   ◆ **Save as PDF.** Creates a PDF document. Enter a name, specify a location, and then click **Save**.

   ◆ **Fax PDF.** Creates and faxes a PDF document.

   ◆ **Mail PDF.** Creates and attaches a PDF document in an e-mail.

   ◆ **Save as PDF-X.** Creates a compacted PDF document for the Print industry. Enter a name, specify a location, and then click **Save**.

   ◆ **Save PDF to iPhoto.** Creates and exports a PDF document to iPhoto.

   ◆ **Save PDF to Web Receipts Folder.** Creates and stores a PDF document in your Web Receipts folder; great for saving Web site receipts.

Specify PDF settings; options vary

A PDF document viewed in Acrobat Reader.

# Using Desktop Printers

The typical method for printing a document goes something like this: You open an application, open a document, click the File menu, and then click Print. While the majority of the time that's exactly what you want to do; especially if you need to make minor corrections to the document before printing, there is an easier way to go from document to printer: Desktop printers. Desktop printers give you the ability to create an icon of a printer, and with a drag and a drop, print a document using any connected printer. Not only is this method fast, it gives you the ability to print from two or more connected printers at a time. Printer icons can be located on the desktop, inside a folder, or even placed in the Dock.

## Use Desktop Printers

1.  Click the **System Preferences** icon in the Dock, and then click the **Print & Fax** icon.

2.  Drag the printer you want to the desktop.

3.  Click the **Close** button.

4.  To print a document, drag a file over the desktop printer icon.

5.  If the application opens, make any changes to your print options, and then click **Print**.

### Did You Know?

*You can instantly check on the status of a particular printer.* Double-click a desktop print icon to check the status of the printer, including items waiting to print.

*You can display all installed printers in the Printers folder.* Open the Home folder, double-click the Library folder, and then double-click the Printers folder.

Drag from here

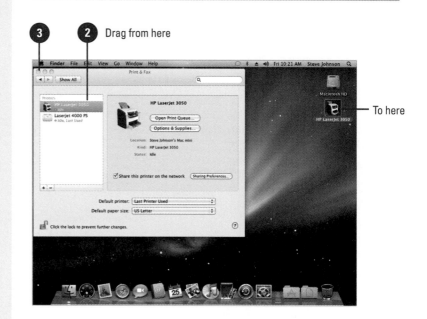

To here

# Managing Print Queues

The definition of a queue is a line. In Great Britain the term is used to describe a line of people waiting to get into a movie or restaurant. In printing terms a **queue** is a group of documents all waiting to be printed on the same printer. Mac OS X handles the queue like a master conductor; keeping everything in order, as it smoothly instructs the printer to print each document in turn. However, sometimes problems can occur that the Print Queue utility doesn't quite know how to handle. For example, it's possible that you want to place a job on hold while other jobs print (preferably yours), or you many want to delete a job. In fact, you can even instruct the printer to stop printing altogether.

## Manage Print Queues

1. Open the Printer window with the print jobs you want to manage:

   ◆ Click the **System Preferences** icon in the Dock, click the **Print & Fax** icon, select the printer, and then click **Open Print Queue**.

   ◆ Double-click the printer's icon in the Dock while the document is printing.

   ◆ Double-click the printer's icon as a desktop printer.

2. Select a job, and then click one of the following:

   ◆ **Delete**. Deletes the job from the queue.

   ◆ **Hold/Resume**. Stops or resumes the printing of the selected job.

   ◆ **Info**. Opens the Options & Supplies dialog box.

   ◆ **Pause/Resume Printer**. Pauses or resumes the printer.

3. To view information about completed print jobs, including the print time and date, click the **Jobs** menu, and then click **Show Completed Jobs**.

4. Click the **Close** button.

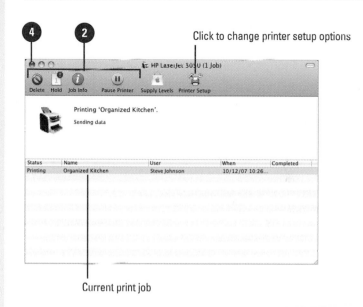

Click to change printer setup options

Current print job

Paused printer

# Scheduling Print Jobs

Sometimes it's just not the best time to print a document. For example, it's 10:00 AM and the network printer is jammed with jobs being printed by fellow office workers, who are attempting to get their documents out before lunchtime. You know that by 12:15 PM everyone is out to lunch, and the printers are free, but you don't want to lose a quarter of your lunch break just to click the Print button. The solution is to instruct the sending application to click the Print button for you, while you enjoy your much-deserved break.

## Schedule Print Jobs

1. Open the document that you want to schedule for printing at a later time.

2. Click the **File** menu, and then click **Print**.

3. Click the **Printer** pop-up, select a printer from the available options, and then specify the specifics for the print job (copies, pages, paper size, and orientation).

4. Click the **Options** pop-up, and then click **Scheduler**.

5. Click the **At** option, and then select a time for printing the document.

   **IMPORTANT** *When you schedule a job for future printing, you can only schedule into the future by 24 hours (23 hours and 59 minutes).*

6. Click the **Priority** pop-up, and then select the importance of this job, over other jobs that may be scheduled to print at the same time.

7. Click **Print**.

8. Quit your application.

---

## For Your Information

### Running Print Jobs

Not only does scheduling a print job help you keep your lunch appointment, they can also save you a lot of time waiting for jobs to print. If you know ahead of time that you have a fifty-page report to print, you could schedule the job to print in the evening, and it'll be ready for you the next day. Just remember the printer will be running solo, so make sure the ink cartridges are okay and there's enough paper in the hopper to handle the job.

# Creating a Cover Page

When you print a document, Mac OS X allows you to create a cover page. When you work with secure information, you can print a cover page that indicates the private nature of a document. For example, you can add a cover page with the following tags: classified, confidential, secret, top secret, and unclassified. Many companies require a cover page to be sent with sensitive documents. Since the decision to use a cover sheet is dependent on the document, Mac OS X gives you the choice to add a cover sheet each time you print a document.

## Create a Cover Page

1. Open a document that you want to print a cover page.

2. Click the **File** menu, and then click **Print**.

3. Click the **Printer** pop-up, and then select a printer from the available options.

4. Click the **Options** pop-up, and then click **Cover Page**.

5. Click the print cover page option you want: **None**, **Before document**, or **After document**.

6. Click the **Cover Page Type** pop-up, and then select the print cover page option you want.

7. Click **Print**.

# Sending Fax Documents

Using your Mac to print and fax is an obvious extension of the normal, everyday computing process. You have a document, and you need to fax it to a co-worker or friend. Once you've decided whom the fax is to be sent to, and what the fax number is, the next step is to send the fax. When you fax a document, Mac OS X allows you to create a cover page. A cover page indicates to the person receiving the fax, the number of pages in the fax, who is sending the fax, the date and time the fax was sent, and a short text paragraph. Since the decision to use a cover sheet is dependent on the document, Mac OS X gives you the choice to add a cover sheet each time you generate a fax.

## Send Fax Documents

1. Open a document that you want to fax.

2. Click the **File** menu, and then click **Print**.

3. Click the **PDF** button, and then click **Fax PDF**.

4. If necessary, click the **Printer** pop-up, and then select your fax modem.

5. Specify the specifics for the fax job (copies, pages, paper size, and orientation).

6. Click the **Options** pop-up, and then select from the following options:

   ◆ **Fax Information**. Type the fax number in the To field. Enter any prefixes into the Dialing Prefix field, such as 9 to get an outside line. Select the **Use Cover page** check box to add a fax cover sheet, and then type the subject and message text you want to display on the Cover Page.

   **IMPORTANT** *You cannot create a new paragraph while typing the cover page text. The Return key only sends the fax prematurely. To get around this, create the cover page text in another application, and then copy and paste it into the field.*

- ◆ **Fax Modem**. Select between tone or pulse phones, whether to hear the dialing through your computer speakers, and if you want the modem to wait for a dial tone before beginning the fax process.

- ◆ **Layout.** When printing large documents, allows you to select how many pages per sheet, the layout direction, border options, and two-sided printing.

- ◆ **Color Matching.** Gives you access to Macintosh's ColorSync management system, and the ability to apply the new Quartz Filters to the printed document.

- ◆ **Paper Handling.** Select to print in reverse order (page 1 prints last), and whether to print all, odd, or even pages.

- ◆ **Scheduler.** Lets you schedule a time for faxing the document.

- ◆ **Printer Features**. Select between low and high quality output.

- ◆ **Summary**. Summarizes all of the current settings.

7 Click **Fax**.

8 Close your document.

Fax modem options

7

## For Your Information

### Saving your Fax Print Options

If you have a combination of faxing options that you frequently use, you can save it as a Preset. After selecting your options, click the Presets pop-up menu, click Save As, and then type a name for the new options. If you want to use the new options to fax a document, click the Presets pop-up, select its name from the Presets pop-up menu, and then click Fax.

## Did You Know?

*You can let other users send faxes through your computer.* Click the System Preferences icon in the Dock, click the Print & Fax icon, select the fax modem you want to share, select the Share This Fax check box, and then click the Close button. The fax is now available for other to use.

# Receiving Faxes Automatically on Your Computer

It's actually pretty easy to set up your computer to receive faxes automatically. All you need is a phone line, and Leopard's Fax utility. You can set up the Fax to answer after a certain number of rings, and you don't have to be logged in; however, your Macintosh needs to be on and not in sleep mode. To make it easier to work with faxes, you can set the option to show the Fax status menu in the menu bar for easy access. After you send and receive some faxes, you can view information about the completed job. You can manage the fax queue just like the print queue.

## Receive Faxes Automatically

① Click the **System Preferences** icon in the Dock, and then click the **Print & Fax** icon.

② Select the fax modem you want to use.

③ To use the Fax status menu, select the **Show fax status in menu bar** check box.

④ Enter your fax number into the field, exactly as you would dial the number.

⑤ Click **Receive Options**.

⑥ Select from the following options:

◆ **Receive faxes on this computer**. Select the check box to receive faxes.

◆ **When a fax arrives answer After**. Enter how many rings are required before the Fax answers the phone.

◆ **Save to**. Select the check box, and then select where to save the faxes.

◆ **Email to**. Select the check box, and then select where to e-mail the faxes.

⑦ Click **OK**.

⑧ Click the **Close** button.

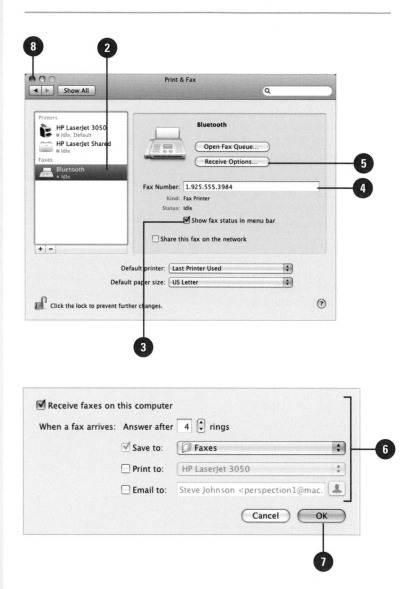

216

## Turn Sleep Mode Off

**1** Click the **System Preferences** icon in the Dock, and then click the **Energy Saver** icon.

**2** Drag the slider to the Never state.

**3** Click the **Close** button.

---

### Did You Know?

***You can check the status of a fax.*** Click the fax modem icon in the Dock while a document is being sent. To pause the printer, click the Pause Printer button; to resume the printer, click the Resume Printer button. To put a fax on hold, select it, and then click the Hold button; to resume the fax, select it, and then click the Resume button.

***You can view fax information about completed jobs.*** Click the System Preferences icon in the Dock, click the Print & Fax icon, double-click the fax modem icon in the Fax list, click the Jobs menu, and then click Show Completed Jobs.

***You can manually receive faxes.*** Wait for the phone to ring, click the Fax status menu, and then click Answer Now.

---

### See Also

*See "Managing the Print Queue" on page 211 for information on using the fax queue.*

Monitor goes to sleep after one hour of inactivity.

# Addressing Faxes from the Address Book

When you send a Fax, you need a document, and a fax number to send it. For example, you have a document that needs to be sent to your co-worker, and you remember that you added her fax number to her address card in the Address Book application (smart move). Do you need to open the Address Book, and write that number down, so that you have it when you send the Fax? No. Mac OS X gives you the ability to pull that information directly from the address card with the click of a button. Remember that in order for an address card to be used for faxing, it must first have a fax number entered into the card.

## Address Faxes from the Address Book

1. Open a document that you want to fax.

2. Click the **File** menu, and then click **Print**.

3. Click the **PDF** button, and then click **Fax PDF**.

4. Click the **Options** pop-up, and then click **Fax Information**.

5. Click the **Address Book** button, and then select a name from your address list.

6. Click the **To** button to add the name and fax number to the current fax request.

7. Select a name.

8. Click the **Close** button.

9. Select the **Use Cover page** check box, and then type a subject and message for the fax.

   Continue on with your fax requirements, and then send it.

# Exploring the Internet

## Introduction

The **Internet** is a global collection of more than a billion computers (and growing) linked together to share information. The Internet's physical structure includes telephone lines, cables, satellites, and other telecommunications media. Using the Internet, computer users can share many types of information, including text, graphics, sounds, videos, and computer programs. The World Wide Web (also known as the Web or www) is a part of the Internet that consists of Web sites located on different computers around the world.

## History of the Internet and the World Wide Web

The Internet has its roots in the Advanced Research Projects Agency Network (ARPANET), which the United States Department of Defense started in 1969. In 1986, the National Science Foundation formed NSFNET, which replaced ARPANET. NSFNET expanded the foundation of the U.S. portion of the Internet with high-speed, long-distance data lines. In 1991, the U.S. Congress expanded the capacity and speed of the Internet further and opened it to commercial use. The Internet is now accessible in almost every country in the world. The World Wide Web was developed in Switzerland in 1991 to make finding documents on the Internet easier. Software programs designed to access the Web, known as Web browsers, use point-and-click interfaces. The first such Web browser, Mosaic, was introduced at the University of Illinois in 1993. Since the release of Mosaic, Microsoft Internet Explorer, Netscape, and AOL have become some of the most popular Web browsers.

## What You'll Do

**Connect to the Internet**

**Set Up a Modem, Ethernet, or AirPort Wireless Connection**

**Set Up Multiple Connections**

**Make an Internet Connection**

**Understand Web Sites and Browsers**

**Start and Customize Safari**

**Browse the Web**

**Change the Home Page**

**View a History List**

**Bookmark a Web Page**

**Work with Bookmarks**

**View and Bookmark RSS Feeds**

**Fill Out Forms on the Web**

**Search the Web**

**Print and Save a Web Page**

**Save Pictures or Text from a Web Page**

**Download Files from the Web**

**Set Safari Preferences**

**Block Pop-Up Windows**

# Connecting to the Internet

Universities and large companies are most likely connected to the Internet via high-speed wiring that transmits data very quickly. Home computer owners usually rely on a modem and the phone lines already in place. In some areas, however, several faster connection options are becoming available and affordable. There are **DSL** (Digital Subscriber Lines), wires that provide a complete digital connection; **cable modems**, which use cable television lines; and **wireless**, which doesn't use wires or phone lines. DSL and cable modems, also known as **broadband** connections, are continually turned on and connected to an Ethernet network so you don't need to establish a connection using a dial-up modem. Data travels more slowly over phone wires than over digital lines and cable modems. Wireless provides a mobile connection to the Internet using an AirPort connection anywhere there is a wireless base station, such as a router or a network hub. Whether you use a phone line, a DSL line, a cable modem, or a wireless device, Mac OS X can help you establish a connection to the Internet.

Before you start the process to set up an Internet connection, you need to select an ISP (Internet Service Provider), which is a company that sets up an Internet account for you and provides Internet access. ISPs maintain servers connected directly to the Internet 24 hours a day. You pay a fee, sometimes by the hour, but more often a flat monthly rate. To connect to the Internet, you need to obtain an Internet account and connection information from your ISP or your system administrator. Each type of Internet connection requires certain connection information, including:

◆ **ISP Phone Number**. A number to create a dial-up connection.

◆ **Account Name**. A user name for the Internet account.

◆ **Password**. A security password for the Internet account.

If your ISP needs it, you may also need the following information:

◆ **IP Address**. An IP (Internet Protocol) address is a unique identifier of your computer on the Internet.

◆ **Subnet Mask**. A filter that helps your computer differentiate between computers on a local network and the Internet.

◆ **Router**. A device address that sends and receives information over the Internet.

◆ **Domain Name Server** (DNS). A computer that translates a Web site name into an IP address.

◆ **Proxy**. A computer your Macintosh uses to access the Internet.

When you have the connection information from your ISP or network administrator, you can use the Network pane in System Preferences to set up, configure, and display status for all your network connections, such as Modem, Ethernet, and AirPort.

Network pane in System Preferences

Get assistance

## Getting Internet Connection Assistance

At the bottom of the Network pane is the **Assist Me** button. When you click the Assist Me button, it starts the Network Setup Assistant, which asks you a series of questions to help you set up your Internet Connection.

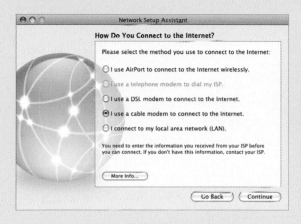

## Creating Multiple Connections

If you have a mobile computer, such as a MacBook, you can set up multiple connections for different locations. Setting up multiple connections allows you to connect to the Internet at home using a dial-up connection, at the office using an ethernet connection, or on the road using a wireless connection.

If you have a dial-up modem or AirPort card, you can use the Internet Connect application located in the Applications folder to help you quickly create an Internet connection to different configurations in your current location.

## Protecting your Computer from the Internet

When you connect to the Internet, you can access Web sites and information on the Internet, but other users on the Internet can also access information on your computer. You can prevent this by activating a firewall, another security layer of protection. A **firewall** is a security system that creates a protective barrier between your computer or network and others on the Internet. The firewall monitors all communication between your computer and the Internet and prevents unsolicited inbound traffic from the Internet from entering your private computer. The firewall discards all unsolicited communication from reaching your computer unless you specifically allow it to come through. If your computer is directly connected to the Internet, you should activate a firewall. If you are sharing an Internet connection on your network to provide Internet access on multiple computers, you should activate the firewall on the computer connected to the Internet only to avoid creating network communication problems. For more information and instructions on setting up a firewall, see "Configuring an Internet Firewall," on page 409 in Chapter 16.

## Sharing an Internet Connection

If you have an Internet connection and work on a network, you can share the Internet connection with other computers on your local area network. For more information and instructions on sharing an Internet connection, see "Sharing an Internet Connection," on page 408 in Chapter 16.

# Setting Up a Modem Connection

If you have a dial-up modem installed on your computer, you can set up and use a modem connection to access the Internet or another computer. You only need to set up a dial-up connection once. After you set up the dial-up connection, you can use the Show Modem Status menu to easily connect and disconnect from the Internet or network, and show modem connection information. When you are connected, the Finder displays a connection icon and connects information in the menu.

## Set Up a Modem Connection

1 Click the **System Preferences** icon in the Dock, and then click the **Network** icon.

2 Click **Modem** in the list.

◆ If a modem is not in the list, click the **Add** (+) button, click Modem from the Interface pop-up, and then click **Create**.

3 Click **Advanced**.

4 Click the **PPP** tab, and then specify your user name, password, and ISP phone number.

◆ Specify PPP Options to redial a busy connection, automatically connect when starting TCP/IP applications, and automatically disconnect if you select Log Out from the Apple menu.

5 Click the **TCP/IP** and **DNS** tabs, and then specify any settings provided by your ISP, such as IP Address, Subnet Mask, Router, and DNS Servers.

6 Click the **Proxies** tab, and then specify any settings provided by your ISP.

7 Click the **Modem** tab, and then specify any settings specific to your computer's modem.

8 Click **OK**.

9 Click **Apply**.

# Setting Up an Ethernet Connection

If you have a DSL or cable modem, you can set up and use an ethernet connection to access the Internet. In addition to connecting to the Internet, you also use ethernet to connect to a local area network (LAN). When you set up an ethernet connection using a cable modem or on a corporate network, some settings are typically configured automatically by a **BOOTP** (boot protocol) or **DHCP** (Dynamic Host Configuration Protocol). If your network supports ones of these services, you can use the Configure IPv4 pop-up in the TCP/IP area to select a protocol. If your ISP uses **PPPoE** (Point to Point Protocol over Ethernet), you need to specify your account and password. Check with your ISP or network administrator to determine if this applies to you.

## Set Up an Ethernet Connection

1. Click the **System Preferences** icon in the Dock, and then click the **Network** icon.

2. Click **Ethernet** in the list.

3. If you want assistance, click **Assist Me**, and then follow the instructions.

4. Click **Advanced**, if needed.

5. Click the **TCP/IP** and **DNS** tabs, and then specify any settings provided by your ISP, such as IP Address, Subnet Mask, Router, and DNS Servers.

   **TROUBLE?** *If your Internet connection is having problems, click Renew DHCP Lease to refresh your IP address.*

6. Click the **Proxies** tab, and then specify any settings provided by your ISP.

7. Click the **Ethernet** tab, and then select a configuration (automatic or manual) and specify settings.

8. Click **OK**.

9. Click **Apply**.

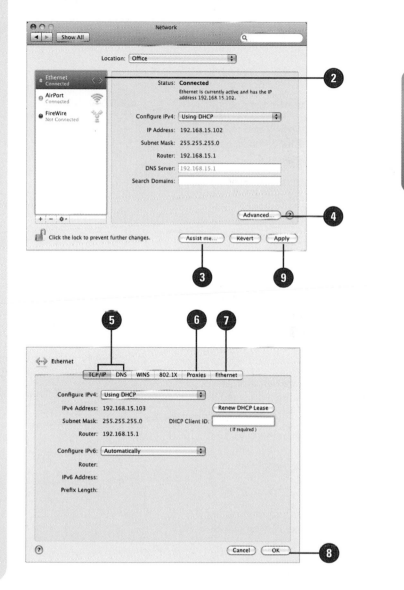

# Setting Up an AirPort Wireless Connection

If you have an AirPort card on your computer and are within range of a wireless base station, such as a router or network hub, you can set up and use an AirPort connection to access the Internet. AirPort is Apple's 802.11b-based wireless networking device that enables you to connect to the Internet without using network wires or phone lines. AirPort networks are identified by a network name. You can join a specific network or select one of the detected AirPort networks. You can join a wireless network quickly with the AirPort status menu, which includes signal strength for all visible wireless networks (**New!**).

## Set Up an AirPort Wireless Connection

1. Click the **System Preferences** icon in the Dock, and then click the **Network** icon.

2. Click **AirPort** in the list.

3. Click **Turn AirPort On**, if needed.

4. Click the **Network Name** pop-up, and then select a wireless network and enter a password.

5. Select or clear the **Ask to join new networks** check box.

6. Click **Advanced**, if needed.

7. Click the **AirPort** tab, and then specify the options you want, such as add or remove a network.

8. Click the **TCP/IP** and **DNS** tabs, and then specify any settings provided by your ISP, such as IP Address, Subnet Mask, Router, and DNS Servers.

9. Click the **Proxies** tab, and then specify any settings provided by your ISP.

10. Click the **Ethernet** tab, and then select a configuration (automatic or manual) and specify settings.

11. Click **OK**.

12. To show the AirPort status menu, select the **Show AirPort status in menu bar** check box.

13. Click **Apply**.

# Setting Up Multiple Connections

If you have a mobile computer, such as a MacBook, you can set up multiple connections. For example, you can use a laptop to access the Internet at home using a dial-up modem, go to work and connect to a network using ethernet, or relax at a coffee shop and browse the Web using AirPort. Each set of network connections is called a **network port configuration**. You can create different port configurations with unique priorities for different locations, which makes switching from one location to another easier. You can quickly access different locations using the Location submenu on the Apple menu.

## Set Network Port Configurations and Locations

① Click the **System Preferences** icon in the Dock, and then click the **Network** icon.

② Click the **Location** pop-up, and then select one of the following options:

- ◆ **Automatic**. Default location.

- ◆ **A location name**. Switches to the location name.

- ◆ **New Location**. Creates a new location, such as "home".

- ◆ **Edit Location**. Changes settings for a location.

③ Select the network you want to disable or enable, click the **Action** button, and then click **Make Service Inactive** or **Make Service Action**.

④ Click **Apply**.

---

## For Your Information

### Understanding Infrared Wireless Communication

Infrared wireless communication technology allows you to transfer files between computers, typically laptops, with infrared ports even when no formal network is available. IrDA is an infrared wireless communication protocol, a set of rules, that enables computer-to-computer interaction.

# Making an Internet Connection

After you set up your connection in the Network Preferences pane, you can also use the pane to connect to the Internet. This is not always convenient, so Mac OS X provides status menus on the right side of the menu bar. The status menus makes it easy to quickly log into different configurations in your current location for dial-up modem, PPPoE for ethernet, Bluetooth, and AirPort connections. You can use the Network Preferences pane to enable the menus.

## Use Status Menus to Connect to the Internet

- **Modem.** Click the **Modem** icon on the menu, and then click a command:
  - ◆ **Connect.**
  - ◆ **Show time connected**, **Show status while connecting**, or **Open Network Preferences**.
- **Bluetooth.** Click the **Bluetooth** icon on the menu, and then click a command:
  - ◆ **Turn Bluetooth On or Off.**
  - ◆ **Discoverable**, **Send File**, **Browse Device**, **Set Up Bluetooth Device**, or **Open Bluetooth Preferences**.
- **PPPoE for Ethernet.** Click the **PPPoE** icon on the menu, and then click a command:
  - ◆ **Connect PPPoE.**
  - ◆ **Show time connected**, **Show status while connecting**, or **Open Network Preferences**.
- **AirPort.** Click the **AirPort** icon on the menu, and then click a command:
  - ◆ **Turn AirPort On or Off.**
  - ◆ **Join Other Network**, **Create Network**, or **Open Network Preferences**.

Bluetooth Status menu

| Bluetooth: On |
| Turn Bluetooth Off |
| ✓ Discoverable |
| Send File... |
| Browse Device... |
| Set up Bluetooth Device... |
| Open Bluetooth Preferences... |

PPPoE for Ethernet Status menu

| Connect PPPoE |
| PPPoE |
| ✓ Default |
| ✓ Show time connected |
| ✓ Show status while connecting |
| Open Network Preferences... |

Modem Status menu

| Modem: Idle |
| Connect |
| ✓ Default |
| ✓ Show time connected |
| ✓ Show status while connecting |
| Open Network Preferences... |

AirPort Status menu

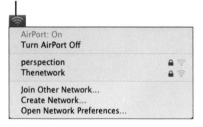

| AirPort: On |
| Turn AirPort Off |
| perspection  🔒 📶 |
| Thenetwork  🔒 📶 |
| Join Other Network... |
| Create Network... |
| Open Network Preferences... |

# Understanding Web Sites and Browsers

A **Web site** contains Web pages linked together to make searching for information on the Internet easier. **Web pages** are documents that contain highlighted words, phrases, and graphics, called **hyperlinks** (or simply **links**) that open other Web pages when you click them. Some Web pages contain frames. A **frame** is a separate window within a Web page that lets you see more than one Web page at a time. **Web browsers** are software programs that you use to "surf the Web," or access and display Web pages. Browsers make the Web easy to navigate by providing a graphical, point-and-click environment. Safari 4.0 is a browser from Apple that is built into Mac OS X Snow Leopard. Microsoft Internet Explorer, Mozilla Firefox, and Netscape Navigator are other popular browsers. With a Web browser, you can display Web pages from all over the world, use links to move from one Web page to another, play audio and video clips, search the Web for information, bookmark Web pages for easy access, and print text and graphics on Web pages.

Web browser   Web site

Web page

Link

# Starting and Customizing Safari

Safari is a Web browser that you use to search the World Wide Web. You can start the Safari application using the Safari button in the Dock or the Safari icon in the Applications folder. After you start Safari, you might need to enter a user name and password when you use a dial-up modem to establish a connection to the Internet. After you establish a connection to the Internet, you are ready to explore Web pages on the Internet. The elements of the Safari window allow you to view, print, and search for information on the Internet. You can customize the Safari window display to conform to the way you work. The View menu allows you to turn on and off different display elements.

## Start the Safari Application and Customize the Window

1. Click the **Safari** icon in the Dock.

2. If necessary, click **Connect** to dial your ISP. You might need to type your user name and password before Safari connects to the Internet.

   The Safari window opens.

   ◆ The first time you start Safari, the application imports your bookmarks from Microsoft Internet Explorer, Netscape Navigator, and Mozilla.

3. Click the **View** menu.

4. Click the menu item with the element you want to show or hide in the Safari window.

   ◆ **Bookmarks Bar**

   ◆ **Status Bar**

   ◆ **Tab Bar**

   ◆ **Toolbar**

   ◆ **Customize Toolbar**

   ◆ To change the display view, select one of the zoom commands: **Actual Size, Zoom In, Zoom Out**, or **Zoom Text Only**.

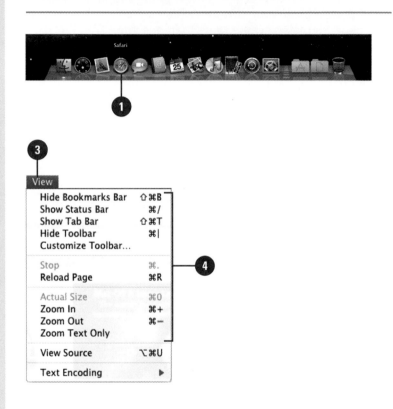

## For Your Information

### Selecting a Text Encoding

Text encoding determines how characters appear in a Web page. When a Web page doesn't specify text encoding, Safari uses the default text encoding specified in the Appearance pane of Safari preferences. Sometimes when the Safari default text encoding doesn't correspond with the desired Web page text encoding, you can see garbled text. If the text in a Web page is garbled, use the View menu to select a text encoding that corresponds to the language used in most of the Web pages you visit. This may fix the problem.

# Viewing the Safari Window

**Menu bar**
Contains all the commands you need to access and move around Web pages, customize Safari, and get Help.

**Address bar**
Provides buttons to locate and move around Web pages, as well as a place to enter or display the address of the current Web page.

**Bookmarks bar**
Contains buttons for quick access of favorite Web sites.

**Google Search bar**
Provides the ability to search the Web using the Google search engine.

**Tabs bar**
Displays Web pages in a tab to make it easier to switch between the pages.

**Browser pane**
Displays the current Web page.

**Status bar**
Displays the address of a link, as well as other messages about selected actions, such as loading a Web page.

# Browsing the Web

A **Web address** (also known as a **URL**) is a unique place on the Internet where you can locate a Web page. With Safari, you can browse sites on the Web with ease by entering a Web address or by clicking a link on a Web page to access a new site. When you type a Web address in the Address bar, Safari tries to find a recently visited page that matches what you've typed so far. If Safari finds a match, it fills in the rest of the address. As Safari opens the Web page, the Address box shows a blue-shaded progress bar as the page loads. If the page opens too slowly or if you decide not to access it, you can stop it. If a Web page loads incorrectly or you want to update page information, you can reload, or refresh the page. As you browse the Web, you can move backward or forward one location at a time to show sites you've previously visited in this session. Safari also stores information about Web sites you visit and information you've entered, which other users can view. You can prevent this by using Private Browsing, which clears the history list, Downloads window, AutoFill information, searches, and cookies are deleted. It's as if you never used Safari.

## Open and View a Web Page

Use any of the following methods to display a Web page:

◆ In the Address box, type the Web address, and then press Return.

  If you have recently entered the Web page address, Safari remembers it and tries to complete the address for you. The suggested match is highlighted. Click the correct address in a list of possibilities or continue to type until the address you want appears in the Address list.

◆ Click any link on the Web page, such as a picture or colored, underlined text. The mouse pointer changes to a hand when it is over a link.

◆ Browse Privately. Click the **Safari** menu, click **Private Browsing**, and then click **OK**. To skip the confirmation, Option-click the Private Browsing command.

  ◆ To turn it off, click the **Safari** menu, and then click **Private Browsing**.

Type a Web address

Click a link

## Navigation Basics

◆ To move back or forward one Web page at a time, click the **Back** button or the **Forward** button on the Address bar.

> **TIMESAVER** *To move back, press ⌃⌘+[ (left bracket). To move forward, press ⌃⌘+] (right bracket).*

◆ To stop a page from loading, click the **Stop** button on the Address bar during the load, or click the **View** menu, and then click **Stop**.

> **TIMESAVER** *Press ⌃⌘+. (period).*

◆ To reload a page, click the **Reload** button on the Address bar, or click the **View** menu, and then click **Reload**.

> **TIMESAVER** *Press ⌃⌘+R.*

◆ To go to the Home page, click the **History** menu, and then click **Home**.

> **TIMESAVER** *Press ⌃⌘+Shift+H.*

### Did You Know?

*You can open a Web page on your hard disk or network server.* Click the File menu, click Open File, type the complete path and file name of the Web page, and then click Open.

*You can open a Web page from a document in another application.* Select the Web address, click the application menu (such as TextEdit), point to Services, and then click Open URL.

Back button

Forward button

Reload button

## For Your Information

### Understanding a Web Address

The address for a Web page is called a URL (Uniform Resource Locator). Each Web page has a unique URL that is typically composed of four parts: the protocol (a set of rules that allow computers to exchange information), the location of the Web site, the name that maintains the Web site, and a suffix that identifies the type of site. A URL begins with a protocol, followed by a colon, two slashes, the location of the Web site, a dot, the name of the Web site, a dot, and a suffix. The Web site is the computer where the Web pages are located. At the end of the Web site name, another slash may appear, followed by one or more folder names and a file name. For example, in the address, http://*www.perspection.com/*downloads/main.htm, the protocol is *http* (HyperText Transfer Protocol), the location of the Web site is *www* (World Wide Web), the name of the Web site is *perspection*, and the suffix is *com* (a commercial organization); a folder at that site is called */downloads*; and within the folder is a file called *main.htm*.

# Browsing the Web Using Tabs

When you open a Web page, it opens in the same window you are using. If you want to view more than one page at a time in a single window, you can open Web pages in separate tabs or new windows. You can also bookmark a set of tabs for easy access in the future or revert to the tabs that were open the last time you used Safari. Before you start opening Web pages in tabs, you can set tab browsing options to specify the way you want to use tabs in Safari. When you open a page in a tab, the Tab bar appears (below the Bookmarks bar) with the name of the Web page along with a box you can use to close the tab. You can also use the View menu to show the Tab bar. If you select a Web page from the History or Bookmarks menu, the page opens in the current tab. When you use the Back and Forward buttons in the Address bar, Safari displays Web pages previously viewed in the current tab.

## Set Tabbed Browsing Options

1. Click the **Safari** menu, and then click **Preferences**.

2. Click **Tabs**.

3. Select the ⌘-**click opens a link in a new tab** check box to open a link in a new tab; clear it to open a link in a new window.

4. Select the **When a new tab or window opens, make it active** check box to open new tabs in front of the current tab.

   **IMPORTANT** *Some keyboard shortcuts change depending on the tab options you select. The bottom of the Tab Preferences window displays the new shortcuts. The shortcuts change revert back when you disable the options.*

5. Select the **Confirm when closing multiple tabs or windows** check box to get a warning alert when you close a Safari window.

6. Click the **Close** button.

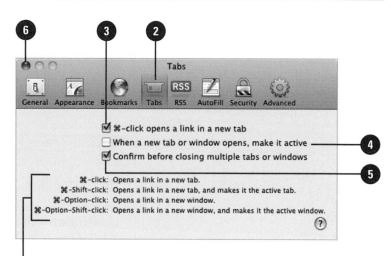

Shortcuts to use when working with tabs.

## Open and View a Web Page in a Tab

◆ To show or hide the Tab bar, click the **View** menu, click **Show/Hide Tab Bar**.

◆ To open a Web page in a tab, click the **File** menu, click **New Tab**, type the Web address, and then press Return.

◆ To open a link or bookmark in a tab, hold down ⌘, and then click the item.

◆ To open a bookmark collection in the Bookmarks bar in tabs, hold down the Control key, click the collection in the Bookmarks bar, and then click **Open In Tabs**.

◆ To open a folder of bookmarks in the Bookmarks Library in tabs, click the **Bookmarks** menu, click **Show All Bookmarks**, hold down the Control key, click the folder in the right pane, and then click **Open In Tabs**.

◆ To switch between Web page tabs, click the tab in the Tab bar.

◆ To close a tab, point to the tab, and then click the **Close** box on the tab.

> **TIMESAVER** *Hold down the Option key and click the Close box to show the Web page and close all other tabs.*

## Did You Know?

*You can change the size of text on a Web page.* Click the View menu, and then click Zoom Text Only. You can also click the View menu, and then click Zoom In (⌘++) or Zoom Out (⌘+-). To view the page at 100%, click the View menu, and then click Actual Size (⌘+0).

Close box    Active tab

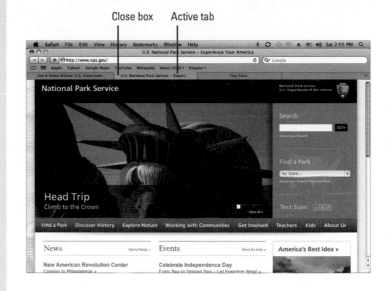

## For Your Information

### Opening a Web Page in a Different Window

You can open a Web page in a different window. Click the File menu, click New Window, type the Web address, and then press Return. To open a Web page in a new window using a link, hold down the Control key, click a link or bookmark, and then click Open Link In New Window. To find out the address of a link, point to it, and then view the Status bar. To switch between open windows, use the Window menu.

# Viewing Top Sites

Top Sites (**New!**) is a visual preview of your favorite Web sites. Safari tracks the sites you visit the most and ranks your favorites, displaying up to 24 thumbnail previews. Simply, click the Show Top Sites button to view and select a Web site to visit. If you don't see a site, you can use the Search History box to visually find it using Cover Flow (**New!**). You can also add or remove sites, mark or unmark sites as permanent, rearrange sites, and change the view to customize Top Sites.

## View and Use Top Sites

◆ **View Top Sites.** Click the **Show Top Sites** button, and then click a thumbnail to visit the page, or use one of the navigation buttons.

   **TIMESAVER** *To view Top Sites, pressShift+⌘+1.*

◆ **Search Top Sites.** In Top Sites, click in the **Search History** box, type keywords to search or drag the slider to flip through Web pages. When you're done, click the **Close** (x) button in the Search History box to exit.

◆ **Add Sites.** In Top Sites, click **Edit**, type the URL site address in Address bar, drag it to the window, and then click **Done**.

◆ **Remove Sites.** In Top Sites, click **Edit**, click the **Never include as top site** button (the X button), and then click **Done**.

◆ **Mark as Permanent Site.** In Top Sites, click **Edit**, click the **Mark as permanent top site** button (the Pin button), and then click **Done**.

◆ **Arrange Sites.** In Top Sites, click **Edit**, click **Small**, **Medium**, or **Large**, and then click **Done**.

◆ **Change View.** In Top Sites, click **Edit**, drag a thumbnail to another location, and then click **Done**.

Show Top Sites button

Click to customize Top Sites

Use to search history

Never include as top site button

Mark as permanent top site button

Type and drag URL to add the site

Click to change the view

# Changing the Home Page

Your **home page** in Safari is the page that opens when you start the program. When you first install Safari, the default home page is the startpage for the Apple Web site. If you want a different page to appear when you start Safari and whenever you click the Home button, you can change your home page. You can select one of the billions of Web pages available throughout the Internet. When you open a new window or tab in Safari, you can specify the default page that you want to view, such as home page, Top Sites (**New!**), empty page, same page, or bookmarks.

## Change the Home Page

1. Open the Web page you want to be the new home page.

2. Click the **Safari** menu, and then click **Preferences**.

3. Click **General**.

4. Click **Set to Current Page**.

5. To specify the page that appears when you open a new window or tab, do any of the following:

   ◆ New Window. Click the **New windows open with** pop-up, and then select a page option.

   ◆ New Tab. Click the **New tabs open with** pop-up, and then select a page option.

6. Click the **Close** button.

### Did You Know?

*You can type a Web address for your home page.* Click the Safari menu, click Preferences, click General, type a Web address in the Home Page box, and then click the Close button.

# Viewing a History List

Sometimes you run across a great Web site and simply forget to add it to your Bookmarks list. With Safari there's no need to try to remember all the sites you visit. The History list keeps track of where you've been for a week organized by the date. Safari deletes Web pages from the History list older than a week. If you no longer need the pages in the History list, you can clear the entire list. To view the History list, click the History menu, and then point to a day or click Show All History. When you show all history or bookmarks, you can visually browse and search sites using Cover Flow (**New!**).

## Open a Web Page from the History List

**1** Click the **History** menu, and then click **Show All History**.

◆ To quickly open a Web page, click the **History** menu, point to a date if desired, and then click a Web page.

**2** Click the **Expand** arrow to display the bookmarks you want to view.

**3** Scroll through the list in Cover Flow or use the Search box to locate the one you want.

**4** Double-click the Web page.

Cover Flow      Full search

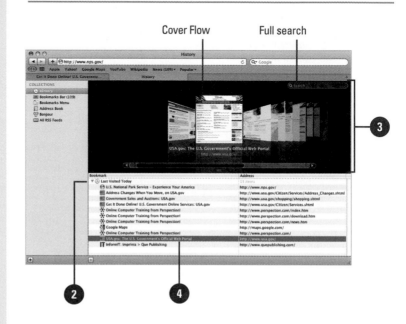

## Did You Know?

***You can delete individual entries in the History list.*** Click the History menu, click Show All History, click History in the Collections column, select the entry you want to remove, press Delete, and then click the Close button.

***You can clear the entire History list.*** Click the History menu, and then click Clear History.

***You can clear the entire History list automatically on a regular basis.*** Click the Safari menu, click Preferences, click General, click the Remove History Items pop-up, select the interval option you want, and then click the Close button.

---

## For Your Information

### Emptying the Cache

As you open Web pages, Safari saves the page content in a temporary location on your local hard disk, known as the **cache**, to make it faster to open the same pages next time. Anytime you display new content, the cache continues to increase in size, taking up valuable hard disk space. You can empty the cache at anytime to remove the local version of the Web page content and free up hard disk space. To empty the cache, click the Safari menu, click Empty Cache, and then click Empty.

# Bookmarking a Web Page

Rather than memorizing URLs or keeping a handwritten list of Web pages you want to visit, you can use the Bookmarks Library to store and organize the addresses. When you display a Web page or a set of tabs that you want to display again at a later time, you can add the Web page or tab set to your Bookmarks Library. After you add the bookmark to the Bookmarks Library, you can quickly return to it by using the Bookmarks bar or Bookmarks menu to select it. If you have bookmarks in other browsers, such as Internet Explorer, Netscape Navigator, and Mozilla Firefox, you can import the bookmarks in the Bookmarks Library using the Import Bookmarks command on the File menu.

## Create Bookmark Pages

1. Open the Web site you want to add to your Bookmark list.

2. Click the **Bookmarks** menu, and then click **Add Bookmark** or **Add Bookmark For These X Tabs**.

   *TIMESAVER Click the Add Bookmark button in the Address bar or drag the icon in the Address box to the Bookmarks bar to quickly add a bookmark.*

3. Type the name for the bookmark, or use the default name supplied.

4. Click the pop up, and then select a bookmark location, either the Top Sites (**New!**), Bookmarks Bar, Bookmarks Menu, or a collection of bookmarks in folders.

5. Click **Add**.

6. To quickly return to a bookmark, use the Bookmarks bar or Bookmarks menu.

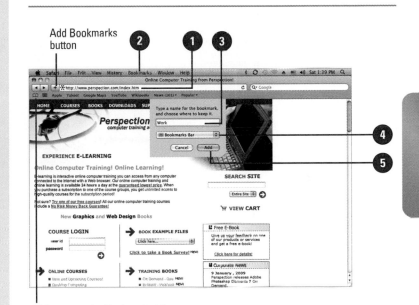

Add Bookmarks button

Click to go to the Bookmarks Library.

## Did You Know?

***You can drag a bookmark to move or delete it.*** Drag a bookmark to another place on the Bookmarks bar to move it, or outside the Safari window to delete it. You can also drag bookmarks and folders from the Bookmarks Library to the Bookmarks bar.

# Working with Bookmarks

If your list of bookmarks grows long, you can use the Bookmarks Library to delete bookmarks you don't visit anymore or move bookmarks into folders to make them easier to find. The Bookmarks Library shows your collections of bookmarks in the left column, and the Cover Flow (**New!**) display at the top and the names and addresses of bookmarks and folders at the bottom in the right column. You also use the Bookmarks Library to work with Web sites from cards in your Address Book, RSS Feeds, and History and Bonjour Web sites. Safari uses Bonjour to find any Web sites on your local network or subnet. Before you can work with the Address Book and Bonjour, you need to enable the options in the Bookmarks pane of Safari preferences.

## Create a Bookmark Folder

1. Click the **Bookmarks** menu, and then click **Add Bookmark Folder**.

   The Bookmarks Library opens, displaying a new untitled folder with the name selected.

2. Type a name for the folder, and then press Return.

3. Display the bookmarks you want to move in the folder in the right column.

4. Drag the bookmarks to the folder.

5. Click the **Bookmarks Library** button on the Bookmarks bar to close it.

   The folder appears on the Bookmarks bar with a triangle next to the name.

### Did You Know?

*You can add Rendezvous Web sites to the Bookmarks bar or menu.* Click the Safari menu, click Preferences, click Bookmarks, select the Include Bonjour check box where appropriate, and then click the Close button.

*You can view a list of Bonjour Web sites.* Click the Bookmarks Library button on the Bookmarks bar, and then click Bonjour in the Collections pane.

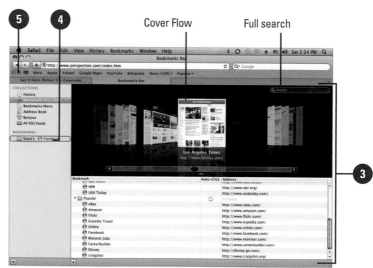

Cover Flow    Full search

## Organize Bookmarks in the Bookmarks Library

◆ **Show and hide Bookmarks Library.** Click the **Bookmarks** menu, and then click **Show All Bookmarks** or **Hide All Bookmarks**.

◆ **Create a collection.** Click the **Add** button (+) at the bottom of the Collections column.

◆ **Rename a collection.** Double-click the name, type a new name, and then press Return.

◆ **Add a folder to a collection.** Select a collection, and then click the **Add** button (+) at the bottom of the Bookmark column.

◆ **Rename a bookmark or folder.** Control-click the name, click **Edit Name**, type a new name, and then press Return.

◆ **Remove a collection, folder, or bookmark.** Select the item, and then press Delete.

◆ **Move or rearrange a collection, folder, or bookmark.** Locate the item, and then drag its icon to the location or icon where you want to place it. To copy it, hold down the Option key as you drag the icon.

Click a collection to display folders and bookmarks

Click to add a folder      Click name and type to change rename item

Click to add a collection

### Did You Know?

*You can add Address Book home pages to the Bookmarks bar or menu.* Click the Safari menu, click Preferences, click Bookmarks, select the Include Address Book check box where appropriate, and then click the Close button.

# Viewing and Bookmarking RSS Feeds

A **feed** delivers frequently updated Web content to your browser on a continuous basis. A feed, also known as RSS (Really Simple Syndication) feed, XML feed, syndicated content, or Web feed, is usually offered on a subscription basis and typically free of charge. A feed can deliver text content in the form of news headlines or blogs, or digital content in the form of pictures, audio, and video. When audio content is delivered usually in the MP3 format, it's referred to as a podcast. When you visit a Web site, Safari checks for available feeds. If it discovers a feed, Safari puts an RSS icon at the right end of the address bar. You can view an individual feed or subscribe to one to get content automatically. When you subscribe to a feed, Safari checks the Web site and downloads new content so you always stay updated with the latest site content.

## Customize RSS Feeds

1 Click the **Safari** menu, and then click **Preferences**.

2 Click the **RSS** button on the toolbar.

3 Specify any of the following options:

◆ **Default RSS Reader**. Select a default reader, such as Safari or Mail.

◆ **Update Articles**. Select the **Bookmarks Bar** and/or **Bookmarks Menu** check boxes to specify where to be notified of automatic updates.

◆ **Mark as Read**. Click **After viewing the RSS page** or **After clicking them** option.

◆ Select or clear the **Highlight unread articles** check box.

◆ **Check Updates**. Select an interval: **Never**, **Every Day**, **Every Hour**, or **Every 30 minutes**.

◆ **Remove Articles**. Select an interval or click **Remove Now**.

4 Click the **Close** button.

## View and Bookmark a RSS Feed

1. Visit a Web site with a feed.

   The RSS button appears in the Address bar.

2. Click the **RSS** button.

   If multiple feeds are available, a list of feeds appears. You can click the **RSS** button again to close it.

3. If available, click the feed you want to see.

4. Click the **Add** (+) button on the toolbar to add an individual or folder bookmark.

   ◆ A bookmark folder shows the total number of new articles.

   **TIMESAVER** Press ⌘+click a bookmark folder to show all feeds.

5. Type the name for the bookmark, or use the default name supplied.

6. Click the pop-up, and then select **Bookmarks Bar**, **Bookmarks Menu**, or a collection of bookmarks in folders.

7. Click **Add**.

8. To view all RSS articles, click the **Bookmarks** menu, point to **Bookmarks Bar**, and then click **View All RSS Articles**.

### Did You Know?

*You can use RSS as a screen saver.* Click the System Preferences icon in the Dock, click the Desktop & Screen Saver icon, click the Screen Saver tab, click RSS Visualizer in the list, click Options, select an RSS feed, click Done, and then click the Close button.

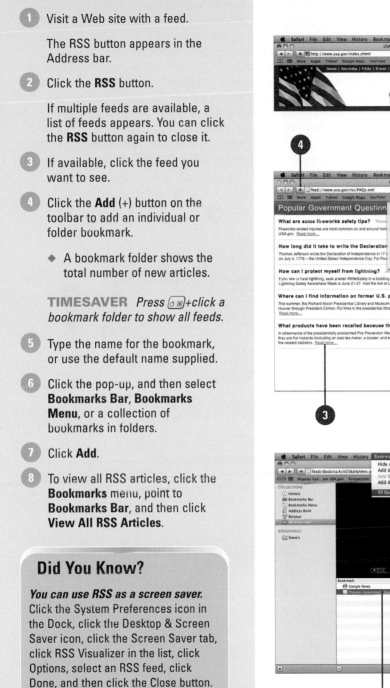

Added RSS feed

# Filling Out Forms on the Web

Safari can use information in your Address Book or data you previously entered in an online form to automatically complete online forms you need to fill out in the future. AutoFill is a service that helps you complete online forms and log in to Web sites with a user name and password. You use the AutoFill pane of the Safari preferences to select, modify, or delete which information AutoFill uses to complete a form or log in. When you use AutoFill to automatically fill in information, Safari highlights the data in yellow so you can see the changes. If you no longer need the AutoFill service, you can keep Safari from automatically completing forms and log ins. If you run out of room in a text field, you can now resize text fields on any Web page by dragging the corner of the field to make more room and reflow the Web page.

## Set AutoFill Preferences

1. Click the **Safari** menu, and then click **Preferences**.

2. Click **AutoFill**.

3. Select or clear the **Using info from my Address Book card** check box to enable or disable AutoFill from information in your Address Book.

4. Select or clear the **User names and passwords** check box to enable or disable AutoFill from Web site log in information you've entered.

5. Select or clear the **Other forms** check box to enable or disable AutoFill based on data from other online forms.

6. For any of the selected check boxes, click **Edit** to view or remove information stored by AutoFill.

7. Click the **Close** button.

### Did You Know?

*You can resize text fields on a Web page.* Drag the corner of a text field to resize it and reflow the Web page.

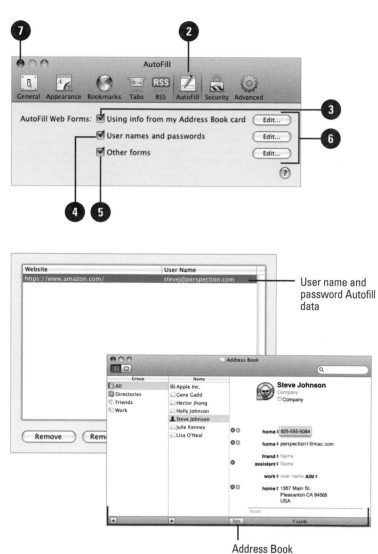

User name and password Autofill data

Address Book Autofill data

## Fill Out Forms in Web Pages

1. Select AutoFill data and options in the AutoFill pane of Safari preferences; click the **Safari** menu, click **Preferences**, and then click **AutoFill**.

2. Use any of the following methods to fill out forms using AutoFill:

   ◆ **Complete user name and password in a log in.** Display a log in screen, enter a user name and password, and then click **Yes** to save the log in information so you don't have to do it again; click **Not Now** to defer saving the log in information until later; and click **Never for this website** to not save log in information for this Web site.

   ◆ **Complete a Web form.** Open the Web page, and then click the AutoFill button in the Address bar.

   ◆ **Complete individual boxes in a form.** Open the Web page, select a text box, and then start typing. If AutoFill retrieves a match, it completes the text. If several items match, a list appears, where you can select the one you want to use.

Enter user name and password

Click an AutoFill save option

## For Your Information

### Checking Spelling and Grammar in Safari

You can't spell check the content of a Web page, but you can spell check any text you enter in a text box on a page. For example, if you type a word in a text box on a form or in the Google box in the Address bar, you can check its spelling before you complete the form or start the search. To check spelling and grammar, click in a text box, click the Edit menu, point to Spelling and Grammar, and then click Check Document Now. If your computer doesn't recognize a word, a dialog opens, asking you to correct, ignore, or add the word to a dictionary. You can also check spelling as you type, like many word processing programs. When you select the Check Spelling While Typing command on the Spelling and Grammar submenu located on the Edit menu, Safari displays a wavy red line under any term your computer doesn't recognize. You can also select the Check Grammar With Spelling to check grammar on demand.

# Searching the Web

You can find all kinds of information on the Web. The best way to find information is to use a search engine. A **search engine** is a program you access through a Web site and use to search through a collection of Internet information to find what you want. Safari comes with the Google search engine built-in to the program. When performing a search, the search engine compares keywords with words that it finds on various Internet Web sites. **Keywords** are words or phrases that best describe the information you want to retrieve. If the search engine finds your keywords in the stored database, it lists links to the matched sites. When you open a link from the results, you can use the SnapBack button to quickly return to your search results. In addition, you can search within a Web page to display the found count and highlight matching terms within a page.

## Search for Information

1. Click the **Google Search** box, type a word or phrase you want to find, and then press Return.

2. Click a link in the list of search results to open a Web page.

3. To return to the last page of Google search results, click the SnapBack button in the Google Search box.

4. To repeat a previous search, click the magnifying glass in the Google Search box, and then select the search term you want.

### Did You Know?

*You can open a Web page in Dashboard.* In Safari, display the Web page you want to open in Dashboard, click the Open This Page In Dashboard button on the toolbar, reposition and resize the highlighted area, and then click Add.

## Search Within a Page

**1** Click the **Edit** menu, point to **Find**, and then click **Find**.

Displays the found count and highlights matching terms within the page.

**2** Click the left and right arrows on the Find bar to highlight the matching terms.

**3** When you're done, click **Done**.

### Did You Know?

*You can revisit search results using SnapBack.* Type a search term or phrase in the Search box, press Return, visit some Web pages, and then click the SnapBack button in the Search box to return to the search results.

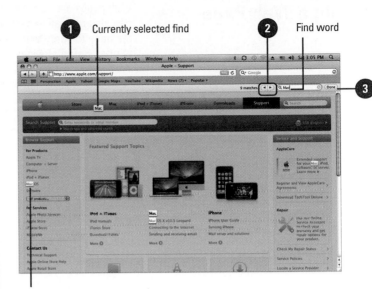

Currently selected find

Find word

Highlighted find word

# Printing a Web Page

Web pages are designed for viewing on a computer screen, but you can also print all or part of one. Before you print, you should preview the page to verify that it looks the way you want. When you are ready to print, Safari provides many options for printing Web pages. If the Web page consists of frames, you can print the specific frame you want to print. You can also use the Print dialog to create a PDF of a Web page or send a Web page as a PDF fax or PDF mail attachment.

## Print a Web Page

1. Open the Web page you want to print, click the **File** menu, and then click **Print**.

2. Click the **Printer** pop-up, and then select from the available printers.

3. Click the **Presets** pop-up, and then select from the available preset options.

4. Click the **Expand/Collapse** button to expand the dialog.

5. Click the **Print Option**s pop-up, and then select from the available print options, such as Safari.

6. Choose the various print options you want.

7. Click the following options to finalize your print: **PDF**, **Supplies**, **Cancel**, or **Print**.

## Did You Know?

*You can print a frame of a Web page.* Hold down the Control key, click the frame you want to print, click Print Frame, specify the options you want, and then click Print.

## See Also

*See Chapter 8, "Printing and Faxing," on page 195 for information on setting up and printing a page.*

246

# Viewing PDF Files

In Safari, you can display a PDF file in the browser window along with a toolbar and sidebar to make it easier to view the file. When you point to the middle of an open PDF page, near the bottom, of the Safari window, a toolbar with PDF tools appears. You can use the tools to zoom in and out to view the screen, open the PDF in Preview, and save the PDF to the Downloads folder. When you no longer want to use the toolbar, simply move the pointer off it.

## View PDF Files in the Browser Window

①  Open the Web page with the link to the PDF you want to view.

②  Click the link for the PDF file.

③  Use any of the following PDF tools:

◆  **View Toolbar.** Point to the middle of the PDF page, near the bottom.

   If you move the pointer off the toolbar, it disappears.

◆  **View Sidebar.** Click the triangle at the left of the toolbar.

◆  **Move Pages.** Click the arrow buttons in the toolbar or click a page in the sidebar.

◆  **Zoom In or Out.** Click the Zoom In (+) or Zoom Out (-) buttons.

◆  **Open PDF in Preview.** Click the button on the toolbar to open the PDF in the Preview application.

◆  **Save PDF to Download Folder.** Click the button on the toolbar to quickly save the file to the Downloads folder in the Home folder.

PDF document in the browser window

# Saving a Web Page

You can save a Web page, and view it later from your local hard drive or use it as source for HTML (HyperText Markup Language) code, which instructs the browser how to display the Web page. When you save a Web page, Safari can save only the HTML text content of the current page, or all the elements on the page, which includes text and images. Before you save a Web page you can view the HTML code to determine if you need it.

## Save Web Page Text

1. Open the Web page you want to save, click the **File** menu, and then click **Save As**.

2. Type a name for the file, or use the suggested name.

3. Select the hard drive and folder in which you want to save the file.

4. Click the **Format** pop-up, and then select a Web format: Web Archive.

   ◆ **Page Source.** Saves only the source text of this page.

   ◆ **Web Archive.** Saves text, images, and other content on this page.

5. Click **Save**.

Click to expand or collapse.

Export As: Apple – Support

Where: Documents

Format: Web Archive

Saves text, images, and other content of this page.

Cancel    Save

## Did You Know?

*You can view the HTML code of a Web page.* Open the Web page, click the View menu, and then click View Source. When you are done viewing, click the Close button.

## See Also

*See "Saving and Closing a Document" on page 190 for more information on using the Save As dialog.*

# Saving Pictures or Text from a Web Page

If you find information on a Web page that you want to save for future reference or share with others, you can copy and paste it to another document or save it on your computer. When you copy information from a Web page, make sure you're not violating any copyright laws.

## Save a Picture from a Web Page

1. Open the Web page with the picture you want to save.

2. Control-click the picture, and then click **Save Image As**.

   **TIMESAVER** *Control-click the picture, and then click Save Image to "Downloads" to quickly save an image to the Downloads folder.*

3. Type a name for the file.

4. Select the drive and folder in which you want to save the file.

5. Click **Save**.

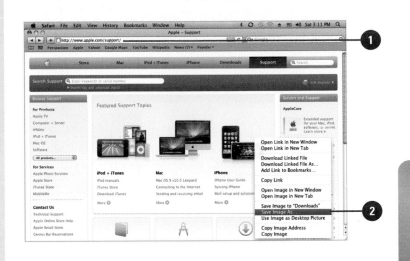

## Copy Text from a Web Page

1. Open the Web page with the text you want to copy.

2. Select the text you want to copy.

3. Control-click the selected text, and then click **Copy**.

4. Switch to where you want to paste the text.

5. Click the **Edit** menu, and then click **Paste**.

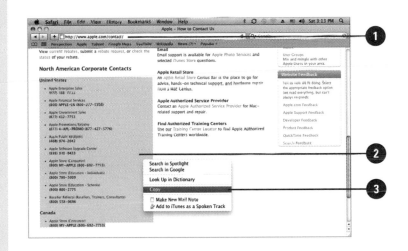

### Did You Know?

*You can copy a picture to the clipboard.* Control-click the picture, and then click Copy Image.

# Downloading Files Safely from the Web

There are thousands of sites on the Internet offering all sorts of files you can download to your computer, from trailers to the latest game demos. You can download files from any Web site by finding the file you want, and then clicking the download link. Safari automatically downloads the file to the location specified in the General pane of Safari preferences. During the downloading process, the Downloads window appears, displaying progress and status information. You can stop downloading a file, view a downloaded file in the Finder, and clear the Downloads window when it gets too full.

## Download a File from a Web Page

**1** Open the Web page that you want to download a file.

**2** Click a download link, or Control+click the link pointing to the actual file, and then click:

   ◆ **Download Linked File** to download the file to the Downloads folder.

   ◆ **Download Linked File As** to specify a download location.

   The Downloads window appears, displaying the estimated time to download the file, along with the estimated transfer time.

   **TROUBLE?** *If the Downloads window doesn't open, click the Window menu, and then click Downloads.*

**3** When the download is complete, click the **Close** button.

   You may need to Quit Preview.

Files downloaded

## Work with Files in the Downloads Window

**1** If necessary, click the **Window** menu, and then click **Downloads**.

◆ The Downloads folder is located in the Home folder. You can click the **Go** menu, click **Home**, and then double-click the **Downloads** folder.

**2** Perform any of the following operations.

◆ **Stop a downloading file.** Click the **Stop** icon to the right of the file name; to restart the download, click the icon again.

◆ **View a downloaded file.** Click the **Magnifying Glass** icon to the right of the file name.

◆ **Clear the Downloads window.** Click the **Clear** button. Clearing the window does not clear files that are being downloaded.

◆ **Remove a downloaded file.** Control-click the file name, and then click **Remove From List**.

**3** Click the **Close** button.

View a downloaded file

Stop a downloading file

Remove a downloaded file

Clear the Downloads window

## See Also

*See "Setting Safari Preferences" on page 252 for information on selecting the download file location and specifying when to remove downloaded items from the Downloads window.*

## For Your Information

### Downloading Disk Images and Installing Software

When you download a disk image, Safari decompresses the file and in some cases mounts a volume, and opens an installer program (if available). There are several different types of disk images. Safari works a little differently for each type. If you download a disk image in the MacBinary, BinHex, or gzip file format, Safari decompresses the file and opens an installer (if available). If you download an Internet Disk Image, Safari decompresses the file, opens an installer (if available), and moves the disk image to the Trash. If you download a disk image file, Safari decompresses the file, mounts the disk image volume, and opens an installer (if available).

# Setting Safari Preferences

Safari preferences help you configure some of the more common features of the program. You can set preferences for General and Advanced options, Appearance, Bookmarks, Tabs, AutoFill, and Security. These preference areas allow you to turn features on and off as well as customize the way Safari works. General, Appearance, and Advanced preferences are covered here, while Bookmarks, Tabs, AutoFill, and Security preferences are covered throughout this chapter.

## Set General Preferences

1. Click the **Safari** menu, and then click **Preferences**.

2. Click **General**.

3. Select or specify the various options you want to use:

   ◆ **Default Web Browser.** Select a default browser.

   ◆ **New Windows open with** or **New tabs open with (New!).** Click the pop-up, and then click Home Page, Same Page, Empty Page, or Bookmarks.

   ◆ **Home page.** Specify a Web address.

   ◆ **Remove history items.** Click pop-up to specify an interval.

   ◆ **Save downloaded files to.** Click the pop-up, and then select Desktop or Choose Other to specify another location.

   ◆ **Remove download list items.** Click the pop-up, and then click Manually, When Safari Quits, or Upon Successful Download.

   ◆ **Open "Safe" files after downloading.** Check to automatically activate safe downloaded files, such as movies, pictures, sounds, PDF and text documents.

   ◆ **Open links from applications.** Select an option to open links in a new window or current tab.

4. Click the **Close** button.

## Set Appearance Preferences

1. Click the **Safari** menu, and then click **Preferences**.

2. Click **Appearance**.

3. For the Standard Font, click **Select** to choose a font for Web pages that don't specify one.

4. For the Fixed-Width Font, click **Select** to choose a fixed-width font for Web pages when you need to align text in a specific way.

5. Select or clear the **Display images when the page opens** check box.

6. Click the **Default Encoding** pop-up, and then select a character encoding set, which tells your browser how to interpret and display characters in a Web page.

7. Click the **Close** button.

## Set Advanced Preferences

1. Click the **Safari** menu, and then click **Preferences**.

2. Click **Advanced**.

3. Click the **Style Sheet** pop-up, and then click **None Selected** or select a style sheet, which specifies a uniform format for the appearance of Web pages.

4. Click **Change Settings** to modify settings for a proxy server. Setting typically required when you use an Internet firewall. See your ISP or network administrator for settings.

5. Select the **Show Development menu in menu bar** check box to use Web development related-commands (**New!**).

6. Click the **Close** button.

# Setting Security Preferences

When you browse the Internet, you can access and gather information from Web sites, but Web sites can also gather information about you and store documents as databases (**New!**) without your knowledge. When you visit a Web site, the site creates a file on your computer, known as a **cookie**, which stores information, such as your Web site preferences or personal information, including your name and e-mail address. Not all cookies are harmful; many cookies save you time re-entering information on a return visit to a Web site. Safari's Security options allow you to block or permit cookies; however, when you block cookies, you might not be able to access all Web site features. You can also get a warning when you visit a fraudulent sites (**New!**).

## Set Security Preferences

1. Click the **Safari** menu, and then click **Preferences**.

2. Click **Security**.

3. Select the **Warn when visiting a fraudulent website** check box to get a warning message (**New!**).

4. Select the Web Content check boxes you want to enable:

   ◆ **Enable plug-ins**. A software module that provides additional functionality outside of HTML.

   ◆ **Enable Java**. A programming language for writing interactive Web pages.

   ◆ **Enable JavaScript**. A simple programming language for displaying simple interaction, such as image mouse rollover, or opening windows.

5. Click the **Accept Cookies** option you want: **Always**, **Never**, or **Only from sites you navigate to**.

6. To show the cookies on your computer and delete any you want to remove, click **Show Cookies**.

7. Select or clear the **Ask before sending a non-secure form to a secure website** check box to enable or disable the option.

8. Click the **Close** button.

Use when a web site stores documents as databases on your computer; set options to show and remove databases and adjust the storage size.

# Blocking Pop-Up Windows

When you open or close a Web page, some pages display pop-up windows to advertise products and services or request login and other information. Pop-up windows can be extremely annoying. Most of the time you end up closing them. To avoid the continual borage of pop-up windows, you can block them in Safari. When you set Safari to block pop-up windows, the program only stops pop-up windows that appear when you open or close a page, but not when you click a link.

## Block Pop-Up Windows

1. Click the **Safari** menu, and then click **Preferences**.

2. Click **Security**.

3. Select the **Block pop-up windows** check box.

   **TIMESAVER** *Click the Safari menu, and then click Block Pop-up Windows to display a check mark on the menu.*

4. Click **Block** to confirm the option selection to block pop-up windows.

5. Click the **Close** button.

## Did You Know?

*You can check security when browsing secure Web sites.* When you enter sensitive information on the Web, you can make sure It's secure. To check security, look for the lock icon in the upper-right corner of the Safari window, or make sure the Web sites address begins with "https," not "http."

## For Your Information

### When Web Pages Don't Work

If you are getting error messages or having problems displaying all or part of a Web page, your security settings may be the cause of the problems. To potentially correct the problems, click the Safari menu, click Preferences, click Security, select the check boxes to use plug-ins, Java, and JavaScript, clear the Block Pop-Up Windows check box, and then click the Close button. A **Plug-in** is a software module developed by a third-party for use with Safari to provide additional functionality outside of HTML. Safari works with common plug-ins including Java, QuickTime and Shockwave Flash. To view which plug-ins recognized by Safari are installed on your computer, click the Help menu, and then click Installed Plug-Ins.

# Selecting a Default Browser

Mac OS X comes with Safari as the default Web browser. If you prefer to use another browser, you can remove Safari from your computer, install another browser, such as Microsoft Internet Explorer, Mozilla Firefox, or Netscape Navigator, and set it as your default Web browser program. When you click links in other applications, such as Mail messages, or double-click a Web Internet Location file icon, your default browser launches and opens the Web page in a new window or tab in the current window.

## Select a Default Browser

1. Click the **Safari** menu, and then click **Preferences**.

2. Click **General**.

3. Click the **Default Web Browser** pop-up, and then select a Web browser.

4. In the Open Links From Applications area, click the **In a new window** or **In a new tab in the current window** option.

5. Click the **Close** button.

## See Also
See "Downloading Files Safely from the Web" on page 250 for information on adding or removing applications.

---

## For Your Information

### Reset Safari Settings

If you use a shared or public computer, you might want to reset Safari to prevent other people from seeing what you have been doing. When you reset Safari, the Web browser program clears the history list, Google search entries, and the Downloads window; removes all cookies saved by Safari and other related applications, such as any saved AutoFill data, such as user names and passwords; and empties the cache. To reset Safari, click the Safari menu, and then click Reset.

# Exchanging Messages Using Mail

## Introduction

If you're like many people today who are using the Internet to communicate with friends and business associates, you probably have piles of information (names, e-mail addresses, phone numbers, etc) that you need often. Unless this information is in one convenient place, and can be accessed immediately, the information becomes ineffective and you become unproductive. Apple's Mail application solves these problems by integrating management and organization tools into one simple system. Mac OS X Snow Leopard includes Mail 4.0, a powerful application for managing **electronic mail** (known as e-mail), and contact information like names, and e-mail addresses.

Using Mail with an Internet connection allows you to accomplish several tasks:

- Create and send e-mail messages
- Manage multiple e-mail accounts with different Internet service providers
- Use the Address Book to store and retrieve e-mail addresses
- Add a personal signature to your e-mail messages
- Attach a file to an e-mail message
- Print e-mail messages
- Create notes and to-do lists

# Starting Mail

Whether you want to exchange e-mail with colleagues and friends or join news feeds to access ideas and information, Mail provides you with all the tools you need. When you install Mac OS X, an icon for Mail appears in the Dock. The first time you start Mail, you need to set up an e-mail account by simply entering your e-mail address and password and letting Mail do the rest. If you are switching from another e-mail application to Mail, you can import your mailboxes and e-mail messages into Mail by answering a few questions. You can set Mail as your default e-mail application so that whenever you click an e-mail link on a Web page or select the mail command in your Web browser, Mail opens.

## Start Mail

1. Click the **Mail** icon in the Dock.

   If you have a MobileMe account, Mail automatically creates an e-mail account using your MobileMe information.

2. When you start Mail for the first time, the application asks you:

   ◆ If you want to import mailboxes from another e-mail client. If so, click **Yes**, and then follow the on-screen instructions (see details on the next page). Otherwise, click **No**.

   ◆ If you want to view new features in this version of Mail. If so, click **Yes** to view a list. Otherwise, click **No**.

   ◆ If you don't have an e-mail account, follow the one step instruction, enter your e-mail address and password.

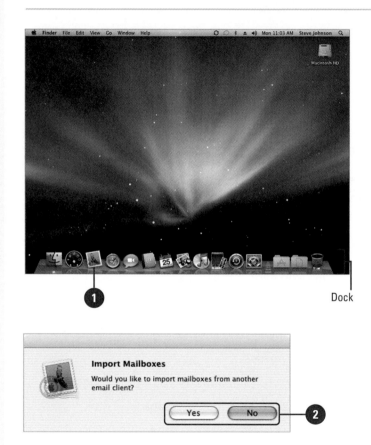

Dock

**Import Mailboxes**

Would you like to import mailboxes from another email client?

Yes    No

## See Also

*See "Setting Up an Account" on page 260 for information on creating an e-mail account.*

## Import Mailboxes and E-Mail

① Click the **File** menu, and then click **Import Mailboxes**.

② Click an option to select the importing application (use Other for Windows or UNIX), and then click **Continue**.

③ Follow the on-screen instructions; the steps to import mailboxes and e-mail vary between applications.

◆ **Import from Apple Mail.** Mailboxes are located in Library/Mail/Mailboxes in your home folder.

◆ **Import from Windows or UNIX.** Use Standard mbox, except for Eudora or Netscape, which use their own. Microsoft Outlook, and Outlook Express for the PC are not supported.

◆ Some options require that you have the importing application, such as Entourage, open.

The imported mail appears in the new Import mailbox.

### Did You Know?

*You can set options to start Mail from your Web browser.* Click the Mail menu, click Preferences, click General, click the Default Email Reader pop-up, click Mail (4.0), and then click the Close button.

# Setting Up an Account

Before you can set up an e-mail account, you need your account name, password, e-mail server type, and the names of your incoming and outgoing e-mail servers from your ISP or network administrator. You can use Add Account to help you set up an e-mail account by answering a series of questions, which is available in the Accounts pane in Mail preferences. Mail allows you to send and retrieve e-mail from different types of **e-mail servers** (including MobileMe and Microsoft Exchange 2007 (**New!**)), which are the locations where e-mail is stored before you access it. MobileMe is an IMAP mail server type, while Microsoft Exchange is a POP or IMAP mail server type. MobileMe and Exchange allow you to have all your messages (in Mail), meetings (in iCal), and contacts (in Address Book) in one place. You can set up Mail to receive e-mail from multiple accounts where each one can have multiple e-mail addresses.

## Set Up an E-Mail Account by Answering Questions

1. Click the **Mail** menu, and then click **Preferences**.

2. Click **Accounts**.

3. Click the **Add** (+) button.

4. Type the information requested (ask your ISP as needed), and then click **Continue**.

   ◆ **Full Name**. The name used in outgoing e-mail.

   ◆ **E-mail Address**. The From address in outgoing e-mail. You can type multiple addresses, each separated by a comma.

   ◆ **Password**. The method that provides secure access to the mail server. If you prefer to type a password every time you check mail, leave this empty.

5. Type the information requested (ask your ISP as needed), and then click **Continue**.

   ◆ **Account Type**. POP, IMAP, Exchange 2007 or Exchange IMAP.

- ◆ **Description**. The account name (appears in mailbox list).

- ◆ **Incoming Mail Server**. The POP or IMAP name.

- ◆ **User Name and Password**. The name and password that identifies you to the mail server.

6 Type the information requested (ask your ISP as needed), and then click **Continue**.

- ◆ **Incoming Mail Security**. Select the Use Secure Sockets Layer (SSL) check box, and then select an authentication option.

7 Type the information requested (ask your ISP as needed), and then click **Continue**.

- ◆ **Outgoing Mail Server**. The SMTP name.

- ◆ **User Name and Password**. The name and password that identifies you to the mail server.

8 Upon completion, click the **Create**.

Review the account information in the Accounts pane in Mail preferences.

## For Your Information

### How Do I Select an E-Mail Server?

Mail supports three types of incoming e-mail servers: **POP** (Post Office Protocol), **IMAP** (Internet Message Access Protocol), and **Microsoft Exchange 2007 (New!)**. A **protocol** is a set of rules that control the transmission of content, format, sequencing, and error management for information over the Internet or network much like rules of the road govern the way you drive. POP servers allow you to access e-mail messages from a single Inbox folder (requires you to log in and download messages), while IMAP servers allow you to access e-mail messages from multiple folder locations or different computers (messages stay on server). An example of an incoming e-mail server is *mail.server.com*. When you use POP or IMAP e-mail servers, you also need to provide an outgoing e-mail server. **SMTP** (Simple Mail Transfer Protocol) is used to send messages between e-mail servers. An example is *smtp.server.com*.

# Managing Accounts

You can set up Mail to receive e-mail from multiple e-mail accounts and from different computers. As you work with multiple accounts, you can use the Accounts pane in Mail preferences to change the order, rename, or delete accounts. Account order indicates the mailbox list order and helps determine which account (if not specified) Mail uses to send an e-mail message. If an account changes, or you no longer need it, you can rename or delete it. If you're using an IMAP or a MobileMe account, mail stays on the mail server so you can access it from any computer. If you're using a POP account, mail downloads to your computer unless you select an Accounts pane option to keep a copy on the mail server.

## Manage E-Mail Accounts

1. Click the **Mail** menu, and then click **Preferences**.

2. Click **Accounts**.

3. Select the account you want to manage.

4. To change the order in which accounts are listed in the Mailbox list, drag the account names.

5. To delete an e-mail account, click the account name, click the **Delete** button (-), and then click **OK**.

6. To rename an e-mail account, click the **Account Information** tab, and then change the name in the Description field.

7. Click the **Close** button, and then click **Save**.

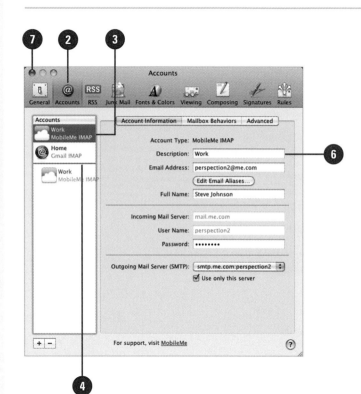

## Did You Know?

*You can view a list of all account and preference information.* Click the Scripts menu, and then click Display All Accounts And Preferences. An e-mail appears with the information.

## Set Advanced Account Options

1. Click the **Mail** menu, and then click **Preferences**.

2. Click **Accounts**.

3. Click the **Advanced** tab.

4. Select from the following options:

   - **Enable this account**. Check or clear to turn this account on or off.

   - **Include when automatically checking for new mail**. Check or clear to check or exclude this account from automatic mail checking.

   - **Keep copies of messages for offline viewing (IMAP only)**. Click the pop-up to download e-mail to your computer for offline viewing.

   - **Remove copy from server after retrieving a message (POP only)**. Check to check e-mail from different computers, and then specify a removal duration.

   - **Prompt me to skip messages Over __ KB (POP only)**. Check to skip retrieval of large e-mail.

   - **Use SSL**. If your mail provider supports Secure Sockets Layer (SSL), check for increased security.

   - **Authentication**. Click the pop-up to specify a security access method. Typically, Password.

5. Click the **Close** button, and then click **Save**.

IMAP specific options

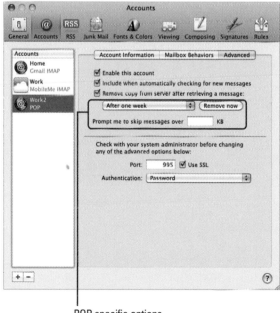

POP specific options

# Viewing the Mail Window

**Mail Toolbar**
The Mail Toolbar contains buttons for the most commonly used commands you need to work with mail messages.

**Search field**
The Search field allows you to find e-mail messages.

**Mailbox list**
The Mailbox list contains all the folders in which Mail stores e-mail messages.

**Message list**
The Message list displays e-mail messages.

**Mail Viewer window**
The Mail Viewer window displays the contents of the current message selected in the Message list.

# Composing and Sending an E-Mail

E-mail is becoming the primary form of written communication for many people. E-mail messages follow a standard memo format, with fields for the sender, recipient, date, and subject of the message. To send an e-mail message, you need to type the recipients e-mail address, type a subject, then type the message itself. You can send the same message to more than one individual, to a contact group, or to a combination of individuals and groups. If you type multiple addresses, you must separate the addresses with a comma (,). If you have multiple accounts, you can select which account you want to use to send the e-mail message.

## Compose and Send an E-Mail

1. Click the **New Message** button on the Mail toolbar.

2. Type the e-mail addresses or names of each recipient or groups.

3. Type the e-mail addresses or names for those recipients or groups who should receive a carbon copy of the message.

4. Type a subject that indicates the purpose of the message.

5. Select a From e-mail address and outgoing server (**New!**).

6. To add custom mail options, click the **Customize** button, and then click an option.

   ◆ **Bcc Address Field.** An address not included in recipients' list.

   ◆ **Reply-To Address Field.** An alternate address for replies.

   ◆ **Priority.** Add mail priority.

   ◆ **Customize.** Use to select from multiple accounts.

7. Type the content of your message.

8. If a red dotted line appears under a word, Control-click the word, and then click the correct spelling.

9. Click the **Send** button on the toolbar.

   Messages are sent out, and then copies appear in the Sent mailbox.

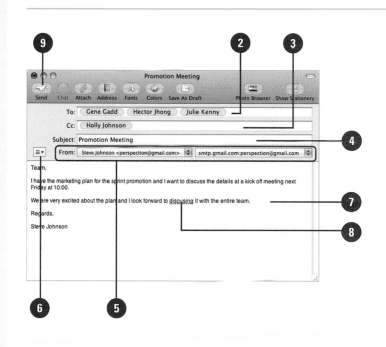

## For Your Information

### Checking the Spelling and Grammar in E-Mail

Before you send an e-mail message, you should spell check the text and grammar to make sure your content is accurate. To start the spell check, click the Edit menu, point to Spelling and Grammar, and then click Show Spelling and Grammar. To have Mail spell check all of your e-mail messages as you type, click While Typing on the Check Spelling submenu (on the Spelling and Grammar submenu) to enable or disable the option. If a word appears with a dotted red line under it, you can Control-click the word, and then click the correct spelling, or other options, such as Ignore or Learn. To include grammar checking, click Check Grammar with Spelling on the Spelling and Grammar submenu.

# Addressing an E-Mail

Mail gives you several ways to address an e-mail. You can type the address manually by typing it in the To or Cc field, or you can select or drag an address from your Address Book. When you begin to type an e-mail address, Mail looks up the name and address in your Address Book, followed by your Previous Recipients list, and then followed by names in the LDAP database (typically for corporate use if specified in the Composing pane of Mail preferences). If Mail finds a match, it automatically completes the recipients name. If you type multiple addresses, you must separate the addresses with a comma (,). You can make addressing easier to view by using Smart Addresses, which displays the recipient name only without the e-mail address for those in your Address Book and Previous Recipients list. You can display the Previous Recipients list to remove addresses you misspelled or don't need anymore, or add addresses to your Address Book.

## Select Names Using Address Complete

1. In the New Message window, type the first few letters of a name, address, or group.

   Mail suggests possible matches.

2. Click the name you want to enter.

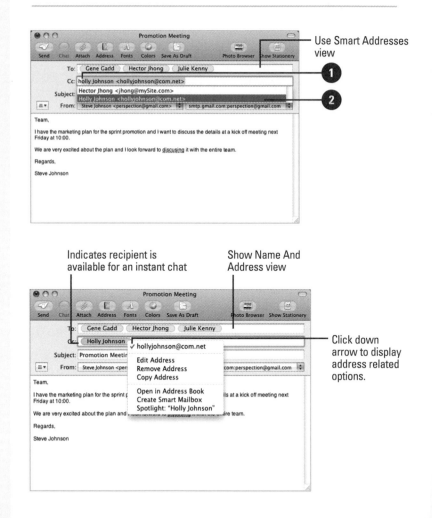

## Did You Know?

*You can use Smart Addresses to show names.* Smart Address are names and addresses in your address book, Previous Recipients list, or any LDAP server. Any names not found in your Address Book or Previous Recipients list still appear in full. To enable it, click the Mail menu, click Preferences, click Viewing, select the Use Smart Addresses check box, and then click OK.

## See Also

*See "Creating an Address Book" on page 138 for information on creating a group of recipients.*

## Select Names from the Address Book

1. In the New Message window, click the **Address** button on the Message toolbar.

2. Click the name of a recipient or group.

3. Click the **To**, **Cc**, or **Bcc** button.

4. Click the **Close** button.

   **TIMESAVER** *You can drag addresses between the To, Cc, or Bcc fields in the message window.*

Addresses from the Address Book

## Work with the Previous Recipients List

1. Click the **Window** menu, and then click **Previous Recipients**.

2. Select an address.

3. To remove the address, click **Remove From List**.

4. To add the address to the Address Book, click the **Add To Address Book**.

5. Click the **Close** button.

## Did You Know?

***You can set addressing preferences.***
Click the Mail menu, click Preferences, click the Composing button, select or clear the following check boxes: Automatically Complete Addresses, When Sending To A Group, Show All Member Address, and Mark Addresses Not In This Domain, and then type a domain name such as *apple.com* to mark it as safe when using LDAP.

# Adding Stationery to E-Mail

Instead of using a standard white background for your e-mail, you can spruce it up with some stationery. If you want to send an e-mail message for a special occasion, such as a birthday, thank you, get well, or just for fun, you can quickly create the look you want by applying stationery templates with professionally designed layouts, fonts, and colors. If you want to use your own photos, you can use the Photo Browser in Mail to find photos in your iPhoto library, Photo Booth or Aperture, and insert them into your e-mail messages.

## Add Stationery and Photos

① Open the message you want to apply a stationery.

② Click the **Show Stationery** button on the Mail toolbar.

③ Click a category.

④ Click the thumbnail of the template you want. To change the background for some templates, click the thumbnail again.

⑤ To add images, use any of the following methods:

◆ **Photo Browser.** Click the Photo Browser button, select/drag the images to the e-mail.

◆ **Finder.** Drag an image file from the desktop or Finder window.

⑥ To remove a template, click the **Stationery** category, and then click **Original**.

⑦ To add a template to your favorites list, drag it to the Favorites category. To remove it, click the **Delete** (x) button in Favorites.

Toggles to Show Stationery

## Did You Know?

*You can have message text read aloud.* Select the text you want to have read, click the Edit menu, point to Speech, and then click Start Speaking or Stop Speaking.

---

### For Your Information

## Using Data Detectors to Manage Information

Mail tries to recognize different types of data, such as an address or a date, so you can effectively manage and use it. When you place your pointer over data in messages, such as an e-mail address, street address, or date and time, you can use the data to create a new contact in your Address Book, map street directions on the Web, or create an event in iCal. In Snow Leopard, data detectors can identify flight numbers, which takes you to the Dashboard Flight Tracker widget (**New!**).

# Formatting Message Text

You can specify a file format for message text. The Plain Text format is one that all e-mail programs recognize, but it doesn't support text formatting. The Rich Text format allows text formatting, but it's not always supported. However, most programs that don't recognize Rich Text, convert the message to plain text. When you use Rich Text, you can use formatting tools, such as bold, italicize, underline, numbered and bulleted lists, indentations, and color text and backgrounds, on the Format menu and in the Fonts and Color dialogs to help draw the reader's attention to key words and emphasize the meaning of your message.

## Format the Message Text

1. Open the message you want to format.

2. Click the **Format** menu, and then click **Make Rich Text**, if available.

3. Select the text you want to format.

4. Click the **Colors** button on the toolbar, use the dialog color wheel to select a color, and then click the **Close** button.

5. Click the **Fonts** button on the toolbar, use the dialog settings (font type, size, style, and effects) to format the message text, and then click the **Close** button.

6. Click the **Format** menu, point to **Lists**, **Style**, **Alignment**, or **Indentation**, and then select a font formatting option you want.

Click to open Colors dialog

Select several font attributes at once.

2 Switches with Make Rich Text; not available here

## Did You Know?

**You can set font preferences.** Click the Mail menu, click Preferences, click Fonts & Colors, select default fonts for the message list, message text (Rich Text), and plain text, and then click the Close button.

# Adding an E-Mail Signature

If you type the same information at the end of each e-mail message, such as Best Regards and your name, then you can automate that task by creating a signature. You can add one signature to all messages or create several and select one when you compose a message. You can customize your signature with a variety of formatting styles, such as font type, size, and color, and you can even include a picture or attach your virtual business card, known as a **vCard**, from your Address Book.

## Create a Signature

1. Click the **Mail** menu, click **Preferences**, and then click **Signatures**.

2. Select an account or **All Signatures**.

3. Click the **Add** (+) button.

4. Type a title for the signature.

5. Type/modify the signature text.

6. For a Rich Text signature, use the **Format** menu to change the text font, color, style, or alignment.

7. If you want, drag a picture or vCard, and then click **OK**.

8. Click the **Choose Signature** pop-up, and then select a signature, **None**, or an option.

9. Select or clear the **Place signature above quoted text** check box to place the signature above or below the quoted text.

10. To remove a signature, select it, and then click the **Remove** (-) button.

11. Click the **Close** button.

### Did You Know?

*You can add your signature to e-mail quickly.* In an e-mail message, click where you want the signature, click the Signature pop-up, and then click a signature.

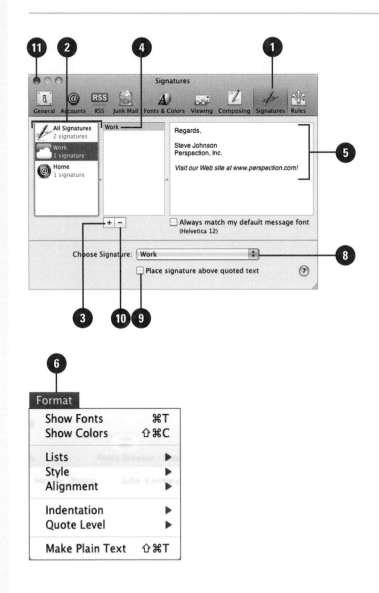

# Creating Notes and Tracking To-Do's

Instead of jotting notes down on paper, you can use Mail to create notes and then to help you organize and track them as to-do's so the things you need done, get done. You can include formatted text, graphics, and attachments in a note. After you create a note, you create a to-do item or send the note to another person. You can select content in a note or message to create a to-do, which can include a due date, reminder alarm, and priorities. The to-do items are automatically added to your iCal calendar.

## Create Notes and Track To-Do's

1. Click the **Note** button on the Mail toolbar.

2. Type the note text you want in the Note window.

   Mail uses the first line of the note as the subject.

3. To format the note, use the **Attach**, **Fonts**, and **Colors** buttons on the Note toolbar.

4. To create a to-do item, select the text you want to use, and then click the **To Do** button on the Note toolbar.

   ◆ To create a to-do item in a message, select the message or its content, click the **To Do** button, type a name if necessary, and then press Return.

5. Click the **Done** or **Send** button on the Note toolbar.

6. To view notes and to-do's, expand Reminders in the Mailbox list, and then click **Notes** or **To Do**.

7. To modify a to-do item (title, date due, priority, iCal calendar, or alarm), point to the item, and then type in the field or use a pop-up.

8. To mark an item complete, select the check box next to it.

9. To delete an item from Mail and iCal, select it, and then click the **Delete** button.

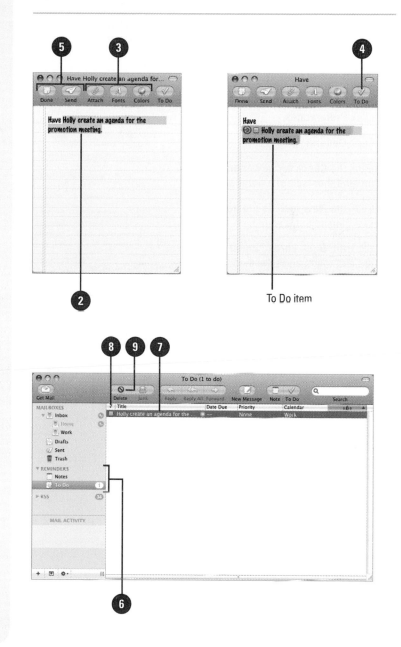

To Do item

# Receiving and Reading E-Mail

You can receive e-mail anytime day or night—even when your computer is turned off. You can retrieve your e-mail manually or set Mail to do so automatically by setting options in Mail preferences. When you start Mail, the application checks for new e-mail. It continues to check periodically while the application is open. New messages appear in the Inbox along with any messages you haven't stored elsewhere or deleted. A blue dot appears next to unread messages in the Mail Viewer window. The Message list displays the subject line of a message and other information, such as date received, senders name, attachments, and priority flags, which you can customize to display the information you need.

## Check for New E-Mail

1. Click the **Mail** menu, and then click **Preferences**.

2. Click **General**.

3. Click the **Check for new mail** pop-up, and then select a duration.

4. Click the **New mail sound** pop-up, and then select a sound.

5. Click the **Dock unread count** pop-up, and then select the mailboxes included in the unread mail count on the Mail icon in the Dock.

6. Click **Accounts**.

7. Select an account, and then click the **Advanced** tab.

8. Select the **Include when automatically checking for new mail** check box.

9. Click the **Close** button.

10. To check for mail manually, click the **Get Mail** button on the Mail toolbar, or click the **Mailbox** menu, point to **Get New Mail**, and then click **In All Accounts** or an account name.

## Open and Read an E-Mail

1. Click the **Inbox** icon in the Mailbox list to view new messages.

2. Click an e-mail message to read it in the Mail Viewer window.

3. Double-click an e-mail message to open it in its own window.

---

### Did You Know?

*You can add a sender to the Address Book.* Select the message in the Message list, click the Message menu, and then click Add Sender To Address Book.

---

## Change the Message List View

1. Click the **View** menu, and then point to **Columns**.

2. Select a column to display:

- **Attachments.** Displays a paper clip for attachments.
- **Buddy Availability.** Displays buddy status information.
- **Date Received.** Displays date received.
- **Date Sent.** Displays date sent.
- **Flags.** Displays a priority flag.
- **From.** Displays sender name.
- **Mailbox.** Displays name/account.
- **Number.** Displays sequential numbers next to the messages.
- **Size.** Displays size of a message or mailbox.
- **To.** Displays recipient name.

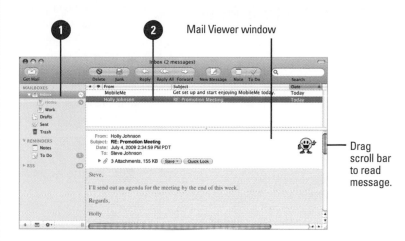

Mail Viewer window

Drag scroll bar to read message.

Drag a column header to change positions.

Status (always available)

Buddy Availability

Attachments

# Responding to E-Mail

You can respond to a message in three ways: reply to it, which creates a new message addressed to the sender(s) and other recipients; forward it, which creates a new message you can send to someone else; or redirect it, which creates a new message from the original sender you can send to someone else (useful when you receive a message by mistake). When you reply or forward a message, the original message appears in the message response. You can reply to the sender only, or to all the people who received the original message.

## Reply to an E-Mail

1.  Select the e-mail message you want to reply to.

2.  If you want, select a portion of the text to include as quoted text.

3.  Click the **Reply** button to respond to the sender only, or click the **Reply All** button to respond to the sender and all recipients listed in the e-mail.

4.  Add or delete names from the To or the Cc field.

5.  Type your message.

6.  Click the **Send** button on the Message toolbar.

    A curved arrow appears in the Status column next to messages you reply to.

**6** Click to toggle between addresses for Reply All and Reply.

Quoted text

---

## Did You Know?

***You can reply with an instant message.*** If you're logged into iChat, Mail displays a green dot indicator next to messages from buddies who are online, or a yellow dot indicator when the person is idle. Click the Mail menu, click Preferences, click the Viewing button, select the Show Online Buddy Status check box, and then click the Close button. Select a message in the Message list, click the Message menu, and then click Reply With iChat.

---

## For Your Information

### Quoting Text in E-Mail

When you reply to an e-mail message, you can include all or part of the original message, known as **quoted text**. The original message appears with a single quote bar to the left of the text. If the original message contained quoted text, you see an additional quote bar. To use quoted text, click the Mail menu, click Preferences, click the Composing button, select the Quote The Text Of The Original Message check box, and then click the Include Selected Text If Any, Otherwise Include All option. To change the color of quoted text, click Fonts & Colors, select the Color Quoted Text check box, and then select colors from the pop-up for Levels One, Two, and Three. When you're done, click the Close button. You can use the Quote Level submenu on the Format menu to change the number of quote bars.

## Redirect an E-Mail

1. Select the e-mail message you want to redirect.

2. Click the **Message** menu, and then click **Redirect**.

3. Type or select names in the To or the Cc field.

4. Click the **Send** button on the Message toolbar.

   A segment arrow appears in the Status column next to messages you redirect.

Message text redirected without a quote bar.

## Forward an E-Mail

1. Select the message(s) or open a message you want to forward.

2. Click the **Forward** button on the toolbar.

3. Type or select names in the To or the Cc field.

4. Type your message.

5. Click the **Send** button on the Message toolbar.

Quoted text

### Did You Know?

***Attachments aren't sent on replies.***
When you reply to a message that has an attachment, the attachment isn't returned to the original sender. You can forward the message to the original sender if you need to send the attachment back.

# Sending and Retrieving a File

You can easily share a file, such as a picture, document, vCard (virtual business card from your Address Book), sound, or movie by attaching it to an e-mail message. Some ISPs have trouble sending attachments between 2 and 10 megabytes MB, so it's a good idea to check with your ISP for limits on file size. Upon receiving the e-mail, the recipient can view it with Quick Look, open the file in the application that created it, or save it on a disk for use in other applications directly from the Mail Viewer window. The Message list displays the number and size of the attachments. If you send an e-mail to a Windows user, the attachment is automatically compressed in a standard zipped (gzip) format so it can be read.

## Send a File Attached to an E-Mail

1. Compose a new message or reply to an existing message.

2. Click the **Attach** button on the Message toolbar.

3. Select the drive and folder that contains the file, and then select it.

4. Select or clear the **Send Windows-Friendly Attachments** check box.

5. Click **Choose File**.

6. Click the **Send** button on the Message toolbar.

## Did You Know?

**You should compress large files before you send them.** Select the file or files you want to compress in the Finder, click the File menu, and then click Archive. Rename the compressed file with a *.zip* extension as necessary.

**You can send a Web link in an e-mail message.** Type or paste the full URL, including "http://" in the body of the message. Your recipients can click the link to go directly to the Web page.

Attached file

276

## View or Open a File in an E-Mail

1. Select the message with the attached file.

2. Click the triangle if necessary to display the attached files.

3. Control-click the attached file icon.

4. Click **Quick Look Attachment**, **Open Attachment**, or point to **Open With**, and then select an application.

## Save Files in an E-Mail

1. Select the message with the attached file.

2. Use one of the following methods:

   ◆ **Save All.** Click the **File** menu, and then click **Save Attachment**, or click **Save All**.

   ◆ **Save Individual.** Click the triangle in the header of the message to see the icons of each attached file. Control+ click an icon, and then click **Save Attachment** or **Save to Downloads Folder** (by passes Steps 3 and 4).

   ◆ **Quick Look.** Click the view attachments in Quick Look.

3. Select the drive and folder where you want to save the files.

4. Click **Save**.

# Managing E-Mail

A common problem with using e-mail is an overcrowded Inbox. To keep your Inbox organized, you should move messages you want to save to other mailboxes and subfolders (a mailbox inside another mailbox), delete messages you no longer want, and create new mailboxes as you need them. A mailbox can store messages on your computer, within a specific account, or within an existing mailbox. When a mailbox contains both messages and other mailboxes, the mailbox icon appears in blue. You can also organize your e-mail by message threads, which is the chain of replies in an e-mail conversation. You can group threads together or highlight them by color to make them easier to see.

## Create a New Mailbox

① To create a subfolder in a mailbox, select the existing mailbox.

② Click the **Add** (+) button at the bottom of the Mailbox list, and then click **New Mailbox**.

③ Click the **Location** pop-up, and then select **On My Mac** (local computer) or an IMAP account (online mail server).

④ Type a name for the new mailbox.

⑤ Click **OK**.

## Did You Know?

***You can show and hide the Mailbox list.*** Click the View menu, and then click Show/Hide Mailboxes.

***You can move items in the Mailbox list.*** Drag the sidebar item to a new location in the Mailbox list (**New!**).

***You can delete a mailbox.*** Control+click it, click Delete Mailbox, and then click Delete.

***You can rename a mailbox.*** Control+click the mailbox, click Rename Mailbox, change it, and then press Return.

***You can change size of mailbox icons.*** Click the View menu, and then click Use Small Mailbox Icons.

## For Your Information

### Learning About the Standard Mailboxes

Mail comes with several standard mailboxes: Inbox, Drafts, Sent, and Trash. **Inbox** stores messages you have received from others; the Drafts mailbox stores messages you have written and saved, but not sent; and the Sent mailbox stores copies of messages you have sent. The Trash mailbox stores all your deleted messages.

## Organize E-Mail in Mailboxes

1. Select the e-mail message you want to move. If necessary, press and hold down ⌘, and click to select multiple e-mail messages.

2. Drag the e-mail message(s) to the new folder.

## Organize E-Mail by Threads

1. Open the mailbox with the e-mail you want to view as threads.

2. Click the **View** menu, and then click **Organize By Thread**.

3. To see all the messages in all threads, click the triangle next to the thread.

4. To collapse a single thread, click the triangle next to the thread.

5. To ungroup, click the **View** menu, and then click **Organize By Thread**.

Click header to sort by subject

Thread original message

Click to open message

Thread history

# Deleting E-Mail

Deleting unwanted messages makes it easier to see the new messages you receive and to keep track of messages to which you have already responded. When you delete an e-mail message, Mail simply moves it into the Trash mailbox. If you want to recover a deleted message, you just have to retrieve it from the Trash mailbox. To get rid of a message permanently, you need to open the Trash mailbox, select the message, and then click Delete. Mail automatically places e-mail messages in the Sent mailbox every time you send them. You'll want to periodically open the Sent mailbox and delete messages so your mail account doesn't get too large. You can also set account options to help you delete messages.

## Delete Unwanted E-Mail

1. Click a mailbox icon in the Mailbox list with the e-mail you want to delete.

2. Click the unwanted e-mail.

3. Click the **Delete** button on the toolbar.

4. To erase messages in the Trash mailbox, click the **Mailbox** menu, point to **Erase Deleted Messages**, click **In All Accounts** or a specific account, and then click **OK**.

## Recover E-Mail from the Trash

1. Click the Trash mailbox in the Mailbox list.

2. Select the e-mail message you want to retrieve.

3. Drag the e-mail message to another folder.

## Change E-Mail Delete Options

1. Click the **Mail** menu, and then click **Preferences**.

2. Click **Accounts**.

3. Select an account.

4. Click the **Mailbox Behaviors** tab.

5. Select any of the following:

   ◆ **Move deleted messages to the trash mailbox**. Check to move deleted messages to the Trash.

   ◆ **Store deleted messages on the server**. Check to keep deleted messages on the mail server for an IMAP account.

   ◆ **Permanently erase deleted messages when**. Click the pop-up, and then select based on the duration you want.

6. Click the **Close** button, and then click **Save**.

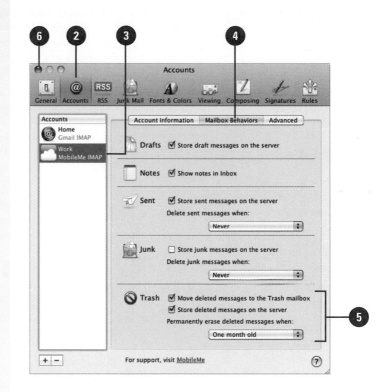

## Did You Know?

*You can save sent messages on the mail server.* Click the Mail menu, click Preferences, click Accounts, click the Special Mailboxes tab, select the Store Sent Messages On The Server check box, and then click the Close button.

*You can print e-mail messages.* Select the message(s) you want to print, click the File menu, click Print, and then click Print. If you select multiple messages, the e-mails are combined into a single document in the order you selected them in the Message list.

## For Your Information

### Backing Up E-Mail

The information in your e-mail messages is important, so making a backup, or **archive**, of a mailbox is a good way to protect it. In Mail, select the mailboxes you want to back up, click the Mailbox menu, click Archive, select a folder to store the files, and then click Choose. Mail backs up the mailboxes as .mbox packages.

Another method is to drag a mailbox from an IMAP account to On My Mac to copy it on your computer. Likewise, you can drag a mailbox from On My Mac to an IMAP account to copy it to your mail server online. To create a copy of a mailbox, drag the mailbox from the Mailbox list to your desktop. In the Finder, you can also backup mailboxes and addresses by copying all files located in the Home/Library/ Mail folder and by copying the folder "AddressBook" located in the Home/Library/Application Support folder. To restore your mail backup, use the Import Mailboxes command on the File menu.

# Saving E-Mail

If you have not finished composing a message, you can save it in the Drafts mailbox and work on it later. If you quit Mail with an open message, Mail automatically saves it as a draft. If you want to use the text from a message in a word processing application, such as TextEdit, you can save a message as a separate file in the Rich Text or Plain Text format. You can also save one or more messages in the Raw Message Source (mbox) format, which is a standard mail message format; you can import mbox into other mail applications, including Mail.

## Save a Draft E-Mail

① Open a new or a reply to an existing e-mail message, and then type a message.

② Click the **Save As Draft** button on the Message toolbar.

③ Close the e-mail message.

④ Click the **Drafts** mailbox in the Mailbox list.

⑤ Double-click the e-mail message to view and change it.

⑥ Click the **Send** button.

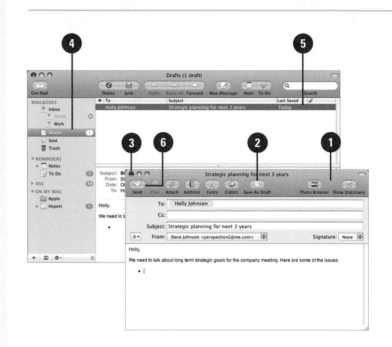

## Save an E-Mail as a File

① Open a new or a reply to an existing e-mail message, and then type a message.

② Click the **File** menu, and then click **Save As**.

③ Select the hard drive and folder where you want to save the file.

④ Type a name for the file.

⑤ Click the **Format** pop-up, and then select a format.

⑥ Click **Save**.

# Searching E-Mail for Text

If you're looking for an e-mail message with specific information, you can use the Mail search field to search for text in an open message, in all messages in a mailbox, in all messages for a specific account, or in all mailboxes. If you search in the From, To, or Subject fields, Mail finds messages that contain the entire search phrase as typed. If you search in mailboxes or the entire message, Mail only finds messages containing the same beginning letters you typed. To refine your search, use the words "and," "or," "not," and parentheses in the Search field. The results appear in the Message list with rankings indicating the best matches. If you frequently search for the same text, you can create a Smart Mailbox to make it quick and easy to find in the future. In addition to the search field, you can also use Spotlight to find e-mails, as well as other text in Mail, such as to-dos and notes.

## Search E-Mail for Text

1 To search in selected mailboxes, select the mailboxes or accounts.

2 Click in the Search field, and then type the text you want to find.

> **TIMESAVER** *Press* ⌘*+Option +F to quickly place the insertion point in the Search field.*

> As you type, Mail starts the search and displays the results.

3 Click **All Mailboxes**, a specific mailbox, **Entire Message**, **From**, **To**, or **Subject** on the Search bar to narrow the results.

4 To save the search as a Smart Mailbox, click the **Save** button on the Search bar, enter a name, and then click **OK**.

5 To broaden the search, click the **Spotlight** icon on the menu bar, type the text you want, and then click the search result you want on the menu.

> **TIMESAVER** *Press* ⌘*+F to find or replace text in an open e-mail.*

## Search Techniques

| Technique | Example |
| --- | --- |
| Use descriptive words | Home improvement |
| Place phrases in quotes | "Home Sense" |
| Use AND to find all words | "meeting and promotion" |
| Use OR to find at least one word | "meeting or promotion" |
| Use NOT to find the first one but not the second one | "meeting not promotion" |
| Use ( ) to find combinations | "meeting and (promotion or fall)" |

# Blocking and Bouncing E-Mail

You can have Mail handle junk e-mail for you. You can specify what should be considered junk e-mail and how Mail should handle that e-mail. You can ensure that e-mail which might seem to be junk e-mail, but is actually from a person or site that you are interested in, gets to you. You can mark messages as junk mail to help train Mail (set rules) to more effectively distinguish between junk and non junk. If you receive annoying mass mailings, you can **bounce**, or reject, the message back to the sender (as long as their return address is valid, which isn't usually the case with spam) and the message appears to the sender as if your address is invalid and the message could not be delivered. Mail also moves the message to the Trash.

## Change Junk E-Mail Options

① Click the **Mail** menu, and then click **Preferences**.

② Click **Junk Mail**.

③ Select the **Enable junk mail filtering** check box.

④ Click the option to leave it in my Inbox and change the text color or move it to the Junk mailbox.

⑤ Select the check boxes to exempt e-mail from junk filtering:

 ◆ **Sender of message is in my Address Book**

 ◆ **Sender of message is in my previous recipients**

 ◆ **Message is addressed using my full name**

 ◆ **Filter junk mail before applying my rules**

⑥ Click **Advanced**.

The default junk mail rule appears, which you can customize.

⑦ Use the pop-ups, fields, and buttons to specify the criteria for the junk rule to apply to messages.

⑧ Click **OK**.

⑨ Click the **Close** button.

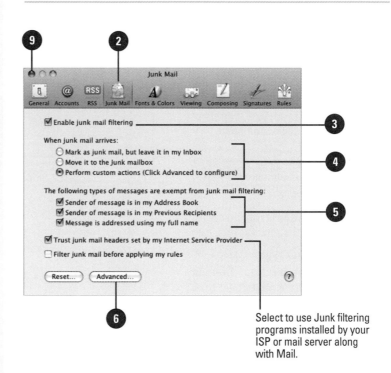

Select to use Junk filtering programs installed by your ISP or mail server along with Mail.

## Mark E-Mail as Junk or Not Junk

① Select the e-mail you want to mark as junk or not as junk.

② Click the **Junk** button or **Not Junk** button on the Mail toolbar.

The button toggles between Junk and Not Junk.

③ To erase messages in the Junk mailbox, click the **Mailbox** menu, click **Erase Junk Mail**, and then click **Yes**.

### Did You Know?

***You can reset junk mail rules to the default.*** Click the Mail menu, click Preferences, click the Junk button, click Reset, click Yes, and then click the Close button.

Message currently marked as Junk mail

## Bounce an E-Mail

① Select the unwanted e-mail message you want to bounce.

② Click the **Message** menu, and then click **Bounce**.

③ Click **Bounce**.

The message is bounced back to the sender and moved to the Trash mailbox.

### Did You Know?

***You can resend a message.*** Select the message in the Sent mailbox, click the Message menu, click Send Again, add or change recipients, and then click the Send button.

# Diverting Incoming E-Mail to Mailboxes

Mail can direct incoming messages that meet criteria to other mailboxes in the Mailbox list rather than to your Inbox. You can set message rules to store any messages you receive from a friend in a different folder so they won't clutter your Inbox. When you are ready to read the messages, you simply open the mailbox and access the messages just as you would messages in the Inbox. You can also set rules to automatically reply to incoming messages, which is useful when you are *out of the office*, or forward incoming messages with additional message text. You can also color-code the messages that you send to or receive from particular people for quick and easy recognition.

## Set Rules for Incoming E-Mail

1. Click the **Mail** menu, and then click **Preferences**.

2. Click **Rules**.

3. Click **Add Rule**.

4. Type a name for this rule.

5. Click the pop-up, and then click **Any** or **All** to set initial criteria.

6. Use the pop-ups and fields, to specify the criteria for the rule to apply to a message.

7. Click the **Add** (+) button or **Remove** (-) button to add or remove criteria.

8. Under the Perform The Following Actions area, use the pop-ups and fields to specify the actions you want to be taken if the criteria is met.

9. Click the **Add** button (+) or **Subtract** button (-) to add or remove actions.

10. Click **OK**, and then click **Apply** or **Don't Apply**.

11. To edit, duplicate, or remove a rule, select a rule, and then click **Edit**, **Duplicate**, or **Remove**.

12. Click the **Close** button.

Select to activate or clear to deactivate.

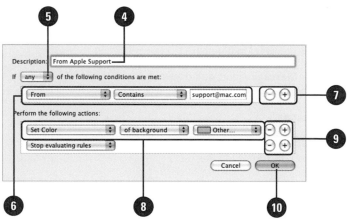

# Creating a Smart Mailbox

A Smart Mailbox displays e-mail messages or to-do items based on a search criteria in an easy to use folder in the Mailboxes list. The message or to-do items are not moved to the Smart Mailboxes. Each time you select a Smart Mailbox, Mail performs a search to create an up-to-date list of results. A Smart Mailbox is like a Smart Folder for Mail. You can create a Smart Mailbox for RSS articles, specific content, or from a specific sender.

## Create a New Smart Mailbox

1. To create a subfolder in a mailbox, select the existing mailbox.

2. Click the **Add** (+) button at the bottom of the Mailbox list, and then click **New Smart Mailbox**.

3. Type a name for the new mailbox.

4. Specify the criteria you want for the Smart Mailbox:

   ◆ **Contents.** Select **messages** or **to-do's**.

   ◆ **That Match.** Select **any** or **all**.

   ◆ **Conditions.** Use the pop-ups to specify the criteria you want for the Smart Mailbox.

   ◆ **Add or Remove Conditions.** Click the **Add** (+) or **Remove** (-) buttons. You can add as many as you want.

5. Select or clear the **Include messages from trash** or **Include messages from sent** check boxes.

6. Click **OK**.

7. To edit a Smart Mailbox, select the mailbox, click the **Mailbox** menu, and then click **Edit Smart Mailbox**.

# Getting RSS Feeds in E-Mail

Since e-mail is an important form of communication, you can use Mail to subscribe to RSS (Really Simple Syndication) feeds and display them in your inbox. A feed delivers frequently updated Web content to your browser on a continuous basis. A feed, is usually offered on a subscription basis and typically free of charge. A feed can deliver text content in the form of news headlines or blogs, or digital content in the form of pictures, audio, and video. When you get feeds in e-mail, a line or two of each articles content and a link to the full article appears for you to quickly and easily view.

## Subscribe to RSS Articles

① Click the **Add** (+) button at the bottom of the Mailbox list, and then click **Add RSS Articles**.

② Browse and select a feed from the ones you bookmarked in Safari, or enter a Web address for a new feed.

◆ **Find Feeds.** Use the Search field to locate the feeds you want.

◆ **Multiple Feed.** Use Shift-click or Command-click to select multiple feeds.

③ Select the **Show in Inbox** check box to include the feeds in your inbox.

④ Click **Add**.

⑤ Click the RSS feed you want to view in the Source pane.

RSS feeds

RSS article

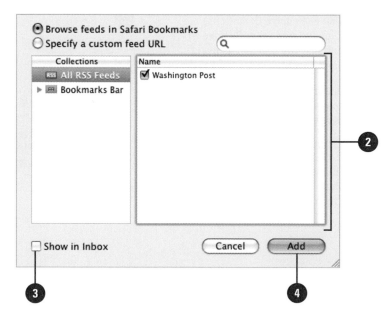

## Did You Know?

*You can RSS feed preferences in Mail.* Click the Mail menu, click Preferences, click the RSS button, use the pop-ups to select a Default RSS Reader, Check For Updates Interval, and Remove Articles Manually or Automatically, and then click the Close button.

# Conducting Live Chats and Video Conferences

## Introduction

Mac OS X Snow Leopard makes communicating with other computers over the Internet easier than ever with iChat 5.0. You can talk to others over the Internet (like you do on a telephone), use full screen video to see and be seen by others while you converse, share programs and files, and collaborate on documents.

You can use iChat to exchange instant messages with a designated list of buddies over the Internet. An **instant message** is an online typewritten conversation in real-time between two or more buddies. Unlike an e-mail message, instant messages require both parties to be online, and the communication is instantaneous.

iChat makes setup effortless. The first time you launch iChat, a setup screen appears to walk you step-by-step through the process. During the setup process, you need to create or provide a screen name, which is your instant messaging address. If you already have an AOL Instant Messenger (AIM), Google Talk or Jabber account, you can use it with iChat. Otherwise, you can setup a MobileMe or Mac.com account to get a screen name. To use the AV features of iChat, you need to have a microphone (for audio only) or FireWire compatible video camera (for audio and video) installed on your computer and a fast Internet connection. iChat allows you to communicate with either AIM, MobileMe, or Mac.com users. Now you can talk to millions more people online.

In addition to using iChat over the Internet, you can also use it on your local network—known as **bonjour messaging**— at the office, school, or home. iChat automatically locates other local users who are logged in, and lets you send messages or files to each other.

# Creating an Instant Message Account

The first time you launch iChat, a setup screen opens to walk you step-by-step through the process. To complete the process, you need to provide or create a screen name (your instant messaging address) to send and receive instant messages with iChat. If you already have a MobileMe (**New!**) or Mac.com (old .Mac) account, an AOL Instant Messenger (AIM) screen name, Google Talk account, or Jabber ID, you can use it with iChat. A MobileMe screen name is your e-mail address, such as perspection@me.com, or an AIM screen name is a handle, such as perspection. If you don't have a screen name, you can sign up for a MobileMe account at during the setup process to get one. If you have multiple accounts, you can switch between them or use them separately. You can't use screen names from other instant messaging systems, such as MSN or Yahoo, with iChat. If you are using iChat over a local network for Bonjour messaging, you don't need a screen name.

## Create an Instant Message Account the First Time

1. If necessary, install a microphone or compatible video camera according to product instructions.

2. Start iChat for the first time; display the Dock on the desktop, and then click the **iChat** icon.

3. Read the Welcome screen, and then click **Continue**.

4. Type your first and last name, if needed.

5. Click the **Account Type** pop-up, and then select an account: **AIM**, **MobileMe**, **Mac.com**, **Jabber**, and **Google Talk**.

   **TROUBLE?** *If you don't have an account, click Get An iChat Account.*

6. Type your Account Name and Password, and then click **Continue**.

7. Select options to setup audio and video for iChat, and then click **Continue**.

8. Click **Done**.

## Create and Enable Accounts

Click the **iChat** menu, and then click **Preferences**.

Click **Accounts**.

**IMPORTANT** *If multiple people use a computer with separate accounts, they use their own screen names.*

To create another account, click the **Add** (+) button, select an account type (**MobileMe**, **Mac.com**, **AIM**, **Jabber**, and **Google Talk**), enter account name and password, and then click **Done**.

Your password is added to your keychain.

Click the **Account Information** tab.

Select one of the following options:

◆ **Enable this account.** Select to enable and display this account.

◆ **Log in automatically when iChat opens.** Select to open this account when you start iChat.

◆ **Allow Multiple logins for this account.** Select to use multiple logins for this account.

Click the **Close** button.

### Did You Know?

*You can get the latest version of iChat online.* Visit the Apple Web site at *www.apple.com* to get updates.

*You can get or change your password and account information.* Visit the AOL Instant Messenger Web site at *www.aim.com*, or visit the MobileMe Web site at *www.me.com*.

### For Your Information

#### Installing and Selecting AV Hardware

Before you can start or join a video chat, you need to connect and install a microphone, a FireWire based video camera, such as iSight by Apple, built-in USB, and a broadband Internet connection (384 Kbps or faster), such as cable or DSL, to your Macintosh computer. If you have a Digital Video (DV) camcorder with a FireWire cable, you can also use it with iChat. Once you attach and install (if necessary) your audio and video equipment, you can set options in the Video pane of iChat Preferences. If you are using a camera with a built-in microphone, iChat automatically uses the camera microphone unless you change it to another one you have attached to your computer.

## Starting iChat

iChat is an instant messaging program that allows you to exchange instant messages with a designated list of buddies over the Internet. An **instant message** is an online typewritten conversation in real time between two or more buddies. Instant messages require both parties to be online, and the communication is instantaneous. After you start iChat, you sign in to let others online know you are connected. When you're done, you sign out.

### Start iChat and Sign In and Out

1 Click the **iChat** icon in the Dock.

A Buddy List window opens, displaying a "Connecting" message. Upon completion, the Buddy List expands to list your buddies and their online status.

2 If you're not automatically signed in, click the **iChat** menu, and then click **Log In To <account>**.

3 To sign out, click the **iChat** menu, and then click **Log Out Of <account>**.

Dock

## Did You Know?

*You can stop signing in automatically.* Click the iChat menu, click Preferences, click Accounts, select an account, clear the Log In Automatically When iChat Opens check box, and then click the Close button.

*Your buddies might need to upgrade their AIM software.* If your buddies are using older versions of the AOL Instant Messaging software, they might need to get a newer version to send messages to your Mac.com screen name.

*You can get help specific to iChat.* Click the Help menu, and then click iChat Help. The application help system works just like Spotlight help.

# Viewing iChat

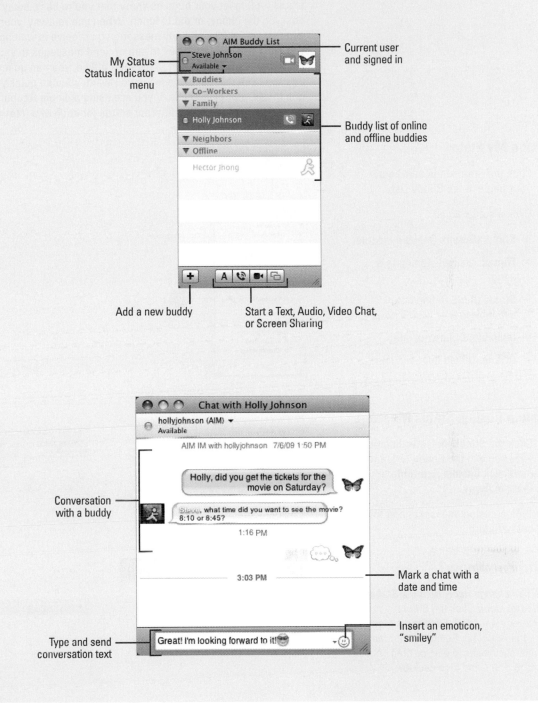

My Status

Status Indicator menu

Current user and signed in

Buddy list of online and offline buddies

Add a new buddy

Start a Text, Audio, Video Chat, or Screen Sharing

Conversation with a buddy

Holly, did you get the tickets for the movie on Saturday?

Steve, what time did you want to see the movie? 8:10 or 8:45?

Mark a chat with a date and time

Insert an emoticon, "smiley"

Type and send conversation text

Great! I'm looking forward to it!

# Changing My Status

When you sign in with iChat, the program notifies buddies currently online from your Buddy list that you are available to chat (green status). While you're signed in, you might need to leave your computer for a meeting or lunch. Instead of signing out, you can change your online status (red) to let your buddies know that you're busy, away from your desk, on the phone, or out to lunch. When you're away, your buddies see that you're idle, and any message you receive is waiting for you. If you don't want your buddies to see or send messages to you, you can go offline. If you don't want to be seen offline, you can go invisible. If you don't see the status message you want, you can quickly customize one to suit your own needs. If you are using multiple Accounts at the same time, you can have different status for each one (**New!**) .

## Change My Status

1 Click the Status Indicator below your name in the Buddy List.

2 Click a status type.

◆ **Status (Green).** Online available.

◆ **iTunes.** Online listening to a song.

◆ **Status (Red).** Online not available.

◆ **Invisible.** Offline not seen.

◆ **Offline.** Offline not available.

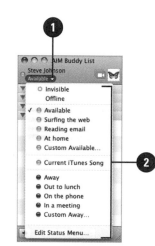

## Create a Custom Status Message

1 Click the Status Indicator below your name in the Buddy List, and then click **Custom Available** or **Custom Away**.

2 Type a custom message, and then press Return.

### Did You Know?

*You can change items from the Status Indicator menu.* Click the Status Indicator menu, click Edit Status Menu, click the Add (+) or Remove (-) buttons, double-click items to edit, or drag items to order, and then click OK.

294

# Using the iChat Status Menu

The iChat Status menu appears as a chat balloon icon on the right side of the menu bar for all applications. When the ballon icon is empty, you're online; when there is a line in the middle, you're away or offline. If you turn on the iChat Status menu, you can still receive instant messages, view online buddies, and change your status when you quit the iChat program. You can turn the Status menu on in the General pane of iChat Preferences, where you set other status options when you switch users or your computer is inactive. When the Status menu is turned off and you quit iChat, you're logged out of AIM and Bonjour messaging.

## Turn On the iChat Status Menu

1. Click the **iChat** menu, and then click **Preferences**.

2. Click **General**.

3. Select the **Show status in menu bar** check box.

4. Select or clear the **At user login, set my status to available** check box.

5. Select or clear the **When I Quit iChat, set my status to offline** check box.

6. Set additional status options after your computer is inactive.

7. Click the **Close** button.

## Use the iChat Status Menu

1. Click the **iChat Status** menu, and then select an available option:

   ♦ **A status.** Click Available, Away, or Offline; you can also select custom available or away messages.

   ♦ **A buddy.** Click the name of an online buddy.

   ♦ **Buddy List.** Click to display your Buddy List.

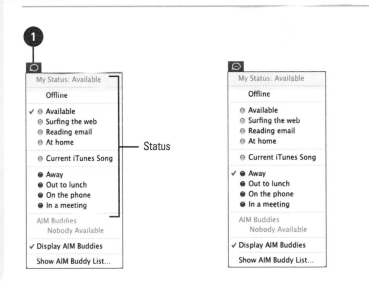

# Adding a Buddy

Before you can send instant messages to other people, they need to be in your Buddy list. Your Buddy list shows you who's currently online and offline, their audio and video capabilities, and if they are available for chatting. You can add a person who has a screen name from a MobileMe or Mac.com account or AIM to your Buddy list. You can add as many buddies as you like to your Buddies list. You can add them from your Address Book or type new ones. When you add a new person to your Buddy list, a new card is added to your Address Book. Your Buddy list is stored on an instant message server, so you can log in to your account from any computer and see if your buddies are online.

## Add a Buddy

1. If necessary, click the **Window** menu, and then click **Buddy List** to display the Buddy List window.

2. Click the **Add** (+) button in the Buddy List window, and then click **Add Buddy**.

3. Type an account name, select a group, type the first and last screen name for the person, or click the **Expand/ Collapse** button, and then select an address from the Address Book.

    **TIMESAVER** *If your buddy uses more than one screen name, you can type more than one by separating each with a comma.*

4. Click **Add**.

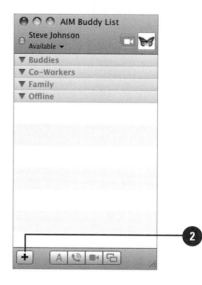

## Did You Know?

*You can quickly delete a buddy from your Buddy list.* Click a buddy in the Buddy list, press Delete, and then click OK. People who are removed from your list can still contact you unless you block them.

*You can view and edit information about a buddy.* Select a buddy in the Buddy list, click the Buddies menu, and then click Show Info. The information shown is typed by your buddy.

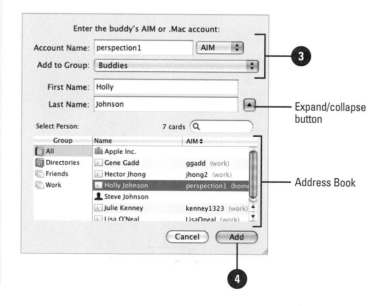

Expand/collapse button

Address Book

# Changing a Buddy Picture

You can change the picture that appears next to your name in the Buddy List and in message windows, along with the ones that appear next to your buddies. The picture is known as the Buddy icon. The Buddy icon you select appears in the Buddy List of those in which you have a chat. To change your Buddy icon, drag an image file—64 x 64 pixels is recommended—to your name in the Buddy List. In addition to an image file, you can also use an animated picture, also known as a GIF or animated GIF, as a buddy picture, which you can also create using Photo Booth.

## Change a Buddy Picture

1. If necessary, click the **Window** menu, and then click **Buddy List** to display the Buddy List window.

2. Select the buddy you want to change.

3. Click the **Buddies** menu, and then click **Show Info**.

4. Click the **Address Card** tab.

5. Clear the **Always use this picture** check box.

6. Drag the image or animated GIF you want to the picture box.

   ◆ **Enable Buddy Picture Animation.** Click the **iChat** menu, click **Preferences**, click **General**, select the **Animate Buddy Pictures** check box, and then click the **Close** button.

7. Select the **Always use this Picture** check box.

8. Click the **Close** button.

## Did You Know?

**You can change your picture.** Click the iChat menu, click Change My Picture, click Choose, select the picture you want, and then click Open. If you want, click the special effects button, select a special effect, and then click Set.

## For Your Information

### Creating an Animated GIF in Photo Booth

If you don't have an animated GIF, you can create one using Photo Booth. Open Photo Booth from the Applications folder, and then click the button for four-up picture format. If you want to add effects, click the Effects button and then select a video effect. Click the Camera button to take a series of four pictures, select the animation, and then export it as a file or set it as a buddy picture. To export it, click the File menu, click Export, specify a name and folder, and then click Save. To set it as a buddy picture, click the Buddy Picture button, specify the size, and then click Set.

# Creating and Managing Buddy Groups

As your Buddy list grows, you may want to organize your buddies into groups. iChat makes it easy to create your own groups and use the one predefined group called Buddies that comes with iChat. Once you have organized your groups, you can simply drag buddies from one group to another. You can use the check boxes next to the group name to hide and display buddies in a group. If a group changes, you can rename it, or if you no longer need a group, you can remove it.

## Turn On or Off the Use of Groups and Offline Groups

1. Click the **View** menu.

2. Click **Use Groups** or **Use Offline Group**.

   **TIMESAVER** *Press Shift*+⌘+H.

3. To turn off the use of Groups or Offline Groups, click the **View** menu, and then click **Use Groups** or **Use Offline Group** again.

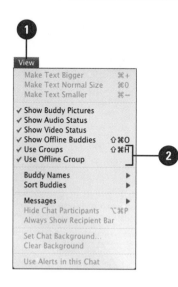

## Create a Buddy Group

1. If necessary, click the **Window** menu, and then click **Buddy List** to display the Buddy List window.

2. Click the **Add** (+) button in the Buddy List window, and then click **Add Group**.

3. Type a name for the group.

4. Click **Add**.

## Manage Buddies and Groups

**1** If necessary, click the **Window** menu, and then click **Buddy List** to display the Buddy List window.

**2** Select from the following options:

- ◆ **Display all group members.** Click the **View** menu, and then click **Use Groups** or **Use Offline Groups**.

- ◆ **Display group members.** Click the arrow next to the group name.

- ◆ **Move a buddy into a group.** Drag the buddy to a group.

- ◆ **Copy a buddy into a group.** Press and hold down the Option key while you drag the buddy to each group.

- ◆ **Move a group.** Drag the buddy group to a new position.

- ◆ **Delete a group.** Click the **Add** (+) button, click **Edit Group**, select the group, click the **Delete** (-) button, and then click **OK**.

  You can't delete a group with buddies in multiple groups, but you can delete a group with the only one buddy in it. You can't delete the last group in the list; you need to always have at least one.

- ◆ **Rename a group.** Click the **Add** (+) button, click **Edit Group**, select the group, click the group again, type a new name, and then click **OK**.

Move a buddy into a group

Use to display

Use to add, delete, or edit a group

## For Your Information

### Changing Buddy List View

If you are having trouble viewing the buddies you want, you can use the View menu to change the buddy list view. There are buddy commands to Show Buddy Pictures and Show Offline Buddies, which shows your entire buddy list, including buddies not currently available. You can also use the submenu Buddy Names to display full names, short name or handles, and the submenu Sort Buddies to sort buddies by availability, first name, or last name. If you want to show all your offline buddies as a group, select Use Offline Group. If you're not sure whether buddies have cameras or microphones, select the Show Audio Status or Show Video Status.

# Sending and Receiving Instant Messages

An instant message is an online typewritten conversation in real-time between two or more buddies. As you type an instant message, you can format your messages by using fonts and color and by inserting graphical symbols called **emoticons**, or "smiley," such as a happy face, which help convey your emotions. You can have instant message conversations with several different buddies at once. When you send a instant message to a group, all participants receive the message and all responses are visible to everyone involved. If a buddy has multiple accounts, you can select the one you want to use to send to and from (**New!**). If you have multiple chat windows open at the same time, you can bring them all together into a single tabbed window; you need to select the *Collect chats into a single window* option in the Messages pane in iChat Preferences.

## Send and Receive Instant Messages

1. If necessary, click the **Window** menu, and then click **Buddy List**.

2. To start a chat, select one or more names in the Buddy list you want to chat with, and then click the **Start A Text Chat** button.

   **TIMESAVER** *Double-click a person in your buddy list to start an individual chat session.*

   To respond to a text chat invitation, click the invitation window, type a message, and then click **Accept**.

3. If the buddy has multiple accounts, click the **Account** menu, and then select a **To** or **From** account.

4. Type your message in the box at the bottom of the window. To start a new line while typing, press Shift+Return.

5. Press Return, and then wait.

6. To add another person to the chat, click the **View** menu, click **Show Chat Participants**, click the **Add** (+) button, and then click a person from your Buddy list or Other.

7. When you're done, click the **Close** button to end the session.

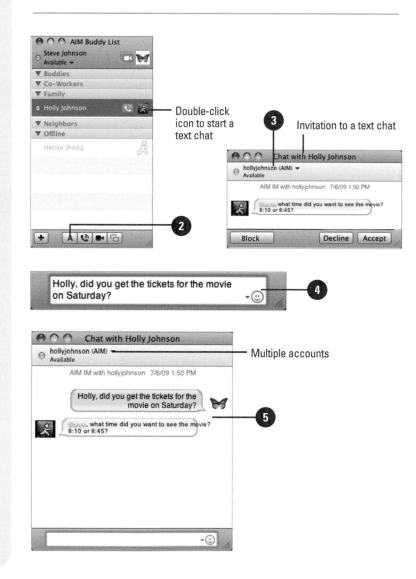

Double-click icon to start a text chat

Invitation to a text chat

Multiple accounts

## Format Message Text

1. Type and then select the text you want to format.

2. Click the **Format** menu, and then click the **Show Fonts**.

3. Specify the font, font style, size, color, and effect you want, and then preview the result in the sample box.

4. Click the **Close** button, and then send the formatted message.

## Insert Emoticons

1. In the Chat window, click the **Emoticons** button.

   **TIMESAVER** *Type a smiley using the keyboard, such as ":-)" and iChat inserts a corresponding graphic. Point to a smiley to view its type.*

2. Type your text, and then click the icon you want to insert into the conversation.

3. Press Return.

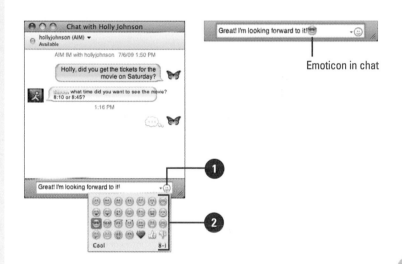

Emoticon in chat

## For Your Information

### Adding Date and Time Stamps

During a long chat, you can insert your date and time stamp to mark a transcript (**New!**). In a chat, click the Edit menu, and then click Mark Transcript. To clear a chat, click the Edit menu, and then click Clear Transcript. This is helpful when you automatically save a transcript for review later. Click the iChat menu, click Preferences, click Messages, select the Automatically Save Chat Transcripts To check box, and then click the pop-up to select a folder location. To specify the number of messages to save, select the In new chat window, show check box, click the pop-up to select an option (**New!**).

# Blocking a Buddy

If you no longer want to receive instant messages from a specific buddy, you can block the buddy from sending you instant messages. When you block a buddy, you appear to be offline to the person, who doesn't know blocking is turned on. Blocking a buddy moves them from your Allow list to your Block list in the Privacy pane of iChat Preferences.

## Block or Unblock a Buddy

1. Click the **iChat** menu, and then click **Preferences**.

   **TIMESAVER** *Select the buddy in the Buddy list, click the Buddies menu, click Block buddy name, and then click Block.*

2. Click **Accounts**, and then select the account with the buddy you want to block.

3. Click the **Security** tab.

4. Click a privacy option:

   ◆ **Allow anyone**. Click to unblock everyone.

   ◆ **Allow people in my Buddy List**. Click to unblock buddies in my Buddy List.

   ◆ **Allow specific people**. Click the option, and then click Edit List to select buddies.

   ◆ **Block everyone**. Click to block everyone.

   ◆ **Block specific people**. Click the option, and then click Edit List to add and remove buddies.

5. Select or clear the **Block others from seeing that I am idle** check box.

6. Click the **Close** button.

## Did You Know?

*You can search for a buddy in Spotlight (**New!**). Select the buddy in the Buddy list, click the Buddies menu, and then click Search in Spotlight.*

List of blocked people

Click to add or remove people in the block list.

Click here after selecting to block a buddy.

# Sending a File During an Instant Message

While you are conversing in iChat, you can send a buddy a file or hyperlink. You can send many different types of files, including pictures, documents, and music. When you send a picture, it's displayed right beside your text in the Chat window, which you can instantly preview with Quick Look (**New!**). When you send any other type of file, a request to transfer the file is sent to your buddy. You are notified when your buddy accepts or declines your request. Before you receive files over the Internet, make sure you have virus protection software to protect your computer. You can also send a hyperlink that points to a Web site. When your buddy receives a message with a link, the person can click it to open the Web address in their Web browser.

## Send a File or Hyperlink

1. Start a chat with the buddy to whom you want to send the file or hyperlink.

2. Type your message in the box at the bottom of the window.

3. Click the **Edit** menu, and then click one of the following:

   ◆ **Send a File.** Click **Attach File**, navigate to and select the file you want to send (for best results, use JPEG or GIF), and then click **Open**. A small icon appears to indicate the picture.

   **TIMESAVER** *Drag the picture file to the area where you type your message.*

   ◆ **Send a Hyperlink.** Click **Add Hyperlink**, type a Web address, and then click **OK**.

4. Type any additional text if you want, and then press Return.

   If you're sending a picture, the image appears in the chat window; if it's a file, wait for the recipient to accept or decline the file; or if it's a hyperlink, the link appears in the chat window.

5. To open a file or hyperlink, click the file (to preview in Quick Look) or link in the chat window.

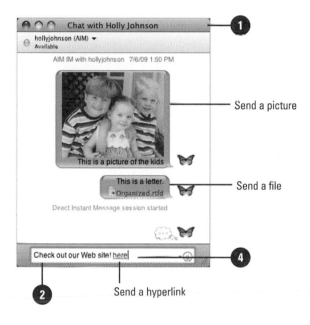

Send a picture

Send a file

Send a hyperlink

# Having an Audio and Video Chat

With iChat, you can talk to others over the Internet as you do on a regular phone, and you can use video to see others and let others see you as you converse. Once you set up your computer hardware and software, you're ready to communicate over the Internet. You have two communication choices: audio only, or audio and video. With audio only, you speak into a microphone and hear the other person's response over your speakers. With audio and video, you send video to others so they receive live images as well as sound. If the buddies you call don't have a video camera, they'll see you, but you won't see them. iChat supports only one video or audio chat at a time.

## Have a Audio or Video Chat

1. If necessary, click the **Window** menu, and then click **Buddy List**.

2. To start a chat, select a name in the Buddy list, and then click the **Start A Video Chat** button or **Start An Audio Chat** button.

   To respond to an audio or video chat invitation, click the invitation window, and then click **Accept**.

   To decline or block a chat invitation, click **Decline** or **Block**.

3. Start talking.

4. Use video controls on the Video menu or use the following:

   ◆ **Size Video Window.** Click the double arrow button to switch between normal and full-screen modes. You can also drag the bottom right corner of the video window.

   ◆ **Invite.** Click the **Invite** button to invite another person to chat.

   ◆ **Pause Video.** Option+click the **Microphone** button. Click the button again to start it.

   ◆ **Mute Audio.** Click the **Microphone** button.

5. When you're done, click the **Close** button to end the session.

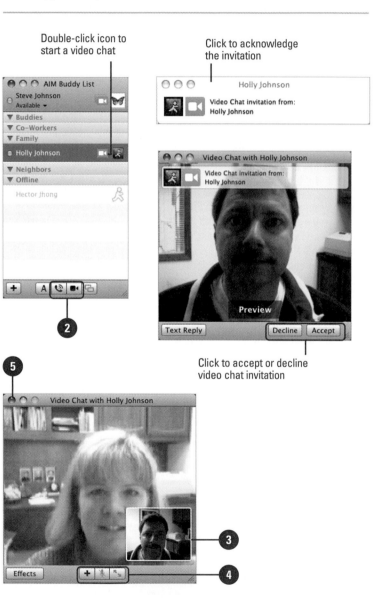

Double-click icon to start a video chat

Click to acknowledge the invitation

Click to accept or decline video chat invitation

## Change Video Bandwidth Speed and Preferences

1. Click the **iChat** menu, and then click **Preferences**.

2. Click **Audio/Video**.

3. Click the **Camera** pop-up, and then select an installed camera.

4. Click the **Microphone** pop-up, and then select an installed microphone.

5. Click the **Bandwidth Limit** pop-up, and then select a video speed option for your computer's performance and quality.

6. Select or clear the check boxes to automatically open iChat when the camera is turned on or play repeated ring sound when invited to a chat.

7. Click the **Close** button.

### iChat Performance and Quality

| Option | Standard | Enhanced | High |
|---|---|---|---|
| Window Size | 352x288 to Full Screen | 352x288 to Full Screen | 352x288 to Full Screen |
| Video Resolution | 176x144 | 176x144 | 352x288 |
| Frames Per Second (fps) | 15 | 20 | 20/30 |
| System Required | > 600 Mhz G3 or 350 Mhz G4 | > 1Ghz G4 | > dual 800 Mhz G4 and any G5 |
| Bandwidth | 100-500 Kbps | 100-500 Kbps | Above 500 Kbps |

# Enhancing a Video Chat

As you hold a video conversation in iChat, you can enhance your experience by adding video effects or backdrops to the video window. The video effects are provided by Photo Booth and the backdrops are professionally designed by Apple. You can use the ones provided, download new ones, or create your own. If you have Snow Leopard and a fast broadband Internet connection (300 Kbps (**New!**) or faster), you can host an iChat theater presentation that contains photos, keynote presentation slides, or movies with high resolution 640 x480 (**New!**) from your desktop while your buddies view it on their computer in an iChat video window.

## Enhance an Audio or Video Chat

1. Start a video chat with one or more buddies.

2. Click **Effects**.

3. To view the video effects and backdrops, click the left and right arrow buttons.

4. Click the video effect thumbnail you want to use.

   ◆ **Photo Booth Effects.** Unique video effects, such as X-Ray, Thermal Camera, and Pop Art.

   ◆ **Backdrops.** Backgrounds you can be in front of.

5. To add your own backdrop, drag it from the desktop or Finder window to a blank backdrop placeholder (User Backdrop 1, etc.) in the Video Effects window.

6. To remove the video effect, click the **Original** thumbnail.

7. When you're done, click the **Close** button to close the Video Effects window.

## Host an iChat Theater Presentation

1. Start a video chat with one or more buddies.

2. Click the **Invite** button, and then click **Share a File With iChat Theater** or **Share iPhoto With iChat Theater**.

   **TIMESAVER** *With an open video chat, you can drag the presentation item to the video chat window.*

3. Select the items you want to present:

   - **Photos, Text, and Other Files.**
   - **QuickTime Movies.**
   - **iPhoto Album Slide Shows.**
   - **Keynote Slide Shows.**

   If you can open an item as a Quick Look, you can use it in iChat Theater.

4. Click **Share**.

5. Deliver the presentation.

6. When you're done, click the **Close** button to end the presentation.

7. Click the **Close** button to end the session.

### Did You Know?

*You can record a video chat.* Start a video chat, click the Video menu, click Record Chat, and then click the Stop button or close the video chat window to stop recording. The recorded chat is saved to the iChats folder in the Documents folder by default.

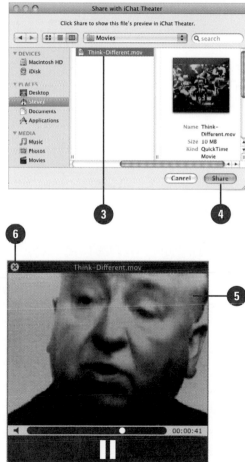

# Chatting on a Local Network

If you don't have an instant message account or server, you can still use iChat to chat with others on your local network. Instead of communicating with a central Internet server, each computer communicates directly with each other over network cables. iChat also works with a wireless connection using AirPort over a local network or the Internet. Bonjour allows you to chat with people on your local network or wireless local community. You can't add a Bonjour user to your Buddy list. The user names are based on the log-in settings on each person's computer and are not AIM screen names. Unlike regular instant message, when you type a Bonjour instant message, each character you type is sent immediately unless you turn off the default setting in the Messages pane of iChat Preferences.

## Turn On Bonjour Instant Messaging

1. Click the **iChat** menu, and then click **Preferences**.

2. Click **Accounts**.

3. Click **Bonjour**.

4. Select the **Enable Bonjour instant messaging** check box.

5. Select or clear the **Log in automatically when iChat opens** check box.

6. Click the **Close** button.

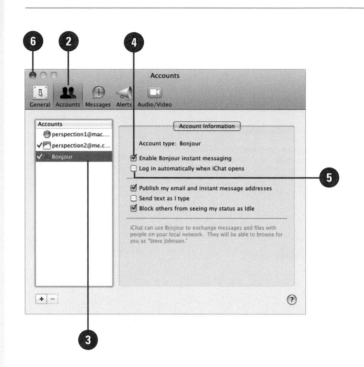

### Did You Know?

*You can send Bonjour message when you're done typing.* Click the iChat menu, click Preferences, click Messages, clear the Send Text As I Type (Bonjour Only) check box, and then click the Close button.

*You can send a SMS (short message service) text message to a mobile phone.* Click the File menu, click Send SMS, click the pop-up, select the account from which you want to send the text message (you can't use Bonjour, Jabber, or Google Talk), type your buddy's cell phone number, and then click OK.

---

### For Your Information

## Having Problems Seeing Bonjour Users

If you're having problems seeing Bonjour users in the Bonjour window, your network connections might be contributing to the problem. If you have firewall protect turned on, you might be unable to receive messages from other users. To use Bonjour, you may need to allow activity on port 5298. If you connect to the Internet using PPP or PPPoE, you won't be able to see other users. Check with your network administrator for information related to your network setup.

## Start Bonjour Messaging

1. Click the **Window** menu, and then click **Bonjour List**.

   The Bonjour window opens, showing iChat local network users who are available for chatting.

2. Double-click the user to whom you want to send an instant message.

3. Type your message in the box at the bottom of the window.

4. Press Return, and then wait for a reply.

5. When you're done, click the **Close** button to end the session.

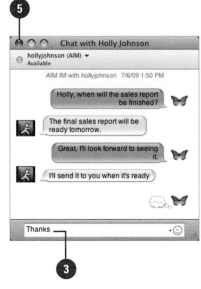

### Did You Know?

*You can use a keyboard shortcut to bring iChat to the front.* Click the iChat menu, click Preferences, click Messages, select the Use A Keyboard Shortcut To Bring iChat To The Front check box, click the pop-up to select a shortcut, and then click the Close button.

*You can quickly close other chats with a click* (**New!**). If you have multiple chats open at the same time, you can close all the other chats except the active one. Control-click the active chat, and then click Close Other Chats.

---

## For Your Information

### Sharing Your Screen with a Buddy

If you and your buddy are using Mac OS X, you can use iChat with any of the support account types to share your screens as if you were sitting in front of it. When you share your screen, your buddy has the same control over your computer as you do. During the screen sharing session, iChat starts an audio chat so you can talk about what your doing. To share your screen, select your buddy, click the Buddies menu, and then click Share My Screen or Ask To Share. You can switch between the two open desktops and copy files between your computers. When you're done, press Control+Esc to end the screen sharing session.

# Changing the Appearance of a Chat

iChat makes it easy to customize the appearance of a chat to suit your own style and preference. You can modify the appearance of the balloons, or change a font style in a chat. The changes you make affect the format of your messages on your screen as well as messages on your buddies screen unless they have chosen to reformat incoming messages. When you reformat incoming messages, you override your chat buddy settings and display all incoming messages using your preferences. You can set your preferences and reformat settings in the Messages pane of iChat Preferences. You can also change the background of the chat window to a picture, which only appears on your computer.

## Change the Appearance of a Chat

1. Click the **iChat** menu, and then click **Preferences**.

2. Click **Messages**.

3. Select or specify the various options you want to use:

   - **My balloon color.** Click the pop-up, and then select a color.

   - **My font color.** Click the pop-up, and then select a font color.

   - **Set Font.** Click to select a font.

   - **Reformat incoming messages.** Check to use your preferred settings, and then select a ballon and font color, and a font for the sender.

4. To highlight your name when its mentioned in a chat, select the **Watch for my name in incoming messages** check box.

5. Click the **Close** button.

## Change the Chat Window Background

1. Click the **View** menu, and then click **Set Chat Background**.

2. Locate and select the background image file you want to use.

3. Click the image file you want to open.

4. Click **Open**.

### Did You Know?

*You can quickly remove a background from the chat window.* Click the View menu, and then click Clear Background.

*You can view a chat as text.* Click the View menu, and then click Show As Text.

*You can save an instant message.* Click the File menu, click Save A Copy As, type a file name, select a location, and then click Save. To review a chat, click the File menu, click Open, select a transcript file, and then click Open.

*You can save chats automatically.* Click the iChat menu, click Preferences, click Messages, select the Automatically Save Chat Transcripts To check box, and then click the pop-up to select a folder location. To specify the number of messages to save, select the In new chat window, show check box, click the pop-up to select an option (**New!**). Click the Close button.

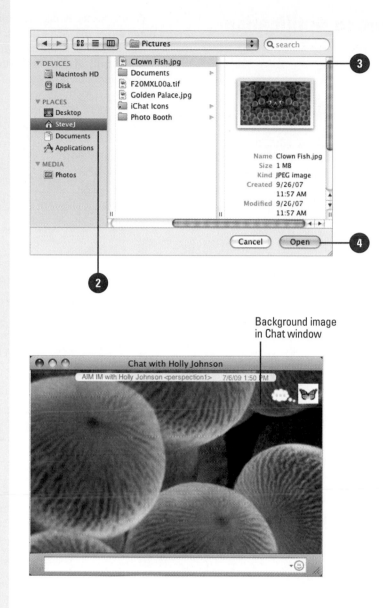

Background image in Chat window

# Getting Notification Alerts

When certain events, such as messages arrive or buddies log in, iChat can notify you with a sound, spoken message, or bounce of the iChat icon in the Dock. You can set alerts that apply to every buddy in the Alerts pane of iChat Preferences, or you can set specific notification alerts for each buddy in the Actions pane of the Show Info dialog.

## Set Up Notification Alerts

1. Click the **iChat** menu, and then click **Preferences**.

2. Click **Alerts**.

3. Click the **Event** pop-up, and then select the type of event you want to be notified of.

4. Select or clear the **Play Sound** check box. If you select it, click the pop-up, select an occurrence, and then select or clear the Repeat check box if you want the alert to occur every time.

5. Select or clear the **Bounce icon in the Dock** check box. If you select the check box, select or clear the **Repeat** check box.

6. Select or clear the **Speak an announcement** check box, and then drag the slider to set the speech volume.

7. Select or clear the **Run AppleScript** check box. If you select it, choose the script you want.

8. Click the **Close** button.

## Did You Know?

*You can specify different alerts for each buddy.* Select a buddy in your Buddy List, click the Buddies menu, click Show Info, click Alerts, select the options you want, and then click the Close button.

# Working with Music and Media

## Introduction

Macs were born for multimedia, and even after 20 years, they're still considered a front runner when it comes to images, movies, and music. Snow Leopard is bundled with several old friends, iTunes, and DVD and QuickTime Players, as well as some new ones, Photo Booth and Front Row.

The **iTunes** application is a software jukebox that comes with Snow Leopard, yet it's also available on Microsoft Windows, so you can share music between Macintosh and Windows. iTunes allows you to sort through and organize your digital music collection, convert CD's into the digital format, and even burn your favorite music onto a CD. If that's not enough, iTunes come complete with a built-in link to the iTunes music store. So if you have an Internet connection, you're one click away from a music store that contains the latest songs, as well as millions (yes, I said millions) of songs from the past. And for those of you that like to listen to the radio while you work, iTunes comes equipped with its own Internet Radio.

If you have an iSight or other camera attached to your computer, you can use Photo Booth to capture photos just like you were sitting in a photo booth at a carnival. You can capture individual photos or create a short movie and add a backdrop or visual effects.

If your Mac includes an Apple Remote, you can use it to control Front Row, where you can access and play iTunes music and playlists, iPhoto slide shows, and videos and DVDs on your Mac or TV. With the Apple Remote, you can navigate menus and lists, start and pause media, and change the volume in Front Row. You can also use the Apple Remote to deliver Keynote presentations and play music with the iPod Hi-Fi. The Apple Remote uses an infrared (IR) reception and works up to 30 feet within an unobstructed line of sight.

## What You'll Do

**Start and Set Up iTunes**

**View the iTunes Window**

**Set up iTunes to Automatically Play CDs**

**Get Music and Media from CDs and the iTunes Music Store**

**Use and Create Playlists**

**Add Media to a Playlist**

**Listen to Internet Radio**

**Subscribe and Play Podcasts**

**Use iPod or iPhone with iTunes**

**Burn CDs and Export to MP3 Players**

**Set iTunes Preferences**

**Capture Photos in Photo Booth**

**Record Movies in Photo Booth**

**Add Photo Booth Effects**

**Play and Browse DVD Movies**

**Customize the DVD Player**

**Play and Create QuickTime Movies**

**Erase a CD or DVD**

**Explore and View Media in Front Row**

**Change Settings in Front Row**

**Explore iMovie, iDVD, and iPhoto**

# Starting and Setting Up iTunes

You can conveniently start iTunes from the Dock. Simply, click the iTunes icon in the Dock to start iTunes. The first time you start iTunes, the programs walks you through the process of setting up an Apple account (it's easy if you have a MobileMe account) and iTunes Store, which helps you discover new music and videos from your iTunes library. When you sign in to iTunes, you authorize your computer to play iTunes store purchases. When you download a media item, Apple lets you copy and play that item on up to five authorized machines (Mac or Windows). If you want to use a sixth computer, you need to deauthorize one and then authorize the other.

## Start and Set Up iTunes

1. Click the **iTunes** icon in the Dock.

   ◆ You can also click the **Applications** folder in the Dock, and then click the **iTunes** icon to start it.

2. If you started iTunes for the first time, follow the iTunes Setup Assistant step by step instructions to set up iTunes.

3. To use the iTunes Store, click the **Store** menu, click **Sign In** or **Create Account**, and then follow the account review or setup process as requested.

4. To download album artwork, click the **Advanced** menu, and then click **Get Album Artwork**.

4. To authorize or deauthorize a computer, click the **Store** menu, and then click **Authorize** or **Deauthorize**.

   ◆ To deauthorize a computer to play items from the Audible Web site, click the **Advanced** menu, and then click **Deauthorize Audible Account**.

   ◆ To deauthorize a computer you no longer own, you can deauthorize all your computers at once (only available once a year). Click the **Store** menu, and then click **View My Account**.

# Viewing the iTunes Window

When you open iTunes, you're working in an organized window that gives you access to your movie and music collections, creates new Playlists, organizes your music, converts existing CD's into an iTunes collection, and burns selected media onto a CD or DVD (a writable CD or DVD drive is required). The same iTunes window that lets you listen and organize your music also lets you listen to Internet Radio and podcasts, or purchase music, movies, TV shows, and other media through the iTunes Music Store. In other words, once you open the iTunes application, everything you need to enhance your music experience, including listening to audio books, is right in front of your eyes.

# Setting Up iTunes to Automatically Play CDs

When you open the iTunes application for the first time you'll be asked a few preference questions. For example, you are asked if you want iTunes to be the application your Mac uses for playing music files from the Internet, whether you want iTunes to ask permission every time it connects to the Internet, and whether you want the program to scan your home folder for all of your music. If you select not to have iTunes automatically scan your home drive for music files, you can always drag a folder into the iTunes window. It will automatically scan the folder for any music files, and then place them within the active Playlist.

## Set Up iTunes to Automatically Play CDs

① Click the **System Preferences** icon in the Dock, and then click the **CDs & DVDs** icon.

② Click the **When you insert a music CD** pop-up, and then select **Open iTunes**.

③ Click the **Close** button to close the System Preferences window.

---

### Did You Know?

*You can select another program to play music CDs.* If you find an application better than iTunes at managing your record collection, you can always select Another Application from the CDs & DVDs pop-up menu.

# Getting and Playing Music from CDs

If you have music on CD, you can quickly import it into iTunes. If you have System Preferences for CDs & DVDs set to automatically open CDs in iTunes, all you need to do is insert the CD and iTunes does the rest. The music on your CD is copied to your computer in your iTunes music library. Importing music can also be accomplished through the iTunes menu system, or it can be as simple as a drag and drop. After you download music from your CD, you can view and work with music displayed in a list, grouped with artwork, or in Cover Flow, a 3D visual approach to flipping through your libraries. When you want to play a song, you can use the playback controls in the upper-left corner of the iTunes window or the ones in the full screen Cover Flow view.

## Get Music from a CD and Play it in iTunes

1. Insert the CD into your drive.

2. If an alert message appears, asking for confirmation, click **Yes**.

   The music automatically downloads to your iTunes Music Library.

3. To view the music in different ways, click one of the view buttons: **List View**, **Album View**, and **Cover Flow View**.

   ◆ **Cover Flow.** Click the cover art Left and Right Arrows or drag the slider to view the music, or click the **Full Screen** button to view and playback music.

4. To play the music, select the tracks you want to play, and then use the playback controls.

### Did You Know?

*You can set CD import options in iTunes.* Click the iTunes menu, click Preferences, click Advanced, click the Importing tab, select the options you want, and then click the Close button.

*You can create multiple libraries.* Hold down the Option key and click the iTunes icon in the Dock, and then click Create Library.

Song importing from a CD

Full Screen button

# Getting Media from the iTunes Music Store

The iTunes music store is a dream come true for all of us that love music, but don't necessarily want to buy the whole album just to get our favorite song. The music store was born out the desire to help musicians get paid for their work (Internet piracy of music is affecting the entire music industry), and to help the end-user (you and me) get what we want. The iTunes music store was not the first to make the purchase of songs or albums and other media easy, but they are considered the best at doing it. All you have to do to get started is open the iTunes application, click the iTunes Store option, and that's it (assuming you have an Internet connection). You're ready to start hunting for the music, movies, TV shows, podcasts, and iPod games you love. Once you download a media item, Apple lets you copy and play that item on up to five authorized machines. When you move media to another computer, you are prompted to type in your Apple Account number, which authorizes that computer to play that media.

## Use the iTunes Music Store

1. Click the **iTunes** icon in the Dock.

2. Click **iTunes Store** in the Source pane.

   ◆ If promoted, setup your payment options (it's easy if you have a MobileMe or Mac.com account).

3. Click on any of the various links to access that particular title.

4. Use the Search field and type a title, artist, or keyword to search, and then press Return.

5. Click an item to open it, if needed.

## Did You Know?

*You can download songs for a buck.* My favorite part of iTunes is the ability to download selected songs from an album, without having to download an entire album. You can download any song for a buck. In addition, the Music Store gives you the ability to download entire albums at a reduced rate over the individual songs.

⑥ To navigate, click the **Back**, **Next**, **Home**, or category buttons below the toolbar.

⑦ To preview an item, double-click the item or click the **Preview** button; availability varies depending on the media item.

⑧ Click the purchase, download, or subscribe button for the type of item you want; the button name varies depending on the media item.

   **IMPORTANT** *If you haven't set up your payment options (credit cards), Mac OS X prompts you to do so at this time.*

   The media item is downloaded to your iTunes library. Click **Downloads** in the Source pane to display progress or pause, resume, or stop the process.

⑨ Quit iTunes.

## Did You Know?

***You can shrink the iTunes window.***
Click the Window menu, and then click Zoom. Click the Zoom command again to enlarge the window.

***You can view different aspects of iTunes.*** Click the View menu, and then click Show Browser, Show Genius Sidebar, or Show Artwork Column. Click the Window menu, and then click Show Equalizer. Show Browser displays a three column view to make it easier to find items and navigate. Show Genius Sidebar displays a pane to recommend music and make playlists. Show Artwork Column displays a column for artwork in the Item list. Show Equalizer displays a dialog where you can adjust sound levels.

Music

Podcast

# Using and Creating Playlists

The iTunes application lets you add media from several different sources. For example, you might have some MP3 songs on your hard drive, and you want them stored within the iTunes application, or you have a music CD that you want converted into MP3 format. Whatever method you select, you'll first want to set up a Playlist to hold and organize your media. A **playlist** is a folder that holds media. For example, you could have a Playlist for all your Country & Western songs, one for your Rock & Roll; even one for audio books. iTunes comes with a set of playlists, or you can create your own. Playlists come in two flavors—Playlists and Smart Playlists. Playlists let you play the songs in the list again, play the songs in random order, or stop when the last song plays. Smart Playlists rebuild themselves according to the criteria you setup. For example, you might create a Smart Playlist that only plays the songs in the library you rate a 4-star or only Christmas songs.

## Play and Create a Playlist in iTunes

① Click the **iTunes** icon in the Dock.

② To play all the songs in a Playlist, click the Playlist you want listen to, and then double-click the first song or click the **Play** button.

③ Click the **File** menu, and then click **New Playlist**.

④ Type a name for the Playlist, and then press Return.

⑤ To rename a playlist, click it once, click it again, type a new name, and then press Return.

⑥ Quit iTunes.

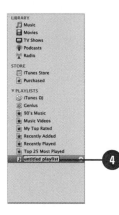

## Did You Know?

*You can drag a music folder from an open window into the Source pane.* iTunes automatically creates a Playlist for the songs, and names the Playlist with the name of the dragged folder.

*You can import your playlists.* Click the File menu, point to Library, and then click Import. Only songs and videos in your iTunes are included in the Playlist.

## Add a Smart Playlist to iTunes

① Click the **iTunes** icon in the Dock.

② Click the **File** menu, and then click **New Smart Playlist**.

③ Click the **Criteria** pop-up, and then select the main selection criteria.

④ Click the **Operator** pop-up, and then choose a selection method.

⑤ Type a word or phrase to search.

⑥ Click the **Add Criteria** (+) button to add an additional search option.

⑦ Select the **Limit To** check box and pop-up to limit the number of songs, time played, or max size.

⑧ Click the **Selected By** pop-up, and then select how to select songs.

⑨ Select the **Match only checked items** check box to limit selection to songs that are checked.

⑩ Select the **Live updating** check box to update the Smart Playlist as you add or subtract songs from the iTunes Library.

⑪ Click **OK**.

⑫ Name your Smart Playlist.

⑬ Quit iTunes.

### See Also

*See "Adding Media to Playlist" on page 322 for more information on creating a playlist using Genius.*

### Did You Know?

*You can delete a playlist.* Select the playlist in the Source pane, click the Edit menu, and then click Delete.

## For Your Information

### Understanding Copyright Laws

When you create Playlists you're working smart. Most iTunes users have hundreds, if not thousands of songs on their hard drives, and Playlists and Smart Playlists are the only way to help organize all those songs. A word of caution, make sure they are your songs. Piracy is a big problem in the music industry today, and it's not just what you take off the Internet. The iTunes application gives you the ability to create music tracks from most music CDs. That does not mean you can borrow all of your friend's music CDs and transfer them to your computer. Enjoy your music, but know the laws involving piracy, and copyright violation. Use your browser to search for the latest information about copyright laws in the U.S.

# Adding Media to a Playlist

Whenever you add media to the iTunes application, it stores the media in a Library, and then creates a link to the selected Playlist. As a matter of fact, Playlists simply create links to the media in the iTunes Library. If you delete a Playlist or a media within a Playlist, it does not remove the song from the iTunes Library, only the link created in the Playlist is removed. If you want help from iTunes, you can create a Genius playlist (**New!**), which sends music information about your libraries to iTunes Store, and creates a personalized playlist for you.

## Add Media to a Playlist

① Click the **iTunes** icon in the Dock.

② Add media using any of the following options:

- ◆ Drag media from other libraries in iTunes to the Playlist.

- ◆ Click the **File** menu, and then click **Add To Library**. Locate the song or songs you want to add, and then click **Open**.

- ◆ Drag media files from an open folder to the Playlist in the iTunes window.

- ◆ Click the **Store** menu, and then click **Turn On Genius**. Follow the online steps to enable it. Select a song from a library, click the **Show/Hide Genius Sidebar** button, and then click the **Start Genius** button. Click **Genius** in the Source pane to view the Genius playlist. When you're done, click the **Store** menu, and then click **Turn Off Genius**.

③ Quit iTunes.

Genius playlists    Genius Sidebar

Drag media

Start Genius    Show/Hide Genius Sidebar

Add to Library

## Did You Know?

*You can export your playlists.* Select the Playlist, click the File menu, point to Library, and then click Export Library. To save all your Playlists, click the File menu, point to Library, and then click Export Library.

# Listening to Internet Radio

Listening to music is great, so is curling up with a cup of hot chocolate and your favorite audio book. However, sometimes you would just like to listen to a radio station. Maybe NPR (National Public Radio) is your thing, or possibly your looking for a radio station that just plays classical music. Whatever direction your tastes run, you are probably able to find it on the Internet radio, and iTunes makes the process of selecting and listening to a radio station as easy as turning on a traditional radio.

## Listen to Internet Radio

1. Click the **iTunes** icon in the Dock.

2. Click **Radio** in the Source pane.

3. Select a group from the available options.

4. Click the expand button (triangle) to open the group.

5. Double-click on a station to begin the broadcast.

6. Use the **Play/Pause** button to turn the selected station on or off.

7. Use the **Previous** and **Next** buttons to move up and down through the radio station list.

8. Drag the volume slider in the upper left corner to adjust the volume.

9. Quit iTunes.

## Did You Know?

*You can add radio stations to the iTunes radio list.* Click the Advanced menu, and then click Open Stream. Type in the station's Web address, and then click OK.

# Subscribing and Playing Podcasts

Podcasts are radio and TV shows you can download from the Internet to your iTunes library. The iTunes Store provides free podcasts you can download at any time. If you like a podcast, you can subscribe to it and have it automatically downloaded as it becomes available. If you have an iPod, you can add podcasts to your player and play them on the go when you're not connected to the Internet.

## Subscribe and Play Podcasts

1. Click the **iTunes** icon in the Dock.

2. Click **iTunes Store** in the Source pane.

3. Search for the podcast you want.

4. To subscribe to a podcast (only need to do once), display the podcast you want, click **Subscribe**, and then click **Subscribe** again if prompted.

   The podcast is downloaded to your iTunes library. Click **Downloads** in the Source pane to display progress or pause, resume, or stop the process.

5. Click **Podcasts** in the Source pane.

6. Click **Podcasts**, **Categories**, or **New** to display the podcasts you want, and then double-click the thumbnail (not "Play Selected").

7. Click the expand/collapse button (triangle) to expand the podcast listing in the iTunes window.

8. Click **Get All** to download all the podcasts or click **Get** to download an individual podcast.

9. To play a podcast, double-click the podcast. Point to the player to display playback controls and Close button to exit.

10. To unsubscribe to a podcast, select the podcast, and then click **Unsubscribe**.

11. Quit iTunes.

# Using iPod or iPhone with iTunes

The iPod digital MP3 music/video player is so unique, it deserves a class all of its own. The iPod is the most successful digital music/video player ever created. More iPod players are sold than any other player. Now you can also use the new iPhone with iTunes. They're made for Macintosh and Windows computers, and it just so happens they work perfectly with the iTunes player. When you plug your iPod or iPhone cable into your computer, it automatically opens the iTunes application and synchronizes playlists, music, videos, podcasts, photos, contacts from your Address Book that you create on your iPod. The iTunes Store also includes games you can purchase and download. You can also manually make changes. It's a simple matter of deleting media you no longer want or dragging media into your iPod or iPhone.

## Use iPod or iPhone with iTunes

1. Plug your iPod or iPhone into your computer (requires a FireWire or USB port). This also recharges your iPod or iPhone.

2. Click the iPod or iPhone device name in the Source pane.

3. Click the tabs to set sync options, and then click **Sync**.

4. Click the expand/collapse button (triangle) to expand the device in the Source pane, and then select a library or Playlist.

5. To remove media, select an item in the iTunes window, and then press Delete.

6. To add media, drag a media item or Playlist from the iTunes window to the device in the Source pane.

7. Click the **Eject** button, to eject and remove the iPod.

    **IMPORTANT** *If you disconnect your iPod without performing an Eject, it could cause the iPod hard drive (and all your songs), to become corrupted.*

8. Quit iTunes.

# Burning CDs and Exporting to MP3 Players

While CD's are still around and popular, digital music players seem to be one of the "newer" technologies set to change how we listen to our tunes. iTunes gives us the option to use CDs and digital music players—we can burn our own customized music CDs or we can transfer the music files to any one of a number of digital music players. When you insert the CD, iTunes gives you the option of choosing the Playlist you want to use. If the playlist is too large to fit on a single CD or DVD, iTunes asks you for another disc. Digital music players, more commonly known as MP3 players, hold music files using the MP3 digital format. MP3 players can be thought of as a hard drive that holds music files, and then plays them back to you through a set of speakers or a headset. When you purchase your MP3 player, it comes with software designed to move music files from your computer hard drive to the drive located on the MP3 player. Some MP3 players, when connected to your computer, appear as an external hard drive.

## Burn a Music CD

① Click the **iTunes** icon in the Dock.

② Create and select the Playlist you want to burn onto the CD.

  iTunes uses the name of the Playlist as the name of the CD.

③ Insert a blank CD into your drive, and then click **Ignore**, if prompted.

  **IMPORTANT** *You must have a writable CD or DVD drive.*

④ Click **Burn Disc** once to open the button, and then click a second time to perform the burning operation.

⑤ Quit iTunes.

### Did You Know?

*You can't burn more than 10 copies of your Playlist.* If you do have a legitimate need for that 11th CD, all you need to do is change the sort order of the songs in the Playlist, and then you can burn 10 more.

## Export to MP3 Players

**1** Navigate to the iTunes music folder:

Main Hard Drive/Home/Music/ iTunes/iTunes Music.

**2** Select a folder or a list of iTunes files that you want to move.

**3** Drag the music files to the hard drive icon of your MP3 music player.

**4** Control-click the MP3 player desktop icon, and then click **Eject**.

> **IMPORTANT** *Not all MP3 music players allow you to drag music files between your hard drive and the player icon. When this occurs you'll have to use the transfer software that came bundled with the player. Simply load the software and follow the onscreen instructions.*

## Did You Know?

***You can backup your iTunes library to a CD or DVD.*** Click the File menu, click Back Up To Disc, select the options you want, insert a blank writable CD or DVD, and then click Back Up.

***You can set CD burn options in iTunes.*** Click the iTunes menu, click Preferences, click Advanced, click the Burning tab, select the options you want, and then click the Close button.

***You can access the names of your songs on the Internet.*** Insert a music CD, click the Advanced menu, and then click Get CD Track Names. The iTunes application accesses the Gracenote music title repository, and then changes the dull Track1 and Track2, with the names of the song.

# Setting iTunes Preferences

Like any application, iTunes gives you a Preferences panel that helps you adjust the software to fit your specific needs. For example, Podcasts preferences give you the option to specify when to check for and download new episodes. The iTunes preferences give you precise control over how the program operates on your computer.

To set your preferences, or to review the defaults that have been set in iTunes, simply open the Applications folder, and then double-click the iTunes application. Click the iTunes menu, and then click Preferences. There you'll find almost every conceivable setting that is used in iTunes. For a summary view, we've shown you commonly used screens and what is contained on that Preference screen. After making any changes to the screens, simply click OK to change the setting or click Cancel to undo your change.

**General:** Controls text within the iTunes window.

**Playback:** Gives you options to play music and movies.

**Advanced:** Controls the Buffer, and helps manage and maintain the iTunes Music folder.

**Sharing:** Lets you share your music files with other users.

# Capturing Photos in Photo Booth

If you have an iSight or other camera attached to your computer, you can use Photo Booth to capture photos just like you were sitting in a photo booth at a carnival. You can capture individual photos or create a short movie. In addition, you can include a backdrop or visual effects to your photo snapshots and movie recordings. When you're done capturing photos, you can use them as a user account or iChat buddy picture, send them as an attachment in an e-mail message, present them in a slide show or print them in a proof sheet. Photo Booth saves your photos and movies in a folder called Photo Booth, located in the Pictures folder in your Home folder. The still photos are saved as JPEG files.

## Capture Photos in Photo Booth

1. Attach an Apple iSight or other video camera to your computer.

2. Click the **Photo Booth** icon in the Dock.

3. Click the **Take a still picture** button.

4. When you're ready to take a still picture, click the **Shutter** button.

   After a 3-second countdown, the screen flashes and Photo Booth takes a photo. The picture appears as a thumbnail in the bottom pane.

5. To preview a photo, select the thumbnail in the bottom pane.

6. To permanently delete a photo, select the thumbnail, and then click the **Delete** button in the bottom left corner of the thumbnail.

7. Click the **Shutter** button again to go back to live images.

8. To e-mail a photo or use a photo in a user account or buddy picture, use the buttons below the preview.

9. To present a slide show, click the **View** menu, click **Start Slideshow**, and then use the toolbar to navigate through the slide show.

Preview

# Recording Movies in Photo Booth

In addition to capturing individual still photos, you can also record a movie in Photo Booth. You can create two types of movies, either a movie clip or a 4-up movie. A movie clip is a continuous recording of frames, while a 4-up movie is four snapshots taken very quickly to simulate a movie. The 4-up movies are saved as four JPEG files, while movie clips are saved as QuickTime MOV files. However, you can export the movie clip or 4-up movie as an animated GIF, which you can also use as an iChat buddy icon.

## Record Videos in Photo Booth

1. Attach an Apple iSight or other video camera to your computer.

2. Click the **Photo Booth** icon in the Dock.

3. Click the **Take four quick pictures** or **Take a movie clip** button.

4. When you're ready to take a still picture, click the **Shutter** button.

   For a 4-up movie, a 3-second countdown and a flash occurs for each photo. The four images appear on the screen at the same time as individual images.

   For a movie clip, the recording starts after a 3-second countdown.

5. When you're done recording a movie clip, click the **Stop** button.

6. To preview a movie, select the thumbnail in the bottom pane, and then point to the bottom of the live image to display and use the slider and Pause/Play button to view a movie clip.

7. To permanently delete a movie, select the thumbnail, and then click the **Delete** button in the bottom left corner of the thumbnail.

8. Click the **Shutter** button again to go back to live images.

# Adding Photo Booth Effects

Photo Booth includes backdrops and visual effects you can add to visuals to have some fun and create more interesting photo effect. A backdrop is a background that appears behind the camera image. You can use one of the backdrops provided by Photo Booth, such as New York, Paris, or Yosemite, to make it seem like your in an another place, or add and use one of your own. In addition to backdrops, Photo Booth also includes a set of visual effects, such as Comic Book, Sepia, X-Ray, and Light Tunnel, that you can use to create a fun and unique effect.

## Add Photo Booth Effects

1. Attach an Apple iSight or other video camera to your computer.

2. Click the **Photo Booth** icon in the Dock.

3. Click the **Effects** button.

4. Click the Left and Right Arrows to display more effects.

5. Select the backdrop or visual effect you want to use.

6. Point to the bottom of the live images. If a slide appears, drag it to adjust the visual effect level.

7. To remove an effect, select the **Normal** effect in the middle.

8. To add your own backdrop, drag it to a "Drag Backdrop Here" place holder.

9. When you're ready, select a picture button, and then click the **Shutter** button.

### Did You Know?

*You can export a movie as an animated GIF.* Select a 4-up movie or movie clip in the bottom pane, click the File menu, click Export, type a name, specify a location, and then click Save.

Backdrops

Visual effects

# Playing and Browsing DVD Movies

Okay, it's time to break out the popcorn and soda, because the DVD player in Sow Leopard is here. Using the DVD player, you can access a movie chapter by chapter, freeze the action, move forward and backward through the movie, and even play a movie in slow motion frame-by-frame. You can even watch your video in full screen mode while you work on another display. In addition, the DVD Player offers closed captioning. All that translates into a great viewing experience—sounds like a winner to me. If you have an Apple Remote, you don't even need to get up to control the DVD player.

## Play and Browse DVD Movies with the DVD Player

① Insert a DVD into the DVD drive of your computer to start the movie.

◆ You can also click the **Application** folder in the Dock, and then click the **DVD Player** icon to start it.

② Select from the following DVD Player options:

◆ Click the **Left**, **Right**, **Up**, **Down**, or **Return** buttons to navigate.

◆ Click the **Previous** or **Next Chapter** buttons to move between movie chapters.

◆ Click the **Play/Pause** or the **Stop** button to play/pause or stop the movie.

◆ Click the **Eject** button to stop the movie and eject the DVD.

◆ Click the **Title** or **Menu** buttons to view the movie title or menu.

◆ Drag the volume control to raise or lower the volume.

◆ Open the Options panel, and then select between Slow Motion, Step Frame, Return, Sub Title, Audio, or Angle.

③ At the top of the window, click the Video menu, and then select between the various viewing options.

④ To exit the movie without using the

Movie Player

Navigate

Volume Control

Slow Motion    Step Frame

Sub Title

Options panel

Audio

Previous; Hold to Fast Rewind

Stop

Return    Angle

Play & Pause

Next; Hold to Fast Forward

# Customizing the DVD Player

In addition to the main DVD player controls, you can also customize your playback experience. With the new full-screen interface and Image Bar, you can quickly access playback controls, subtitles, and audio tracks, change the screen view and scale, and browse DVD content. You can also create video snippets from any DVD and set bookmarks, also known as key points, you can view again later.

## Customize the DVD Player

① Insert a DVD into the DVD drive of your computer to start the movie.

② Select from the following Movie Player options:

◆ **Show/Hide Full Screen**. Press ⌘+F.

◆ **Image Bar**. Point to the bottom of the screen in Full Screen.

◆ **Create Video Clip**. Position the video, click the **Controls** menu, click **New Video Clip**, set the start and end frame, and then click **Save**.

◆ **Bookmark**. Position the video, click the **Controls** menu, click **New Bookmark**, enter a name, and then click **Add**.

◆ **View Bookmarks, Video Clips, and Chapters**. Click the **Window** menu, and then click **Bookmarks**, **Video Clips**, or **Chapters**.

◆ **Video Zoom or Color**. Click the **Window** menu, and then click **Video Zoom** or **Video Color**, select the **On** check box, and then adjust the levels.

◆ **Keyboard Shortcuts**. **Play**: Space bar, **Stop**: ⌘+. (period), **screen size**: ⌘+0 thru ⌘+3, **Switch to Finder**: Option+⌘+F.

③ To exit the movie without using the controller, press ⌘+Q.

Full Screen

Image bar          Movie controls

# Playing QuickTime Movies

QuickTime Player supports H.264 video decoding capabilities using the GPU (Graphics Processing Unit) instead of the CPU (**New!**), which is considered the standard for creating, delivering, and playing multimedia at the lowest data rates possible with hindering quality. Now, you can share content with others via both computers and mobile devices all over the world. QuickTime works with the MPEG4 format and other common formats, giving you access to movie clips. In addition, QuickTime delivers several performance enhancements, including ColorSync management (**New!**), live resize, zero-configuration streaming at the best connection speed, surround sound in up to 24 channels, full screen playback, additional keyboard shortcuts to mirror Final Cut Pro, improved A/V controls, and closed captioning with up-to-date standards, and timecode or frame count display instead of movie time. QuickTime Player plays movies in a redesigned window with fade away playback controls (**New!**). If your movie contains chapter markers, QuickTime Player displays them in frame-based thumbnail images (**New!**).

## Play QuickTime Movies

1. Click the **Applications** folder in the Dock, and then click the **QuickTime Player** icon.

2. Click the **File** menu, and then click **Open** to load individual QuickTime (or other formatted) movies or click **Open URL** to load URLs.

   ◆ To open a recent movie, click the **File**, point to **Open Recent**, and then select a movie.

3. Point to the movie to display movie controls (if necessary), and then click the movie controls to **Play/Pause** and **Rewind** or **Forward** the movie.

   ◆ You can also drag the slider to adjust the movie position.

   **TIMESAVER** *Press the Spacebar to play/pause a movie.*

4. To adjust the volume, drag the Volume slider.

5. Click the **View** menu, and then select from the available viewing options.

6. Quit QuickTime Player.

Opened movie

Trim movie or add it to iTunes, MobileMe, or YouTube

Toggle full screen

Adjust play position

## Customize QuickTime Playback

1. In the QuickTime Player, select from the following options:

- **Show/Hide Full Screen.** Press ⌘+F.

- **Change Screen View.** Press ⌘+1 for Actual Size; press ⌘+3 for Fit to Screen; press ⌘+4 for Fill Screen; press ⌘+5 for Panoramic; press ⌘++ or ⌘+- for Increase Size or Decrease Size.

- **Show/Hide Chapters.** Click the **View** menu, and then click **Show Chapters**.

- **Closed Captioning.** Click the **View** menu, and then click **Show Closed Captioning**.

- **Show Movie Inspector.** Click the **Window** menu, and then click **Show Movie Inspector** to display movie information (Source, Format, FPS, Data Size, Data Rate, and Current Size), and then click the **Close** button.

- **Show Export Progress.** Click the **Window** menu, and then click **Show Export Progress** to display progress information, and then click the **Close** button.

### Did You Know?

***You can listen to a movie in a different language.*** Click the View menu, point to Languages, and then select a language. If the languages are grayed out, the movie doesn't support it.

***You can show movie subtitles while a movie plays.*** Click the View menu, point to Subtitles, and then select a language. If the languages are grayed out, the movie doesn't have subtitles.

Full screen

Movie controls

Show Movie Inspector

Think Different—Inspector

**Think Different**
Chiat/Day Advertising
© 1997 Apple Computer, Inc.

| | |
|---|---|
| **Source:** | /Users/stevejohnson/Movies/thinkdif.mov |
| **Format:** | Apple Cinepak, 320 x 240, Millions IMA 4:1, Mono, 44.100 kHz |
| **FPS:** | 15.44 |
| **Data Size:** | 14.3 MB |
| **Data Rate:** | 1,974.93 kbit/s |
| **Current Size:** | 382 x 287 pixels |

# Creating QuickTime Movies

QuickTime 10 provides powerful commands (**New!**) to record live video and audio directly from an iSight camera, FireWire camcorder, or microphone or capture movement on your desktop to disk. After you create a QuickTime movie, you can edit the beginning or end of the movie, trim it shorter, or remove unwanted content, such as silence. QuickTime also allows you to convert and share your media in iTunes, iPhone, iPod, or Apple TV, and publish your media to YouTube (no longer than 10 minutes or larger than 1 GB in size), and MobileMe. QuickTime also provides HTTP live streaming to playback live video online using Web server and firewall technology for seamless use.

## Create Movies, Audio, or Screens

1. Click the **Applications** folder in the Dock, and then click the **QuickTime Player** icon.

2. Click the **File** menu, and then click **New Movie Recording**, **New Audio Recording**, or **New Screen Recording**.

3. Click the **Down** arrow to select commands to adjust recording devices, quality, and destination.

4. Click the **Record** button.

   ◆ For a Screen Recording, click **Start Recording**.

5. When you're done, click the **Stop** button.

   ◆ For a Screen Recording, click the Stop button on the menu bar. You can also press ⌘+Control-Esc.

   The media is automatically saved in the Movies folder.

5. To save the movie is another format, click the **File** menu, click **Save As**, type a name, select a format and destination, and then click **Save**.

6. To export the movie to the Web, click the **File** menu, click **Save for Web** (**New!**), type a name, select a destination and export format, and then click **Save**.

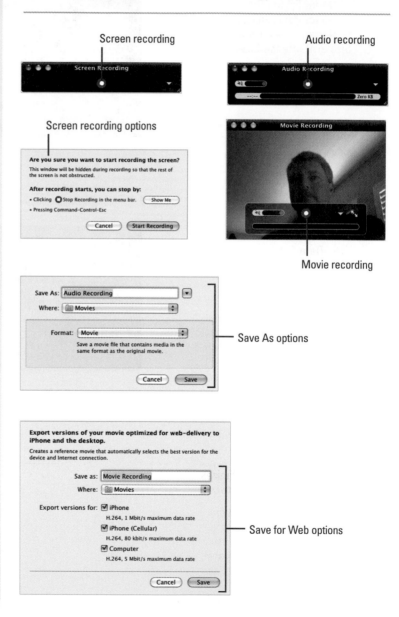

Screen recording

Audio recording

Screen recording options

Movie recording

Save As options

Save for Web options

## Edit QuickTime Movies

1. In the QuickTime Player, click the **File** menu, and then click **Open File**, select the movie you want to edit, and then click **Open**.

2. Click the **Edit** menu, and then click **Trim**.

3. Edit the movie using any of the following commands:

   ◆ Drag the play head (red vertical line) to locate the part of the movie you want to remove.

   ◆ Drag the start and end of the trimming bar (yellow handles) to select the part of the movie you want to keep.

   ◆ Click the **Edit** menu, and then click **Select All Excluding Silence** to exclude the silent part of the movie.

4. Click **Trim**.

## Share QuickTime Movies

1. In the QuickTime Player, click the **File** menu, and then click **Open File**, select the movie you want to edit, and then click **Open**.

2. Click the **Share** menu, and then select a sharing option:

   ◆ **iTunes.** Converts the movie to the iTunes library format, which is compatible with iPod, iPhone, and Apple TV.

   ◆ **MobileMe Gallery.** Optimizes and uploads the movie to your MobileMe account.

   ◆ **YouTube.** Optimizes and uploads the movie to your YouTube account. The movie is limited to 10 minutes or larger than 1 GB in size.

iTunes options

MobileMe Galley options

YouTube options

# Erasing a CD or DVD

If you want to reuse a CD-RW or DVD-RW disc, you need to erase it first, which you can do with Disk Utility. Before you start, there is one thing you need to know. You can't erase a standard CD or DVD that was a previously recorded CD-R or DVD-R disc. During the process, you have the option to select Quick Erase. When you select Quick Erase setting, the contents on the CD or DVD gets overwritten when new information is placed over it. If you don't select Quick Erase setting, the contents is overwritten with zeros to completely erase the CD or DVD, which takes longer to finish.

## Erase a CD or DVD

1. Click the **Applications** folder in the Dock, clck the **Utilities** folder, and then click the **Disk Utility** icon.

2. Select the disc in the left column you want to erase.

3. Click the **Erase** tab.

4. Click the **Quickly** or **Completely** option.

5. Click **Erase**.

6. Click **Erase** to confirm you want to erase the CD.

7. Click the **Disk Utility** menu, and then click **Quit Disk Utility**.

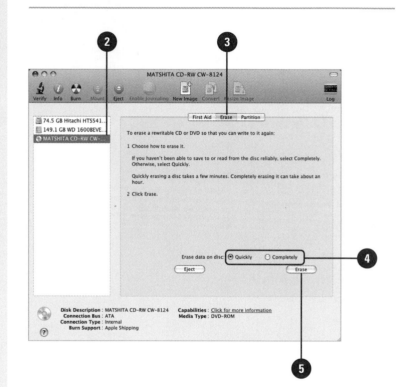

# Starting and Exploring Front Row

Front Row is an entertainment system integrated into your computer that lets you watch movies, TV shows, iPhoto slide shows, and listen to iTunes music and podcasts. Because Front Row is designed to be used as an entertainment system, the display and navigation are unlike any other program. When you start Front Row, the program uses the entire screen and doesn't use standard Macintosh program menus or tool-bars. You navigate by using the up and down arrows to specify a main category, and then the left and right arrows to specify a subcategory. You can use your keyboard or a Apple Remote to navigate the system.

## Start and Navigate Front Row

◆ **Start and Quit Front Row.** Hold down the **Menu** button on your Apple Remote or press ⌘+Esc.

◆ **Navigate menus and lists.** Press the **Plus (+)** or **Minus (-)** buttons on your Apple Remote or press Up or Down Arrows.

◆ **Return to previous menu.** Press the **Menu** button on your Apple Remote or press Esc.

◆ **Select an item in a menu or list.** Press the **Play/Pause** button on your Apple Remote or press Space bar or Return.

◆ **Play and pause audio or video.** Press the **Play/Pause** button on your Apple Remote or press Space bar or Return.

◆ **Change volume.** Press the **Plus (+)** or **Minus (-)** buttons on your Apple Remote or press Up or Down Arrows.

◆ **Go to next or previous song, photo, or DVD chapter.** Press the **Next/Fast-Forward** or **Previous/Rewind** buttons on your Apple Remote or press Right or Left Arrows. You can also hold down the buttons and keys to fast-forward or rewind a video or DVD.

Front Row main screen

Navigate menus

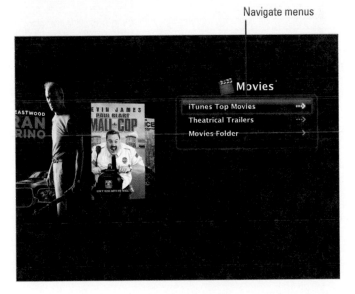

# Viewing Media in Front Row

With Front Row, you can watch movies, TV shows, and iPhoto slide shows, and listen to iTunes music, and podcasts. From a music stand point, you can play music videos, audiobooks, and playlists, which is very convenient with the Apple Remote. If you like movies, you can watch movie trailers (provided by Front Row) or movies you have on your computer. If you want to deliver a slide show, you need access to iPhoto on your computer or a shared iPhoto library on a network. To make the most of Front Row, you need to populate your Mac with media. You can use iTunes to purchase and download media from the iTunes Store, or search the Web and download the compatible media you want. You can play DVDs with Front Row. However, the Main menu in Front Row doesn't display the DVD menu until you insert a DVD in your disc drive.

## View Media in Front Row

1 Hold down the **Menu** button on your Apple Remote or press ⌘+Esc.

2 Press the **Plus** (+) or **Minus** (-) buttons on your Apple Remote or use the Up and Down Arrows to select the media type you want to play:

- ◆ **DVD.**
- ◆ **Movies.**
- ◆ **TV Shows.**
- ◆ **Music.**
- ◆ **Podcasts.**
- ◆ **Photos.**

3 Press the **Next/Fast-Forward** or **Previous/ Rewind** buttons on your Apple Remote or press Right or Left Arrows.

4 To play an audio or video, press the **Play/Pause** button on your Apple Remote or press Space bar or Return.

5 To quit Front Row, hold down the **Menu** button on your Apple Remote or press ⌘+Esc.

# Changing Settings in Front Row

If you leave Front Row open for a while without any activity, your screen saver turns on like it does with any other program on your Mac. If you don't want this to happen, you can turn off the screen saver just for Front Row. Front Row also provides sounds effects as you navigate around the program. If you don't want to hear them, you can turn off the sound effects too. You can turn these options on or off using the Settings command on the Main menu. Front Row delivers media content from different sources, either your local computer or shared network, which you can change using the Sources command on the Main menu.

## Change Settings in Front Row

◆ **Turn on/off the screen saver.** Select **Settings**, select **Screen Saver**, and then press the Space bar or Return key, or press Play/Pause on the remote to turn it on or off.

◆ **Turn on/off the sound effects.** Select **Settings**, select **Sound Effects**, and then press the Space bar or Return key, or press Play/Pause on the remote to turn it on or off.

◆ **Stream from a shared iTunes or iPhoto library.** Select **Sources**, select an shared iTunes or iPhoto library on your network using built-in Bonjour technologies.

◆ **Stream from a local iTunes or iPhoto library.** Select **Sources**, select an iTunes or iPhoto library on your computer.

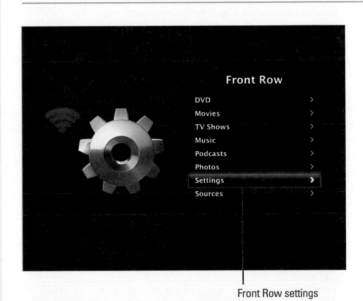

Front Row settings

Screen Saver and
Sounds Effects options

# Exploring iMovie, iDVD, and iPhoto

The **iPhoto** application lets you organize your images into user-defined folders, edit them, and even distribute them to your friends, by placing them on a CD or DVD, or directly over the Internet. iPhoto is part of the iLife suite of application, which is sold separately from Mac OS X.

When you open the iPhoto application, you're treated to the ultimate in organization and simplicity. For example, you own a digital camera, and you want to move the images from the camera to your computer. Most digital cameras come with their own proprietary programs that let you hook your camera up (USB or FireWire port), and then organize and manage your files. Fortunately, iPhoto does away with camera-specific programs. When you plug your camera in, iPhoto recognizes the device and lets you move the image files from the camera to iPhoto.

The **iMovie** application lets you create high-quality, professional movies. Using footage from your digital camcorder (MiniDV or Digital 8 format), you can edit and combine different movie files, create transitions between scenes, even capture live video, and then add an audio track (voice or music). iMovie is part of the iLife suite of application, which is sold separately from Mac OS X.

The iMovie application is simple to operate, yet powerful when it comes to creating professional movies, using footage from your digital movie camera, or any other digital multimedia files; including image stills and audio files.

The iMovie window is your working studio. Inside this one window, you have the ability to draw together all of the elements of your movie, and then arrange them by adding titles and transitions; you can even use special effects. For example, you could create a movie of a family members birthday, using a dozen movie clips, plus background music and narration. You can also add still images, create seamless fades between photos, and movies. It's all here inside the iMovie window.

The **iDVD** application comes bundled on all Macintosh computers that have a DVD burner. Using iDVD, you can create slideshows of pictures, or become a director and create your own DVD movies, using a digital camcorder. You even have iMovie to help you edit your home movies. iDVD is part of the iLife suite of application, which is sold separately from Mac OS X.

If you've ever wanted to test your skills at movie production, then the iDVD application is just what you've been waiting for all these years. There are all kinds of layout applications, such as applications for laying material out on paper (Adobe InDesign and Quark Xpress), and there are programs that layout Web pages (Adobe Dreamweaver). With that in mind, think of iDVD as a layout application for the creation of your Oscar-winning production. This gives you the ability to generate slideshows, videos, or a combination of both, along with menus, buttons (just like any other DVD), and then burn it onto a blank DVD that can be viewed by anyone that owns a DVD player.

The iDVD application is powerful, but just like any other layout program, it requires material to use for the layout. For example, when you open iDVD, you need access to video files, audio files, and graphics. The iDVD application doesn't create the materials that make up the DVD; it only organizes them. And, not all DVD players are created equal. Some DVD disks do not work in all the players on the market; especially older DVD players. For information on compatibility issues between DVD writers and DVD players, point your browser to: *http://www.dvdrhelp.com*.

# Exploring MobileMe

## Introduction

MobileMe provides a centralized place on the Web to manage and synchronize e-mail, contacts, calendar, photo albums, and documents that you can access from a Mac, PC, iPhone, or iPod touch. Synchronization is the process of keeping information updated in multiple places. When you make changes on one computer or device, your changes are automatically updated on other synchronized computers or devices so you always have up-to-date information where ever you go. For example, if you create and send e-mail in Mail, create a contact in Address Book, or schedule a meeting in iCal on your main Mac, the changes you make are synchronized with MobileMe (Mail, Contacts, and Calendar) and then synchronized with other computers and devices, such as your iPhone.

In addition to keeping information up-to-date, you can also use MobileMe to store documents and create photo albums that you can share with others on the Web. For example, if you have a large file that you can't send in an e-mail, you can use a virtual hard drive, known as an iDisk, available with MobileMe to store the file so you or someone else can access it from another computer or device. If you take a lot photos, you can create an online photo album that that others can access on the Web.

You can join the MobileMe community on a trial basis, and receive some limited features; however, if you want to utilize the full power of MobileMe, you'll need to purchase a subscription, which runs about a hundred dollars a year. While that may seem like a substantial chunk of change, the benefits of the services are great and if you do the math, it breaks down to about eight dollars a month.

## What You'll Do

# Joining the MobileMe Community

When you join the MobileMe community, you're immediately connected with thousands of other happy Macintosh users. Not only does a subscription to MobileMe give you access to all kinds of cool stuff, it also gives you access to web-based e-mail, contacts, calendar, and disk storage that you can synchronize with a Mac, PC, iPhone, or iPod touch. Joining the MobileMe community is quick and simple. If you're not sure whether to join, you can try it out first. If you want to join, you'll need a credit card to complete the online purchase.

## Join the MobileMe Community

1. Open your browser, and then go to *www.apple.com/mobileme/*.

2. Click the **Free Trial** or **Join Now** button.

3. Fill out the registration information screens.

4. Click **Submit**, and then follow any additional online instructions.

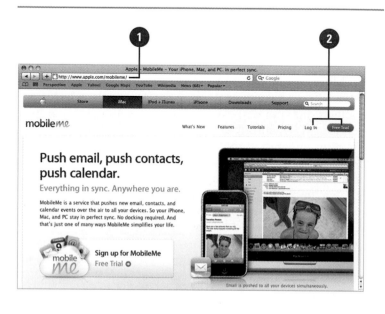

# Accessing Your MobileMe Account

Once you've filled out all the information on the registration form, and then clicked Submit, you now have instant access to the full power of the MobileMe community and the Web. The good news is that you can access your account from any computer, anywhere, at any time of the day or night. You might say that the MobileMe community never sleeps. Your MobileMe account is not measured by time spent online. Once you pay your subscription fee, you can use the account as often as you want. The process of signing on is simple and painless; in fact, you could create a bookmark in your browser, and automate the entire process.

## Access Your MobileMe Account

1. Open your browser, and then go to *www.mobileme.com*.

2. Type your MobileMe member name and password.

3. Click **Log In**.

4. A message appears asking you if you'd like to save your password. Click an option:

   ◆ **Never For This Website**

   ◆ **Not Now**

   ◆ **Yes**

   You are now signed in and ready to begin.

   **IMPORTANT** *If you leave your account logged in with no activity for a while, MobileMe asks you to re-enter your password.*

5. To get help using MobileMe, click the **Help** button (with the question mark icon) on the right side of the MobileMe toolbar.

6. When you're done, click **logout** on the right side of the MobileMe toolbar.

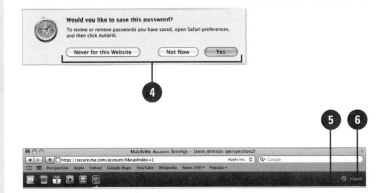

# Changing MobileMe Account Preferences

Once you're registered as a user, all of the advantages of the MobileMe site become instantly available; including the ability to read and send e-mail from your new mail account, manage contacts and a calendar, store and share your photos online, manage and backup files online, and synchronize MobileMe content across multiple computers and devices. You can access your MobileMe account settings from MobileMe preferences in System Preferences or online at the MobileMe Web site. When you login in to your online MobileMe account, you can set account preferences in the following areas: personal information, account options, billing info, password and storage settings, personal domain, security certificate, and Find My iPhone.

## View MobileMe Account Preferences

1 Click the **System Preferences** icon in the Dock, and then click the **MobileMe** icon.

◆ If prompted, type your MobileMe member name and password, and then click **Sign In**.

2 Click **Account** tab.

A quick summary of account details appears in MobileMe preferences. You can get more account details online.

3 Click **Account Details**.

4 Type your MobileMe member name and password, and then click **Log In**.

MobileMe Account Settings Web page appears, displaying a summary of your account.

5 Click one of the category buttons in the left column to view your current settings.

## Change MobileMe Account Preferences

1. Open your browser, and sign onto your MobileMe account.

   ◆ You can access MobileMe log in at *www.mobileme.com*.

2. Click the **Account Settings** button.

3. Select from the following online MobileMe account options, and then change the options you want:

   ◆ **Summary Info.** Displays your account name and e-mail address, current disk usage, account details, help, and announcements.

   ◆ **Personal Info.** Sets account name and e-mail address, language and time, and update notifications.

   ◆ **Account Options.** Sets account subscription options.

   ◆ **Billing Info.** Accepts credit card information.

   ◆ **Password Settings.** Changes account password and sets security information.

   ◆ **Storage Settings.** Allocates online storage for iDisk and Mail.

   ◆ **Personal Domain.** Adds a Web domain so you can host a Web site using MobileMe.

   ◆ **Security Certificates.** Creates a certificate to keep your iChat information secure online.

   ◆ **Find My iPhone.** Helps you find your iPhone or iPod touch in case it gets lost.

4. Click **Save**, if needed.

MobileMe password settings

MobileMe storage settings

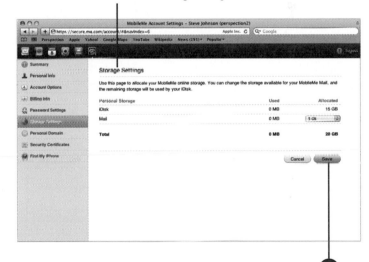

# Managing MobileMe Mail

The MobileMe Mail service gives you a way to keep in touch with friends, family, and clients at home, or wherever you travel. And you don't even have to have your own computer. You can access, read, and save your e-mail using a Web browser on any computer, anywhere, through the *www.mobileme.com* Web site. After you setup or sign-in to a MobileMe account, you are now ready to receive and send e-mail to other MobileMe members, or to anyone with an Internet e-mail address. MobileMe Mail work in a similar way as Mac OS X Mail. MobileMe Mail also provides preferences, so you can customize the way it works.

## Work with MobileMe Mail

1. Open your browser and sign onto your MobileMe account.

   ◆ You can access MobileMe log in at *www.mobileme.com*.

2. Click the **Mail** button.

3. Click the **Get New Mail** button to check for e-mail.

4. Click on an e-mail in your Inbox to open and read it in the preview pane below.

5. If you want, click the **Reply**, **Reply All** or **Forward** button to respond to an e-mail, and then click the **Send** button.

6. To put selected e-mail in the Trash folder, click the **Delete** button.

7. To create a new e-mail, click the **New Message** button to write an e-mail, and then click the **Send** button.

   ◆ Click the **Add Contacts** button to use contacts from the Address Book.

   ◆ Click the **Spelling** button to check spelling in the e-mail.

   ◆ If you're not finished with an e-mail, you can click the **Save Draft** button to store it in the Drafts folder for use later.

Drafts button    Spelling button

Send button    Contacts button

Message

## Change MobileMe Mail Preferences

1. Open your browser and sign onto your MobileMe account.

2. Click the **Mail** button.

3. Click the **Actions** button, and then click **Preferences**.

4. Select any of the following preference categories:

   ◆ **General.** Sets appearance, mailbox, and junk mail options.

   ◆ **Composing.** Sets options to customize new e-mail, check spelling, and add a signature.

   ◆ **Viewing.** Sets options to view e-mail from your Inbox and folders.

   ◆ **Aliases.** Creates alias e-mail addresses to keep your MobileMe one protected against unwanted e-mails.

   ◆ **Other.** Sets options to check mail from an external POP account, forward e-mail to another e-mail account, and automatically reply to e-mail.

5. Click **Save**.

MobileMe Mail general preferences

MobileMe Mail composing preferences

### Did You Know?

*You can empty the Trash folder.* In MobileMe Mail, click the Trash folder, click the Actions button, click Empty Folder, and then click Empty Folder.

*You can view mail disk use by folder.* In MobileMe Mail, click the Actions button, click Manage Folders to view the information, and then click Done.

# Creating a MobileMe Address Book

Your MobileMe Address Book lets you store personal and business information on all your friends, relatives, and contacts, in one safe place. In truth, you might actually have two or three other places where this same information is stored, maybe Safari, the Address Book application that comes bundled with the Snow Leopard operating system, or even your iPod. The MobileMe address book is used to maintain your mailing lists and e-mail contacts. However, before you despair of having to type in all those contacts again, Macintosh gives you a way to Sync all of the contacts and keep them up-to-date, no matter what application performed the changes.

## Create a MobileMe Address Book

1. Open your browser and sign onto your MobileMe account.

   ◆ You can access MobileMe log in at *www.mobileme.com*.

2. Click the **Contacts** button.

3. To create a group for contacts, **New Group** button, type a name, and then press Return.

   ◆ To add a contact to a group, select the group and create a new contact or drag it to the group name.

4. To create a new contact, click **New Contact**, enter information, and then click **Save**.

5. To display contact information, click the contact name.

6. To modify the contact info, select the contact, click the **Edit Contact** button, and then click **Save**.

7. To remove a contact from the list, select the contact, click the **Delete Contact** button, and then click **Delete**.

8. To generate an e-mail for the selected contact, click the **Actions** button, and then click **Email Contact**.

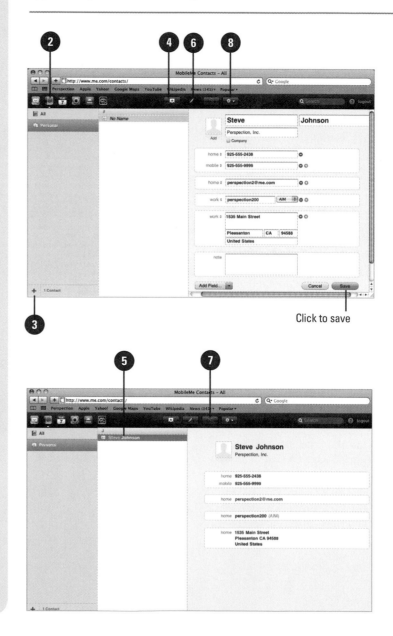

Click to save

## Change MobileMe Address Book Preferences

1. Open your browser and sign onto your MobileMe account.

2. Click the **Contacts** button.

3. Click the **Actions** button, and then click **Preferences**.

4. Select from the following MobileMe Address Book options:

   ◆ **Show contact names like this.** Select the option you want: **First name Last name** or **Last name, First name**.

   ◆ **Sort by.** Click the pop-up, and then select the option you want.

   ◆ **Address Layout.** Click the pop-up, and then select a language.

   ◆ **Format phone numbers.** Select the **Automatically format phone numbers** check box to have MobileMe do it for you, click the pop-up, and then select a format.

5. Click **Save**.

# Working with MobileMe Calendar

With MobileMe Calendar, you can keep track of all your activities, either work or personal. You can create separate calendars for different people, such as your family, or a team, or different types of activities. MobileMe Calendar gives you the ability to add new events or modify existing events directly in the Calendar window just like iCal. In fact, MobileMe Calendar works in a similar way as Mac OS X iCal. MobileMe Calendar also provides preferences, so you can customize the way it works.

## Work with MobileMe Calendars

1. Open your browser and sign onto your MobileMe account.

   ◆ You can access MobileMe log in at *www.mobileme.com*.

2. Click the **Calendar** button.

3. To add a calendar or calendar group, click the **Add** (+) button, click **New Calendar** or **New Calendar Group**, type a name for the calendar, and then press Return.

4. Click a view button to find a date.

   ◆ Today. Click to display the current day.

   ◆ Day, Week, and Month. Click to display a day, week, or month at a glance. Use the Left or Right Arrows to move by the selected view.

   ◆ Mini-Month. Click a day or use the Left or Right Arrows. Click the **Show/Hide Mini-Month** button to show or hide the mini-month calendar.

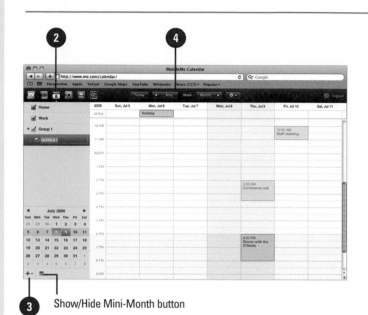

Show/Hide Mini-Month button

## Did You Know?

*You can delete a MobileMe calendar or event.* In Calendar, select the calendar or event you want to delete, click the Actions button, and then click Delete.

## Add or Edit MobileMe Calendar Events

1. Open your browser and sign onto your MobileMe account.

2. Click the **Calendar** button.

3. Click the calendar you want to add an event.

4. Click a view button to find the date to add.

5. Drag a time interval on the day you want to add an event.

6. Type a title for the event.

7. To adjust the time and day, drag the top or bottom edge of the event item, or drag the title to a new location.

8. To edit event details, double-click the event, make changes, and then click **OK**.

## Change MobileMe Calendar Preferences

1. Open your browser and sign onto your MobileMe account.

2. Click the **Calendar** button.

3. Click the **Actions** button, and then click **Preferences**.

4. Select any of the following preference categories:

   ◆ **General.** Sets appearance and format options.

   ◆ **Advanced.** Sets options for time zone support and whether to hide or delete past events and to do items.

5. Click **Save**.

# Creating a MobileMe Gallery

With MobileMe Gallery, you can create and manage an online gallery of photos and movies that you can share with other people from any computer, iPhone, iPod touch, or Apple TV. If you have iLife 08 or Aperture 2 on your Mac, you can create and publish photos to MobileMe. You can use .JPG, .PNG, or .GIF photo formats and the .MOV movie format in your gallery. However, you cannot directly use RAW images; you need to use Aperture 2 or later. When you share a gallery with MobileMe, you can set options to allow visitors to upload or download photos, add photos via e-mail, or see photo titles or the Gallery e-mail address.

## Create a MobileMe Gallery

① Open your browser and sign onto your MobileMe account.

◆ You can access MobileMe log in at *www.mobileme.com*.

② Click the **Gallery** button.

③ To add a calendar, click the **Add** (+) button, type a name for the gallery, and then press Return.

④ Type a name for your album.

⑤ Select the check boxes you want to allow visitors to download photos, upload photos via the Web, or add photos via e-mail or iPhone.

⑥ Select the check boxes you want to show photo titles or the e-mail for uploading photos.

⑦ Select the Advanced options you want to hide the album or syncs with iPhoto or Aperture.

⑧ Click **Create**.

⑨ Click the **Upload** button, and then select the photos or video clips you want to add.

⑩ Click **Choose**, select the files that you want to add, and then click Select.

⑪ Click **Done**.

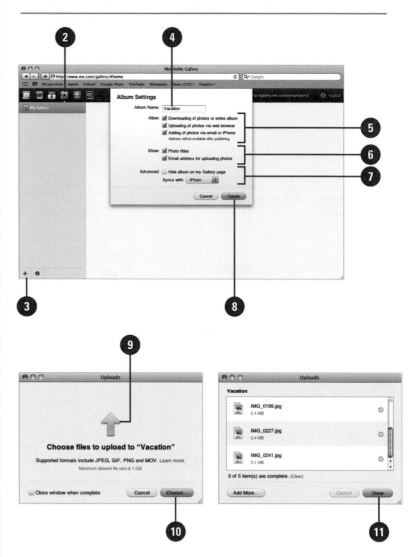

## Modify a MobileMe Gallery

1. Open your browser and sign onto your MobileMe account.

2. Click the **Gallery** button.

3. Click **My Gallery**, if necessary to display the available albums.

4. Double-click the album you want to edit.

   ◆ To quickly view the images in the album, move your pointer in the album thumbnail in My Gallery.

5. Edit the album using any of the following:

   ◆ **Edit Item Title.** Click the title, edit the text, and then press Return.

   ◆ **Arrange Items.** Drag the items to another position.

   ◆ **Delete Items.** Select the items, and then click the **Delete** button.

   ◆ **Rotate Items.** Select the items, and then click the **Rotate Clockwise** button.

   ◆ **Settings.** Click the **Setting** button, change the options you want, and then click **Publish**.

### Did You Know?

*You can add photos from your iPhone to a gallery.* In iPhone, setup a MobileMe account, select the photo you want in Camera or Photos, tap the Send Photo button, tap Send To MobileMe, tap the Gallery album to which you want to add a photo, type a title for the photo in the subject of the e-mail, and then tap the Send button.

# Viewing and Sharing a MobileMe Gallery

You can view your MobileMe gallery using a browser on your computer, either Mac or PC, iPhone, iPod touch, or on Apple TV. When you view a MobileMe gallery, you can change view options to display it as a grid, mosaic, carousel, or slideshow; select color options to change the background; or drag the Zoom slider to change the view size. Depending on your gallery settings, you can allows visitors to download the entire gallery or an individual photos or movies, subscribe to the RSS gallery feed, upload photos or movies, upload the gallery by mobile phone or e-mail, or send an e-mail with a link to this gallery. A blue dot in an album indicates an album change.

## View a MobileMe Gallery

1 Access a MobileMe gallery using any of the following methods:

◆ **Computer.** Open your browser (Mac or PC) and go to *http://gallery.me.com/member name*.

◆ **iPhone or iPod touch.** Open Safari, and then go to *http://gallery.me.com/member name*.

◆ **Apple TV.** Select **Photos** from the main menu, and then click **MobileMe**. Click **Add MobileMe Gallery**, and then type your MobileMe member name, and then select an album or movie to view it.

2 Click the album you want to view.

3 Use any of the following viewing options:

◆ **View.** Click **Grid**, **Mosaic**, or **Carousel** to view the album.

◆ **Color.** Click a color option to change the background.

◆ **Zoom.** Drag the **Zoom** slider to change the view percentage.

4 To view a slide show, click **Slideshow** to play a slide show, move your mouse to display playback controls, and then click buttons to pause, play, and exit full screen.

## Share a MobileMe Gallery

**①** Open your browser and go to *http://gallery.me.com/member name*.

**②** Click the album you want to view.

**③** Use any of the following options:

◆ **Download.** To download the entire gallery, deselect all items, click **Download**, click **Download**. To download a photo, click the photo, click the **Download** button.

◆ **Subscribe.** To open the feed for the selected album in your RSS feed reader, click **Subscribe**, and then click **OK**.

◆ **Upload.** To upload photos or movie, click **Upload**, type your name and address, type security characters, click **Choose Files**, select the files you want, and then click **Select**.

◆ **Send to Album.** To upload to the selected album by mobile phone or e-mail, send photos or movies to a Web address, click **Send to Album**, write down the Web address, and then click **OK**.

◆ **Tell a Friend.** To send an e-mail with a link to the selected album, click **Tell a Friend**, type your name, friend's e-mail address, and message, type security characters, and then click **Send**.

### Did You Know?

*You can add photos from your mobile phone to a gallery.* Send an e-mail with a photo attached to your gallery address. (*http://gallery.me.com/your membername*).

Download gallery or file

Upload files

Subscribe to RSS feed

Tell a Friend via e-mail

Send to Album

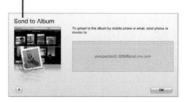

# Managing Files with iDisk

Probably one of the coolest, and most-used features of a MobileMe account is iDisk. The iDisk service is like having up to 20 GB hard drive available to you anytime and anywhere you can plug into the Internet. The iDisk is perfect for performing off-site backups, or for storing large files for later use. For example, you could place large files in your iDisk (files that are too big to e-mail), and then download them when you get to your destination. Or if you have a high-speed Internet connection, you could simply use it as a secondary storage device. In addition, if you need more room, you can always upgrade and purchase more space. The good news is that once iDisk is open, you can treat it just like any other storage device on your computer. In fact, the Public folder located in your iDisk can be accessed by anyone owning a MobileMe account. This is the perfect place for placing a document that needs to be distributed to co-workers, or as a place to store photos for other MobileMe users to see.

## Manage Files with iDisk

① Click the **Go** menu, point to **iDisk**, and then click **My iDisk** (it is not necessary to be logged into your MobileMe account.)

② If necessary, double-click on a folder to display its contents.

③ Drag items, files, or folders into any of the existing folders.

④ Click the **Close** button to close the iDisk window.

### Did You Know?

**You can't add folders to the iDisk window.** If you try to drag a folder from your hard drive directly into the iDisk window, you'll be told that you don't have sufficient privileges; however, if you drop the folder inside of one of the pre-existing folders, the operation is successful.

## Display Files from MobileMe iDisk

**①** Open your browser and sign on to your MobileMe account.

**②** Click the **iDisk** button.

- ◆ You can access the iDisk Home folder at *http://idisk.me.com/ membername*.

- ◆ You can access the iDisk Public folder at *http://public.me.com/ membername*. If prompted, type *public* for the user name, and then type the password.

The MobileMe iDisk window opens, displaying a file hierarchy of the iDisk hard disk online.

**③** Click the **Home** or **Public** folder, and then click folders to navigate to the location with the files you want to display from iDisk.

All the files you copied into the iDisk folders on your Mac now appear in MobileMe iDisk.

**④** To create a new folder, select a folder location, click the **Actions** button, click **New Folder**, type a name, and then press Return.

**⑤** To upload a file from your computer to iDisk (say from another computer), click the **Upload** button, click **Choose**, select the file, and then click **Select**.

**⑥** To download a file or folder to the Downloads folder on your computer, select the file or folder, click the **Downloads** buttons, and then click **Download**.

Home folder

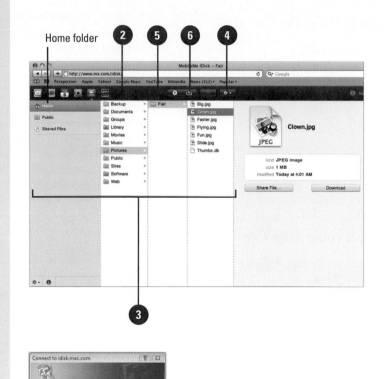

Access to Public folder

Public folder displayed on a PC in Windows

# Setting iDisk Preferences

If you're not connected to the Internet, you can create a local copy of your iDisk on your computer, so you can make changes to it at any time. The next time you connect to the Internet, the local changes you made on your computer are synchronized with your iDisk online. If you need more iDisk space online, you can add more space for iDisk and MobileMe mail storage. You can find out current iDisk storage usage information on the iDisk tab in MobileMe Preferences. If you change the size of your iDisk storage, your local iDisk storage is automatically changed. If you are away from your computer, you can access your iDisk public folder online. The Web address is *http://public.me.com/membername*. The public folder is available to anyone who knows how to access it unless you add password protection, which you can set in the MobileMe Preferences.

## Create a Local iDisk Copy

1. Click the **System Preferences** icon in the Dock, and then click the **MobileMe** icon.

2. Click the **iDisk** tab.

3. Click **Start**.

4. Click the **Update** pop-up, and then click **Automatically** or **Manually** to sync the content the next time you get online.

5. To stop the iDisk local sync, click **Stop**.

6. Click the **Close** button.

### Did You Know?

*You can access iDisk Public folder using Windows.* For Windows 7 or Vista, create a mapped drive to the following address: *http://public.me.com/membername*. For Windows XP, download the iDisk Utility for Windows at *www.apple.com/mobileme*.

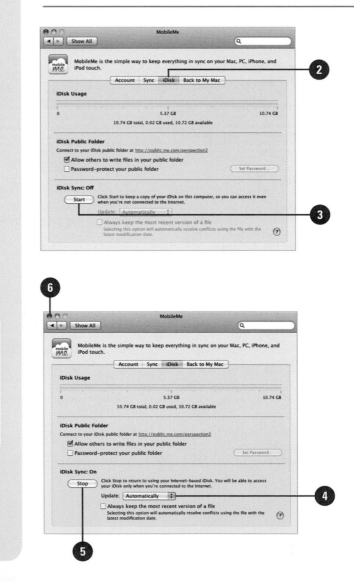

## Change iDisk Public Folder Permissions

1. Click the **System Preferences** icon in the Dock, and then click the **MobileMe** icon.

2. Click the **iDisk** tab.

3. Select the **Allow others to write files in your public folder** check box or clear it to allow read only access.

   If you selected the Read and Write option, it's important to set a password.

4. Select the **Password-protect your public folder** check box.

5. Type a password 6 to 8 characters, and then type it again to confirm it.

6. Click **OK**.

7. To change the password, click **Set Password**, type a new password, confirm it, and then click **OK**.

8. Click the **Close** button.

### Did You Know?

*You can connect to your iDisk public folder in MobileMe preferences.* Click the System Preferences icon in the Dock, click the MobileMe icon, click the iDisk tab, and then click the link to your iDisk public folder.

iDisk copy

Mounted copy of iDisk

# Sharing Files with MobileMe iDisk

MobileMe iDisk makes it easy to share files with other people. You can share files by using the Public folder or the Share File command. The Public folder in MobileMe iDisk is available to anyone who knows how to access it unless you add password protection, which you can set in the MobileMe preferences. You can access a public folder at *http://public.me.com/ membername*. If prompted, type *public* for the user name, and then type the password. You can share a folder or file by simply copying it to your Public folder on your Mac or in MobileMe iDisk. If you want to share a file to a specific person, you can use the Share File command to send an access link to the file via e-mail.

## Share Files from MobileMe iDisk Public Folder

1. Open your browser and sign on to your MobileMe account.

2. Click the **iDisk** button.

   ◆ You can access the iDisk Home folder at *http://idisk.me.com/ membername*.

3. To create a new folder, select a folder location in the Public folder, click the **Actions** button, click **New Folder**, type a name, and then press Return.

4. Drag folders or files to the Public folder on iDisk to copy them over.

5. To upload a file from your computer to iDisk, select the Public folder, click the **Upload** button, click **Choose**, select the file, and then click **Select**.

6. To rename a folder or file, click it, edit the name, and then press Return.

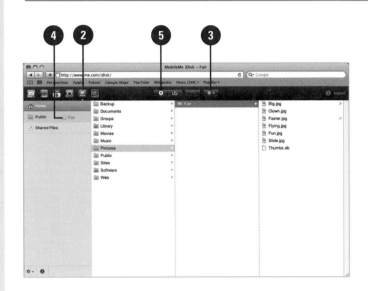

## Did You Know?

*You can compress files in MobileMe iDisk to save space.* In MobileMe, select a folder or file, click the Actions menu, click Compress *folder* or *file name*.

## Share Files from MobileMe iDisk via E-mail

1. Open your browser and sign on to your MobileMe account.

2. Click the **iDisk** button.

   ◆ You can access the iDisk Home folder at *http://idisk.me.com/membername*.

   ◆ You can access the iDisk Public folder at *http://public.me.com/membername*. If prompted, type *public* for the user name, and then type the password.

3. Click the **Home** or **Public** folder, and then click folders to navigate to display the files from iDisk you want to share.

4. Select the file you want to share.

5. Click **Share File**.

6. Type contact names or e-mail address, and a message.

7. To add an expiration date, select the **Link expires after X** check box, click the pop-up, and then select a duration.

8. To add a password, select the Password-protect file check box, and then type a password.

9. Click **Share**.

Icon indicates shared file

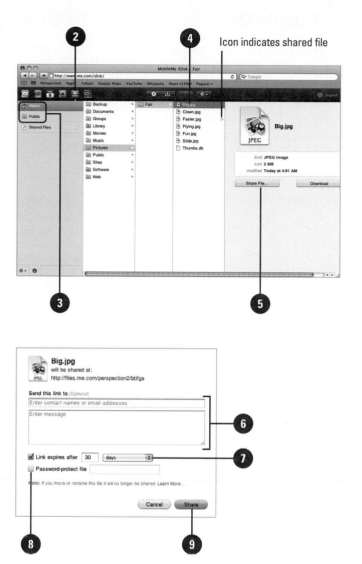

### Did You Know?

***You can check available iDisk storage space.*** In MobileMe, click the iDisk button, and then click the Info button (i) in the lower-left corner.

# Getting MobileMe Online Support

Having difficulty working with MobileMe? Not sure what to do. Don't worry, Apple's online support system is available to help you find answers to your nagging questions or contact a support representative. You can find answers by browsing through MobileMe help categories or frequently asked questions, or by performing a search. Apple's support system is constantly being updated to reflect the state of the current Macintosh software and hardware so finding the information you need isn't too far away.

## Get MobileMe Online Support

1. Open your browser and go to *www.apple.com/support/mobileme*.

2. If you want to find specific information, click in the Search Support field, type what you want, and then press Return.

3. Click the specific Help links for information on:
   - ◆ **Account & Billing.**
   - ◆ **MobileMe Mail.**
   - ◆ **Syncing with MobileMe.**
   - ◆ **MobileMe Contacts.**
   - ◆ **MobileMe Calendar.**
   - ◆ **iDisk.**
   - ◆ **Gallery.**
   - ◆ **Sites & iWeb.**
   - ◆ **Back to My Mac.**
   - ◆ **Backup & iChat.**

4. Click a link under Top Support Issues to find answers to the most frequently asked questions.

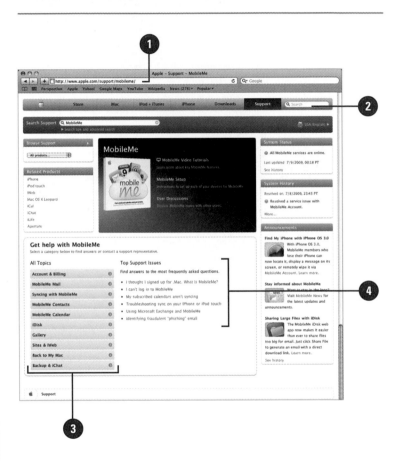

# Tracking and Synchronizing Information

## Introduction

Computers can indeed be a blessing and a curse. On the one hand they give you instant access to mountains of information; on the other hand you're the one who has to organize and keep track of all that data. There are a lot of programs out there that claim to help you stay organized, using everything from day-planner software to relational databases. There's only one problem, you have to actually use those programs. That typically means learning new third party software, loading all your data and schedules, and then trying to keep it current, even if you move it to a different computer. This paragraph defined the problem; the next provides the solution.

When Apple introduced OS X, they touted it as a **digital hub**. The concept of a digital hub involves placing your daily schedules and contact data into the system one time. Then the hub would keep the data up-to-date and in sync with any other places the same data is stored. With the release of OS X, and applications such as: iSync and iCal, the folks at Apple achieved the dream of creating a true, easy-to-use digital hub. I have a graveyard of applications that promised to organize and make my life easier. However, the programs were difficult to manage, and they didn't move information easily between systems. In short, the promise was not the reality. When Snow Leopard was released, along with improved versions of its syncing and management programs, I was finally able to get control of the mountains of information that make up my daily life.

## What You'll Do

View the iCal Window

Create a To Do List

Create and Work with Calendars

Add and Edit Calendar Events

Publish and Subscribe to a Calendar

Print Calendars and To Do Lists

Add Portable Devices to iSync

Set iSync Preferences

Set Device Synchronization Options

Set Up MobileMe Synchronization

Reset MobileMe Synchronization

Keep Track of Passwords with Keychain

Work with Keychains

Modify Keychains

Add Keychains

# Viewing the iCal Window

iCal is the Macintosh version of a scheduling and time-management application. There are other programs out there that schedules and manages your time; however, iCal's native architecture (built by Apple), it's stability, and ability to transfer and sync information easily across multiple applications, makes it an easy choice for the busy executive, the harried designer/animator, or anyone who owns a Macintosh, and wants to keep track of what they're doing. iCal assists you by helping you automate repetitive events such as: Yoga every Friday at 8pm, the kids soccer practice, or that quarterly conference call with management. In addition, iCal notifies you of an event by using an alarm sound, pop-up note, or even e-mail. iCal uses a new look user interface and iTunes style-style sidebar to make it easier to use. To access iCal, click the iCal icon in the Dock or open the Applications folder, and then double-click the iCal icon.

## Adding Calendar Accounts

If you use Google, Yahoo, and Gmail, calendars, iCal can automatically set them up (**New!**). Click the iCal menu, click Preferences, click Accounts, click the Add (+) button, enter your account e-mail address, and then click Create. iCal account assistance looks for any calendar accounts associated with the e-mail address. You can also add a calendar account for Exchange 2007 and CalDAV, however, you need to provide account details.

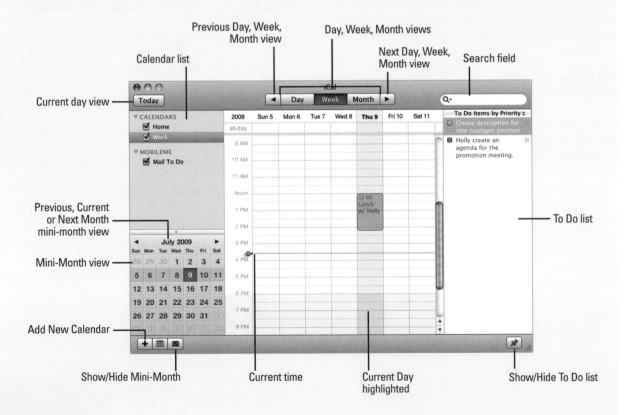

Previous Day, Week, Month view — Day, Week, Month views — Next Day, Week, Month view — Search field — Calendar list — Current day view — Previous, Current or Next Month mini-month view — Mini-Month view — Add New Calendar — Show/Hide Mini-Month — Current time — Current Day highlighted — To Do list — Show/Hide To Do list

# Creating a To Do List

Okay, you've created this awesome calendar that lists all of your appointments, plus things that you have to do (my wife calls this a honey do list). Not only does the iCal application let you create a To Do list, complete with every task on your list; it also helps you stay on schedule using audio or pop-up reminders. This is an easier solution than your wife tapping you on the shoulder, and asking you if you remembered to fix the screen on the back porch door.

## Create a To Do List

1. Click the **iCal** icon in the Dock.

2. Click the **Pushpin** button.

3. To add an event, double-click in the **To Do Items** pane, and then press Return.

4. Click the **Edit** menu, and then click **Get Info**.

5. Add or modify the following To Do information, and then click the **Close** button:

   ◆ **Completed**. Select the check box when the task is complete.

   ◆ **Priority**. Click to select a priority setting.

   ◆ **Due Date**. Select the check box, and then enter a due date.

   ◆ **Alarm**. If Due Date is checked, Alarm notifies using a Message, Message With A Sound, E-mail, or Open A File.

   ◆ **Calendar**. Click to select the calendar this list is linked to.

   ◆ **URL**. Click to add a URL address to the To Do.

   ◆ **Note**. Click to add any notes.

6. To sort To Dos, click the **To Do Items pane** pop-up, and then select a sort command.

7. To remove, select an item, and then press Delete.

8. Click the **Pushpin** button to close the To Do Items pane.

New To Do item

# Creating and Working with Calendars

With iCal, you can keep track of all your activities, either work or personal. You can create separate calendars for different people, such as your family, or a team, or different types of activities. Separating your calendars makes it easy to focus on the information for a specific activity and share only that calendar with the people you want. You can also group related calendars together to make it easier to manage. iCal is not just a standard, one-size-fits-all calendar. As a matter of fact, you can customize the calendar to fit your particular needs. iCal gives you the ability to change how the calendar displays days and weeks, and months. In addition, you can instruct iCal when to delete old events and To Do items, and even turn off alarms and time zone support.

## Create and Work Calendars

1. Click the **iCal** icon in the Dock.

2. To add a calendar, click the **Add** (+) button, type a name for the calendar, and then press Return.

3. Use the following buttons to navigate a calendar:

   ◆ **Today.** Click to display the current day.

   ◆ **Day, Week, and Month.** Click to display a day, week, or month at a glance. Use the Left or Right Arrows to move by the selected view.

   ◆ **Mini-Month.** Click a day or use the Left or Right Arrows. Click the **Show/Hide Mini-Month** button to show or hide the mini-month calendar.

4. Use the following to work with calendars:

   ◆ **Rename.** Click the calendar name, click it again, type a new name, and then press Return.

   ◆ **Delete.** Control-click the calendar, and then click **Delete**.

   ◆ **Color.** Control-click the calendar, click **Show Info**, change the color, and then click **OK**.

New calendar

Show/Hide Mini-Month button

Change color

Show Info dialog

## Create a Calendar Group

1. Click the **File** menu, and then click **New Calendar Group**.

   **TIMESAVER** *Hold down the Shift key, and then click the Add (+) button to create a calendar group.*

2. Type a name for the group, and then press Return.

3. Drag existing calendars into the group or click the **Add** (+) button to create a new calendar.

4. To remove a calendar from the group, drag it out of the list.

## Change iCal Preferences

1. Click the **iCal** menu, and then click **Preferences**.

2. Click **General**.

3. Select from the following iCal preferences:

   ◆ **Day and Week Defaults.** Use the pop-ups to specify defaults.

   ◆ **Show Time and Birthdays Calendar.** Select to show time in month view and the birthdays calendar.

   ◆ **Default Alarm.** Select to add a default alarm to all new events and invitations.

   ◆ **Synchronize with MobileMe.** Select to sync calendars with MobileMe. Click **MobileMe** to specify settings.

4. Click **Advanced**, and then select to options you want to enable.

5. Click the **Close** button.

# Adding and Editing Calendar Events

When you first create your iCal calendar, it represents where you are with your schedule at that moment in time. Unfortunately, things change and they can change often. Therefore, iCal gives you the ability to add new events or modify existing events directly in the Calendar window. The beauty of iCal is that it makes calendar modifications easy, and once complete, they can be transferred to other applications and devices. If you need detailed information for multiple events, you don't have to edit each one, you can use the Inspector window (**New!**) to display you what you need by simply clicking it.

## Add or Edit Calendar Events

① Click the **iCal** icon in the Dock.

② Click the calendar you want to add an event.

③ Click a view button to find the date to add.

④ Drag a time interval on the day you want to add an event.

⑤ Type a title for the event.

⑥ To adjust the time and day, use the following options:

◆ **Adjust Event Time.** Drag the top or bottom edge of the event item.

◆ **Move Event Day.** Drag the title to a new location.

## Did You Know?

*You can quickly delete an iCal event.* In iCal, select the event you want to delete, and then press Delete.

*You can export or import events.* To export as a .ICS file, click the File menu, point to Export, click Export, type a name, specify a location, and then click Export. To import a .ICS file, click the File menu, click Import, select an import option (iCal, vCal, or Entourage data), click Import, select the file, and then click Import.

---

### For Your Information

## Working with Attachments for an Event

If you have an attachment you want to include with an event, you can quickly attach it by dragging it to the event in the iCal window just like a drop box. When you send e-mail invitations to your attendees, the attachments go along with it. While you edit an event, you can also preview an attachment. Simply select it in the Edit dialog, and then press the Space bar. Click the Close button to exit it. To delete an attachment, select it, and then press Delete.

## Show or Edit Calendar Events Details

1. Click the **iCal** icon in the Dock.

2. To show event details, click the **Edit** menu, click **Show Inspector**, and then click an event.

3. Double-click the event you want to edit.

4. Click **Edit**.

5. Add the following event options:

   - ◆ **Location.** Enter a location for the event.
   - ◆ **All-day.** Check for all day event.
   - ◆ **From/To.** Enter a From/To date.
   - ◆ **Repeat.** Sets this to a repeating event.
   - ◆ **Calendar.** Click to select the calendar this event is linked.
   - ◆ **Alarm.** Lets you be notified before the event.
   - ◆ **Attendees.** Adds attendees to the event list.
   - ◆ **Attachments.** Adds file attachments to the event.
   - ◆ **URL.** Click to add a URL address to the event.
   - ◆ **Note.** Click to add any notes.

6. Click **Done**.

## Did You Know?

***You can back up or import calendars.***
To backup all your calendars, click the File menu, point to Export, click iCal Archive, type a name, select a location, and then click Save. To import all your calendars, click the File menu, point to Import, click Import, select the backup file, and then click Import.

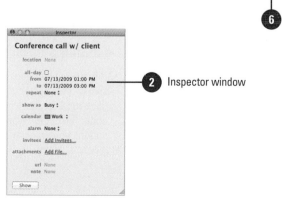

② Inspector window

# Publishing and Subscribing to a Calendar

You can create a calendar that lists all of your appointments with detailed information and a To Do list that helps you keep track of everything from household chores to the research you need to do for next week's big funding conference. But what good is that information, if you're out of town, and you forgot to bring your trusty MacBook? By publishing your iCal calendar, you wouldn't have a problem. If you have a MobileMe account or a CalDAV workplace calendar server, publishing your calendar gives you access to that information anywhere there's a computer and an Internet connection. With CalDAV, you can also check the availability of people and resources. In addition, if someone else has published a calendar, you can gain access to it by subscribing. Not only does this give you access to your calendar, but any one that requires your scheduling information.

## Publish a Calendar

1. Click the **iCal** icon in the Dock.

2. Select a calendar to publish.

3. Click the **Calendar** menu, and then click **Publish**.

4. Type a name for the calendar.

5. Click the **Publish on** pop-up, and then select a server location, such as MobileMe or CalDAV.

6. Select from the following options:

   ◆ **Publish changes automatically**

   ◆ **Publish titles and notes**

   ◆ **Publish To Do items**

   ◆ **Publish alarms**

   ◆ **Publish attachments**

7. Click **Publish**.

8. Write down the URL as it appears. This is very important if you want to view your calendar or allow someone else to subscribe to it.

9. Click **Visit Page**, **Send Mail** or **OK** in the confirmation message.

10. To unpublish a calendar, select it, click the **Calendar** menu, click **Unpublish**, and then click **Unpublish**.

## Subscribe to a Calendar

1. Click the **iCal** icon in the Dock.

2. Click the **Calendar** menu, and then click **Subscribe**.

3. Type the URL full path name to the calendar with an ICS extension. You need to get the exact URL to the calendar from the person who published it.

4. Click **Subscribe**.

5. Select from the following options:

   ◆ **Name and Description**. Type a name and description for the calendar subscription.

   ◆ **Remove Alarms, Attachments, or To Do items**. Check to remove any of the items.

   ◆ **Auto-refresh**. Select to update the calendar, and then select how often the update occurs.

6. Click **OK**.

7. To unsubscribe to a calendar, Control-click the calendar you want to remove in the Calendar list, and then click **Delete**.

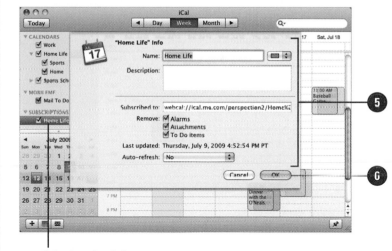

Calendar subscription

# Printing Calendars and To Do Lists

Just like you can print documents and photographs, you can also print any of your calendars and To Do lists. iCal gives you the flexibility to specify the calendars you want to print and the related details you want to include, such as To Do items with due dates, all-day events, mini-months (next and previous calendar months in the upper right corner of the page), and calendar keys (a print legend).

## Print Calendars and To Do Lists

1. Click the **iCal** icon in the Dock.

2. Click the **File** menu, and then click **Print**.

3. Click the **View** pop-up, and then select the print layout you want.

4. Use the **Starts** and **Ends** pop-up to specify the date range you want.

5. Select the check boxes next to the calendars you want to print.

   If you select a calendar group, all the calendars are included.

6. Specify any other print options you want.

   ◆ **All-Day Events.** Includes all day events.

   ◆ **To Do items with Due Dates.** Includes To Do items with due dates.

   ◆ **Mini-Months.** Includes the next and previous months.

   ◆ **Calendar Keys.** Includes a calendar legend.

   ◆ **Black and White.** Prints in black and white.

7. Click the **Text size** pop-up, and then select a text size for event headings.

8. Click **Continue**.

9. Select a printer and any print presets, and then click **Print**.

# Adding Portable Devices to iSync

When you have a contact and calendar list on multiple devices, such as your Mac computer and a mobile device, it's hard to keep them both up-to-date. Not any more. Apple gives you the iSync application to help you keep your contact and calendar information on your computer in Address Book and iCal up-to-date with the contact and calendar information on your other devices, such as an iSync-compatible Bluetooth, or USB mobile phone. The iSync application makes it easy to update all your devices in one place with the click of a button.

## Add Portable Devices to iSync

1. Plug-in an iSync compatible device.

   **IMPORTANT** *To find out if your device is compatible, point your browser to www.apple.com/isync /devices.html.*

2. Click the **Applications** folder in the Dock, and then click the **iSync** icon.

3. Click the **Devices** menu, and then click **Add Device**.

4. Double click on the device to add it to the iSync application.

5. Click the **Scan** button to scan for more devices.

6. Close the Add Device window.

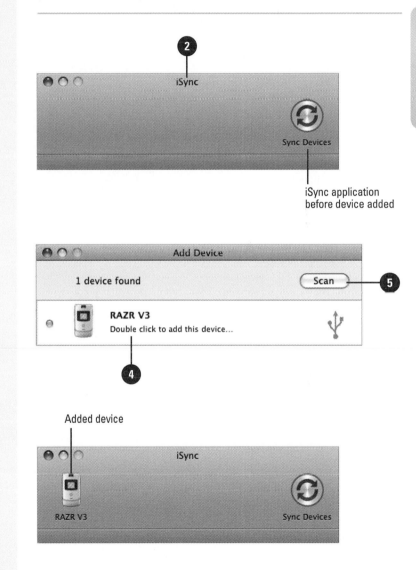

iSync application before device added

Added device

## Did You Know?

*You don't have to synchronize all your devices.* Click on the individual devices and temporarily turn off synchronizing. Remember to turn it back on.

*You can remove a device from iSync.* Select the device in the iSync window, click the Devices menu, and then click Remove Device.

*You can reset the information on a device.* Select the device in the iSync window, click the Devices menu, and then click Reset *Device Name*.

# Setting Device Synchronization Options

When you add devices such as a cell phone or a PDA, each item has its own unique set of synchronization options. Once you've added the device, it's important to open the options, and decide exactly what you want to happen, when you click the Sync Now button. For example, you own a PDA, and you want the PDA to sync with your iCal calendar, but with your contacts. Device Synchronization options give you the control to decide exactly what does and does not sync.

## Set Device Synchronization Options

1. Click the **Applications** folder in the Dock, and then click the **iSync** icon.

2. Click the button of the device that you want to modify.

3. Select from the following options:

   ◆ **Turn on Synchronization**. Activates synchronization (default: checked).

   ◆ **Automatically Synchronize**. Most devices give you the option to synchronize the device when it's first plugged in, or after a certain amount of time (default: unchecked).

   ◆ **Contacts**. Synchronizes all the contacts on the device (default: on).

   ◆ **Calendars**. Synchronizes all the calendars on the device (default: on).

4. Click the device button to collapse the Options panel.

5. Click the **Sync Now** button to perform the sync operation.

Sync Alert to synchronize the device

# Setting iSync Preferences

When you synchronize your computer with devices using iSync or a MobileMe account, the Data Change Alert appears, displaying the information you want to add, remove, or modify, and asking you to confirm the change. You can cancel or allow the synchronization. The Data Change Alert appears when you enable it and when a specified amount of data on your computer will change. You can set iSync Preferences to specify when you want the Data Change Alert to appear as well as other syncing options.

## Set iSync Preferences

1. Click the **Applications** folder in the Dock, and then click the **iSync** icon.

2. Click the **iSync** menu, and then click **Preferences**.

3. Select from the following iSync preferences:

   ◆ **Enable syncing on this computer.** Select to enable syncing with your MobileMe account. This option enables the Synchronize With MobileMe option in MobileMe Preferences.

   ◆ **Show status in menu.** Select to show the iSync Status menu in the menu bar.

   ◆ **Show Data Change Alert when.** Select to display the Data Change Alert, and then specify the amount of change needed to display the alert.

4. To clear the sync log, click **Reset Sync History**.

5. Click the **Close** button.

# Setting Up MobileMe Synchronization

If you've setup a MobileMe account, then you'll want to keep your off-site information up-to-date. You'll accomplish this by setting sync options on the MobileMe pane in System Preferences. You can specify exactly what you want updated, and even let your Macintosh perform automatic updates. You can sync any of the following items on your computer: Bookmarks, Calendars, Contacts, Dashboard Widgets, Dock Items, Keychains, Mail Accounts, Mail Rules, Signatures, and Smart Mailboxes, Notes, and System Preferences. When you synchronize the information on your computer with your MobileMe account online, you can access it from any Mac, which you can also synchronize.

## Set Up MobileMe Synchronization

1. Click the **System Preferences** icon in the Dock, and then click the **MobileMe** icon.

2. Click the **Sync** tab.

3. Select or clear the **Synchronize with MobileMe** check box.

4. Click the **Synchronize with MobileMe** pop-up, and then select one of the following sync options:

   ◆ **Automatically.** Sync selected items when you make changes and connect to the Internet.

   ◆ **Every Hour, Day, or Week.** Sync selected items when you make changes at the specified interval.

   ◆ **Manually.** Sync selected items when you make changes and click **Sync Now**.

5. Select the check boxes next to the items you want to synchronize.

6. To use the MobileMe Sync menu in the menu bar, select the **Show status in menu bar** check box.

7. To manually sync the selected items, click **Sync Now**.

   ◆ Your can also select the **Sync Now** command on the MobileMe Sync menu.

8. Click the **Close** button.

# Resetting MobileMe Synchronization

If you're having problems synchronizing information or you're not sure whether you want to keep all the changes you have made, you can reset the information on your computer to match the information on your MobileMe account. You can select the information you want to reset, including bookmarks, calendars, contacts, dashboard widgets, dock items, keychains, Mail accounts and rules, notes, and system preferences. When you reset data, Snow Leopard erases all the information on the destination device with the information on the source, so make sure this operation is what you want to do.

## Reset MobileMe Synchronization

1. Click the **System Preferences** icon in the Dock, and then click the **MobileMe** icon.

2. Click the **Sync** tab.

3. Click **Advanced**.

4. Select the computer you want to reset sync information.

5. Click **Reset Sync Data**.

6. Click the **Replace** pop-up, and then click **All Sync Info** or select a specific item.

7. Select the Left or Right Arrow to specify the direction you want to replace. Left updates your Mac with MobileMe information and Right updates your MobileMe account with your Mac information.

8. Click **Replace**.

9. Click **OK** to confirm the replacement.

10. Click the **Close** button.

# Keeping Track of Passwords with Keychain

The computer is a fantastic tool, however, the birth of the computer brought along another necessary evil, the creation of passwords. You have passwords for the Internet, FTP sites, login, and your MobileMe site. Passwords, passwords, and more passwords, they multiply like rabbits. Even cars and homes have password entrance systems (called keyless entry). The solution to the problem is to create keychains.

Apple's Keychain works in the background; every time you type your login password, you're typing in the master key, and Keychain responds by filling in all the passwords blanks from that point forward. Since Keychain functions in the background, it's invisible to most users. If Keychain were not available, every time you moved around the Internet, or accessed a hard drive, or almost any device, you would be required to type in the proper password.

If you need to make changes to individual keychains, you can use the Keychain Access utility application, which is located in the Utilities folder within the Applications folder.

Keychains and certificates

Categories

Passwords

# Working with Keychains

When you open Keychain Access, you'll probably already have a list of keychains. If you don't see any keychains, you can use commands on the View menu to view and organize your keychains. With keychains in view, you can unlock and lock access to them, delete them, and add secure notes. If you receive a digital certificate from the Internet, you can add it to your keychain for easier access next time. A **digital certificate** validates users and Web sites on the Internet for credibility.

## Work with Keychains

◆ **Show/Hide Keychains.** Click the **View** menu, and then click **Show Keychains** or **Hide Keychains**.

◆ **Unlock Keychain Access.** Select the keychain (such as login or System), click the **Lock** icon, type your password, and then click **OK**.

◆ **Lock Keychain Access.** Select the keychain (such as login or System), and then click the **Unlock** icon.

   To change the password for Keychain access, click the **Edit** menu, and then click **Change Password for Keychain** *name*.

◆ **Delete Keychain Access.** Select the keychain (such as login or System), click the **File** menu, click **Delete Keychain** *name*, and then click **Delete References & Files** or **Delete References.**

◆ **Add a Secure Note.** Click the **File** menu, click **New Secure Note Item**, type a keychain name, type the note, and then click **Add**.

◆ **Change Default Keychain.** Select a new keychain, click the **File** menu, and then click **Make Keychain** *name* **Default**.

◆ **Remove a Keychain.** Select a keychain, press Delete, and then click **Delete**.

◆ **Add a Certificate to a Keychain.** Drag the certificate file onto the Keychain Access icon or double-click the certificate file, select a keychain, and then click **OK**.

Unlocked keychain        Keychain description

Certificates        Secure Notes

# Modifying Keychains

The Keychain Access application gives you the ability to modify the elements within a keychain. For example, you could add an additional level of password protection, or insert a secure note. It would even be possible to delete or change the parameters of an existing element within the keychain. Since your Macintosh manages the keychain quite well in the background, it just depends on how much control you wish to exert over the Keychain already setup by your computer.

## Modify Keychains

1. Open the **Utilities** folder, and then double-click the **Keychain Access** icon.

2. Click the **View** menu, click **Show Keychains**, and then select the keychain you want to manage.

3. Double-click a keychain password from the list.

4. Click the **Attributes** tab.

5. Select from the following options:

   ◆ **Name**. Type a new name for the keychain item.

   ◆ **Kind**. Type a new kind such as a MobileMe password or an Internet Connect.

   ◆ **Account**. Type a new account name for the keychain item.

   ◆ **Where**. Type a new location for the keychain item.

   ◆ **Comments**. Type any comments into the comments field.

6. Select or clear the **Show password** check box to show the password for this keychain item.

7. Click **Save Changes**.

**8** Click the **Access Control** tab.

**9** Select from the following options:

- **Allow all applications To access this item**. When selected, this item is not restricted.

- **Confirm before allowing access**. When selected, users have to click through to get to the item.

- **Ask for keychain password**. Select or clear the check box to require users to type the keychain password.

  **IMPORTANT** *When you click the check box to show the keychain items password, you'll first be prompted for the keychain's master password.*

**10** To add specific applications, click **Add** (+) button, and then select the applications.

**11** To remove specific applications, click the application, and then click the **Remove** (-) button.

**12** Click **Save Changes** to record your changes to the active keychain.

# Adding Keychains

Although the Keychain application runs in the background, and is therefore invisible to most Mac users, you have the ability to add additional keychains to the current set. To do this you'll need detailed information on the keychain that you want to add, and an application to perform the addition. In your Utilities folder is a program called Keychain Access. This program allows you to add addition keychains to the existing set. For example, you might want a keychain to manage your computer (default keychain), and another keychain to manage and secure your business documents. Since the keychain application allows you to modify existing elements within a keychain, you could easily wind up locking yourself out of devices or Web sites. Caution is advised when accessing the Keychain Access application.

## Add a Keychain and Password

1. Open the **Utilities** folder, and then double-click the **Keychain Access** icon.

2. Click the **File** menu, and then click **New Keychain**.

3. Type a keychain access name, and then select a save location.

4. Click **Create**.

5. Type a password for the keychain, verify it, and then click **OK**.

6. Click the **File** menu, and then click **New Password Item**.

7. Type the keychain name or URL for easy reference, an account name, and password.

    **NOTE** *Keychain passwords are case sensitive. Click the Show Typing check box to make sure your password is accurate.*

8. Click **Add**, type a password, and then click **OK**.

    **IMPORTANT** *Keychains store all of their information as encrypted data, and the password is part of the cipher that restores the information. If you forget your password, there is nothing you can do to restore the information.*

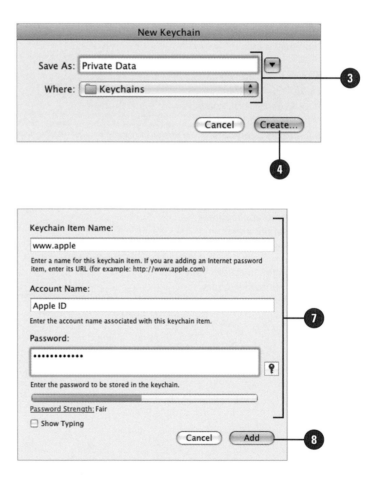

# Setting Up Accounts and Maintaining Security

## 15

## Introduction

Mac OS X was designed from the ground up for sharing, and it really doesn't matter what you want to share. For example, you might want to set up a simple home-based network to share files between family members, or even hook your Macintosh into a major network using a combination of Windows, Unix, and Mac machines. In Chapter 16, "Managing Files Using a Network," you'll learn how to set up a functional network using a variety of methods; however in this chapter you'll learn how to create user accounts, manage those accounts, and even protect your information from being accessed by unauthorized individuals, using Snow Leopard's File Vault application. In addition, Snow Leopard lets multiple users log in and switch between accounts with the click of a button.

Correctly setting up user accounts is important to the security of your computer, so each account is assigned its own name, and individual password. Take care when setting up accounts that you don't give the user more privileges (access) than needed to perform their job. Also, when setting up accounts and passwords, make sure to be accurate in your typing of passwords. Passwords are case-sensitive, and if forgotten, data can be lost forever. When setting up accounts, you can have shared files that can be available for all users on your computer or network.

## What You'll Do

**Understand User Accounts**

**Activate the Login Window**

**Add a User Account**

**Delete a User Account**

**Set File Access Permissions**

**Set Account Access Privileges**

**Set Account Parental Controls**

**Specify Log In and Start Up Items**

**Set Fast User Switching**

**Set System Security Preferences**

**Restore the Administrator Password**

**Manage Files with the Home Folder**

**Protect the Home Folder with FileVault**

**Share Files with Other Users**

# Understanding User Accounts

When Macs were new, they didn't share very well; however, a lot has changed since then. OS X was designed for multi-users, and Snow Leopard has continued that tradition with the inclusion of easy user swapping and tighter file security. Think of a user account as a file drawer within a large file cabinet. A specific individual owns each file drawer, and they have access to that drawer through a unique key. That key gives them access to the contents of their drawer, and no other. Controlling the file cabinet is one person, who has a master key that gives her access to all of the file drawers; including her own. Individuals can do anything they please within their own drawer; including throwing away or adding files, but they can't access the other drawers. A User Account is a file drawer that holds all of the user's folders, files, applications; anything they select to add or subtract from their account.

The interesting thing is that on a Mac, the user account is more than just a file drawer; it's the whole user environment. Users create their own world—including desktop, fonts, and folders. For example, one user logs in and sees a background picture of her dog, while another user, logging in on the same computer, has a background of a beach in the Bahamas. In addition, users are assigned privileges that define where they can go, and what they can access. Let's say one user has access to the accounting system; including all the applications and files, and another user is locked out; all determined by the Administrator. The Administrator holds all the keys to all the accounts; they're the ones that set up the other user accounts and decide who can do what. If you're the owner of the computer, you're the Administrator. It's up to you to decide who does what on your computer.

Individual users

Main hard drive

Users folder

Folder contents

# Activating the Login Window

When you turn on your Macintosh for the first time, it's set up for instant access. You were asked during the initial setup to name your computer and assign a password. By default, the password protection system is not activated, so the next time you start up your Macintosh, you are granted access without having to select your account and type in your password. Before setting up User Accounts, it's a good idea to first activate password login, and then set up any additional accounts. When active, the login window appears every time you start up your computer and contains a list of all those with valid user accounts.

## Activate the Login Window

1. Click the **System Preferences** icon in the Dock, and then click the **Accounts** icon.

2. If the screen is locked, click the **Lock** icon, type your password, and then click **OK**.

3. Click **Login Options**.

4. Click the **Automatic login** pop-up, and then select **Disabled** or a user.

    When you select a user, your computer automatically starts with this user account.

5. Click the **List of users** or **Name and password** options.

6. Select or clear the following settings to show options in the Login window:

    ◆ **Show the Restart, Sleep, and Shut Down buttons.**

    ◆ **Show Input Menu in login window.**

    ◆ **Show password hints.**

7. Select or clear the **Use VoiceOver at login window** check box.

8. Select the **Show fast user switching menu as** check box if there is more than one user, and then use the pop-up to select a view.

9. Click the **Close** button.

# Adding a User Account

Setting up user accounts involves careful consideration as to who is this person, and what they'll be able to access and do on the computer. Mac OS X makes the process of setting up accounts easy; but don't let the ease fool you into thinking it's unsecured. Mac OS X creates a tight wall of protection around each account. When you create a standard account, the security settings are set to their default values. Which means the account user has access to their own personal Home folder, and they are able to access applications on the hard drive. They don't have access to any other account, nor are they able to modify or delete any files or applications on the hard drive.

## Add a User Account

1. Click the **System Preferences** icon in the Dock, and then click the **Accounts** icon.

2. Click the **New Account** pop-up, and then select an account type.

3. Click the **Add** (+) button.

4. Type a name for the new account, and then type a Short Name for the Account (used by the server).

   **IMPORTANT** *The Short Name cannot contain any spaces and is case sensitive. System administrators in the corporate world typically come up with a naming convention so that all the users are set up in a consistent way. For example, Steve Johnson might be SteveJ to the server.*

5. Type and verify the password for the account.

6. Type a Hint for the password (optional).

7. Click **Create Account**.

8. Click the picture icon, and then select a picture for the account, or drag a picture file from a window or the desktop.

9. Click the **Close** button.

   The Account has been added.

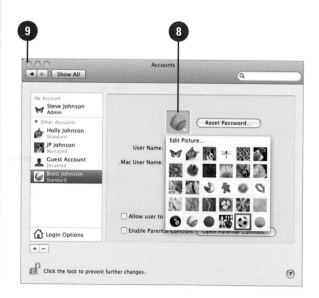

# Deleting a User Account

Things change quickly in the computer world; an account for an employee that was valid a week ago is now invalid due to the employee quitting. Deleting user accounts is easy, and if planned correctly does not mean that the user's data and files are deleted. You can specify to hold all of the deleted account information in a temporary holding area; where it can be accessed for as long as necessary.

## Delete a User Account

1. Click the **System Preferences** icon in the Dock, and then click the **Accounts** icon.

2. Select an account from the available users.

3. Click the **Delete** (-) button.

4. Select from the following options:

   ◆ **Save the home folder in a disk image**. Click to save the home if you want the user back later.

   ◆ **Do not change the home folder**. Click to deactivate the account and keep the home folder.

   ◆ **Delete the home folder**. Permanently delete the home folder.

5. Click **OK**.

6. Type your password, and then click **OK** to delete the account.

7. Click the **Close** button.

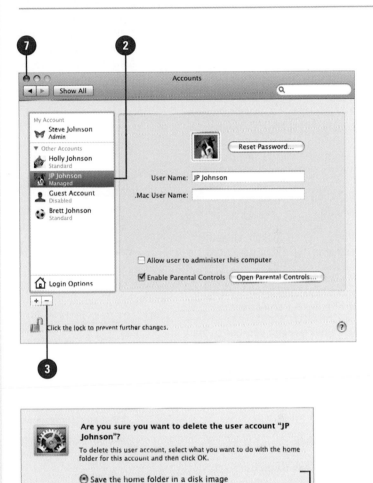

# Setting File Access Permissions

As the Administrator, you have one additional area where you can control what users have access to is the File Info. The **File Info** window lets you, as the Administrator, decide who has access to which files and folders on your computer. For example, you could create a folder on the hard drive and give every user account access, or you could select one file within that folder and restrict access. In fact, you can give users the ability to read a file, but not modify, or let them read and modify the file. Since handling individual files would be a bit time consuming (computers typically hold thousands of files), your Macintosh helps out by assuming users do not have access to the hard drive's files and folders (it's up to you to give them access), and you can apply general access settings to all the files and folders nested within a folder (this saves you time).

## Set File Permissions

1. Open the hard drive and then select a folder, application, or file.

2. Click the **File** menu, and then click **Get Info**.

3. If the screen is locked, click the **Lock** icon, type your password, and then click **OK**.

4. Click the expand button (triangle) for Sharing & Permissions.

5. Click the **Privilege** pop-ups to the right of system, admin, and everyone, and then select what type of access you want assigned to the selected item.

   - **Read & Write**

   - **Read Only**

   - **Write Only (Drop Box)**

   - **No Access**

6. Click the **Close** button.

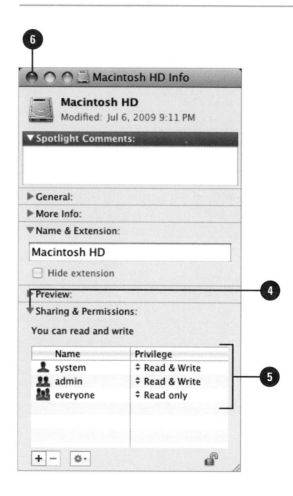

# Setting Account Access Privileges

Once you have set up a user account, it's up to you to decide exactly what that particular user can and cannot have access to. For example, you might create a user account for a graphic designer and give them access to all the design applications such as Adobe Photoshop and Illustrator; however, you don't want them messing around with the accounting programs, so you deny access to those specific applications. Once the access privileges are set for an account, they can be changed at a later date, but the Administrator is the only person authorized to change them.

## Set Account Access Privileges

1. Click the **System Preferences** icon in the Dock, and then click the **Parental Controls** icon.

2. Select the account you want to modify.

3. Click **Enable Parental Controls**, if necessary.

4. Click the **System** tab.

5. Select the **Only allow selected applications** check box, and then select the check boxes for the application you want this user to access.

6. Select to restrict the user's ability to perform certain functions such as **Can administer printers**, **Can change password**, **Can burn CDs or DVDs**, or **Can modify the Dock**.

7. Click the **Close** button.

> ### See Also
> See "Using Simple Finder" on page 94 for information on limiting the available items in the Finder. Great for kids!

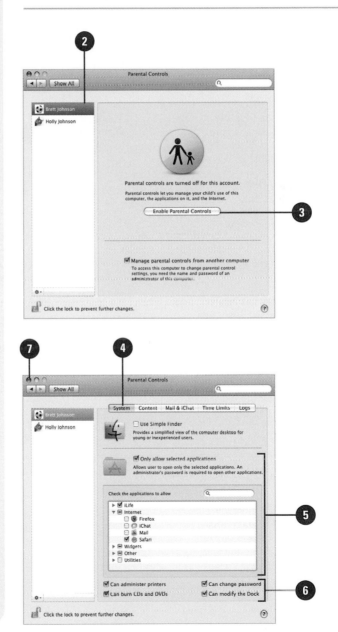

# Setting Account Parental Controls

After you have set up a user account as the Administrator, you can enable and set parental controls. Parental Controls help you manage how your children use the computer. Parental Controls allows you to set limits on your children's Web access, Mail and iChat usage, the amount of time spent logged on the computer, and which games and programs they can use. You can set different settings for each user account on your computer, so you can adjust the level you want for each child. You can also review activity reports on a periodic basis to see what your children are doing on the computer.

## Set Account Content Controls

1. Click the **System Preferences** icon in the Dock, and then click the **Parental Controls** icon.

2. Select the account you want to modify, and then click **Enable Parental Controls**, if necessary.

3. Click the **Content** tab.

4. Select or clear the **Hide profanity in Dictionary** check box.

5. Select one of the following options:

   ◆ **Allow unrestricted access to websites.**

   ◆ **Try to limit access to adult websites automatically.** Click **Customize** to specify sites.

   ◆ **Allow access to only these websites.** Click the **Add** (+) and **Remove** (-) buttons to add and delete items from the allowable Web site list.

6. Click the **Close** button.

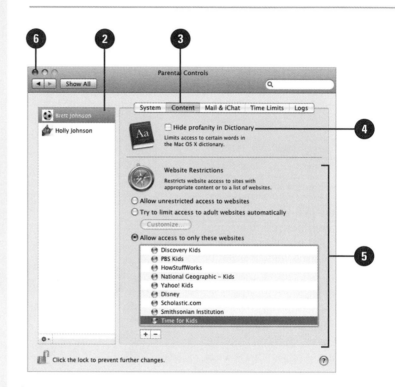

## Did You Know?

*You can view user account log activity.* In Parental Controls Preferences, click the Logs tab, use the pop-ups to show activity for a certain period and group the results, select a log collection and log, and then click Open.

## Set Mail and iChat Controls

1. Click the **System Preferences** icon in the Dock, and then click the **Parental Controls** icon.

2. Select the account you want to modify, and then click **Enable Parental Controls**, if necessary.

3. Click the **Mail & iChat** tab.

4. Select or clear the **Limit Mail** and **Limit iChat** check boxes.

5. Click the **Add** (+) and **Remove** (-) buttons to add and delete addresses from the allowable list.

6. Select the **Send permission requests to** check box, and then type an e-mail address.

7. Click the **Close** button.

## Set Time Limits

1. Click the **System Preferences** icon in the Dock, and then click the **Parental Controls** icon.

2. Select the account you want to modify, and then click **Enable Parental Controls**, if necessary.

3. Click the **Time Limits** tab.

4. Specify options for the following time limits:

    ◆ **Weekday time limits.**

    ◆ **Weekend time limits.**

    ◆ **Bedtime.**

5. Click the **Close** button.

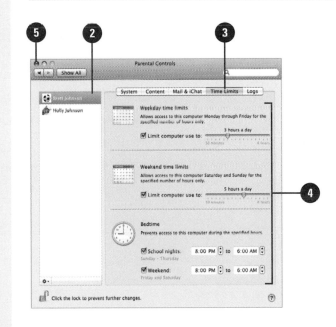

# Specifying Log In and Start Up Items

When you first turn on your computer, it begins by access the operating system and performing a standard start up. A normal start up involves performing a system check, and then if login is activated, opening the login window and requiring you to select your account and type in your password. At that point, Mac OS X opens your desktop and it's off to work. However, there is a way that you can alter the start up procedure, by specifying Start Up, and/or Log In items. **Start Up items** are applications or scripts that you decide to launch every time your computer is turned on. **Log In items** are specified by individual users, and launch whenever their account is accessed. For example, you might have a Start Up item (a script) that accesses the company network. In addition, you have a Log In item (a file) that launches your personal day planner, when you log in. The network script launches each time the computer is turned on, but the day planner only launches when you log in to your account. The individuals who own accounts on your computer set up log in items. In fact, log in items are one of the few things the Administrator cannot do—the user must set them up.

## Work with Log In Items

1. Click the **System Preferences** icon in the Dock, and then click the **Accounts** icon.

2. Select your account (Administrator only).

3. Click the **Login Items** tab.

4. Click the **Add** (+) button to locate a particular application or file you want opened every time you log in.

5. If necessary, click the **Remove** (-) button to remove an item from the startup list.

6. Select the **Hide** check box to open the application or file but hide it until you're ready to work.

7. Click the **Close** button.

   **TIMESAVER** *To see a list of all hidden applications or files, press* ⌘+Tab. *You'll see a list of all open applications. Continue to press A, and then press Tab to move through and select any hidden application.*

Adds or Deletes an account.

## Work with Start Up Items

① Double-click the **System** folder to open it.

② Open the Startup Items folder.

③ Add items to the folder by dragging and dropping.

④ Remove items by dragging them out of the folder.

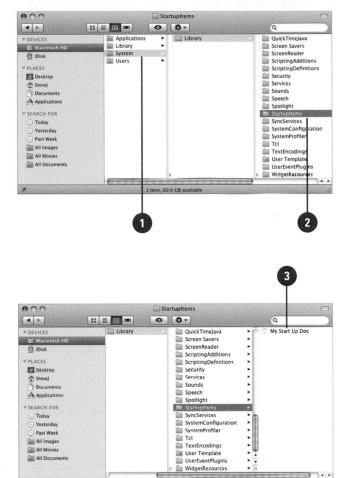

### Did You Know?

*If you don't want to drop an application into the Startup Items folder, create an alias of the application (or file), and place the alias into the folder.* That way, you still have access to the original item, and if you no longer want the item in the Startup Items folder, all you have to do is move it to the trash.

*You can create Startup commands.* Since Start Up items load every time your computer is running; it's a great way to perform routine maintenance and security. For example, you can create a script that instructs the system to perform hard drive diagnostics every seven days. Since the items are placed within the Startup Items folder, it doesn't matter who logs into the computer; the functions load and perform as instructed.

### See Also

*See "Creating Aliases" on page 90 for information on how to create and use an alias.*

# Setting Fast User Switching

One of the advantages to having multiple users and owning Mac OS X, is the ability to quickly switch between users. For example, one of your users wants to quickly check her e-mail. Before Leopard, you would have to close out all your files, log out, and then let her log in, but not any more. Mac OS X allows more than one user access to your computer, and lets you switch back and forth on the fly without closing anything. Think of a large box, and each side of the box represents a user account, along with their personalized desktop, specific folders and applications. To access a new account you simply rotate the box to display another face. That's exactly how it looks when you switch users using Fast User Switching. As you watch, the screen rotates to another face on the box displaying another user, and your account is still active. When she's finished checking her e-mail, all you have to do is switch back. It's that simple, and on systems with multiple users, this one feature can save you a lot of wasted time.

## Enable Fast User Switching

1. Click the **System Preferences** icon in the Dock, and then click the **Accounts** icon.

2. If the screen is locked, click the **Lock** icon, type your password, and then click **OK**.

3. Click the **Login Options** button.

4. Select the **Show fast user switching menu as** check box.

5. Click the pop-up, and then select a user view option: **Name**, **Short name**, or **Icon**.

6. Click the **Close** button.

## See Also

See "Switching Users" on page 22 for information on switching between different users.

# Setting System Security Preferences

The Security pane in System Preferences allows you to set options that prevent others from using your computer, such as requiring a password to unlock and change system preferences or wake your computer from sleep or screen saver, logging you out automatically if you're inactive for a certain amount of time (make sure you save all documents to complete logging you out), and disabling automatic login all together. The Security pane also lets you turn on or off FileVault, which protects your Home folder using encryption (secrets codes) from unauthorized users. Your files are encrypted using your login password. If you forget your login password and don't have the master password (a safety net password that lets you unlock any FileVault account), your files are lost forever.

## Set System Security Preferences

1. Click the **System Preferences** icon in the Dock, and then click the **Security** icon.

2. Click the **General** tab.

3. Select or clear the **Require password after sleep or screen save begin** check box, click the pop-up, and then select a delay interval (**New!**).

4. Select or clear the check boxes related to all user accounts:

   ◆ **Disable automatic login.**

   ◆ **Require password to unlock each System Preferences pane.**

   ◆ **Log out after *X* minutes of inactivity.**

   ◆ **Use secure virtual memory.**

   ◆ **Disable Location Services.**

   ◆ **Disable remote control infrared receiver.**

5. Click the **FileVault** tab.

6. To set or change a master password (*something you never want to forget*), click **Set Master Password** or **Change**, type the information, and then click **OK**.

7. Click the **Close** button.

# Restoring the Administrator Password

System Administrators are the ones that control the computer; they're the ones that set up other user accounts, and they are the ones, that tell you what you can and cannot access on that particular computer. The System Administrator knows all... sees all. However, what if the System Administrator forgets their password? Well first of all, don't tell anyone and don't worry, because you have two possible ways to get back to work. Your operating system has an Administrator password, and a Master password. If you know the master password, you have no problems whatsoever. However, if you set up a master password, turned on FileVault, and then forgot your Master password... well, not even Mac OS X can help you out of that situation, you're data is lost forever. If you didn't set up the master password, don't despair because OS X gives you another way to reset your Administrator password—by using the original install DVD. It's fairly straight forward, but understand others that have an install DVD can perform the same operation, and gain access to your information. It is therefore recommended that you create a Master password, and use FileVault to secure your sensitive documents.

## Use the Master Password

1. Turn on your computer.

2. Type anything into the password login option three times.

    **IMPORTANT** *After three unsuccessful attempts at typing in your password, you'll be asked if you want to reset the Administrator password.*

3. Click **Reset Password**.

4. Type in a new Administrator password.

    **IMPORTANT** *Do not make passwords common items such as your birthday, or mother's maiden name; those passwords will be the first someone tries to get into your system.*

5. Verify by typing in your Master Password.

6. Click **Log In** to restore the Administrator Password, and launch the operating system.

## Use the OS X DVD

1. Insert the Mac OS X DVD.

2. Restart your computer, and then hold down the C key (instructs Mac to start up from the DVD).

   ◆ Click the arrow button to the open installer screen to display menus.

3. Click the **Utilities** menu, and then click **Reset Password**.

4. Select the hard drive you want to reset.

5. Click the **Account** pop-up, and then select the name of your account.

6. Type and verify a new Administrator password.

7. Click **Save**, and then close the window.

8. Click **Mac OS X Installer**, click **Quit Mac OS X Installer**, and then click **Restart** to restart your computer.

### Did You Know?

**The Installer includes several utilities.** The utilities include Startup Disk, Fireware Password Utility, Disk Utility, Terminal, System Profiler, Network Utility, and Restore System From Backup.

Close

### For Your Information

#### Creating Start Up Commands

The Snow Leopard OS X DVD allows you to start your computer, even if the operating system on the hard drive completely fails. Sometimes it's possible to revive a crashed disk (assuming the problem is the operating system), by reinstalling the operating system over the old system, using the OS X DVD. If you travel with a MacBook, it's a good idea to burn a copy of the OS X DVD and take it with you on the road. An ounce of prevention is worth a pound of cure.

# Managing Files with the Home Folder

In a further attempt to organize, as well as secure your computer, each user account is assigned a Home folder. The **Home folder** is where all your account stuff is stored. That means all of your files, images; anything that you've created within your personal account, is stored in this folder. When users sign on to their accounts, they have the ability to add or delete files to their Home folder; however, they cannot access the Home folder of any other user, and they cannot add folders or delete files from any place else but their own Home folder. This gives you a tremendous degree of control over users, and prevents them from accidentally (or purposely) deleting or reading sensitive data. For example, users cannot create folders on the main hard drive, nor can they delete applications from the Applications folder. The other areas of the computer are effectively locked out.

Main hard drive    User folder

Home folder         Home folder documents

## Protecting the Home Folder with FileVault

Leopard's FileVault feature finally gives you total security over your sensitive files and applications. Macintosh computers have always had security, but there were ways to get around it. That was before Leopard came up with FileVault. FileVault gives you the ability to encrypt the files in your Home folder using password encryption (your log in password). It's so strong, that if you forget your password and don't know the master password, no one is able to open the files—they are lost forever. It's theorized that breaking the FileVault encryption would take a password-guessing program over 100 trillion years to figure it out. Therefore, if you decide to use FileVault, please don't forget your password. After you set FileVault, the security encryption and decryption happens on the fly, so you don't have to worry about doing anything; simply use your files normally. If someone else tries to access them, FileVault keeps them out.

### Protect Your Home Folder with FileVault

1. Click the **System Preferences** icon in the Dock, and then click the **Security** icon.

   **IMPORTANT** *Encrypting the entire contents of your hard drive requires the System Administrator.*

2. Click the **FileVault** tab.

3. Click **Turn On FileVault** (all other uses must be logged off the computer).

4. Read the alert message if users are logged in, and then click **OK**.

5. Type your password, and then click **OK**.

6. Another alert message appears, please read it carefully, select the secure check box options you want, and then click **Cancel** or **Turn On FileVault**.

   Leopard then goes through a creation procedure that can take 10 minutes or more to complete.

7. When the process is complete, you are brought back to the Login window.

# Sharing Files with Other Users

When you set up a user account, that person has access to the files in his Home folder. Depending on the level of access, he can open applications, possibly read or access information on the hard drive, but he won't have access to any sensitive areas, or anyone else's Home folder. What if you want to give a file to another co-worker, but you can't drop it into their folder, and the co-worker can't access your Home folder. That's where Macintosh comes to the rescue with shared folders.

When you open your Home folder you'll see two folders named Public and Sites. The Public folder contains a nested folder named Drop Box. The **Drop Box folder** is a place where anyone can drop items for you to use. As another user, I can place things into your

Drop Box, and you can place things in my Drop Box, but I can't see what's in your Drop Box, nor can I change any items. In other words, files check in but they don't check out.

The **Sites folder** is a place where you can create a Web site, and anyone can open the Sites folder, and launch your site. You can even publish it out to the Internet or on a Local Network. As a user with an account on this system, I can launch your Web site, but I can't modify or place any items within the Sites folder.

Finally, there is a **Shared folder**, located in the Users folder. The Shared folder is the only folder (other than your own Home folder) where you have full access to the files it contains.

Public folder     Sites folder            Drop Box folder

Universal Shared folder

# Managing Files Using a Network

## Introduction

Networks are interesting systems. Not too many years ago, a network was defined as two or more computers, connected together by physical cables or telephone lines. They were slow, and they went down (crashed) as much as they were up. The word, network, could bring fear to the hearts of even the stoutest computer system managers. Today, networks are rock solid and reliable. The Web can be defined as one huge network of interconnected computers around the world.

Networks connect more than computers; they work with PDA's, cell phones, televisions, and even wristwatches. And no longer do networks require physical cables. If your computer is equipped with a wireless port, you can connect to the Internet and surf the Web or even check your e-mail, from most major airports and hotel lobbies, without plugging your computer into anything.

In addition, the speed of today's networks allows us to move massive amounts of information, and even conduct real-time video-conferences. Macintosh computers were born to network, even when networking was a difficult proposition, the minds at Apple were working hard to make it fast, easy, and secure; and with the release of Snow Leopard, the ability to set up a local network, or one that stretches around the world, is becoming easier and easier.

Using Snow Leopard's built-in systems, you can even configure a wireless network—using an AirPort or Bluetooth (wireless technologies). You can share files and information with other computers with ease and even set up protection (firewalls) to guard against unauthorized access or potential viruses. It's all made possible with a Macintosh, and the Snow Leopard operating system.

## What You'll Do

**Use Network Sharing Services**

**Set Up File Sharing**

**Share an Internet Connection**

**Configure an Internet Firewall**

**Set Up a Local Area Network**

**Set Up a Network Connection**

**Set Up for Different Network Connections**

**Set Up a Bluetooth Wireless Network**

**Move Items with Bluetooth**

**Set Bluetooth Preferences**

**Browse the Network with the Finder**

**Connect to Another Computer**

**Connect to Your Mac Using a MobileMe Account**

**Set Up Mac and Windows to Share Files**

**Connect from a Windows 7, Vista, or XP Computer**

**Connect to a Network Over the Internet**

**Explore Additional Utility Applications**

# Using Network Sharing Services

Sharing Services are a collection of options that allow you to define what your computer shares with other computers over a network. For example, if you want to use your computer as a Web server, you would select the Web Sharing service, or by selecting the Printer Sharing service, you can share the printers on your computer with anyone else on the network. When you share files on a network, you need to tell other users your computer's Internet Protocol (IP) address or name. If your computer goes to sleep, you can continue to share its files with other computers and devices (**New!**). If you're on a local network, you can use the .local hostname as an alternative to a network address. You can find and change your computer name in Sharing Preferences. To prevent accidental changes to your settings, click the Lock button, located in the bottom-left corner of the Sharing window. The next time you try to make changes, you'll be prompted for your Administrator's password.

## Use Network Sharing Services

1. Click the **System Preferences** icon in the Dock, and then click the **Sharing** icon.

    Your computer's name appears at the top of the Sharing pane. The network location for this computer appears below the name.

2. To change your computer's name, modify the text in the Computer Name field.

3. Select or clear the check box next to any of the following network services to activate or disable it:

    ◆ **DVD or CD Sharing**. Select to allow other users to access this computer's DVD or CD.

    ◆ **Screen Sharing**. Select to allow other users to access and control your computer.

    ◆ **File Sharing**. Select to allow other users to access this computer's Public folders.

    ◆ **Printer Sharing**. Select to allow other users to share this computer's printers.

Click to prevent accidental changes to your settings.

◆ **Scanner Sharing**. Select to allow users to access this computer's scanner.

◆ **Web Sharing**. Select to allow users access to the Web pages, located in the Sites folders.

◆ **Remote Login**. Select to allow others to login to this computer.

◆ **Remote Management**. Select to allow users access to this computer through the Apple Remote Desktop application.

◆ **Remote Apple Events**. Select to allow users to send Apple Events to this computer (optional password protection).

◆ **Xgrid Sharing**. Select to allow Windows users access to the computer's Public folders.

◆ **Internet Sharing**. Select to allow users access to the Internet through your connection.

◆ **Bluetooth Sharing**. Select to allow users access to connected Bluetooth wireless devices.

4 Select or specify the options you want for the selected network service; options vary depending on the service.

5 Click the **Close** button.

## Did You Know?

*You can change your computer's local name.* Click the Edit button to change the name of your local computer. The local computer name is the name that displays with all the other computer names in a network listing.

# Setting Up File Sharing

Whenever you set up a network, regardless of the type, you'll have to configure your computer to communicate with the network. Macintosh computers are big on security, and they won't let your computer talk to any other computer unless you give the other computers permission. Permission involves setting up file sharing options, and then creating accounts with specific user names, passwords, and permissions.

## Set Up File Sharing and Permissions

1. Click the **System Preferences** icon in the Dock, and then click the **Sharing** icon.

2. Select the **Personal File Sharing** check box.

3. Select the shared folder you want to set permissions.

   ◆ To add a shared folder to the list, click the **Add** (+) button, select the folder, and then click **Add**.

4. Select the user you want to change permissions.

   ◆ To add a user to the list, click the **Add** (+) button, select a user from your Address Book, and then click **Add**.

5. Use the pop-ups to the right of the user name to set any of the following permissions:

   ◆ **Read & Write.**

   ◆ **Read Only.**

   ◆ **Write Only (Drop Box).**

   ◆ **No Access.**

6. Click the **Close** button.

## For Your Information

### Creating Privileges for Users and Groups

You can decide who gets to go where and do what. There are four levels of access—Read & Write (allows user to access and change the file), Read Only (allows user to access the file, but not make changes), Write Only (Drop Box), and No Access. The levels are pretty self-explanatory; however, if you give someone Read & Write privileges, you're giving them full control over the file. For example, someone could open a text document and basically erase the contents of the letter or completely rewrite it.

## Set Advanced File Sharing Options

1. Click the **System Preferences** icon in the Dock, and then click the **Sharing** icon.

2. Select the **Personal File Sharing** service; the option doesn't have to be turned on (checked).

3. Click **Options**.

4. Select from the following options:

   ◆ **Share files and folders using AFP.** Select to share files with Mac computers using AFP (Apple Filing Protocol).

   ◆ **Share files and folders using FTP.** Select to share files with an FTP (File Transfer Protocol) site.

   ◆ **Share files and folders using SMB.** Select to share files with Microsoft Windows computers. Select the user accounts you want to use, and type a password upon request.

5. Click **Done**.

6. Click the **Close** button.

# Sharing an Internet Connection

If you have an always-on Internet connection, such as a cable modem or DSL, you can share that connection with all the other people in your network in two ways: purchase a router and gate everyone into the connection, or use the built-in Internet Sharing (it's free). The one requirement is that Internet Sharing must be activated on the Macintosh that's connected to the Internet.

## Share an Internet Connection

① Click the **System Preferences** icon in the Dock, and then click the **Sharing** icon.

② Select **Internet Sharing**.

③ Click the **Share Your Connection From** pop-up, and then select the method used for sharing.

④ Check Ports that other computers are using.

⑤ Select the **Internet Sharing** check box.

⑥ Click **Start**.

**IMPORTANT** *If the Internet computer is shut down or in Sleep mode, the other network users won't be able to access the Internet.*

⑦ Click the **Close** button.

# Configuring an Internet Firewall

If you're using a broadband Internet connection (always on), it's possible that a hacker could gain entrance to your system without your knowledge, and do some extensive damage or make off with your secret recipe for beef paprikash. Fortunately, Mac OS X comes equipped with Firewall protection. A **Firewall** is a gatekeeper that in essence, stands guard over your computer; keeping it safe from all attackers. If vandals try to gain entrance to your computer, the Firewall attempts to shut them out. While no Firewall provides perfect protection from all Internet attacks, you can probably sleep soundly, knowing you probably have one of the most sophisticated protection systems on the market today.

## Configure an Internet Firewall

1. Click the **System Preferences** icon in the Dock, and then click the **Security** icon.

2. Click the **Firewall** tab.

3. Click **Start** to enable firewall settings or click **Stop** to disable it.

4. To set specific firewall settings, click **Advanced**, set the options you want, and then click **OK**.

   ◆ **Block all incoming connections.** Select to block all Incoming connections.

   ◆ Click the **Add** (+) and **Remove** (-) button to modify the applications list of allowable incoming connections.

   ◆ **Automatically allow signed software to receive incoming connections.** Select to allow an incoming connection for certified signed software.

   ◆ **Enable stealth mode.** Select to provide no response from uninvited traffic.

5. Click the **Close** button.

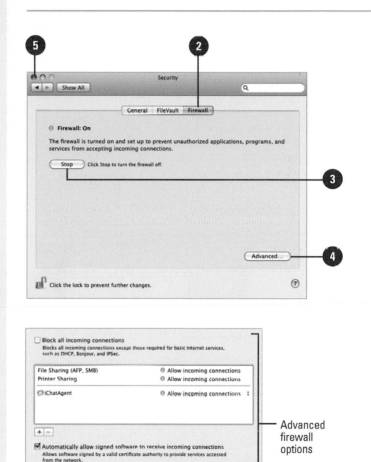

Advanced firewall options

# Setting Up a Local Area Network

Almost any Macintosh computer comes out of the box network ready. Setting up a Local Area Network or LAN, is fairly straightforward. **Local Area Networks** are a group of local computers hooked together. For example, you could create a LAN for the computers in your office or create a LAN for your home computers. Macintosh even allows you to connect with Windows computers without having to purchase additional software. In fact, all of the software you'll need to create and maintain a LAN is built into Macintosh OS X. All you have to do is buy a couple of cables, connect two or more computers together, and you're ready to network. Let's complicate the situation and say that you're going to hook up more than two computers.

In that case, you'll need an Ethernet cable for each computer and an Ethernet hub. A **hub** is a device that lets you connect multiple computers together. Every Macintosh sold comes with an Ethernet port. To set up a LAN, draw out the layout for the network to determine where the computers are and the distance between each unit. Purchase the cables (make sure they're long enough), and the Ethernet hub (you can purchase Ethernet supplies at almost any electronic store). Plug one end of the Ethernet cables into each of the computers, and the other end into the hub (make sure you plug the hub into an electrical outlet). Once the network is established, you'll need to set up the individual computers for file sharing and to recognize the LAN.

**Local Area Network**

Hub device

# Setting Up a Network Connection

With Mac OS X, you can connect to other computers, local and wide area networks and to the Internet. You can can connect to other computers or networks using an Ethernet, FireWire, or AirPort connection. If you are connecting to the Internet, you can connect with a DSL or cable modem, an AirPort wireless connection, or a telephone modem. After you set up the physical network hardware, you can use the Network pane in System Preferences to setup a network connection. To make the process easy, you can use the Network Setup Assistant to walk you through the steps. If you're having problems with a network, you can also use the Network Setup Assistant to help you fix the problem.

## Set Up a Network

1. Click the **System Preferences** icon in the Dock, and then click the **Network** icon.

2. Click **Assist Me**.

3. Click **Assistant**.

   ◆ **Diagnostics**. If you're having problems with a network connection, click **Diagnostics**, and the follow the instructions.

4. Type a location name, such as Home or Work, and then click **Continue**.

5. Click the option with the network connection you want to make.

6. Click **Continue**.

7. Enter network specific information for the selected network, and then click **Continue**; the requested information varies depending on the selected network.

8. Click **Done**.

Click for diagnostics

### See Also

*See "Setting Up an Ethernet Connection" on page 223 or "Setting Up an AirPort Wireless Connection" on page 224 for information on manually setting up networks.*

# Setting Up for Different Network Connections

If you connect to networks and the Internet in different ways, you can save network connects to suit your needs. For example, you connect to your network at home with a wireless AirPort connection and your network at the office with an Ethernet connection. You can save different network configurations for different purposes, so you can optimize your network connections. When you have multiple network connections, Mac OS X tries to connect in the order provided in Network Preferences. You can change the network connection order and save the network connection as a new location, so you only need to do this once. The default location, Automatic, provides setting for each of your computer's network services, including Ethernet, AirPort, or a dial-up modem.

## Set Up or Modify Different Networks Connections

1. Click the **System Preferences** icon in the Dock, and then click the **Network** icon.

2. Use the following methods to work with your connections:

   ◆ **Edit a Location.** Click the Location pop-up, and then select the location you want to modify.

   ◆ **Create a Location.** Click the **Location** pop-up, click **Edit Location**, click the **Add** (+) button, type a name, and then click **Done**.

     ◆ **Remove, Rename or Duplicate.** Use the Edit Location dialog to delete, rename or duplicate a network location.

3. To change the connection priority, click the **Actions** button, click **Set Service Order**, drag the network service icons to the positions you want, and then click **OK**.

4. To remove a network connection, click the **Remove** (-) button.

5. To revert your changes, click the **Revert**.

6. Click the **Close** button.

Edit Location

Set Service Order

# Setting Up a Bluetooth Wireless Network

Macintosh computers have several methods for creating networks. There are standard networks using Ethernet cables, and hubs; there are wireless networks; and then there are Bluetooth networks. **Bluetooth** technology is not so much a network, as it is a simple wireless technology that lets you transmit files and data to any other Bluetooth equipped device. For example, you could use Bluetooth to sync to your Bluetooth PDA, or even use your Address Book, and Bluetooth to automatically dial your Bluetooth cell phone. If you really want to throw away the cables, Apple makes a Bluetooth enabled keyboard and mouse. Bluetooth uses radio signals to communicate with any other Bluetooth device, up to a maximum range of thirty feet. Think of it this way, any Bluetooth device can communicate with any other Bluetooth device, if they are both turned on and within thirty feet of each other. And setup is a breeze with the Bluetooth Setup Assistant.

## Set Up a Bluetooth Wireless Network

1. Click the **System Preferences** icon in the Dock, and then click the **Network** icon.

2. Select Bluetooth in the list.

   ◆ If Bluetooth is not available, click the **Add** (+) button, select Bluetooth DUN as the network, and then click **Create**.

3. Turn on the Bluetooth device and place it within 30 feet of your computer.

4. Click **Set Up Bluetooth Device**.

   The Bluetooth Setup Assistant appears.

5. Click **Continue**, and the step through the assistant specifying the device type and passkey to pair the device and the computer.

   The Bluetooth Preferences dialog appears.

6. To delete a pairing, select it, and then click the **Delete** (-) button.

7. Click the **Close** button.

# Moving Items with Bluetooth

Once you've set up your Bluetooth devices, it's a simple matter to transfer files to the Bluetooth device. For example, you have a PDA device and you want to move a text file from your computer to the device. The process of moving a file from your computer to your Bluetooth device is the same; however, since each Bluetooth device is different, the process of moving a file from the device to your computer is different for each device. Consult your owner's manual for information on how to move information to your computer, from the Bluetooth device.

## Move Items with Bluetooth

1. Turn on the device and place it within 30 feet of your computer.

2. Click the **Applications** folder in the Dock, click the **Utilities** folder, and then click the **Bluetooth File Exchange** icon.

3. Select the file you want to send.

4. Click **Send**.

5. Select the Bluetooth device from the available list.

6. Click **Send**.

7. Click the **Close** button.

# Setting Bluetooth Preferences

After you set up a Bluetooth wireless network on your computer, you can use System Preferences to control how to send and receive files between your computer and other Bluetooth devices. You can use the Settings tab to make your Mac discoverable by other Bluetooth devices and specify whether you want to require a password. The File Exchange tab allows you to indicate what happens when someone sends you a document: accept it, refuse it, or ask what to do. Finally, the Devices tab lets you set up the use of other Bluetooth devices; use pairing to set passwords for security purposes.

## Set Bluetooth Preferences

1. Click the **System Preferences** icon in the Dock, and then click the **Bluetooth** icon.

2. Select or clear the check boxes you want:

   ◆ **Bluetooth Power.**

   ◆ **Discoverable.**

3. To set the following advanced options, click **Advanced**, and the click **OK**.

   ◆ **Open Bluetooth Setup Assistant at startup when no input device is present.**

   ◆ **Allow Bluetooth devices to wake this computer.**

   ◆ **Prompt for all incoming audio requests.**

   ◆ **Share my internet connection with other Bluetooth devices.**

4. To use the Bluetooth Status menu, select the **Show Bluetooth Status in the menu bar** check box.

5. Click the **Close** button.

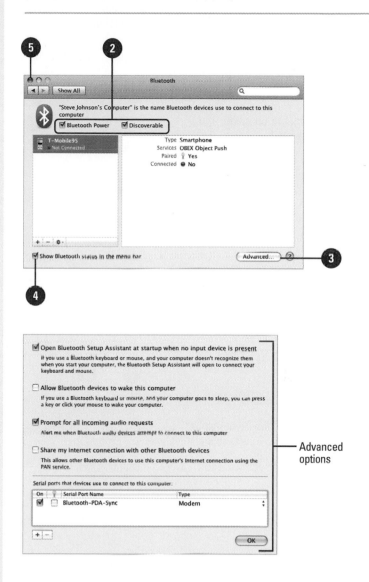

Advanced options

# Browsing the Network with the Finder

The Finder serves as a focused network browser application. From the Go menu, you can access the Network window, which displays all the computers available on your network. If you're not sure what is available, this is the place to browse the network. You can also access a network from the Sidebar, which displays all shared computers. After you display a networked computer, you can use all the find tools available on your Mac to locate files. For example, you're looking for a file with a specific name. You've used the Finder application, and checked on your machine, but can't seem to find it. The other option is that it's on your co-workers computer. The good news is that with the Finder application, not only can you search your computer; you can search any other computer on the network.

## Browse All Networks with the Finder

1  In Finder, click the **Go** menu, and then click **Network**.

2  Double-click a network computer to browse its contents.

## Browse a Specific Network with the Finder

1  Open a Finder window.

2  Click the Shared triangle to display available networks, if necessary.

3  Select the network you want to view.

4  Double-click a folder to browse its contents.

## Search for Files in a Network

① Login to another computer on the network.

② Open the Finder window.

③ Select the network in which you want to search in the Sidebar under Shared For.

④ In the Search field, type the search criteria.

⑤ In the Search bar, select the network name.

⑥ Select **Contents** or **File Name** to specify how you want to perform the search.

## Access Networks from the Finder Sidebar

① Click the **Finder** menu, and then click **Preferences**.

② Click **Sidebar**.

③ Select the check boxes under Shared that you want to display:

♦ **Back to My Mac**

♦ **Connected Servers**

♦ **Bonjour Computers**

④ Click the **Close** button.

# Connecting to Another Computer

Once you've connected several computers together into a network, and configured your computer for file sharing, the next step is to begin communicating. In order to communicate with another computer, you'll need access to a user account. Typically a user account defines you with a specific name, password, and permissions. Once you log into the other computer, you'll be able to access the areas (permissions) granted to you by the Systems Administrator.

## Connect to Another Computer

1. Turn on all the computers.

2. Click the **Go** menu, and then click **Connect To Server**.

3. Connect using one of the following methods:

   ◆ Click **Browse**, and then double-click on one of the available server icons.

   ◆ Type the computer's Server Address, and then click **Connect**.

      ◆ **Windows (SMB/CIFS).** Example: *smb://DNSname/sharename*; *smb://IPaddress/sharename*

      ◆ **Macintosh (AFP)**. Example: *afp://ComputerName.CompanyName.com*

      ◆ **FTP**. Example: *ftp://user@DNSname*; *ftp://DNSname*; *ftp://user:password@DNSname*

      ◆ **NFS**. Example: *nfs://DNSname/pathname*

   ◆ Click the **Recent Servers** button, and then select a server address from the list of available options.

4. Type your Name and Password.

5. Click **Connect**.

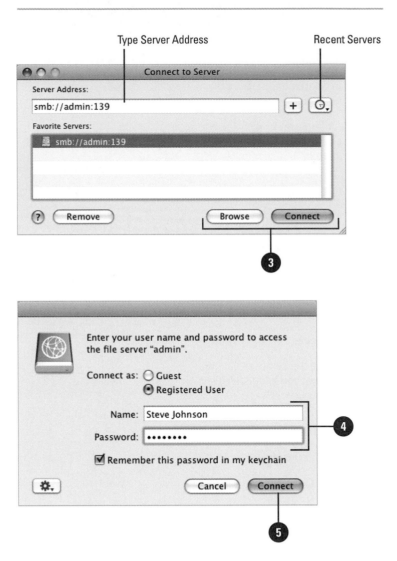

Type Server Address

Recent Servers

6  Select the area of the other computer you want to access.

7  Click **OK**.

**IMPORTANT** *The other computer now functions and acts as a hard drive on your computer.*

8  Click the network computer icon in the Sidebar to display its contents.

9  Work with your computer; drag files from your computer to the networked computer or vice versa.

## Did You Know?

*You can identify the IP (Internet Protocol) address of your computer.* Click the Apple menu, and then click System Preferences. Click Network, and then select the network connection in the list. The current IP address is displayed next to the network connection when available.

# Connecting to Your Mac Using a MobileMe Account

If you have a MobileMe account, you can use Back to My Mac to access your computer and other services, such as file sharing and screen sharing, from another computer on the Internet. Before you can use Back to My Mac, you need to start it on the computer you want to access and all the other computers you want to use to access it. You can start Back to My Mac in the MobileMe pane in System Preferences. If you want to use file and screen sharing, you need to enable those services using the Sharing pane in System Preferences. With Sidebar, you can view and access a shared Mac on your network and control it with permission of the owner.

## Start or Stop Back to My Mac

1 Click the **System Preferences** icon in the Dock, and then click the MobileMe icon.

2 Click the **Back to My Mac** tab.

3 Click **Start** or **Stop**.

4 To setup file sharing options, click **Open Sharing Preferences**.

5 Click the **Close** button.

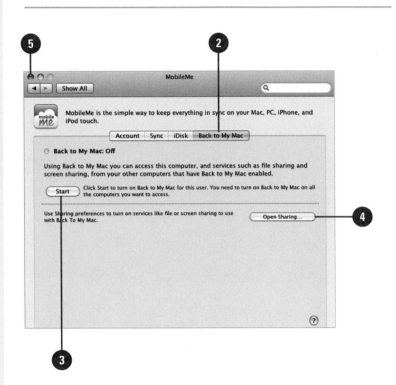

### Did You Know?

*You can display shared devices in the Sidebar.* Click the Finder menu, click Preferences, click Shared, select the Back To My Mac check box, and then click the Close button.

## Access Your Mac with Back to My Mac

1. Open a Finder window.

2. Click your Mac computer in the Sidebar under Shared For.

   The files on your Mac computer appears in the Finder window.

3. Work with your computer as you normally do; drag files from your computer to the networked computer or vice versa.

### See Also

*See "Controlling a Computer with Screen Sharing" on page 422 for information on taking control of your computer from another computer.*

Back to My Mac connection

# Controlling a Computer with Screen Sharing

With Snow Leopard, you can now share your computer with other users. In fact, you can let other users display your computer screen on their monitor and control your computer as if they were sitting in front of it. This is very useful when you need to access your computer at the office when you're at home. If a friend needs assistance, you can use screen sharing to take control and provide online help. While you control another computer, you have full access to everything on the machine, so be aware of the changes you want to make. Before you can use screen sharing, you need to enable the option in Sharing Preferences. Screen sharing uses Virtual Network Computing (VNC) to make the network connection using TCP/IP, an industry standard for networking.

## Set Permissions for Screen Sharing

1. Click the **System Preferences** icon in the Dock, and then click the **Sharing** icon.

2. Select the **Screen Sharing** check box.

   **TROUBLE?** *If Remote Management is already selected, you don't need to select Screen Sharing. Remote Management includes screen sharing.*

3. Select from the following screen sharing options:

   ◆ **All users**. Select to allow all users to access and control your computer.

   ◆ **Only these users**. Select to allow specific users access to access and control your computer. Click the **Add** (+) button and then select the users you want from your Address Book.

4. To set access options, click **Computer Settings**, select the check box settings you want for access permission, and then click **OK**.

5. Click the **Close** button.

Computer settings

## Share Another Computer's Screen

① Enable screen sharing on the computer you want to share in Sharing Preferences.

② Click your Mac computer in the Sidebar under Shared For.

The files on your Mac computer appears in the Finder window.

③ Click **Share Screen**.

④ Select the sharing option you want:

◆ **As a registered user**. Connects to another computer using a login name and password; if the remote computer is set to the *Only these users* option, the login name needs to be in the list.

◆ **By asking for permission**. Asks permission from the current user to share their screen.

⑤ Specify the options you want based on your setup.

The screen for the other computer appears with the Snow Leopard's built-in screen sharing viewer.

⑥ Use your Mac computer as if you were in front of it.

⑦ When you're done, close your session.

⑥ Shared screen

# Setting Up Mac and Windows to Share Files

Before you can share files between Macintosh and Windows computers, you need to set up file sharing options. When you enable file sharing on a Mac computer to share files with Windows users, Mac OS X uses the Samba server software to provide SMB/CIFS file services. Now Windows users can connect to a Mac computer using normal network services. After you share a folder on a Windows computer, you can share files with Mac users. You may need to disable the Internet Connection Firewall or make sure the TCP port 445 is open. To connect to the Windows computer, users need the network address, workgroup name, and the user name and password for the shared folder.

## Set Up a Mac to Share Files with Windows

1. Click the **System Preferences** icon in the Dock, and then click the **Sharing** icon.

2. Select the **File Sharing** check box.

3. Click **Options**.

4. Select the **Share files and folders using SMB** check box.

5. Select the check boxes to enable a user account for sharing.

6. Type a password, and then click **OK**.

7. Click **Done**.

8. Provide the address of your computer displayed in the Sharing pane to Windows users you want to share your computer.

9. Click the **Close** button.

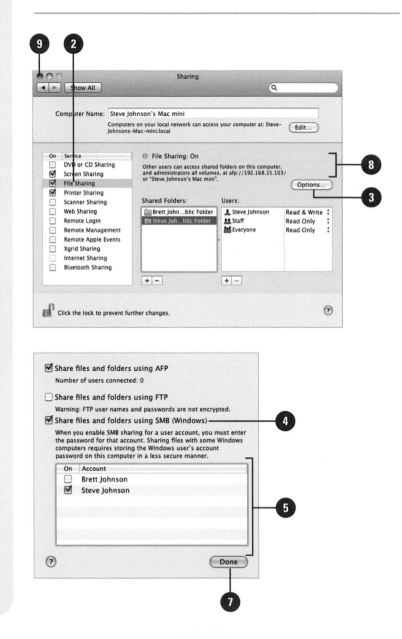

# Connecting from a Windows 7 or Vista Computer

After you enable File Sharing in the Sharing Services area of the System Preferences, Windows computers can connect to your computer. Most networks consist of multiple types of computers and operating systems. For Windows 7 or Vista, the Network window lets you view the entire network, including servers, domains, and workgroups. For a Windows 7 or Vista computer on your immediate network, you can browse the network to access the Macintosh computer.

## Connect from a Windows 7 or Vista Computer on a Local Network

1. Display the Networks connected to your computer.

   ◆ **Windows 7.** Click the **Start** button, click **Computer**, and then click **Network** in the Navigation pane.

   ◆ **Windows Vista.** Click the **Start** button, and then click **Network**.

   **TROUBLE?** *For those using different versions of Windows, consult the online help system for specific instructions.*

2. Double-click the Mac Computer icon to display the shared files, folders, and devices on the computer. If necessary, type a user name and password for the Mac account.

3. Double-click a Mac drive or shared folder.

4. When you're done, click the **Close** button.

Windows 7

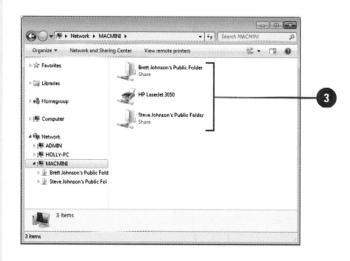

# Connecting from a Windows XP Computer

After you enable File Sharing in the Sharing Services area of the System Preferences, Windows computers can connect to your computer. Most networks consist of multiple types of computers and operating systems. For Windows XP, My Network Places lets you view the entire network or just your part of the network to give you access to the servers, domains, and workgroups on the network. For a Windows XP computer on your immediate network, you can browse the network to access the Macintosh computer. If the Windows XP computer is outside your immediate network, you need to add a network place using the Macintosh computer address displayed in the Sharing pane when you enabled Windows Sharing.

## Connect from a Windows XP Computer on a Local Network

1. Click the **Start** button, and then click **My Network Places**.

   **TROUBLE?** *For those using different versions of Windows, consult the online help system for specific instructions.*

2. In the Network Tasks area, click **View Workgroup Computers**.

3. If the computers are not in the same workgroup, click **Microsoft Windows Network**, and then double-click **Workgroup**.

4. Double-click the Mac Computer icon to display the shared files, folders, and devices on the computer. If necessary, type a user name and password for the Mac account.

5. When you're done, click the **Close** button.

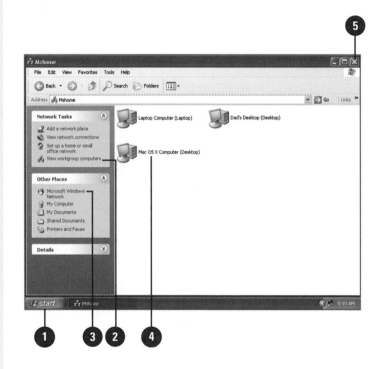

## Connect from a Windows XP Computer Outside Your Network

**1** Click the **Start** button, and then click **My Network Places**.

**2** In the Network Tasks area, click **Add A Network Place**, and then click **Next**.

**3** Click **Choose Another Network Location**, and then click **Next**.

**4** Type the network address of your Macintosh computer. You can find the address in the Sharing pane under Services. Be sure to type it exactly as shown.

**5** Click **Next** to continue.

> **TROUBLE?** *If the addresses are not working, click View Some Examples for help.*

**6** Type a name for the network place or use the suggested one, and then click **Next**.

**7** To open the network, select the **Open This Network Place When I Click Finish** check box.

**8** Click **Finish**.

### See Also

*See "Using Network Sharing Services" on page 404 for information on enabling Windows sharing and find the network address of your Macintosh computer.*

Shortcut to a network

# Connecting to a Network Over the Internet

You can create a VPN (Virtual Private Network) connection to securely connect your computer to a network over the Internet. The computer you want to connect to must support a VPN and Internet connection. Before you create a connection, you need to have the server or IP address of the VPN computer. The first time you setup a VPN, you need to select a VPN protocol, either L2TP Over IPSec or PPTP. Use L2TP (Layer Two Tunneling Protocol) over IPSec (Internet Protocol Security), where security is a concern between your computer and Windows XP, or use PPTP (Point-to-Point Tunneling Protocol) where security issues are not as much a problem, but where backward compatibility with older systems is a concern. You can use the Show VPN Status menu to easily connect and disconnect from the VPN, and show connection information. If you want a create a private connection within your physical network, you can create a VLAN (Virtual Local Area Network).

## Create a VPN Connection

1. Click the **System Preferences** icon in the Dock, and then click the **Network** icon.

2. Click the **Add** (+) button.

3. Click the **Interface** pop-up, and then click **VPN**.

4. Click the **VPN Type** pop-up, and then click **L2TP Over IPSec** or **PPTP**.

5. Type a name for the connection.

6. Click **Create**.

7. Type the Server Address and Account Name.

8. Click **Authentication Settings** to specify a password or other credentials.

9. To display the modem menu for easy connection access, select the **Show VPN Status In Menu Bar** check box.

10. Click **Connect** to start a VPN connection.

11. When you're done, click the **Close** button, and then save the configuration, if necessary.

## Create a VLAN Connection

① Click the **System Preferences** icon in the Dock, and then click the **Network** icon.

② Click the **Actions** button, and then click **Manage Virtual Interfaces**.

③ Click the **Add** (+) button, and then click **New VLAN**.

④ Type a name for the VLAN connection.

⑤ Click the **Interface** pop-up, and then click a network connection.

⑥ Click **Create**.

⑦ Click **Done**.

⑧ Specify any settings provided for the network, such as IP Address, Subnet Mask, and Router, and DNS Servers.

◆ If you want assistance, click **Assist Me**, and then follow the instructions.

⑨ When you're done, click the **Close** button, and then save the configuration, if necessary.

### See Also

*See "Setting Up an Ethernet Connection" on page 223 for information on setting up a LAN connection.*

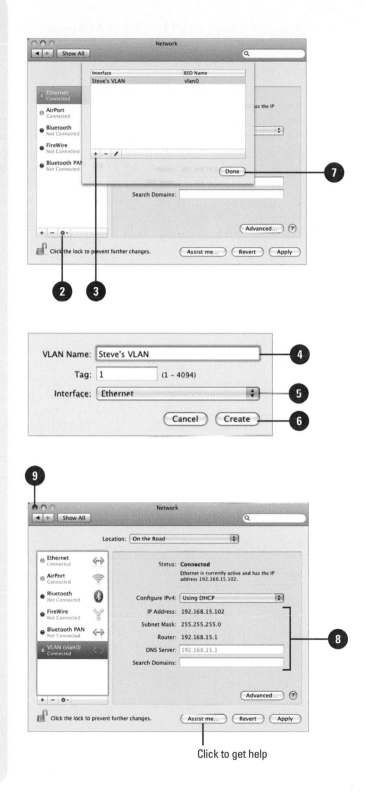

Click to get help

# Exploring Additional Utility Applications

The Utilities folder, located within the Applications folder, is host to several dozen applications and utilities that help you manage the daily activities with running your Macintosh computer system, internet and wireless connections, and troubleshooting. It's possible that you might go your entire life and never access some of the more obscure utilities located in this folder; however you should explore the available options, because some of them are useful.

## Network Utility

The Network Utility holds information on Web sites, and offers the ability to perform standard Internet services such as: Info, NetStat, Ping, Finger, and Whois. Info displays your IP (Internet Protocol) address and other network information. NetStat displays technical information about your network. Ping allows you to test an Internet connection. Finger allows you to find out about an e-mail address, while Whois allows you to find out about a domain. When you're experiencing problems with your service, it's possible that a service technician may ask you some of this information.

## AirPort Admin Utility

The AirPort Admin Utility lets you monitor the connections within an existing AirPort network. In addition, you can use the utility to manually setup new connections.

Info

NetStat

Ping

Whois

# Maintaining Your Computer

## Introduction

Once you've bought your Macintosh computer, installed the operating system and all your applications, it's important to be able to keep all that software up-to-date; especially the operating system software. With the consistent updates that Apple is making to the Snow Leopard operating system, Mac OS X helps you keep all the software up-to-date with the click of a button.

In addition, loss of data can be a tragic occurrence, so Snow Leopard lets you archive or copy data from your computer to an external disk (just remember to keep your backups offsite). Snow Leopard also helps you monitor activities on your system, see who is currently using your computer, and how much processing power each program is using. This gives you the ability to fine-tune your system for maximum performance. If your system seems to be slowing down, or you're experiencing more crashes than usual (a rare occurrence on a Mac), Snow Leopard gives you the programs to optimize and repair day-to-day problems, and keep your system in tiptop shape.

Remember that maintaining your computer requires more on your part than the launching of a couple of programs. The Macintosh computer comes with several internal fans that help keep the inner workings cool; however, those fans also pull in dust. You should open your computer and vacuum out the interior about once a year, and dust the exterior surface about once a month. In addition, make sure the computer has enough room around it for air to circulate. Finally, make sure all the cables you have strung from the computer to all your peripherals are out of harms way, and in good condition. In past years, attempting to maintain your computer system was a challenge; however, today it's easy to keep things running smoothly.

## What You'll Do

**Download and Install Software**

**Automate Software Updates**

**Open Compressed Files**

**Compress and Uncompress Files and Folders**

**Use Application Services**

**Understand Disk File Systems**

**Format and Copy a Disk**

**Fix Disk Problems**

**Optimize a Disk**

**Start Your Computer From a Mac OS 9 Disk**

**Migrate Information Between Macs**

**Monitor System Activities**

**View System Messages with the Console**

**View System Information with System Profiler**

**Force a Restart**

# Downloading and Installing Software

Let's face it, a computer without software is simply a very expensive boat anchor. On the other hand, software without a computer is useless. Once you install your software, it's important to keep up with all the updates, patches, and fixes. The Snow Leopard operating system comes bundled with literally dozens of software packages—everything from disk repair utilities to image-capture applications. In addition, hackers are causing problems and Apple stays on top of them with updates to Snow Leopard, which you can download from the Internet. After you download a software package, you can re-use the package file (.pkg) to install it on another Mac without re-downloading.

## Download and Install Software

1. Click the **Apple** menu, and then click **Software Update**.

   A screen appears with a status bar checking for software updates.

   **IMPORTANT** *Performing software updates requires an Internet connection.*

2. Click **Show Details**, if necessary.

3. Check the software updates you want to load (if available).

4. Select an update, to read more information about that specific product.

5. Click the **Install Items** button.

6. Type your Administrator name and password.

7. Click **OK**.

   Mac OS X begins installing the software. Follow any onscreen instructions, and then close it

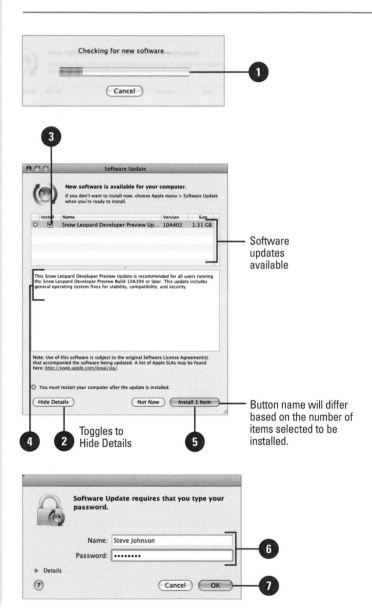

Software updates available

Button name will differ based on the number of items selected to be installed.

Toggles to Hide Details

# Automating Software Updates

Trying to keep up with all your software updates use to be a hassle, but not any more. Not only does Snow Leopard let you quickly download all your operating system software updates; it lets you automate the process. When you automate software updates, you select a specific time interval between checks. For example, you could instruct Snow Leopard to check for available updates every month. Snow Leopard even lets you download important updates in the background, so it doesn't interrupt your workflow. With the ability not only to update your software, but also to automate the entire process, there is no longer any excuse for not having up-to-date software.

## Automate Software Updates

1. Click the **System Preferences** icon in the Dock, and then click the **Software Update** icon.

2. Click the **Scheduled Check** tab.

3. Select the **Check For Updates** check box.

4. Click the **Updates** pop-up, and then select how often Snow Leopard checks for updates.

5. Select the **Download important updates automatically** check box to download updates without interrupting your workflow.

6. Click **Check Now** to check for any current updates.

7. To check all the updates you've currently installed, click the **Installed Updates** tab.

8. A list of updated files appears.

   You can scroll through the updates to view any changes to your system.

9. Click the **Close** button.

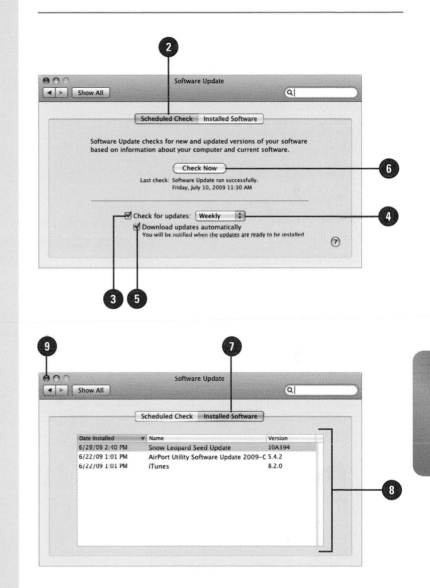

# Opening Compressed Files

Not all compressed file formats are self-extracting. For those files you'll need a program capable of uncompressing (extracting) the files. Stuffit Expander is a universal utility that helps you open up all those pesky compressed files that other users and companies send you. The latest version (Stuffit 2009 v13), opens almost any compressed format including: .sit, .sea, .hqx, and, .bin. In addition, Stuffit can open files compressed using WinZip (Windows compression utility), and the UNIX formats: .tar, .gzip, and .bzip. For example, you receive a WinZip file from your parents showing pictures of their trip to Hawaii or you download the latest software patch for your word-processing program, and it came in the .hqz format. With Stuffit Expander, you're only seconds away from viewing those pictures and updating that word processor.

## Open Compressed Files with Stuffit Expander

1 Click the **Applications** folder in the Dock, and then click the **Utilities** folder or the **Stuffit** folder to locate the Stuffit Expander.

2 Select a compressed file.

3 Drag and drop the file over the **Stuffit Expander** icon.

4 Stuffit Expander uncompresses the file, and places it in the same location as the compressed file.

Mounted drive

# Compressing and Uncompressing Files and Folders

You can compress files and folder in special files that compress the contents to decrease the size of the files they contain. Compressed folders are useful for reducing the file size of one or more large files, thus freeing disk space and reducing the time it takes to transfer files to another computer over the Internet or network. A compressed file is denoted by a ZIP icon. You can compress one or more files in a compressed file by using the Compress command on the File menu. When a file is compressed, a copy is used in the compression, and the original remains intact. You can uncompress, or extract, a file from the compressed folder by double-clicking the compressed file icon. The compressed files and folder are uncompressed into a folder called Archive.

## Compress and Uncompress Files and Folders

1. Select a file, group of files, or a folder.

2. Click the **File** menu, and then click **Compress.**

   Archive creates a zipped file with the same name as the original item.

3. To restore an archived zip, double-click its icon.

   **IMPORTANT** *Remember that a back up of your data is your insurance of recovery after a disk crash or other catastrophic system failure. Always keep your backups offsite, or in a protected location, such as a fireproof safe. As tragic as a fire would be, the damage would be compounded if your backups were also destroyed.*

## See Also

*See "Opening Compressed Files" on page 434 for information on opening compressed files with Stuffit Expander.*

Compressed file    Uncompressed files

# Using Application Services

Application Services are a Mac OS X feature that lets you efficiently use content from one application to another application. Services are available on the Application menu in an application, such as TextEdit or Finder, based on the situation or in a shortcut (context) menu (**New!**). For example, you could use the Services option to send selected text information in an e-mail, or make a sticky note in TextEdit. In Snow Leopard, you can individually disable or enable each service in the Keyboard preferences (**New!**). With Automator, you can now build your own services, making a repetitive task simple to use (**New!**).

## Use Application Services

1. Open an application.

2. Click the **Application** menu, and then point to **Services**.

3. Select from the available commands in the Services application you want.

## Change Services Preferences

1. Click the **System Preferences** icon in the Dock, and then click the **Keyboard** icon.

2. Click the **Keyboard Shortcuts** tab.

3. Click **Services** in the left column.

4. Select or clear the check boxes next to the services you do or don't want under the task type, such as Text, Internet, or Pictures.

5. To add services, click the **Add** (+) button, select an application, type a menu title, and specify a keyboard shortcut, and then click **Add**.

6. Click the **Close** button.

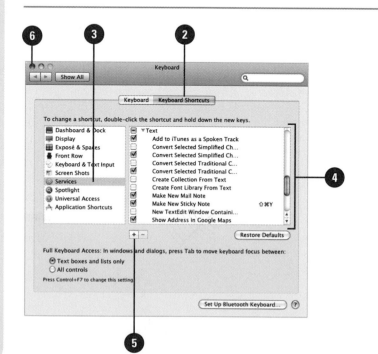

# Understanding Disk File Systems

When you work on a computer, you're utilizing applications that are stored on the computer's hard drive. As you work, you're accessing and writing files back to the hard drive. For example, you open MS Word, create a document, and then save it using the name: MyLetter.doc.

Mac OS X stores files and programs on your hard drive using a system of tracks and sectors; similar to a pie cut into equal triangular pieces. In addition, Mac OS X divides the hard drive into logical file systems, which can help you organize your files and projects.

When you open your hard drive, you'll see that Mac OS X has created several folders to organize your creative efforts. There's a folder for applications, and a folder for the System files—there's even a folder that contains all the users for the particular computer, and another for your documents.

Typically, when you load an application for the first time, you're asked to hold the application within the Applications folder. This gives Mac OS X the ability to control the program, and even helps you when it comes time to check for updates. As you use your computer, you'll probably begin adding folders for your various projects. It's important that you create a disk file system that's well organized. Well organized file systems help you locate and retrieve files quicker and, if properly created, help you to move them from machine to machine. For example, you create a project folder for a major video project: everything that pertains to that project (video, audio, files, text, graphics), are all organized into folders within that one folder. When it come times to publish, move, or archive that information, all your files are conveniently organized in one location.

Tracks

Sectors

Organized contents with folders

File folder

# Formatting and Copying a Disk

Computers are wonderful devices; however, it's the information they hold that makes them important. Not only is that information important on your computer, it might also be something you want to send to someone else or archive. In order to send or archive, you'll first need a disk. When you format a disk, you're actually telling the operating system to scrub the disk of all information, and prepare it for use. Make sure you backup any important data before performing the formatting operation. When using the Disk Utility to copy, Mac OS X creates a mirror copy of the original. This differs from dragging and dropping a file onto a disk icon. When you drag and drop, the OS places the new files in whatever space is available. However, when you use Disk Utility, it places the files in exactly the same tracks and sectors as the original.

## Format a Disk

1. Click the **Applications** folder in the Dock, click the **Utilities** folder, and then click the **Disk Utility** icon.

2. Select the volume (disk) you want to format (you cannot format the startup drive).

3. Click the **Erase** tab.

4. Click the **Volume Format** pop-up, and then select from the following options:

   ◆ **Mac OS Extended (Journaled).** Uses the same HFS Plus filing system as Mac OS Extended, and keeps a journal of your activities. Journaling makes for shortened startup times, and helps in the event of a crash.

   ◆ **Mac OS Extended.** Formats the disk using HFS Plus filing system (helps to compress files and maximize file space).

   ◆ **UNIX File System.** Formats a disk for use on a UNIX system.

   ◆ **MS-DOS File System.** If available, formats a disk for use on a Windows (MS-DOS) system.

5. Type a Name for the formatted disk.

6. Click **Erase**.

Warning message

Volume or disk statistics

438

## Copy a Disk

1. Click the **Applications** folder in the Dock, click the **Utilities** folder, and then click the **Disk Utility** icon.

2. Click the **Restore** tab.

3. Drag a disk image into the Source input box (the disk to copy).

4. Drag a disk image from the Disk Volume column into the Destination input box (the disk to copy onto).

5. Select the **Erase Destination** check box to instruct the OS to erase the Destination drive before performing the copy (recommended).

6. Click **Restore**.

### Did You Know?

*You can copy information from a disk over the Internet.* Type the URL of the disk you want to restore from into the Source input box.

*You can create a new disk image.* Select a disk or folder icon in the Disk Volume column, and then click the New Image button.

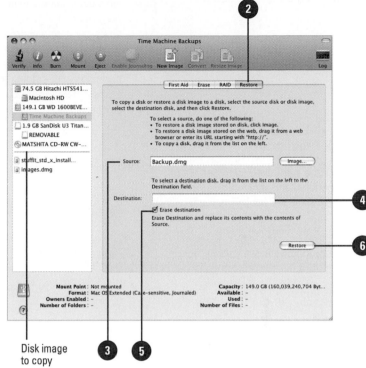

Disk image to copy

# Fixing Disk Problems

It's not unusual for a hard drive to experience problems. When problems occur on the main hard drive, it can produce lock ups and slower performance. Apple helps to solve this problem by letting you perform disk repairs to any drives with the exception of the start up drive. For example, you could use disk repair to fix problems on a damaged JAZZ drive, or a secondary hard drive. Apple's Disk Utility locates and fixes problems with catalog and storage files. When information in these areas is damaged, it can cause trouble opening files and slowing down performance.

## Fix Disk Problems

① Click the **Applications** folder in the Dock, click the **Utilities** folder, and then click the **Disk Utility** icon.

② Click the **First Aid** tab.

③ Select a non-startup volume (you cannot repair the startup drive).

④ Click **Repair Disk**.

> **IMPORTANT** *You cannot repair the Startup volume. To perform a Repair Disk on the Startup volume, you'll have to reboot from a different disk.*

⑤ Repeat steps 3 and 4 until all your disks have been repaired.

> **TIMESAVER** *Applications such as Norton Utilities and Tech Tools can help to further enhance and optimize your hard drives, by performing a defrag, or by performing error checks to files not available with the Apple Disk Utility.*

# Optimizing a Disk

Your computer uses a storage device to hold applications and data. Typically this would be the main hard drive. Not only is the storage of that information important, but timely retrieval is also an important consideration. Every computer user wants their system to run as efficiently as possible. Faster computers should perform operations such as: opening applications, saving files, and performing normal operations faster than older computers. However, you may notice that after a while your computer doesn't seem to be operating as fast as it did previously—files that took a few seconds to open now take a minute. The problem lies in the optimization of the hard drive, and Snow Leopard gives you several ways to optimize your hard drive. Benchmark tests reveal that keeping your hard drive in tiptop shape, actually makes the drive perform eight to ten percent faster. That means programs operate faster, opening and working on graphic files is faster; everything is faster. Time spent in optimizing your hard drive is time well spent.

## Optimize a Disk

1. Click the **Applications** folder in the Dock, click the **Utilities** folder, and then click the **Disk Utility** icon.

2. Click the **First Aid** tab.

3. Select the Startup volume from the available options.

4. Click **Repair Disk Permissions** (available only for volumes with Mac OS X installed).

> **IMPORTANT** *Disk Permissions are required by the operating system, and can become damaged. When they are damaged, normal operations become slower.*

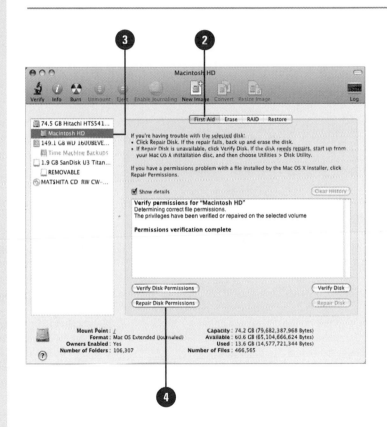

# Starting Your Computer From a Mac OS 9 Disk

Mac OS X Snow Leopard doesn't support the Classic environment, so if you want to use Mac OS 9, you need to install it on a different disk or partition disk. When you want to use Mac OS 9, you can use the Startup Disk pane in System Preferences to set Mac OS 9 as your startup disk. When you restart your computer, Mac OS 9 starts. In Mac OS 9, you need to use the Startup Disk control panel in the Apple menu to switch back to your Mac OS X startup disk and use Mac OS X features. If Mac OS 9 is not available in the Startup Disk preference pane, your computer only starts in Mac OS X, which happens on some newer computers. Check your documentation or Apple support for details.

## Restart with Mac OS 9

1. Click the **System Preferences** icon in the Dock, and then click the **Startup Disk** icon.

2. Click the Mac OS 9 icon system folder you want to use as the startup disk.

   An alert message appears, asking for confirmation.

3. Click **Restart**, and then click Restart again as confirmation.

   **TIMESAVER** *Hold down the Option key while you restart your computer, select a startup disk, and then click Restart.*

## Did You Know?

**You can quickly restart with Mac OS X.** In Mac OS 9, click the Apple menu, point to Control Panel, and then click Startup Disk. In the control panel, select the folder icon for the Mac OS X System folder, and then click Restart.

## For Your Information

### Fast Startup Switch in Mac OS X or Mac OS 9

If you have both Mac OS X and Mac OS 9 installed on the same hard disk or partition (divide one hard disk into two sections), while the Mac is starting up, hold down the X key to start up in Mac OS X. If you have installed Mac OS X and Mac OS 9 on different hard disks or partitions (where the Mac OS 9 system is on the internal disk or first partition, and Mac OS X is the startup disk), you can hold down the D key while the Mac starts up to start up in Mac OS 9. With the same set up, you can also hold down the Option key to display the Startup Manager, where you can select the OS you want to start.

# Migrating Information Between Macs

Instead of trying to re-create Macintosh settings manually from an old computer on a new Macintosh computer, you can use the Migration Assistant. With a FireWire cable connecting the two computers using Mac OS X, you can use the Migration Assistant to transfer important files and Macintosh settings from one computer to another. The Migration Assistance can transfer user accounts, applications, network and computer settings, files, and volumes. Before you can use the Migration Assistant, you need the administrator user name and password to gain access.

## Use the Migration Assistant

1. Click the **Applications** folder in the Dock, click the **Utilities** folder, and then click the **Migration Assistant** icon.

2. Read the welcome screen, and then click **Continue**.

3. Enter the administrator name and password, and then click **OK**.

4. Select the migration method you want to use:

   ◆ **From another Mac.** Transfers information from another Mac using a FireWire.

   ◆ **From another volume on this Mac.** Transfers information from another volume on this Mac.

   ◆ **From a Time Machine backup.** Restores information from a Time Machine backup.

5. Click **Continue**.

6. Follow the on-screen instructions for your migration option, which includes selecting the information you want to transfer; steps vary depending on your migration method.

7. Click **Transfer**.

8. When the process is complete, click **Done**.

# Monitoring System Activities

Mac OS X lets you view exactly how much processor power the various files and applications you have open are using, by utilizing the Activity Monitor. The Activity Monitor is a highly accurate tool that gives you up-to-date information on the various operations currently being used on your computer. It gives you the ability to view the process on a live graph, and even to halt various processes. In addition, if you own a multi-processor Mac, you'll see a separate graph for each processor to let you know how well the operating system is dividing the load.

## Monitor System Activities

1. Click the **Applications** folder in the Dock, click the **Utilities** folder, and then click the **Activity Monitor** icon.

2. Select a process from the available options.

3. To view more information, click the **Inspect** button.

4. To save the current process list, click the **File** menu, and then click **Save**.

5. To force a quit of the selected process, click the **Quit Process** button.

6. To search for a specific process, enter a search string in the Filter field.

CPU statistics

System Memory statistics

⑦ To view selected processes, click the **Process** pop-up.

⑧ Select from the following monitoring tabs:

◆ **CPU.** Select to view a graph of the process currently active.

◆ **System Memory.** Select to view the current distribution of system memory.

◆ **Disk Activity.** Select to view information on the current disk activities.

◆ **Disk Usage.** Select to view disk usage on the selected disk (click the Disk pop-up to select a disk).

◆ **Network.** Select to view the current activity across the network.

⑨ Click the **Close** button.

Disk Activity statistics

Disk Usage statistics

Network statistics

# Viewing System Messages with the Console

The Console utility is a viewer that displays all the text-based messages sent between the Macintosh operating system, and all open applications. While this utility may seem a bit much for the average Macintosh user, it's of great value to programmers, or would-be programmers, because it gives you information on how the operating system communicates with OS X applications.

## View System Messages with the Console

1. Click the **Applications** folder in the Dock, click the **Utilities** folder, and then click the **Console** icon.

2. Click **Show Log Lists**, and then select from the available Console logs.

3. To erase the current log, click **Clear Display**.

4. To reload the active log, click **Reload**.

5. To add a day/date stamp to the log, click **Insert Marker**.

6. To look for a specific function, type a search value into the Filter field.

7. To add or subtract buttons from the Console toolbar, click the **View** menu, and then click **Customize Toolbar**. Select the item to add or subtract.

8. To change the font used in displaying Console messages, click the **Font** menu, and then click **Show Fonts**.

9. If necessary, make any changes to the Font family and size.

10. Click the **Close** button.

11. Click **Done**.

# Viewing System Information with System Profiler

The System Profiler gives you an exact record of what applications you have installed on your computer; along with information on the installed hardware, system extensions, and current network. It's a great place to go, if you're curious about what you've got. For example, the System Profiler not only gives you information on your installed applications, it also tells what version (including patches) you've got, and the last time you updated it. The System Profiler also gives you detailed information on your processor; its speed, and any external devices, such as your hard drives and scanners.

## View System Information with System Profiler

① Click the **Applications** folder in the Dock, click the **Utilities** folder, and then click the **System Profiler** icon.

② Select an item from the Contents column.

③ View information on the selected item in the Info window.

④ Click the **View** menu, and then select from **Short Report**, **Standard Report** (default), or **Extended Report**.

⑤ Click the **File** menu, and then click **Save Print** or **Export** the current report.

⑥ Click the **Close** button.

Selected application

### Did You Know?

*You can use System Profiler to check if you have a CD or DVD recordable drive on your computer.* Launch System Profiler from the Utilities folder, click the triangle to expand the Hardware category, click the ATA (internal), USB, FireWire, or SCSI category, and then look for CD-R, DVD-R, CD-RW, or DVD-RW. Any of these means you can burn a CD or DVD. If it says simply CD or DVD, then you can't.

# Forcing a Restart

When OS X was first unveiled to the Apple community, many users sat back and waited to see how this new operating system would fit into the Mac world, and over the years, it has won over even its harshest critics. With its ability to process information ultra fast, and its UNIX base, it has become the system of choice for the discriminating Mac user. Apple OS X is the first "true" multi-processing operating system to appear in the Mac market. When you open a program, the UNIX-based operating system runs the application within a protected area of the CPU memory. When a second program is opened, it gets its own CPU working areas. What that means to you is that a program crash no longer means restarting your computer. All you have to do is force the program to quit. In the event of a system lockup, you can even instruct the operating system to force a restart.

## Force a Restart

1. Click the **Apple** menu, and then click **Force Quit**.

2. Click **Finder**.

3. Click **Relaunch** to conduct a mini restart of the operating system.

   **TIMESAVER** *If your system is so locked up that you can't access the Force Quit command, just hold down the ⌘+Control+Power keys to force your computer to restart.*

4. Follow any onscreen instructions for restarting.

## Did You Know?

**When you perform a mini restart, you're just relaunching the Finder.** Any other programs that were open remain open.

# Managing Hardware

## Introduction

Computer systems are composed of more than just a computer (that's why they're called systems). A computer houses a hard drive, and is connected to a keyboard, mouse, and video display. All of these hardware devices are required to operate your computer. For most users that's just the start, you'll probably have one or more printers, a scanner; maybe even a second monitor. Then of course, there are digital cameras, fax machines... you get the idea.

Computers are made up of a group of hardware devices, and like a conductor at a symphony, Snow Leopard helps you work with those devices, by making the installation, management, and removal easy. In addition, Snow Leopard can help you manage color between devices, help you install MIDI (audio) devices, and even make Internet communications easy. If the worst of the worst problems occur (a system crash), there are steps you can perform to bring your computer system back on line, and you don't even have to be a techie.

## What You'll Do

**Install Hardware Devices**

**View Hardware Settings**

**Change Mouse Settings**

**Change Keyboard Settings**

**Change Monitor Display Settings**

**Measure Display Colors with the Digital Color Meter**

**Select Colors with the Color Picker**

**Match Colors to Devices with ColorSync**

**Configure Audio MIDI Devices**

**Prevent Hardware Problems**

**Remove Hardware Devices**

# Installing Hardware Devices

Years ago, hardware installation required all kinds of techniques and special skills. A hardware device such as a printer, could take hours to set up. There were all kinds of cabling problems, and even after it was installed, there were numerous settings to complete before you could use the device. Today, many devices are plug-and-play. You can now go out to your local computer store, pick up a FireWire hard drive, plug it in to your computer, and immediately begin using it. The same is true for many other devices, such as card readers and digital cameras. Even if the device requires the installation of a driver (printers and scanners usually do), a double-click on the install application and answering a few simple questions is typically all that's needed.

## Install Hardware Devices

1. Insert the install CD or DVD into your computer (assuming the device is not plug-and-play) or navigate to the installer on your computer or network.

2. Launch the installation application.

   **TROUBLE?** *Some installations require the device be plugged into your computer. Make sure the device is plugged in, and if necessary, powered on.*

3. Follow the instructions for installing the device (some devices may require a reboot of the system).

4. When the installation is finished, follow the on-screen instructions to end the process.

## Did You Know?

*You can purchase a power strip (also known as a surge protector) to help with all those power plugs.* If you install several hardware devices that require their own external power supplies, such as printers and scanners, you can invest in a power strip, and to protect against power spikes, make sure it's a surge-protected power strip.

# Viewing Hardware Settings

Most hardware devices have settings that control how the device operates. For example, all ink-jet printers have settings that control the type of paper used, how the inks are applied to the paper and, if your printer has more than a single paper tray, which tray is used for the current printing process. Snow Leopard uses the System Preferences panel to display all of the available hardware settings for the major components of the operating system. In addition, when you install specific hardware devices such as a third-party mouse or video-control board, you'll see an icon for controlling the device in the System Preferences.

## View Hardware Settings

1. Click **System Preferences** icon in the Dock.

   The Hardware section holds the icons to the standard hardware devices for Mac OS X.

2. Click an icon to view or modify the hardware settings of the selected device.

3. When you're finished viewing or modifying the settings, select the following options:

   ◆ **About.** Provides information on the manufacturer of the device; including the hardware version and Web site (if any).

   ◆ **Help.** Gives you access to the Help dialog for the selected device.

   ◆ **Revert.** Puts the settings back to their previous selections.

   ◆ **Apply Now.** Applies the changes to the settings.

   ◆ **Close.** Closes the pop-up.

Hardware section

# Changing Mouse Settings

When you use any computer, a mouse is an important part of the computing experience. Computers communicate with the user through a series of Graphical User Interfaces or a G.U.I. (pronounced Gooey). The user communicates with the computer through several devices, such as: a touch screen, a keyboard, a drawing tablet and a mouse. Using a mouse requires a bit of hand-to-eye coordination: You see something on the screen (a button perhaps), and you move the mouse pointer over the object and click. Apple understands the importance of the mouse, and gives you ways to control its movement and sensitivity through preferences located in System Preferences. If you have a Bluetooth wireless mouse, you can set it up a new device, check battery levels, and select other Bluetooth-related options.

## Change Mouse Settings

1. Click **System Preferences** icon in the Dock, and then click the **Mouse** icon.

2. Drag to adjust the following options:

   ◆ **Tracking Speed.** Controls the speed of the mouse as you drag across your mouse pad.

   ◆ **Scrolling Speed.** Controls the scrolling speed of the mouse.

   ◆ **Double-Click Speed.** Controls the speed at which you must double-click your mouse.

3. To use the scroll wheel on your mouse, select the **Zoom using scroll wheel while holding** check box, click the pop-up, and then select a shortcut key. To set additional zoom options, click **Options**.

4. To set Bluetooth wireless options, click **Set Up Bluetooth Mouse**, and then follow the on-screen instructions.

5. Click the **Close** button.

## For Your Information

### Performing Finder Gestures

If you're using a Mac notebook with a Multi-Touch trackpad, you can use it to perform three- or four-finder gestures (**New!**).

# Changing Keyboard Settings

Your keyboard is another one of those wonderful devices that help us communicate with a computer. Keyboards have what is called a **tactile feel** (the way the keys bounce back when they're pressed). Although you can't control the tactile feel of a keyboard, you can control how the keyboard's repeat functions work through System Preferences. Keyboard shortcuts allow you to quickly perform a task by pressing keys on your keyboard. You can change or disable many global keyboard shortcuts, the same shortcuts in all applications, to avoid conflicts or customize to suit your own work preferences (**New!**).

## Change Keyboard Settings

1. Click **System Preferences** icon in the Dock, and then click the **Keyboard** icon.

2. Click the **Keyboard** tab.

3. Drag the **Key Repeat Rate** slider to adjust the speed at which a repeating key is typed.

4. Drag the **Delay Until Repeat** slider to adjust the length of time you have to hold down a key before it begins repeating.

5. Click the **Close** button.

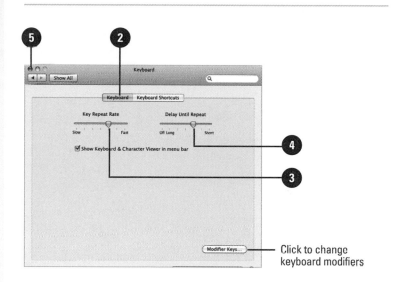

Click to change keyboard modifiers

## Customize Keyboard Shortcuts

1. Click **System Preferences** icon in the Dock, and then click the **Keyboard** icon.

2. Click the **Keyboard Shortcuts** tab.

3. Click the category (**New!**) with the shortcuts you want to customize.

4. To disable a shortcut, clear the check box next to the description.

5. To change a key combination, click the characters, hold down the new shortcut key combination you want.

6. Click the **Close** button, and then restart any application that uses it.

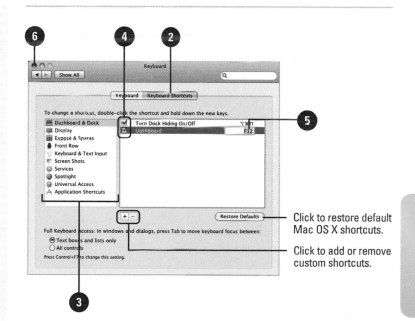

Click to restore default Mac OS X shortcuts.

Click to add or remove custom shortcuts.

# Changing Monitor Display Settings

Your monitor is the main interface between you and your computer. A monitor displays all your programs and mouse movements. Without a monitor, you would in fact be attempting to operate your computer with your eyes closed. Apple, in a effort to give you the best possible view of its wonderful operating system interface, gives you the ability to modify how your monitor displays data, through options located in System Preferences.

## Change Monitor Display Settings

**1** Click **System Preferences** icon in the Dock, and then click the **Displays** icon.

**2** Click the **Display** tab.

**3** Select from the following options:

◆ **Resolutions.** Select a display resolution from the options.

◆ **Colors.** Click the pop-up, and then select the number of colors to display.

◆ **Refresh Rate.** Click the pop-up to set a refresh rate.

◆ **Detect Displays.** Searches for any additional displays attached to the computer.

◆ **Show Displays In Menu Bar.** Check to display the Displays icon on the Apple menu bar.

◆ **Number Of Recent Modes.** Click the pop-up, and then select how many recent modes to display.

◆ **Brightness.** Changes the brightness of the monitor (a Mac laptop feature).

◆ **Automatically Adjust Brightness As Ambient Light Changes.** Automatically adjusts the brightness of the monitor to compensate for external lights (a Mac laptop feature).

④ Click the **Color** tab.

⑤ Select from the following color options:

◆ **Show Profiles For This Display Only.** Check to display profiles for the current monitor.

◆ **Open Profile.** Click to open a profile.

◆ **Delete Profile.** Click to delete a profile.

◆ **Calibrate.** Click to calibrate the color of the monitor.

⑥ Click the **Close** button.

Display Calibrator Assistant

---

### For Your Information

#### Smoothing Fonts On-Screen

If the fonts on your screen look fuzzy, you can set a screen option to smooth the fonts appearance. Click the System Preferences icon in the Dock, click the Appearance icon, click the Font Smoothing Style pop-up, and then select the best option for your monitor. Automatic is best for the main display, while Standard works the best for an old style CRT monitor. If you have a flat panel display, Medium is the best option. When text smoothing, also known as antialiasing, is enabled, smaller fonts can be harder to read. If you need to use small fonts in your documents, set the font size you want before text smoothing kicks in. When you're done, click the Close button.

# Measuring Display Colors with the Digital Color Meter

Have you ever wondered what the exact color value of an item on your monitor would be if measured using RGB (red, green, and blue) values? Or how about the hexadecimal value of a color (useful if you design Web pages)? Color is an important part of any designer's life, and the Digital Color meter lets you accurately sample colors from your monitor. Since the cursor determines the sampled color, you'll need to learn a few shortcut keys to lock, print, and save the color information.

## Measure Display Colors with the Digital Color Meter

① Click the **Applications** folder in the Dock, click the **Utilities** folder, and then click the **Digital Color Meter** icon.

② Click the **Color** pop-up, and then select a color space to measure.

③ Drag the **Aperture Size** slider left or right, to decrease or increase the area used for the taking of a screen shot.

④ Move the mouse over the monitor to measure the color directly underneath the cursor.

⑤ To hold a color into the color swatch box, press ⌘+Shift+H.

⑥ To lock the screen shot of the current image, press ⌘+L.

⑦ Click the **Image** menu, and then click **Save As TIFF** to save the current locked screen shot as a TIFF image.

⑧ Click the **Color** menu, and then click **Copy Color As Text** or **Copy Color As Image** to save the held color in clipboard memory. The color can then be copied into another program.

**456**

# Selecting Colors with the Color Picker

The world of color on a computer is a very subjective place to live. For example, you might be using a new Macintosh Studio Display, and someone else might be using a Sony LCD monitor. What this means to you is, a color displayed on your hardware device (monitor) might look slightly different on another computer using a different monitor. In addition, it's possible that two people, owning the same monitor, may have them adjusted differently. While creating consistent color output is a difficult thing, Mac OS X gives you a stable color picking system, which helps to stabilize colors systems. The Macintosh Color Picker is accessed through an application, such as TextEdit, MS Word or Photoshop, or any application that lets you select colors.

## Select Colors with the Color Picker

1. Open an application, such as MS Word or TextEdit.

2. Display the Colors window.

   ◆ In MS Word, select a button, such as text color, and then click **More Colors**.

   ◆ In TextEdit, click the **Format** menu, point to **Font**, and then click **Show Colors**.

3. Click a palette, and then select a color from the available color profiles:

   ◆ **Color Wheel.** Drag the scroll bar vertically to adjust the brightness, and then click inside the ball, to select a color.

   ◆ **Color Slider.** Select a color mixing method from the pop-up, and then drag the sliders to select a color.

   ◆ **Color Palettes.** Select a pre-designed color palette from the pop-up, and then select the color from the available list.

   ◆ **Image Palettes.** Displays a spectrum of colors. Click in the spectrum to select a color.

   ◆ **Crayons.** Select a color from the available crayons.

4. Click the **Close** button.

Color Wheel   3            Color Palettes            Crayons

# Matching Colors to Devices with ColorSync

The ColorSync utility gives the designer the ability to match up colors between devices, and to check on and repair the device color profiles present on the computer. As you might have figured out by now, computer monitors are not the best at maintaining color accuracy; especially between monitor and print. The ColorSync utility strives to maintain a color standard between devices, by acting as a translator between different devices. The original scanned image, your monitor, and the output printing device are all examples of where color needs to be synced, and it is achieved though the ColorSync utility.

## Match Colors to Devices with ColorSync

1.  Click the **Applications** folder in the Dock, click the **Utilities** folder, and then click the **ColorSync Utility** icon.

2.  Click **Profile First Aid**.

3.  Click **Verify** (to view) or **Repair** (to fix) the color profiles installed on your computer.

4.  Click **Profiles**.

5.  View a gamut grid of the color profiles installed for your computer (click the user option to view color profiles created by you).

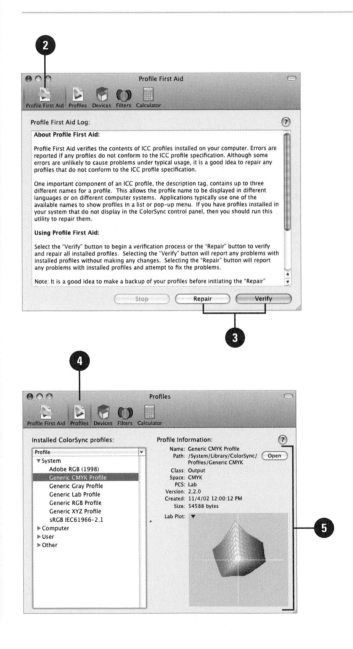

6. To select and assign color profiles to all installed devices, click **Devices**.

7. To view information on the currently installed filters, click **Filters**.

8. Click **Add** (+) or **Remove** (-) button to add a new filter, or delete the selected filter.

9. Click the **Down Arrow** icon, point to any of the following commands, and then select the option you want:

   ◆ **Duplicate Filter.**

   ◆ **Add Color Management Component.**

   ◆ **Add Image Effects Component.**

   ◆ **Add PDF Retouch Component.**

   ◆ **Add Domain Information.**

   ◆ **Add Comments.**

   **IMPORTANT** *The ColorSync Utility gives you the ability to view and change the color profiles used by different devices. This is an area where you don't want to experiment. Have a good understanding of color theory, before attempting to change any of the ColorSync settings.*

10. Click the **Close** button.

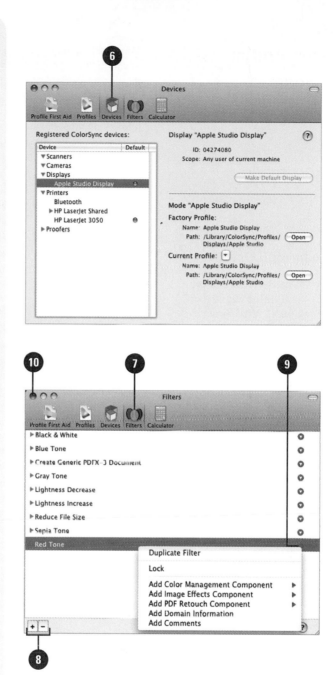

# Configuring Audio MIDI Devices

Macintosh computers were born to work with music, and as the years advanced they got better and better. The Audio MIDI (Musical Instrument Digital Interface) Setup utility is designed to help you setup all your input and output sound equipment, such as microphones, speakers, and multichannel audio interfaces, either built-in or external (**New!**). In most cases, the default settings work the best. However, if you do work a lot with audio, Apple has made the process of adding, monitoring, and adjusting external devices, such as electronic keyboards and speakers, a snap. If you have multiple audio devices, you can combine them together, known as aggregating devices, to add capacity. For example, if you have an two 6 channel audio devices, you can combine them to work as a single 12 channel audio device.

## Configure Audio MIDI Devices

① Click the **Applications** folder in the Dock, click the **Utilities** folder, and then click the **Audio MIDI Setup** icon.

② To create an aggregate device, click the **Add** (+) button.

- ◆ To remove an aggregate device, select it, and then click the **Remove** (-) button.

③ Select the audio device you want to configure.

④ To use the selected device for sound input or sound output, or to play system sounds, click the **Actions** button, and then select an option.

⑤ If you're using an audio device that sends its own timing messages, click the **Clock source** pop-up, and then select an option.

⑥ Click the **Input** or **Output** tab, if available.

⑦ If you prefer a different source option, click the **Source** pop-up, and then select an option.

The Mac automatically selects the appropriate source option for you.

8  Based on your audio device, click the **Sample Rate** and **Bit Depth** pop-ups (under Format), and then select an appropriate setting.

9  To set the volume for each channel, drag the **Volume** sliders.

10 To configure surround sound (multichannel) speakers, click **Configure Speakers**, select the options you want, click **Apply**, and then click **Done**.

   ◆ Select **Stereo** or **Multichannel** device type, and then select a surround sound version for multichannel.

   ◆ Select the device channel for each speaker.

   ◆ To test the speaker connection, click a speaker to play a sound.

11 Click the **Close** button.

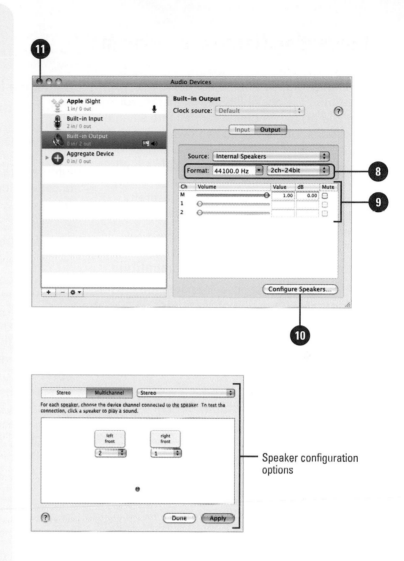

Speaker configuration options

# Preventing Hardware Problems

Whenever you add hardware devices to your computer, the possibility exists that a problem will occur. Problems can fall into several categories: The device doesn't work, the device doesn't work the way you expect, or the computer refuses to boot. Apple's built-in management systems make hardware problems a rare event. However, a few careful steps on your part can help to make problems almost non-existent.

## Check for hardware device compatibility

Not all hardware devices are compatible with your particular version of Macintosh. For example, you could purchase a video driver board, which works fine in a G4 model, but won't function in a G5 or later. Make sure the user's manual lists your model of Macintosh.

## Check for software compatibility

Many hardware devices require installation software to operate. Even though OS X has been in the market for a couple of years, there are still hardware devices with accompanying installation software that is not compatible with the OS X operating system. In addition, the Snow Leopard operating system changed the rules on computer architecture; therefore, make sure the software is not just OS X compatible, but is also Snow Leopard compatible.

## Check the Internet

Software changes (almost on a weekly basis), when you purchase a piece of hardware, that box may have been sitting on the shelf for months. Make sure you access the device's Internet site, and determine if you have the latest version of the software. It's easy and it's free.

## Plan for the future

If you haven't purchased an Intel-based Mac (yet), you probably will in the future. Be advised that some of your hardware devices may not work with the new architecture. Many times it's the software for the device. Some hardware manufacturers can take months to develop the software necessary to operate your hardware devices on the new computers, and some have no plans to upgrade at all. When you purchase new hardware, check the manufacturer's Web site, and see if they plan on supporting future Macintosh computers.

## When the worst happens

Sometimes you install a hardware device, and your Macintosh refuses to startup. Many times it's because you just installed a new hardware device. Unfortunately, when you disconnect the device your Mac still won't startup. The reason is because the software that runs the device is still installed. When this happens you can attempt a fix by performing a "Safe" boot.

First, you'll need to power down your computer. After your computer has shut off, go ahead and press the power button. After you hear the startup tone, immediately press and hold the Shift key. You'll release the Shift key when you see the gray Apple and progress indicator (looks like a spinning gear).

The Safe Mode takes awhile to boot (several minutes). That's because Safe Mode performs a system check before starting. Then, you'll use the hardware device's installation CD to remove the installed hardware. After that is done, restart your computer the normal way (without holding the Shift key).

If removing the device software does not solve the problem, your glitch may be caused by something more serious. You can attempt a reinstall of the OS X operating system, but before doing that, go online and check out the Apple Web site and search for help on your problem. When there is no solution but to start over, or get a new device, you'll need to remove the hardware device and the software that controls it.

Perform a safe boot

# Removing Hardware Devices

Installing hardware can be relatively easy: you insert the installation CD or DVD and follow the onscreen instructions. However, when you remove a hardware device, the software that ran the device is still on your computer. It's important to remove any software that is no longer needed for two reasons: it takes up space on your hard drive, and it could cause problems in the future with the installation of other hardware devices.

## Remove Hardware Devices

① Startup your computer.

② Use the third-party software's installer CD or DVD to remove the recently installed software.

> **IMPORTANT** *If you do not have the original CD or DVD, check the manufacturer's Web site. Most have an uninstall program that you can download for free.*

③ If you are uncertain about which software was installed last, perform the following steps:

◆ Open the Startup Items folder, located in the Systems folder, and temporarily remove one or more items.

◆ Perform a restart and see if the problem goes away.

④ If the problem still exists, perform the additional steps:

◆ Open the Extensions folder, located in the Systems/Library/Extensions folder.

◆ View files by Date Modified.

◆ Temporarily move into a folder any relevant, recently modified, third-party .kext files, and then restart the computer.

◆ Add back the moved .kext files one at a time and restart, until the problem reoccurs.

⑤ Click the **Close** button.

Startup items

Extensions

464

# Working with Mac OS X Along with Windows

## Introduction

If you have an Intel-based Mac computer, you can install and run Microsoft Windows XP (Service Pack 2 or later), Windows Vista, or Windows 7 on your computer. All you need is Boot Camp Assistant, related drivers, and your Microsoft Windows installation disc.

The Boot Camp Assistant helps you set up a Windows partition on your computer's hard drive and then start the Windows operating system installation. After you complete the initial installation, you need to install Boot Camp drivers to complete the installation and start your Mac in either Windows or Mac OS X. The Boot Camp drivers, available on your Mac OS X Snow Leopard installation disc, allow you to use your Apple keyboard to emulate a standard PC keyboard, an Apple Remote (if your computer is equipped with one) to control iTunes and Windows Media, Bluetooth wireless devices, an iSight camera, and AirPort wireless network connectivity, and change brightness and contrast controls for built-in displays. After you finish the Windows installation and Boot Camp driver update, you can use Windows on your Mac.

If you no longer want to run Microsoft Windows on your Mac computer, you can remove it using Boot Camp Assistant. When you remove Windows, the Boot Camp Assistant removes the Windows software and restores your hard disk back to a single partition.

# Preparing a Mac for Windows

Before you can install Microsoft Windows XP (Service Pack 2 or later), Windows Vista, or Windows 7 on your Mac, you need to meet the minimum hardware requirement for your Mac, create a partition on your hard disk for the Windows software, and have a single-full Windows (32-bit version) installation disc. You can use the About This Mac command on the Apple menu to check your hardware configuration and Boot Camp Assistant to create a partition for the Windows software. Before you install Windows on your Mac computer, it's critical to make a back up of the important files on your computer; better safe than sorry.

## Prepare a Mac for Windows

1. Before you can install and set up Windows on your Mac, your computer needs to meet the following minimum requirements:

   - An Intel-based Mac computer.

   - A USB keyboard and mouse, or a built-in keyboard and touch pad.

   - Mac OS X version 10.5 or later; the lastest version of the Mac OS X is recommended.

   - At least 10 GB of free space on the installation disk.

   - Internal disk with a single partition, formatted as a Mac OS X Extended (Journaled) volume.

   - 2 GB or more of RAM when running Windows 7 or Vista on a Mac Pro computer.

   - A licensed copy of Windows XP Home Edition or Professional, Windows Vista, or Windows 7.

2. Click the **Applications** folder in the Dock, click the **Utilities** folder, and then click the **Boot Camp Assistant** icon.

About This Mac computer information

3 Read the Introduction screen, and then click **Print Installation & Setup Guide** to have this important document handy during your Windows installation.

4 Click **Continue**.

5 If your computer has more than one internal disk, select the disk you want to use, select the partition option you want, and then click **Continue**.

6 Use the default size (recommended), or specify the size you want. Either, drag the divider to set the size of the partition or click **Divide Equally** or **Use 32 GB**.

The partition must be at least 5 GB and leave at least 5 GB of free space on the Mac OS X partition.

**IMPORTANT** *A partition larger than 32 GB cannot be formatted as a FAT volume.*

7 Click **Partition**, and then wait for the completion of the partition.

8 Click **Quit and Install Later** to perform the Windows install at another time, or go to the next page and follow the instructions to start the installation.

## Did You Know?

***You can upgrade from Boot Camp beta.*** If you already installed Boot Camp beta on your computer, all you need to do is update the Boot Camp drivers for Windows. You don't need to repartition your hard disk or reinstall Windows. Simply, restart your Mac using Windows, insert the Mac OS X Snow Leopard disc, and then follow the on-screen instructions as needed to update the drivers.

## Have a Problem?

### Having Trouble Partitioning a Disk

If you have a problem creating a partition, you may need to update your system software and the firmware on your computer. Firmware is software embedded in hardware components. Boot Camp requires Mac OS X 10.4.6 or later and the latest firmware. To update your system software, click the Apple menu, and then click Software Update. To update your firmware, go to the Apple Downloads Web site at *www.apple.com/support/downloads*, search for firmware updates for your computer and follow the instructions.

# Installing Windows on a Mac

After you create a partition on your Mac computer for the Windows software, you can start the Microsoft Windows XP (Service Pack 2 or later), Windows Vista, or Windows 7 installation on your Mac with a single-full Windows (32-bit version) installation disc. During the Windows installation, you need to reformat the new Windows partition, so you can boot (startup) from Windows. You can reformat the Windows partition with the NTFS (XP, Vista, or 7) or FAT (XP only) format. NTFS provides reliability and security, while FAT provides compatibility, which allows you to read and write file on the Windows partition from Mac OS X. After you complete the Windows installation, you need to update Boot Camp drivers on your Mac computer, which are available on your Mac OS X Snow Leopard installation disc, to install Mac-specific drivers for graphics, networking, audio, AirPort wireless connectivity, Bluetooth, iSight camera, Apple keyboards, Apple Remote, and brightness control for built-in displays.

## Install Windows on a Mac

1. Create a partition on your Mac computer for the Windows software; see "Preparing a Mac for Windows Software" on page 466 for specific details.

   **IMPORTANT** *To install Windows using Boot Camp, you must be logged in as an administrator.*

2. If you quit Boot Camp Assistant without installing Windows, click the **Applications** folder in the Dock, click the **Utilities** folder, click the **Boot Camp Assistant** icon, and then click the **Start the Windows installer** option.

3. Click **Continue**.

4. Insert your Windows installation disc, and then click **Start Installation**.

   **IMPORTANT** *Do not install an earlier version of Windows XP and try to update it.*

**5** Follow the Windows installation instructions until you need to decide where to install Windows.

◆ **Windows XP.** Select **C:Partition3 <BOOTCAMP> [FAT32]**, and then select an NTFS or FAT format partition option.

◆ **Windows 7 or Vista.** Click **Disk 0 Partition 3 BOOTCAMP**, click **Drive option (advanced)**, click **Format**, and then click **OK**.

**6** Finish the Windows installation, and then eject the Windows Installation disc.

**7** Insert your Mac OS X Snow Leopard installation disc.

◆ If the installer doesn't automatically start, double-click the setup.exe file on the disc to start installing drivers.

**8** Follow the on-screen instructions. Don't click Cancel in any of the dialog boxes; click **Continue**. Click **Finish**, and then click **Yes** to restart.

**9** After your computer restarts, follow the instructions in the Found New Hardware Wizard to update your software drivers (Windows XP only).

## Did You Know?

*You can upgrade Windows XP to Windows 7 or Vista.* Restart your Mac using Windows, insert your Windows 7 or Vista installation or upgrade disc, follow the on-screen instructions, insert the Mac OS X Snow Leopard disc, and then follow the on-screen instructions as needed to update the drivers.

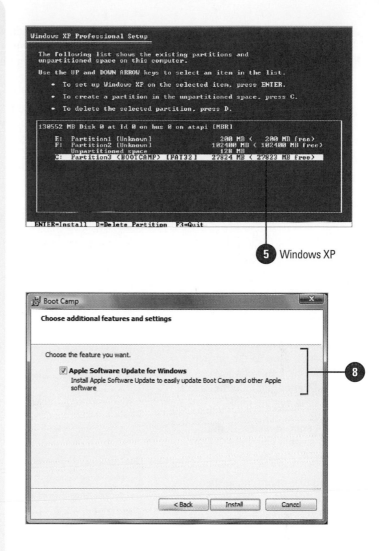

**5** Windows XP

# Starting Up with Mac OS X or Windows

After you install Microsoft Windows and Boot Camp drivers, you can start up your Mac computer in either Mac OS X or Windows. You can set the default operating system you want to use on a regular basis using Startup Disk preferences on the Mac or the Boot Camp Control Panel on Windows, and then use quick controls to directly restart your computer in the other operating system or select an operating system while starting your Mac computer.

## Set the Startup Disk for Mac OS X or Windows

1.  Start up using either of the following:

    ◆ **In the Mac OS X.** Click the **Apple** menu, click **System Preferences**, and then click **Startup Disk**.

    ◆ **In Windows.** Click the **Start** button on the taskbar, click the **Boot Camp** icon in the notification area on the taskbar, and then click **Boot Camp Control Panel**. Click **Continue** to access the system utility.

2.  Select the startup disk with the operating system you want to use by default.

3.  To start up that operating system now, click **Restart**.

4.  Click the **Close** button (Mac) or **OK** (Win).

470

## Start Up with Mac OS X or Windows

◆ **Select an OS when you startup.** As your computer starts up, hold down the Option key until disk icons appear, select the startup disk with the operating system you want, and then click the arrow below the icon.

◆ **Restart to Mac from Windows.** In Windows, click the **Boot Camp** icon in the notification area, click **Restart in Mac OS X**, and then click **OK**.

◆ **Restart to Windows from Mac.** In Mac OS X, click the **Apple** menu, click **Restart**, click **Restart**, hold down the Option key until disk icons appear, select Windows, and then click the arrow below the icon.

Select an OS when you start up

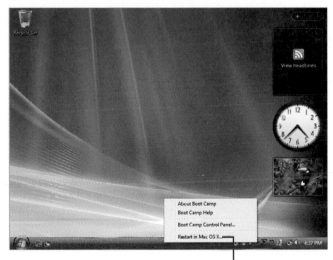

Restart to Mac from Windows

# Using Windows on a Mac

After you finish the Windows installation and Boot Camp driver update, you can use Windows on your Mac. The Boot Camp drivers allow you to use your Apple keyboard to emulate a standard PC keyboard, use function keys, eject discs using the Eject key on the keyboard, change the volume using the Volume Down or Up keys, right-click using an Apple Mighty Mouse or trackpad, use an Apple Remote (if your computer is equipped with one) to control iTunes and Windows Media, use Bluetooth wireless devices, attach and use an iSight camera, and connect to a wireless network using AirPort. In addition, you can work with files between your Mac OS X and Windows disks. Due to HFS+ support, you can now access files (read-only) on your Mac from Windows (**New!**) for review or save with a different name to make changes.

## Use Windows on a Mac

◆ **Disable remote control.** In Windows, click the **Boot Camp** icon in the notification area, and then click **Boot Camp Control Panel**, click the **Remote** tab, select the **Disable remote control infrared receiver** check box, and then click **OK**.

◆ **Pair or Unpair a remote control.** A Mac computer can only use one remote at a time. Use a remote, you need to pair it with the computer. Hold the remote close to the computer (3 to 4 inches) and point the remote at the front, press and hold down Menu and Next buttons on the remote for 5 seconds until a chain link symbol appears.

If you want to change remotes, you need to unpair the current one first. In Windows, click the **Boot Camp** icon in the notification area, and then click **Boot Camp Control Panel**, click the **Remote** tab, click **Unpair**, and then click **OK**.

◆ **Restart after a power failure.** In Windows, click the **Boot Camp** icon in the notification area, and then click **Boot Camp Control Panel**, click the **Power** tab, select the **Restart automatically after a power failure** check box, and then click **OK**.

Remote control options

Restart after a power failure

- **Use a Bluetooth Device.** In order to use a Bluetooth wireless device with Windows, you need to pair the device with your computer.

  In Windows, open the Bluetooth Devices control panel, click the **Devices** tab, click **Add**, and then follow the wizard instructions.

  Use the following numeric passkeys: Wireless Mighty Mouse, enter four zeros: *0000.* Apple Wireless keyboard, enter six to sixteen digits.

- **Copy Files Between Mac OS X and Windows.** If you installed Windows XP on a partition formatted with FAT, you can open and save files on your Windows disk, or copy files between your Mac OS X disk and Windows disk.

  If you installed Windows XP, Vista, or 7 on a partition formatted with NTFS, you can open files on your Windows disk from Mac OS X, or copy files from Windows to Mac OS X. However, you cannot copy or save any files to the protected Windows disk.

  **IMPORTANT** *Windows files need extensions (for example, .doc) to identify the file type. Most programs come in both Mac and Windows versions, so there should be no problem there. If it's a Mac only file type, you may need to convert it for Windows use.*

- **Use the Apple Keyboard with Windows.** Refer to the table for specific keyboard commands you can use on your Apple keyboard to emulate a standard PC keyboard.

  You can also use the Eject key and Volume Down and Up keys on the Apple keyboard to perform commands not available on the standard PC keyboard.

File on Mac disk    Windows Disk    Mac disk

Files on Windows disk

## Apple Keyboard with Windows

| PC Key Command | Apple External | Built-in Mac |
| --- | --- | --- |
| Control+Alt+Delete | Control-Option-Delete | Control-Option-Delete |
| Alt | Option | Option |
| AltGr | Control-Option | Control-Option |
| Backspace | Delete | Delete |
| Delete | Delete | Fn-Delete |
| Enter | Return | Return |
| Enter (num keypad) | Enter | Enter |
| Insert | Help | Fn-Enter |
| Num lock | Clear | Fn-F6 |
| Pause/Break | F16 | Fn-Esc |
| Print Screen | F14 | Fn-F11 |
| Print active window | Option-F14 | Option-Fn-F11 |
| Scroll/Lock | F15 | Fn-F12 |

# Removing Windows

If you no longer want to run Microsoft Windows on your Mac computer, you can remove it using Boot Camp Assistant. When you remove Windows, the Boot Camp Assistant removes the Windows software and restores your hard disk back to a single partition. All the information on the Windows partition is erased, so it's critical to make a back up of the important files on your computer before you start the removal process.

## Remove Windows from a Computer with a Single Internal Disk

① Start your Mac computer in Mac OS X.

② Click the **Applications** folder in the Dock, click the **Utilities** folder, and then click the **Boot Camp Assistant** icon.

③ Click **Continue**.

④ Click the **Create or remove a Windows partition** option.

⑤ Click **Continue**.

⑥ Enter your name and password, and then click **OK**.

⑦ Click **Restore**.

⑧ When you're done, click **Quit**.

### Did You Know?

*You can use Disk Utility to remove Windows on a single-volume disk.* Open the Applications folder, open the Utilities folder, and then double-click the Disk Utility icon to erase the disk and reformat it as a Mac OS X volume.

## Remove Windows from a Computer with Multiple Internal Disks

1. Start your Mac computer in Mac OS X.

2. Click the **Applications** folder in the Dock, click the **Utilities** folder, and then click the **Boot Camp Assistant** icon.

3. Click **Continue**.

4. Click the **Create or remove a Windows partition** option.

5. Click **Continue**.

6. Select the disk with the Windows software.

7. Click the **Restore to a single Mac OS partition** option.

8. Click **Continue**.

9. Enter your name and password, and then click **OK**.

10. Click **Restore**.

11. When you're done, click **Quit**.

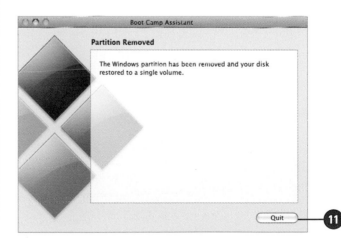

# Backing Up Everything with Time Machine

## Introduction

Backing up your files is an important part of protecting and maintaining your computer. If you accidentally deleted a file or lose files due to a computer problem, you can recover them with a backup.

Time Machine is a Mac OS X application that allows you to back up everything on your computer on a regular basis without any additional work on your part after the initial set up. The first time you use Time Machine, it backs up everything on your computer, including system files, applications, accounts, preferences, music, photos, movies, and documents. As you work and make changes on your computer, Time Machine backs up only the things that have changed.

Time Machine works best when you dedicate and use the same disk for you backups. You can use an internal or external disk as the back up disk. When you attach an external disk to your Mac computer, Time Machine asks if you want to use the device for backups and automatically sets everything up for you.

Backups are organized and store by date. You can browse and recover individual files, folders, or your entire computer. You can also burn backup CDs and DVDs, copy files onto another disk, or use your iDisk if you have a MobileMe account.

## What You'll Do

**Set Up Time Machine for Backups**

**Perform a Backup**

**Exclude Items from a Backup**

**Work with a Backup**

**Recover Backed Up Items**

**Recover an Entire Computer System**

**Create a Disk Image to Backup Files**

**Burn a CD or DVD from a Disk Image**

**Restore a Disk Image**

**Back Up Files onto a CD or DVD**

# Setting Up Time Machine for Backups

Time Machine works best when you dedicate and use the same disk for your backups. You can use an internal (except for your startup disk) or external disk (such as a FireWire or USB disk) as the back up disk. If you have partitioned a disk, you can use the partition as a back up disk too. The disk you use must be in the Mac OS Extended (Journaled) format, and must have Access Control Lists (ACLs) enabled. When you attach an external disk to your Mac computer, Time Machine asks if you want to use the device for backups and automatically sets everything up for you. The first time you start Time Machine, the program backs up everything on your computer. This may take a while, so it would good to start the initial set up and use for a time when your computer is idle, such as a late evening or weekend, so it can work overnight. However, if you use Time Capsule (a wireless hard drive designed to work with Time Machine), it's about 50 percent faster (**New!**). As you work and make changes on your computer, Time Machine backs up only the things that have changed.

## Set Up Time Machine Preferences

1. Click **System Preferences** icon in the Dock, and then click the **Time Machine** icon.

   ◆ On first use, you can click the **Time Machine** icon in the Dock, and then click **Start Preferences**.

2. To show a status menu, select the **Show Time Machine status in the menu bar** check box (**New!**).

3. Slide the switch to **ON**.

4. Click **Select Backup Disk**.

   ◆ If you have Time Capsule, click **Set Up Time Capsule** to use the AirPort Utility to set it up.

5. Click one of the available disks you can use for backups.

6. Click **Use for Backup**.

7. If your disk needs to be erased before you can use it with Time Machine, click **Erase** or **Choose Another Disk**.

8. Click the **Close** button.

Click to set up Time Capsule using the AirPort Utility

# Performing a Backup

Time Machine keeps track of everything on your Mac computer. The first time you start Time Machine, the program backs up everything on your computer. As you work and make changes on your computer, Time Machine backs up only the things that have changed. If you want to manually perform a backup, you can Control-click the Time Machine icon in the Dock or click the Time Machine Status menu (**New!**) to access the Back Up Now command.

## Start a Manual Back Up

① Control-click the **Time Machine** icon in the Dock or click the **Time Machine Status** menu.

② Click **Back Up Now**.

Time Machine status information appears in the Time Machine Status menu.

③ To stop the backup, Control-click the **Time Machine** icon in the Dock or click the **Time Machine Status** menu, and then click **Stop Backing Up**.

◆ You can also click the **Stop** button (X) in the Time Machine preferences window.

### Did You Know?

**You can backup files to your iDisk.** If you have an iDisk, you can't use it with Time Machine. Instead, you can use the Backup utility to copy files to your iDisk; check the MobileMe Web site at *www.apple.com/mobileme/*. In addition, Backup can also copy files to CDs or DVDs.

Time Machine Status menu

Latest Backup: Today, 12:10 AM

Back Up Now
Enter Time Machine

Open Time Machine Preferences...

Open Time Machine Preferences...
Back Up Now
Browse Other Time Machine Disks...
Remove from Dock

Enter Time Machine

Current status of the back up

Backing Up: 9.91 GB of 45.08 GB

Stop Backing Up
Enter Time Machine

Open Time Machine Preferences...

# Excluding Items from a Backup

If you already have copies of files, such as third-party programs (Microsoft Office, Adobe Creative Suite, etc.), on CD, DVD, or in another location, you can exclude them from regular backups to save space on your backup disk. Time Machine assumes you want to back everything up unless you specifically add it to the nonbackup list, which you can modify using Time Machine preferences.

## Exclude Items from a Backup

**1** Click **System Preferences** icon in the Dock, and then click the **Time Machine** icon.

**2** Click **Options**.

A list appears with the available disks you can use for backups with Time Machine.

**3** Click **Add** (+), and then select the items you don't want to be backed up, and then click **Exclude**.

◆ If you select the System folder, an alert appears, asking you for confirmation.

The backup disk is automatically included in the list.

**4** To remove an item from the list, select the items you want to be backed up, and then click **Remove** (-).

**5** Select or clear the **Notify after old backups are deleted** check box.

**6** Click **Done**.

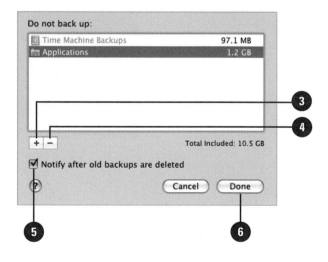

# Working with a Backup

If a backup is interrupted for some reason, such as a network connection problem, detached external disk, or power outage, Time Machine tries to automatically resume the backup when the problem is corrected. If Time Machine doesn't automatically resume, you can manually restart it. If you want to pause a backup, you can also manually stop it by Time Machine icon in the Dock or by using the Time Machine Status menu (**New!**). The Time Machine Status menu icon rotates as the takes place. If a problem occurs, the icons changes to an alert symbol. Also, the first item on the menu displays status information about the current or last back up.

## Work with a Backup

◆ **Pause/stop a backup.** Press the Control key while you click the **Time Machine** icon in the Dock or click the **Time Machine Status** menu, and then click **Stop Backing Up**.

◆ **Resume/start a backup.** Press the Control key while you click the **Time Machine** icon in the Dock or click the **Time Machine Status** menu, and then click **Back Up Now**.

◆ **Run out of space.** As the backup disk fills up, Time Machine deletes older backups to make room for new ones. If you run out of space, you can attach a new backup disk to complete the process.

### Did You Know?

*You can back up all the Macs in your wireless network.* If you have a hard disk connected to your AirPort Extreme Base Station or Time Capsule, you can use Time Machine to back up all your Macs wirelessly. All you need to do is select your AirPort Disk or Time Capsule as the backup disk for each computer connected to the wireless network.

Time Machine Status menu

> Latest Backup: Today, 12:10 AM
>
> Back Up Now
> Enter Time Machine
>
> Open Time Machine Preferences...

Resume/start a backup

Current status of the back up

> Backing Up: 9.91 GB of 45.08 GB
>
> Stop Backing Up
> Enter Time Machine
>
> Open Time Machine Preferences...

Icon changes to indicate a problem

> Latest Backup: Failed...
>
> Back Up Now
> Enter Time Machine
>
> Open Time Machine Preferences...

Pause/stop a backup

Click to find out the problem

# Recovering Backed Up Items

If you've been using Time Machine to back up your computer, and you lose or accidentally delete a file or folder, you can use Time Machine or Time Machine along with Spotlight to recover it. You can even recover older versions of files that you have changed. Spotlight makes it easy to perform a search for the backup file or folder you want to recover, and Time Machine allows you to recover it. The recovered item is restored to its original location on your computer. Time Machine may ask if you want to overwrite one or more folders so it can restore an item to its original location.

## Recover Items Using Time Machine and Spotlight

1. Open a Finder window.

2. Type a search word or phrase in the Search box from the item you want to recover.

3. Click the **Time Machine** icon in the Dock.

4. Use the arrows and the timeline to browse through the Time Machine backups. Your search is performed in every window.

5. Narrow down your search to find the item you want to restore, and then select it.

6. Click **Restore**.

   The window appears on the desktop along with a Copy dialog box.

7. Click **Keep Original** to keep the original file instead of the backup, **Keep Both** to keep the original and the backup, or **Replace** to replace the original with the backup.

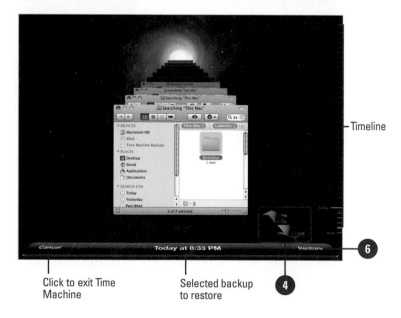

Timeline

Click to exit Time Machine

Selected backup to restore

## Recover Items Using Time Machine

① Open the window or location (desktop or e-mail Inbox) where the recovered item will appear.

② Click the **Time Machine** icon in the Dock.

③ Use the arrows and the timeline to browse through the Time Machine backups. Your search is performed in every window.

④ When you find the item you want to restore, select it.

⑤ Click **Restore**.

The window appears on the desktop along with a Copy dialog box.

⑥ Click **Keep Original** to keep the original file instead of the backup, **Keep Both** to keep the original and the backup, or **Replace** to replace the original with the backup.

Click to exit Time Machine

Selected backup

# Recovering an Entire Computer System

If your entire computer system or startup disk becomes corrupt or damaged, you can recover it using Time Machine. If you're experiencing problems after you install a Mac OS X software update, you can use Time Machine to revert back to a previous version of the Mac OS to fix the problem. Remember, any additional changes you've made to your computer after installing the Mac OS X software update will be removed, so you need to make copies of those changes on another disk. To perform a recovery, you'll need your Mac OS X Installation disc to start the process.

## Recover an Entire System Using Time Machine

**1** Connect your Time Machine backup disk to your computer, if necessary.

**2** Insert the Mac OS X Install disc, double-click the **Install Mac OS X** icon.

**3** Click **Utilities**, and then click **Restart**.

**4** In the installer, click the **Utilities** menu, and then click **Restore System from Backup**.

The Restore Your System dialog box appears.

**5** Click **Continue**.

**6** Select the Time Machine backup volume you want to use.

**7** Click **Continue**.

**8** Select the Time Machine backup you want to restore.

**9** Click **Continue**.

**10** Select the restore destination volume.

**11** Click **Restore**.

## Revert Back to a Previous Version of Mac OS X

1. Connect your Time Machine backup disk to your computer, if necessary.

2. Insert the Mac OS X Install disc, double-click the **Install Mac OS X** icon, and then click **Restart**.

3. Click **Utilities**, and then click **Restart**.

4. In the installer, click the **Utilities** menu, and then click **Restore System from Backup**.

   The Restore Your System dialog box appears.

5. Click **Continue**.

6. Select the Time Machine backup volume you want to use.

7. Click **Continue**.

8. Select the most recent Time Machine backup to restore your computer to the state it was before you installed an update.

9. Click **Continue**.

10. Select the restore destination volume.

11. Click **Restore**.

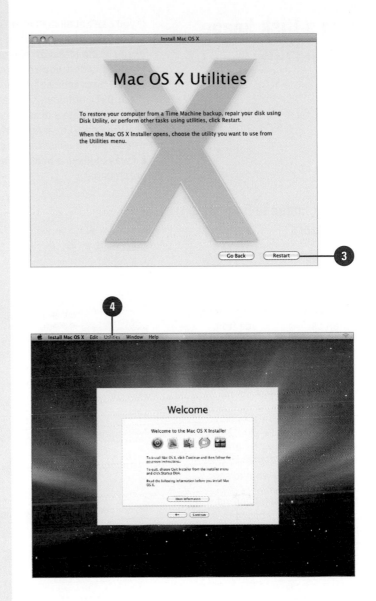

# Creating a Disk Image to Backup Files

If you can't fit all the files and folders you want to backup onto a single CD or DVD, you can use the Disk Utility to create a compressed disk image of the files and folders. A **disk image** is a file that contains other files and folders you can mount on your desktop like a hard disk or CD or DVD disc. You can create a disk image with an existing disk, volume, CD or DVD, or folder, or create a blank one, and then drag files to it. After you create a disk image (.dmg extension), you can burn it on a CD or DVD, copy it to another Mac or network, or e-mail it to another Mac user. Creating a disk image of your Mac OS X installation disc is a useful way to make a backup copy of your Mac OS X installation for added protection.

## Create a Disk Image to Backup Files and Folders

1. Click the **Applications** folder in the Dock, click the **Utilities** folder, and then click the **Disk Utility** icon.

2. Click the **File** menu, point to **New**, and then click **Disk Image from Folder** or **Disk Image from <disk name>**.

3. If you want to create a disk image from a folder, select it.

4. Click **Image**.

5. Type the name you want for the disk image, and then specify the location where you want to save it.

6. Click the **Image Format** pop-up, and then click **compressed** to create a smaller disk image or **read-only** to create a faster disk to create and open.

7. To require a password to open the disk image, click the **Encryption** pop-up, and then select the option you want.

8. Click **Save**. If you required a password, enter it twice, and then click **OK**.

9. To restore a disk image, select the disk image, click the **Images** menu, and then click **Scan Image for Restore**.

## Create a Blank Disk Image as a Backup

① Click the **Applications** folder in the Dock, click the **Utilities** folder, and then click the **Disk Utility** icon.

② Click the **File** menu, point to **New**, and then click **Blank Disk Image**.

③ Type a name for the disk image, and then specify the location where you want to save it.

④ Select from the following options:

  ◆ Enter a name or use the default.

  ◆ Click the **Size** pop-up, and then select the size you want.

  ◆ Select the **Format** pop-up, and then select **Mac OS Extended (Journaled)** for Mac computers or **MS-DOS (FAT)** for Windows or Mac computers.

  ◆ To require a password to open the disk image, click the **Encryption** pop-up, and then select the option you want.

  ◆ Click the **Partitions** pop-up, and then select the partition scheme that matches the type you want to create.

  ◆ Click the **Image Format** pop-up, and then click **read/write disk image**.

⑤ Click **Create**.

⑥ If you required a password, enter it twice, and then click **OK**.

The blank new disk image mounts on your desktop.

⑦ Drag the files and folders you want to include in the disk image onto the mounted disk on your desktop.

---

**New Blank Image**

Save As: My Music

Where: Desktop ③

Name: My iTunes

Size: 100 MB

Format: Mac OS Extended (Journaled)

Encryption: 128-bit AES encryption (recommended)

Partitions: No partition map

Image Format: read/write disk image

④

Cancel   Create ⑤

---

Enter a new password to secure My Music.dmg. If you forget this password you will not be able to access the files stored on this image. Forgotten passwords cannot be retrieved.

Password: ••••••••••

Verify: ••••••••••

Password Strength: Fair

☑ Remember password in my keychain

⑥

▶ Details

② Cancel   OK

---

## For Your Information

### Recording or Duplicating a Data CD or DVD

You can use Disk Utility to quickly create a CD or DVD from data on your computer or make a copy of a CD or DVD that contains information. Once you create a disk image, you can make multiple copies from the same disk image. If you select the Leave Disc Appendable option during the process, you can create a **multisession CD** or **DVD**; you burn data on a CD-R or DVD-R now, and then add to it later until there is no more room, just like a CD-RW or DVD-RW. You can use the CD or DVD to transfer files from one computer to another, backup data for safekeeping, or restore the files on a disk.

# Burning a CD or DVD from a Disk Image

After you create a disk image, you can burn it on a CD or DVD, which makes it easy to make a backup copy of important files, move files to another computer, or share files with other Mac users. This is also a useful way to make a backup of your Mac OS X installation DVD from a disk image of the installation DVD disc. After you select the disk image you want to burn to a CD or DVD in Disk Utility, you can select the Burn options you want before the actual burn takes place.

## Burn a CD or DVD from a Disk Image

1. Click the **Applications** folder in the Dock, click the **Utilities** folder, and then click the **Disk Utility** icon.

2. Click the **Burn** button on the toolbar.

3. Navigate to and select the disk image you want to burn.

4. Click **Burn**.

5. Click the **Down Arrow** button to show advanced burn options.

6. Select the Burn Options and After Burning settings you want.

7. Insert a writable CD or DVD disc into your read/writable drive.

8. Click **Burn**.

   A status bar appears, indicating the current progress of the burn.

9. Click **OK**.

# Restoring a Disk Image

After you create a disk image, you can use Disk Utility to restore it to a disk. This is useful when you want to re-create all the contents of the disk image to a disk. Disk Utility allows you to select the source and destination for the restored files. You can even erase the destination before the restoration occurs. If you only want to restore only a few files, you can access the content of the mounted disk image on your desktop like any other hard disk and copy it to another location.

## Restore a Disk Image to a Disk

1. Click the **Applications** folder in the Dock, click the **Utilities** folder, and then click the **Disk Utility** icon.

2. Select the disk in the list at the left.

3. Click the **Restore** tab.

4. Drag the disk image to the Source field or click **Image**, and then select the disk image.

5. Drag the destination disk you want to the Destination field.

6. If you want to erase the disk before copying to it, select the **Erase destination** check box.

   If you want to add the disk image's content to the destination disk without erasing it, clear the **Erase Destination** check box.

7. Click **Restore**, and then click **Restore** again to confirm the restoration.

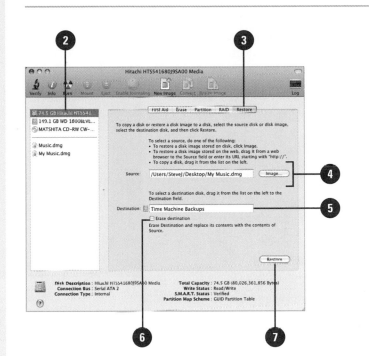

## Did You Know?

*You can get information about your disk.* Open the Utilities folder, double-click the Disk Utility icon, select the disk or volume in the list at the left, click the Info button. When you're done, click the Close button twice.

# Backing Up Files onto a CD or DVD

If you can write (burn) files to a CD or DVD, you can create and use a burn folder to backup important files. Burn folders are useful for regularly backing up a set of files or for burning multiple copies of a folder. You can create a burn folder from the Finder. The files and folders you drag into the burn folder are ready to be written to a CD or DVD. The Finder creates aliases to the items in the burn folder. The original items are not moved. When you burn the files to a CD or DVD, the original files are burned to the disc.

## Copy Files onto a CD or DVD from the Finder

1. Click the desktop background or open the window where you want to create and use a burn folder.

2. Click the **File** menu, and then click **New Burn Folder**.

3. Type a name for the burn folder.

4. Drag the items you want to burn to a disc into the burn folder.

    The Finder creates aliases to the items in the burn folder. The original items are not moved.

5. Open the burn folder to burn a CD or DVD.

6. Click **Burn**.

    **TIMESAVER** *If the burn folder is in the sidebar of the Finder window, click the burn icon next to the burn folder name.*

7. Insert a writable CD or DVD disc into your read/writable drive.

    The original files and any folders are burned to the disc.

    ◆ If the Finder can't find an original file, it asks you to cancel the burn or continue without the file.

8. Type a name for the CD or DVD, and then select a burn speed.

9. Click **Burn**.

# Automating Your Work

## Introduction

Automator is a program that lets you automate the things you frequently like to do on your Mac. You don't need to be a programmer to create automations. With Automator, all you need to do is assemble a series of **actions** into a workflow to complete a task. Each action performs an individual step, such as opening a file, creating an event in iCal, or importing photos in Image Capture. You can create your own actions or use one of the many pre-built ones available in Automator library.

When you start Automator, a dialog box appears asking you to choose from a group of templates, also known as starting points, that help you create the first part of your workflow. There are several templates you can use to help you get started (**New!**): Workflow, Application, Service, Folder Action, Print Plugin, iCal Alarm, and Image Capture Plugin. After you choose a template, you see an untitled workflow with a blank workflow action in the Workflow pane you can fill in. You create a workflow by dragging additional actions or variables into the Workflow pane, arranging them into the order you want from top to bottom, and specifying the settings you want for each action or variable.

When you have more than one action in a workflow, Automator frequently passes information from one action to another starting from the top. When you run a workflow, each action receives information from the previous action (input) and passes information to the following action (output). If an action needs to receive a certain type of information, it needs to be placed in the workflow following an action that outputs that type of information.

In addition to Automator, you can also use AppleScript, an English-like scripting language, to run prebuilt or custom-made scripts to automate actions performed by the computer. AppleScript lets you write your own mini applications to help with repetitious tasks.

# Introducing Automator

Anyone can create a workflow in Automator. All it requires is the Automator application available in the Applications folder, and a little knowledge about the process.

When you start Automator, a dialog box appears asking you to choose from a group of templates that help you create the first part of your workflow. There are several templates you can use to help you get started (**New!**): Workflow, Application, Service, Folder Action, Print Plugin, iCal Alarm, and Image Capture Plugin. If you already have an existing workflow, you can open it from the dialog box.

After you choose a template, you see an untitled workflow with a blank workflow action (except for Custom) in the Workflow pane you can fill in. You create a workflow by displaying Actions or Variables in the Library pane, selecting the name of the application or category you want to use from the Library list, specifying what you want it to do with it in the Action or Variable list, and dragging it into the Workflow pane to assemble the steps you want to automate.

## Automator Window

The Automator window consists of different parts, including Toolbar buttons, Library pane, Library list, Action or Variable list, Search box, Description view, and Workflow pane.

### Toolbar buttons

The top part of the Automator window displays a toolbar with buttons you can use to make it easier to work with Automator. On the left side of the toolbar, Automator provides two default buttons: Hide/Show Library and Media. The Hide/Show Library button) hides or shows the Library pane, while the Media but-

ton makes it easy to add media to your workflows. On the right-side of the toolbar, Automator provides three default buttons, known as Workflow control buttons: Record, Stop, and Run. The Record button creates a workflow by recording of your mouse movements, while the Stop and Run buttons stop and play back the current workflow. These are not the only toolbar buttons available in Automator. You can use the Customize Toolbar command on the View menu to add and remove the buttons you want and change the button size and display.

### Library pane

The left side of the Automator window is the Library pane, which displays the available actions and variables you can use to create Automator workflows.

### Action list

When you click the Actions button at the top of the Library pane, a Library list and Action list appear. The Library list displays every program, including some OS utilities, on your Mac that you can use to create Automator workflows. When you select a program, the Action list changes to show the actions related to the program. Snow Leopard provides improved and new actions, for Preview, the Internet, RSS, and the Finder. At the bottom of the Library list, you can use Smart Groups, including Most Relevant, Most Used, and Recently Added, or create your own to make it easier to displays the actions you want to use.

### Variable list

When you click the Variables button at the top of the Library pane, a Library list and Variable list appear. The Library list displays OS utilities categories on your Mac that you can use to create Automator workflows. When you select a program, the Variable list changes to show the available variables you can use to store values and create more flexible workflows.

## Search box

The Search box at the top of the Library pane is similar to the one you find in other parts of Mac OS X. In Automator, the Search box makes it easier to find the actions or variables you want to use. Before you start a search, select a category from the Library list. As you type in the Search box, Automator displays the actions or variables that match your criteria from the selected category. If you want to search through more than one category, you can press ⌘ to select the ones you want. If you want to search all the categories, click Library at the top of the Library list. The results of your search appear in the Action or Variable list in order of relevance to your search criteria. When you're done, you can click the small gray X button in the Search box to return to the complete list of actions.

## Description view

The Description view at the bottom of the Library pane displays a description of the selected action or variable. The description provides information about what the action or variable does, what requirements it needs to get started, what kind of data it needs as input, what options are available, and what kind of action it performs as a result. If you need more room to display the Action or Variable list, you can click the Show Or Hide The Description View button at the bottom of the Library pane.

## Workflow pane

The Workflow pane is where you place the actions and variables you want to use to create a workflow. The Workflow pane displays and tracks a flow of information from one action or variable to the next creating the results you want. In the Workflow pane, you can change the order of items, set item specific settings and options, display item descriptions, and show the results for specific ones.

## Workflow log

The Show Or Hide The Workflow Log button at the bottom of the Workflow pane shows or hides the workflow log, which allows you to track what your workflow is doing.

## Workflow variable list

The Show Or Hide The Workflow Variable List button at the bottom of the Workflow pane shows or hides the workflow variable list, which allows you to track the current values for the variables you use in your workflow.

## More to come

Developers are always creating new actions for you to use. Check out the Apple Web site at *www.apple.com/downloads/macosx /automator* for more information and details, or visit *www.automatorworld.com/category /actions*. After you download them to your computer, you can use the Import Actions command on the File menu to add them to your Library list in Automator. Writing your own actions is out of the scope of this book. For details, see the Apple Developer Web site at *www.apple.com/macosx/features /automator*.

# Viewing the Automator Window

Search box

Toolbar

Action and Variable lists

Description view

Library pane

Workflow pane

Workflow log

# Getting Started with Automator

When you start Automator, a dialog box appears asking you to choose from a group of templates, also known as starting points, that help you create the first part of your workflow. You can use any of the following templates (**New!**) to help you get started: Workflow, Application, Service (**New!**), Folder Action, Print Plugin, iCal Alarm, and Image Capture Plugin. After you choose a template, you see an untitled workflow with an action in the Workflow pane you can fill in.

## Get Started with Automator

1.  Click the **Applications** folder in the Dock, and then click the **Automator** icon.

    Automator opens, displaying the Templates dialog.

2.  Click a template icon:

    ◆ **Workflow.** Use to creates a workflow document.

    ◆ **Application.** Use to create an executable workflow application.

    ◆ **Service.** Use to create a service (**New!**) for use in another application or the Finder; a plug-in workflow.

    ◆ **Folder Actions.** Use to perform batch folder operations, such as opening or adding files; a plug-in workflow.

    ◆ **Print Plugin.** Use to run a workflow when you print a file. An item appears on the PDF menu in the Print dialog box; a plug-in workflow.

    ◆ **iCal Alarm.** Use to open iCal and create a new event; a plug-in workflow.

    ◆ **Image Capture Plugin.** Use to import photos from a camera or scanner with Image Capture; a plug-in workflow.

3.  Click **Choose**. If prompted, select your content, and then click **Add**.

    ◆ Click **Close** to exit the dialog without taking any action.

Description of selected template

## For Your Information

### Starting a Workflow with a Set of Files

If you wanted to create a new workflow with a specific set of files, you can use the shortcut menu in the Finder to quickly get started. In Finder, select the files you want to use in the new workflow. Control-click the selected files, point to Automator, and then click Create Workflow. Automator opens with a new workflow and the selected files are in the first action.

# Opening an Existing Workflow

After you save a workflow as a Workflow (.workflow) or Application (.app) file, you can open either one at any time to modify or run it. You can open a workflow by using the standard Open dialog box in Automator. You can access the Open dialog box from the New dialog box when you start Automator from the Finder or from the Open command on the File menu in Automator.

## Open an Existing Workflow

1. Use one of the following methods:

   ◆ **In Finder.** Click the **Applications** folder in the Dock, click the **Automator** icon, and then click **Open an Existing Workflow**.

   ◆ **In Automator.** Click the **File** menu, and then click **Open**.

   **TIMESAVER** *Press ⌘+O to open the Open dialog.*

2. Click the **Type** pop-up, and then select **All** or a workflow type.

3. Select the place from which you want to open the file.

   **TIMESAVER** *Click the Where pop-up to select from a list of recent places you already visited.*

4. Click the document you want to open.

5. Click **Open**.

6. To close a workflow, click the **File** menu, and then click **Close**.

## Did You Know?

*You can open a workflow file directly.* In Finder, double-click the workflow file icon (.workflow) you want to open.

*You can create a new workflow.* Click the File menu, and then click New. The templates dialog box appears or a blank custom workflow appears.

# Opening an Example Workflow

Automator comes with four example workflows you can open to see what a completed one looks like. The examples show you how to a workflow can copy new unread mail into your iPod's text-notes folder, display movie trailers in Safari (**New!**), import photos from a Photo Album posted on your MobileMe site into iPhoto, and process images with the Quartz composition filter. The process images workflow may not be a real useful workflow at first glance. However, it's a good example of batch processing.

## Open an Example Workflow

1. Start Automator, click the **Workflow** icon, and then click **Choose** to open Automator with a blank workflow.

2. Click the **Help** menu, and then click **Open Examples Folder**.

   The Workflows folder opens, displaying four example workflows.

   ◆ **Copy Unread Mail to iPod Notes.** Copies new unread mail into your iPod's text-notes folder.

   ◆ **Display Trailers in Safari.** Displays movie trailers from *www.apple.com* in Safari (**New!**).

   ◆ **Import MobileMe Photo Album into iPhoto.** Imports photos from a Photo Album posted on your MobileMe site into iPhoto.

   ◆ **Process Images.** Batch process images with the Quartz composition filter.

3. Double-click the workflow file you want to open.

   The workflow file opens, displaying actions in the Workflow pane.

4. To close a workflow, click the **File** menu, and then click **Close**.

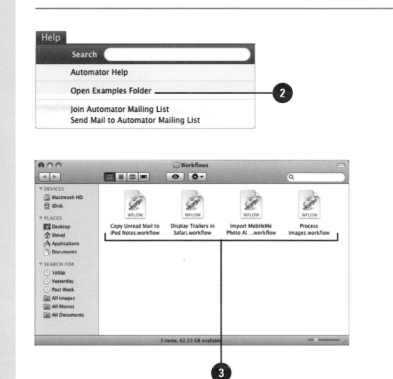

# Working with an Example Workflow

The best way to learn how to create a workflow is to go through an example. Automator comes with three example workflows you can open to see what a completed one looks like. The process images workflow is a good example of batch processing images. The example processes images with the Quartz composition filter. However, you can easily change the workflow to modify the image size or convert it to another format.

## Work with an Example Workflow

① Start Automator, click the **Workflow** icon, and then click **Choose** to open Automator with a blank workflow.

② Click the **Help** menu, and then click **Open Example Folder**.

③ Double-click the **Process Images .workflow** icon.

④ Examine the following actions in the Workflow pane:

◆ **Ask for Confirmation.** Displays a dialog box with information you provide for the user's benefit. You can change the button names and click the Robot icon to change it.

◆ **Get Specified Finder Items.** Lets you specify the files you want to process. You can use the Add or Remove buttons or drag files directly from the Finder.

◆ **Copy Finder Items.** Makes copies of the files to protect the originals.

◆ **Apply Quartz Composition Filter to Image Files.** Applies the filter to the selected image files.

◆ **Open Images in Preview.** Opens the specified image file in Preview.

⑤ To execute the workflow, click the **Run** button on the toolbar.

## For Your Information

### Controlling Input and Output

You can control the input and output within a workflow. Some actions allow you to choose whether you want to receive results from a previous action. If so, select this check box (names vary depending on action). If available, select the Use Results from Previous Action option from the pop-up menu on the action in the Workflow pane. When you start a workflow from the shortcut menu in Finder (see "Using a Workflow as Plug-ins" on page 506), any items you select are passed into the workflow as input. If you don't want this to happen, you can set the first action to ignore input. Control-click the title bar for the first action, and then click Ignore Input.

## Modify an Example Workflow

1. Start Automator, click the **Workflow** icon, and then click **Choose** to open Automator with a blank workflow.

2. Click the **Help** menu, and then click **Open Example Folder**.

3. Double-click the **Process Images .workflow** icon.

4. Instead of working from a specified folder, let's have the Finder ask you where to get the image files.

   ◆ **Get Specified Finder Items.** Click the **Delete** button (X) on the Get Specified Finder Items title bar, click **Files & Folders** in the Library list, and then drag the **Ask for Finder Items** action to the same place as the deleted action.

5. Instead of applying the Quartz filter, let's change the image type.

   ◆ **Change Type of Images.** Click the **Delete** button (X) on the Apply Quartz Composition Filter to Image Files title bar, click **Photos** in the Library list, and then drag the **Change Type of Images** action to the same place as the deleted action.

6. Click the **File** menu, click **Save As**, specify a new name, and then click **Save**.

7. To execute the workflow, click the **Run** button on the toolbar.

Ask for Finder Items action

# Adding Actions to a Workflow

You can add one or more actions to create the workflow you want. When you have more than one action in a workflow, Automator frequently passes information from one action to another starting from the top. When you run a workflow, each action receives information from the previous action (input) and passes information to the following action (output). If an action needs to receive a certain type of information, it needs to be placed in the workflow following an action that outputs that type of information. The type of input an action needs appears in the title bar. If the input and output don't match or it's not being received from the previous action, the information appears in red to indicate a problem.

## Add Actions to a Workflow

1. Start Automator and use a template or open the workflow you want.

2. Click the **Actions** button in the Library pane.

3. Click the category or application from the Library list to display the actions you want.

4. Drag the action you want to the Workflow pane.

5. Enter information and specify the settings you want for the action; the information and settings vary depending on the action.

6. To show and set additional options, click the **Options** button, and then specify the ones you want to set. To hide the options, click the **Options** button again.

   ◆ To allow a user to select action settings, select the **Show Action When Run** check box.

   The availability of the Options button varies depending on the action.

# Adding Variables to an Action

A variable stores a value that you can use in a workflow. For example, you can use variables to get the current time or today's date, unique text and data, or even a script. You can add variables directly to a workflow or to a compatible editable field or pop-up of an action. If you need a variable, yet you're not ready to use it, you can declare it in the Variables log for later use. In some cases, you can declare or create a a variable directly in an action.

## Add Variables to an Action

1. Start Automator and use a template or open the workflow you want to add variables to an action.

2. Click the **Variables** button in the Library pane.

3. Click the category from the Library list to display the actions you want.

4. Use any of the following methods to add a variable to an action:

   ◆ **Add to Workflow.** Drag variable into the Workflow pane. The "Get Value of Variable" action appears.

   ◆ **Add to Action.** Drag variable into an editable field or pop-up menu of an action. The variable is added to the Variables log.

   ◆ **Declare in Log.** Drag the variable to the Variables log. You can declare it without using it immediately.

5. Enter information and specify the settings you want for the variable; the information and settings vary depending on the variable.

6. To show and set additional options, click the **Options** button, and then specify the ones you want to set. To hide the options, click the **Options** button again.

Selected variable

Drag variable into an editable pop-up

# Recording an Action

If you can't find a pre-built action that meets your needs, you can record your own. Automator records your keyboard and mouse event to create a custom action, known as the "Watch Me Do" action. After you record the "Watch Me Do" action, you can adjust the playback speed and timeout settings, as well as delete any events you don't want. Before you can record an action, you need to select the "Enable access for assistive devices" check box in the Universal Access preferences.

## Record an Action

1 Set up your environment the way you expect it to be before you start to record.

2 Start Automator and create or open the workflow you want to add a recorded action.

◆ If a dialog appears, click the **Open Universal Access** button, select the **Enable access for assistive device** check box, and then click the **Close** button.

3 Click the **Record** button on the toolbar.

The Automator Recording message appears with the Stop button.

4 Perform the steps you want to record, and then click the **Stop** button.

5 To test your recording, click the **Run** button on the toolbar.

6 Adjust the settings you want for the recorded action.

◆ **Delete Event.** Select the event, and then type Delete.

◆ **Rearrange Event.** Drag an event to change the order.

◆ **Adjust Timeout.** Click the Timeout up and down arrows.

◆ **Adjust Speed.** Drag the **Playback speed** slider.

# Working with Workflows

After you add actions to your workflow, you can work with them to create the results you want. In the Workflow pane you can arrange actions in a different order; remember the input and output needs to match. If you need the same action in another place, you can copy and paste it. If you don't always need an action, you can disable it for now and then enable later. If you want to add media to a workflow, you can use the Media browser. If you can't locate a certain action, you can use the Search box to try and find it. If you still can't find it, you can import actions developed by others.

## Work with Workflows

◆ **Collapse/Expand.** Click the triangle to the left of the action title.

◆ **Arrange.** Drag the action title bar in the Workflow pane to a new place.

◆ **Copy.** Select the action in the Workflow pane, click the **Edit** menu, click **Copy**, click in the workflow where you want to insert the action, click the **Edit** menu, and then click **Paste**.

◆ **Disable.** Control-click the action title bar, then click **Disable**.

◆ **Enable.** Control-click the action title bar, then click **Enable**.

◆ **Delete.** Click the **Delete** button (X) on the title bar of the action in the Workflow pane.

◆ **Browse Media.** Click the **Media** button on the toolbar. Displays the media browser where you can select and use audio, photos, and movies.

◆ **Import.** Click the **File** menu, click **Import Actions**, navigate to and select the actions you want, and then click **Import**.

◆ **Find.** Enter a word or phrase in the Search box, and then press Return. To clear the search, click the **Delete** button (X) in the Search box.

◆ **View Events.** Click the **View** menu, and then click **Show Log**. You can also use the View Results action in a workflow.

Find     Collapse/Expand     Enable/Disable

View events

Browse Media

# Running and Stopping a Workflow

When you finishing creating a workflow, it's important to test (run) it to make sure it works the way you want it to. When you run a workflow (all at once with the Run button or one step at a time with the Step button(**New!**)), Automator executes each action from top to bottom, displaying status messages at the bottom of the window. As each action completes, a green checkmark appears in the bottom left-corner of the action indicating the action worked correctly. If a problem occurred, such as the input and output not matching, a red x appears.

## Run and Stop a Workflow

1 Start Automator and create or open the workflow you want to run.

2 To view the values stored in variables as a debugging tool, click the **Show or hide the workflow log** button to display the log.

3 Click the **Run** button on the toolbar to play the entire workflow or click the **Step** button to play the workflow one step at a time.

Automator executes each action from top to bottom, displaying status messages at the bottom of the window.

**TIMESAVER** *Click the View menu, and then click Show Log to view all the status messages.*

4 If a dialog box appears, requesting information or files, fulfill the request.

As each action completes, a green checkmark appears in the bottom left-corner of the action indicating the action worked correctly. If a problem occurred, such as the input and output not matching, a red x appears.

5 To stop the workflow, click the **Stop** button on the toolbar.

6 To show the results of a specific action, click the **Results** button at the bottom of the action. To hide the results, click the **Results** button again.

# Saving a Workflow

After you finish creating a workflow, you can save it for use at any time or share it with others as you would any file. When you create a workflow with the template type Workflow or Application (**New!**), you can save it as a Workflow (.workflow) or Application (.app) file. A Workflow file is one you open, modify, and run in Automator. An Application file is one you can double-click from anywhere on your Mac, drag it to the Dock, and assign a keyboard shortcut to make it easier to launch. When you save a workflow as an Application file, the size of the file gets larger, as much as 20 times larger.

## Save a Workflow

1. Start Automator and create (Workflow or Application) or open the workflow you want to save.

2. Click the **File** menu, and then click **Save As**.

3. Type the name you want for the workflow file.

4. Click the **Where** pop-up, and then select the location where you want to save the file.

5. Click the **File Format** pop-up, and then click **Workflow** or **Application**.

6. Click **Save**.

Click to expand dialog box

## Did You Know?

*You can revert to the previously saved workflow.* Click the File menu, click Revert, and then click Revert to confirm the operation.

*You can customize the toolbar.* Click the View menu, click Customize Toolbar, drag toolbar items to the toolbar, specify the options to display toolbar items as text, icons, or both, and to use the small size or not, and then click Done.

*You can print a workflow.* Click the File menu, click Print, select the print options you want, and then click Print.

# Using a Workflow as Plug-ins

When you create a workflow with the template type Folder Actions, Print Plugin, iCal Alarm, or Image Capture Plugin, Automator saves it as a plug-in type (**New!**). Saving your workflows as a plug-in allows you to automate tasks in different places and situations on your Mac. For example, you can run a workflow from the Finder's shortcut menu, an event in iCal, the import feature in Image Capture, or a print dialog box.

## Use a Workflow as a Plug-in

1 Start Automator and create or open the workflow with the following type:

◆ **Service.** Use to create a service for use in another application or the Finder.

◆ **Folder Actions.** Use to perform batch folder operations, such as opening or adding files.

◆ **Print Plugin.** Use to run a workflow when you print a file. An item appears on the PDF menu in the Print dialog box.

◆ **iCal Alarm.** Use to open iCal and create a new event named after plug-in.

◆ **Image Capture Plugin.** Use to import photos from a camera or scanner with Image Capture.

2 Click the **File** menu, and then click **Save As**.

3 Type the name you want for the plug-in.

4 Click **Save**.

# Understanding AppleScript Basics

The AppleScript language is your way of communicating with your operating system; instructing it to perform specific tasks. Who wants to do the same tasks over and over again... no one. For example, adding the .jpg extension to 150 graphic files that have to move to a system that requires extensions. There is an easier way to perform repetitive tasks, and that's with AppleScript. **AppleScript** is an English-like scripting language that is used to write script files, and those files automate actions performed by the computer (like adding an extension 150 times).

ActionScripting is more than a language that repeats recorded actions; AppleScript can make decisions based on user-interaction or by analyzing data, documents, or situations. And with Mac OS X Snow Leopard and the AppleScript Studio, you can create powerful Mac OS X applications with the Aqua look-and-feel written entirely in AppleScript. AppleScript is an automation language that helps us get through the mundane tasks of working on a computer and that's more than worth the time and effort spent in learning AppleScript.

AppleScript provides shortcuts for complex tasks such as naming files, resetting preferences, or connecting to the Internet, and the AppleScript Studio comes bundled with dozens of pre-written scripts that can immediately help you with your daily computer tasks. In addition, the automated workflow gives consistency, and speed to any Macintosh project. Since more can be accomplished in the same amount of time, you become more efficient—all through the power of AppleScript. To create your own AppleScripts, open the AppleScript editor, and type the script using precise language limitations.

Script Editor command buttons

Script Editor

Displays the results (if any) of the last running of the script.

Displays a short description of the current script.

Displays data on the performance of the script (aids in script editing).

# Using Ready-Made AppleScripts

You can use AppleScript right away, by working with AppleScripts created by the friendly folks at Apple. To gain access to the ready-made scripts, open the Applications folder, select the AppleScript folder, and then select Example Scripts, or do it the easy way by activating the built-in Script menu. When you activate (display) the Script menu, the Script icon appears on the right side of the menu bar and is available in the Finder and whenever you open an application. For example, you can click the Scripts icon, point to Printing Scripts, and then click Convert To PDF.

## Display the Script menu

1. Click the **Applications** folder in the Dock, click the **Utilities** folder, and then click the **AppleScript Editor** icon.

2. Click the **AppleScript Editor** menu, and then click **Preferences**.

3. Click **General**.

4. Select the **Show Script menu in menu bar** check box.

5. Select or clear the **Show Computer scripts** check box to show or hide library scripts.

6. Click the **top** or **bottom** option to specify where to show application scripts on the menu.

7. Click the **Close** button.

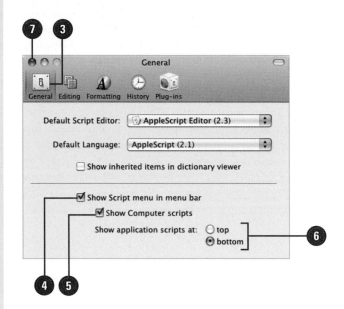

## Did You Know?

*You can remove the Script menu from the Mac desktop menu.* Click the Script menu on the menu bar, click Open AppleScript Editor, click the AppleScript Editor menu, click Preferences, clear the Show Script Menu In Menu Bar check box, and then click the Close button.

## Use Ready-Made AppleScripts

① On the right side of the menu bar, click the **Scripts** icon.

② Point to a script category, if necessary.

③ Select a script option. Some of the useful scripts include:

◆ **Add to File Names** and **Add to Folder Names**. Add text to the beginning or end of every file or folder in the active Finder window.

◆ **Replace Text in Item Names**. Replaces text in file and folder names.

◆ **Trim File Names** and **Trim Folder Names**. Removes file extensions or text from the beginning or end of every file or folder in the active Finder window.

## Open Example Scripts Folder

① On the right side of the menu bar, click the **Scripts** icon.

② Point to **Open Scripts Folder**, and then click one of the Scripts Folder (Finder, User, or Computer).

③ Double-click the example folder you want, if necessary.

④ Double-click the script you want to execute.

### Did You Know?

*You can add your scripts to the Scripts menu.* Open the Example Scripts folder in the AppleScripts folder, create a folder with the name you want on the Scripts menu, and then drag your script into the folder. The script name appears on the Scripts menu.

# Writing and Recording AppleScripts

Anyone can write AppleScripts. All it requires is the Script Editor application available with Snow Leopard, and knowledge of the AppleScript language. The AppleScript editor lets you type script directly into the editor window, or you can click the Record button, and then perform some Mac operation, as the editor records each step as you work. There are many places where you can go to increase your AppleScript understanding; however, point your browser to *http://www.apple.com/applescript/*, and then click the Resources link to access current resources dealing the creative techniques for AppleScript.

## Write and Record AppleScripts

1. Click the **Applications** folder in the Dock, click the **Utilities** folder, and then click the **AppleScript Editor** icon.

2. Type the Script directly into the Script Editor window.

3. Click the **Record** button to record within the active script.

4. Click the **Run** button to run the active script.

5. Click the **Stop** button to stop the running of the active script.

6. Click the **Compile** button to create a version of the active script.

7. Click the **File** menu, and then click **Save**, or **Save As** to save the script using a unique name and location.

## Did You Know?

*You can create AppleScript beyond the capabilities of the Script Editor Application.* The AppleScript Studio is a solution for creating total applications, using the Aqua interface and all the other elements associated with the Macintosh operating system. Point your browser to *http://www.apple.com/applescript/*, and then click the AppleScript Studio link for more information.

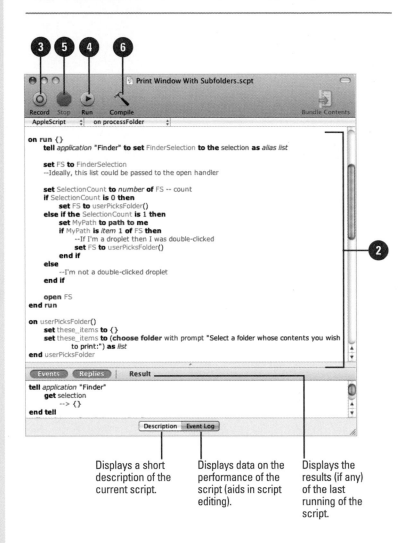

Displays a short description of the current script.

Displays data on the performance of the script (aids in script editing).

Displays the results (if any) of the last running of the script.

## Open and Modify a Script from the Scripts Menu

1. On the right side of the menu bar, click the **Scripts** icon.

2. Point to a script category, if necessary.

3. Option-click the script you want to open.

   The Script Editor opens, displaying the selected script.

4. Modify the script as you want.

5. Click the **Run** button to run the active script.

6. Click the **Stop** button to stop the running of the active script.

7. Click the **Compile** button to create a version of the active script.

8. Click the **File** menu, and then click **Save As** to save the script using a unique name and location.

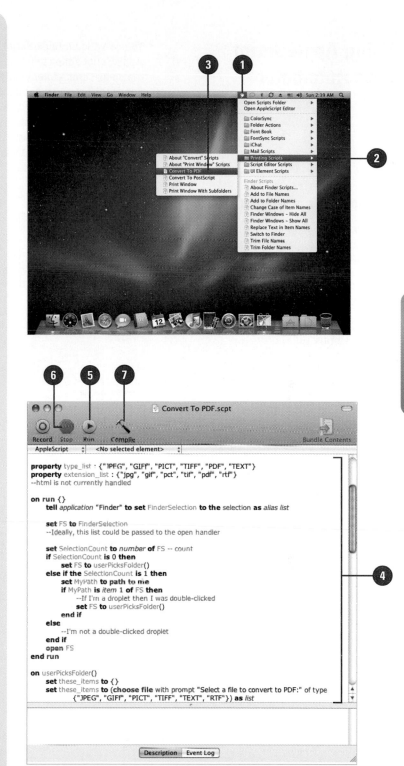

# Using AppleScript with Automator

You can add an AppleScript script to a workflow. Simply, drag the Run AppleScript action into your workflow, and then enter your script into the small script editor within the action. Automator is a scriptable application. You can use AppleScript in the Script Editor to develop and execute workflows. To help you write the scripts, you can view the Automator's AppleScript dictionary. Open the Utilities folder window, open another window with the Applications window. Drag the Automator icon (located in the Applications folder) onto the Script Editor icon (located in the Utilities folder).

## Use AppleScript with Automator

1. Start Automator and use a template or open the workflow you want.

2. Click the **Actions** button in the Library pane.

3. Click the **Utilities** category from the Library list.

4. Drag the **Run AppleScript** action you want to the Workflow pane.

5. Type the script you want in the action.

6. To run the script, click the **Run** button in the action below the title bar.

7. To compile the script, click the **Compile** button to create a version of the active script.

8. To run the workflow, click the **Run** button on the toolbar.

# Appendix: Installing Mac OS X Snow Leopard

## Introduction

If you're upgrading to Mac OS X Snow Leopard from a previous version of Mac OS, this appendix describes how to prepare and install Mac OS X Snow Leopard. The temptation is to insert the Installation DVD and start the installation, but you can avoid problems by making sure your computer is ready for Mac OS X Snow Leopard. Before you install Snow Leopard, you need to check your computer hardware and software and make several setup decisions that relate to your computer. The Mac OS X Snow Leopard Installer walks you through the installation process. If your computer doesn't have an optical drive, you can use Remote Install Mac OS X to install Mac OS X using another computer's optical drive.

# Preparing to Install Mac OS X Snow Leopard

The Apple Installer guides you through many of the choices you need to make, but there are some decisions and actions you need to make before you start the installation. In order to run Mac OS X, you'll need at least 1 GB of physical RAM, and at least 5 GB of available space on your hard disk for the installation. And your Mac needs to be one of the models that can run Mac OS X.

## Confirm that your hardware can run Mac OS X Snow Leopard Version 10.6

Mac OS X Snow Leopard Version 10.6 requires a Macintosh with an Intel processor, a DVD drive, at least 1 GB MB of physical RAM and a built-in display or a display connected to an Apple-supplied video card supported by your computer. Mac OS X does not support processor upgrade cards.

## Verify you have enough hard drive space.

While the amount of disk space required depends on your computer and the way you are installing Mac OS X, you are recommended to have at least 5 GB (**New!**) of available space on your hard drive (which is less than half of the space of Leopard), or 8 GB of disk space if you install developer tools.

## Update computer firmware.

You may need to update your computer's firmware. You can check the Apple Software Updates web site at *www.apple.com/support/downloads* to see if your computer needs it.

## Check out third party hardware compatibility

Third Party Hardware. Mac OS X Version 10.6 Snow Leopard includes out-of-the-box functionality for many hardware devices. Mac OS X will automatically configure itself to support most hardware. However, some devices may need additional driver support from the man-ufacturer. Please check with the manufacturer of your product to see if Mac OS X Version 10.6-compatible drivers are available.

Third Party Hardware Specifics. If you have a third-party SCSI card or video card attached to your computer and the installer or Mac OS indicates there are problems, try removing the cards or adding a terminator or disk drive to the SCSI card.

If you have a UFS-formatted volume, you cannot install Mac OS X Snow Leopard as a new installation or as an upgrade from an older version to Snow Leopard. You need to back up your computer hard disk, and then reformat your startup volume. To perform the install, start the installer, click the Utilities menu, click Disk Utility, click Restore, drag your startup volume to the Source field, drag the external disk to the Destination field, click Restore, and then Quit the Disk Utility. Continue with the installation using the Erase and Install option.

## Reinstall Mac OS X Snow Leopard.

If you have problems with your installation and want to reinstall the Mac OS X Snow Leopard software to correct it, insert the Mac OS X Install DVD, start the installer, and then click Options in the Select a Destination pane to use the Archive and Install option to save your existing system files or the Erase and Install option to erase the destination volume and install a new copy of Mac OS X.

## Uninstall Mac OS X Snow Leopard.

Unfortunately, there isn't any clean way, like an uninstall application, to uninstall Mac OS X10.6. The only real way is to backup your Home folder, Applications folder, Library folder, and anything else you want to save, and then erase the hard drive and install the operating system you want to use.

# Determining the Current Mac OS Version

If you're not sure what version of the Mac operating system you've currently installed on your computer, you can use the About This Mac command or the Startup Disk utility to find out. The About This Mac command on the Apple menu displays the currently installed version and provides access to Software Update to upgrade it and More Info about the hardware with the System Profile application. If you have multiple versions installed on different drives, you can use the Startup Disk Utility to quickly find out what is installed. You can access the Startup Disk utility from System Preferences in the Dock.

## Check About This Mac for Mac OS X Version

1 Click the **Apple** menu.

2 Click **About This Mac**.

The OS version appears in the window.

3 Click the **Close** button.

Mac OS version

## Check Startup Disk Utility for Mac OS X Version

1 Click the **System Preferences** in the Dock.

2 Click the **Startup Disk** icon.

The OS version for the connected hard drives appear in the pane.

3 Click the **Close** button.

Mac OS versions

# Installing Mac OS X Snow Leopard

There are several different kinds of installation: clean (new or erased disk), upgrade from Mac OS 10.0 through 10.5, reinstall Mac OS 10.6, or restore Mac OS 10.6 using Time Machine. If you don't have a drive, you can also use DVD or CD Sharing to upgrade a Mac to Snow Leopard using another computer's drive. The Installer guides you step-by-step through the process of installing Mac OS X Snow Leopard no matter what the installation type. You insert the installation DVD, and then follow the on-screen instructions (read the instructions, select options, and then click Continue) to complete the process. As you go through the process, you can click the Go Back button at any time to change option in previous screens. The installation process takes about 45 minutes if all goes well (**New!**), which is faster than Leopard.

## Install Mac OS X Snow Leopard

1. Insert the Mac OS X Snow Leopard installation disc into your DVD drive.

2. Double-click the **Install Mac OS X** icon in the DVDs window.

3. To perform a clean install, click **Utilities**, click **Restart**. In the Language screen, select a language, and then click **Continue**.

4. Step through the intro screens:

   ◆ **Welcome.** Read, and then click **Continue**.

   ◆ **Software License Agreement.** Read, click **Continue**, and then click **Agree**.

5. If an Authenticate dialog appears, enter the administrator name and password, and then click **OK**.

6. In the Select Destination screen, click to select the icon for the disk or partition to install Mac OS X.

   A green arrow appears on the disk or partition. If a yellow exclamation appears, there is an install issue with the drive.

7. To perform a custom install, click **Customize**, and then select or clear the components you want or don't want, and then click **OK**.

**IMPORTANT** *This is the last step in which you can back out of the installation. Click the Installer menu, click Quit Installer, and then click Quit to confirm. Hold down the mouse button to eject the Mac OS X DVD.*

8. Click **Install**, and then wait for the Installer to copy files.

9. Follow the on-screen instructions to complete the process. Your computer restarts and displays the first screen for the Setup Assistant.

## Did You Know?

*You can use Time Machine to back up and restore your Mac OS X.* After you have created a back up using Time Machine, you can use it to restore everything on your computer. Insert the install DVD, double-click the Install icon, and click Utilities, click Restart. Select a language, click Continue, click the Utilities menu, click Restore System From Backup, click Continue, select a backup source, and then follow the on-screen instructions.

*You can use another computer's drive to upgrade Mac OS X.* Connect both computer to the same network, install DVD or CD Sharing software (available at apple.com for Mac or Windows) on the computer with the drive, turn on DVD or CD Sharing in Sharing preferences. Insert the install DVD in the drive. On the computer where you want to install Mac OS X, select the Remote Disc under Devices in a Finder window sidebar. On the computer with the install DVD, click Accept, select the disc, open the installer, and then follow the onscreen instructions.

Custom options

## For Your Information

### Erasing and Partitioning a Hard Disk

During the Mac OS X install, you can erase the hard disk you plan to install Snow Leopard and install a clean version with the factory settings. Insert the install DVD, double-click the Install icon, and click Utilities, click Restart. Select a language, click Continue, click the Utilities menu, click Disk Utility, select a hard drive, and then click the Erase tab. Click the Format pop-up menu, select Mac OS Extended (Journaled), type a name for the disk, and then click Erase. In addition, you can partition your hard disk into several volumes before you install Mac OS X. When you partition a disk into volumes, the entire disk is erases, so it's important to back up your files first. In Disk Utility, click Partition. When you partition the disk, you need to select a disk format. The typical choice in most cases is Mac OS Extended (Journaled). Upon completion, quit Disk Utility, and then follow the remaining on-screen instructions to complete the install.

# Configuring Mac OS X Snow Leopard

After you install Mac OS X Snow Leopard, your computer restarts and displays the Setup Assistant, which helps you configure Snow Leopard to your specific needs. The Setup Assistant is a program that steps you through the process using a simple question and answer format. The information you enter is automatically used in System Preferences to customize your Mac OS X environment. The Setup Assistant allows you to configure options for personal identification, Internet account, telephone or DSL modem connection, network usage, e-mail account, and the date & time. Unfortunately, there is not a way to take screen shots of the configuration process, so illustrations are not available for the configuration parts.

## Configure Mac OS X Snow Leopard

① Install Mac OS X Snow Leopard.

Your computer restarts and displays the first screen for the Setup Assistant.

② In the Welcome window, select a country or region, and then click **Continue**.

③ Select a transfer information from another Mac option, click **Continue**, and then follow the on-screen instructions to complete the transfer.

④ Select a keyboard layout, and then click **Continue**.

⑤ Specify the requested Apple ID information, and then click **Continue**.

◆ **Already have an Apple ID.** Type your Apple ID and password (if you registered for a .Mac account or on the Apple Web site).

◆ **Create an Apple ID for me.** Creates an Apple ID for you later. Leave the Apple ID and password blank.

**6** Step through the following screens:

◆ **Registration.** Read, and then click **Continue**.

◆ **A Few More Questions.** Read, and then click **Continue**.

**7** Step through the following screens:

◆ **Create Your Account.** Specify the requested information to create your user account, and then click **Continue**.

◆ **Select a Picture For This Account.** Take a snapshot or select a picture, and then click **Continue**.

**8** When the Thank You window appears, click **Go** to complete the process.

**9** The Software Update utility may automatically start after installing Mac OS X Snow Leopard if there are any software updates available from Apple. Select the items you want to install, and then click Install X Items.

**10** To eject the Install DVD, right-click or Option-click the Mac OS X Install DVD icon on the desktop, and then click Eject "Mac OS X Install DVD."

---

**Software Update**

**New software is available for your computer.**

If you don't want to install now, choose Apple menu > Software Update when you're ready to install.

| Install | Name | Version | Size |
|---------|------|---------|------|
| ☑ | Snow Leopard Developer Preview Up... | 10A402 | 1.31 GB |

This Snow Leopard Developer Preview Update is recommended for all users running the Snow Leopard Developer Preview Build 10A394 or later. This update includes general operating system fixes for stability, compatibility, and security.

Note: Use of this software is subject to the original Software License Agreement(s) that accompanied the software being updated. A list of Apple SLAs may be found here: http://www.apple.com/legal/sla/.

○ You must restart your computer after the update is installed.

( Hide Details )          ( Not Now )  ( Install 1 Item )

**9**

# Downloading Mac OS X Tools from Apple

Mac OS X provides additional programs and tools you can download from the Web that may not be included in the Automatic Software Update. These programs include the non essentials that are not required by the system, but make computer life easier and much more fun. You can download screen savers, icons, system/disk utilities, productivity tools, games, and much more. Developers are continually upgrading applications, utilities, and games, so check the Apple Web site from time to time for the latest and greatest stuff.

## Download and Install Mac OS X Tools, Etc.

1. Open your Web browser.

2. Go to *www.apple.com*.

3. Click the **Downloads** tab.

    **TIMESAVER** *Click the Apple menu, and then click Mac OS X Software to access this Web page directly.*

4. Click a category link to narrow down the list of downloads.

5. Explore the page, and then click any of the links to find out more about a product and download it to your computer.

6. When you're done, quit your Web browser.

# New! Features

## Mac OS X Snow Leopard

Mac OS X Snow Leopard means superior results faster, with new features and enhancements that help you build Web sites and Internet applications. It provides a combination of visual layout tools, application development features, and code editing support, enabling developers and designers at every skill level to create visually appealing, standards-based sites and applications quickly and easily.

## Only New Features

If you're already familiar with Mac OS X Leopard, you can access and download Mac OS X Snow Leopard New Features to help make your transition to the new version simple and smooth. The Mac OS X Snow Leopard New Features as well as other Mac OS X Leopard to Mac OS X Snow Leopard transition helpers are available on the Web at *www.perspection.com*.

## What's New

If you're searching for what's new in Mac OS X Snow Leopard, just look for the icon: New!. The new icon appears in the table of contents and throughout this book so you can quickly and easily identify a new or improved feature in Mac OS X Snow Leopard. The following is a brief description of each new feature and it's location in this book.

## Mac OS X Snow Leopard

- ◆ **Faster Shutdown and Wake Up  (p. 24)**   Snow Leopard is up to 75 percent faster when shutting down, twice as fast when waking up from sleep and 55 percent faster joining wireless networks.

- ◆ **Date in Menu Bar  (p. 105)**   You can display the date alongside the time in the menu bar.

- ◆ **Text Substitution  (p. 108-109)**   You can create symbol and text substitution that automatically change as you type. For example, you can type (c) to insert ©.

- ◆ **More Synchronization Options  (p. 142)**   You can now synchronize contacts through MobileMe, Yahoo!, and Google.

- ◆ **New Fonts (p. 153)**   Snow Leopard includes more fonts: Terminal, Chalkduster (Heiti J, K, SC, and TC), and Hiragino Sans GB.

- ◆ **Chinese Handwriting Input (p. 169)**   You can use the Multi-Touch trackpad to draw Chinese characters.

- ◆ **Updated Thesaurus (p. 174)**   Snow Leopard includes the Oxford American Writer's Thesaurus, second edition.

- ◆ **Bidirectional Text (p. 177)**   You can use a split-cursor to work with languages written right to left, such as Hebrew and Arabic, along with languages written left to right.

- ◆ **Automatic Updates for Printer Drivers (p. 197)**   When you plug in a new printer, Snow Leopard downloads the appropriate driver. Periodically, Snow Leopard checks to make sure it has the lastest driver using Software Update as needed.

- ◆ **AirPort Menu Signal Strength (p. 224)**   The AirPort item in the menu bar includes signal strength for all visible wireless networks.

- ◆ **Improved File Sharing (p. 404-405)**   When your computer goes to sleep, you can continue to share its files with other computers and devices.

- ◆ **Redesigned Services Menu (p. 436, 495)**   The Services menu is context based for the selected application and customizable. You can also create automated services using Automator.

- ◆ **HFS+ Read Support in Book Camp (p. 472)**   Boot Camp allows you to access the files on your Mac OS X partition from Windows.

- ◆ **Faster Time Machine Backup (p. 478)**   The initial backup time when using time Capsule is up to 50 percent faster.

- ◆ **Starting Points for Automator (p. 495)**   You can create workflows using new templates: Workflow, Applications, Services, Folder Actions, Print Plugin, iCal Alarm, and Image Capture Plugin.

- ◆ **Smaller Installation (p. 514)**   Snow Leopard takes up less hard disk space (up to 6 GB) than Leopard.

- ◆ **Faster Installer (p. 516)**   Snow Leopard includes the Oxford American Writer's Thesaurus, second edition.

- ◆ **Digital Asset Exchange Support**   Collada Digital Asset Exchange (.dae) files support 3D models, which you can zoom and rotate in a 3D scene and play viewpoint animations. You can also use Quick Look to display them.

- ◆ **Split Pane Terminal**   In Terminal, you can use a split window for different terminal sessions so you can compare information.

## Finder

- ◆ **Enhanced Icon View (p. 11, 30)**   You can thumb through a multipage document, such as a PDF, or watch a QuickTime movie in Icon view.

- ◆ **Larger Icon Sizes  (p. 12)**   In Icon view, you can use a slider to adjust the size of the icon previews up to 512 by 512 pixels.

- ◆ **Remove Sidebar Headers  (p. 16)**   If you remove all the items under a header, such as Devices, in the side, the header disappears. When you add an item back to the sidebar, the header appears.

- ◆ **Restore Deleted Items  (p. 48-49)**   If you put an item in the Trash, then change your mind, you can restore it to its original location by using the Put Back command.

- ◆ **Show/Hide Sidebar  (p. 86)**   You can show or hide the sidebar in a Finder window.

## Dock

- ◆ **Activate Expose from the Dock  (p. 14, 18, 20)**   You can click and hold an application icon in the Dock to start Expose. Press the tab key to move to the next application.

- ◆ **Scroll Through Stacks (p. 19)**   In Grid view, you can scroll through stacks from the Dock.

- ◆ **Navigate Folders in Stacks  (p. 19)**   In Grid view, you can open a folder in a stack to view the files inside. When you're done, you can use the return path icon to return to the previous folder location.

- ◆ **Assign Applications to Spaces  (p. 21, 93)**   You can spread out your work in different spaces by assigning an application to a space from its icon in the Dock.

## Spotlight

- ◆ **View Options  (p. 62)**   You can adjust view options for Spotlight results just like the Finder.

- ◆ **Sort Search Results  (p. 62)**   You can sort search results by name, date modified, dated created, size, kind, and label. Use the Action menu and Keep Arranged By submenu to select a sort field.

- ◆ **Change Search Locations  (p. 64, 78)**   You can change the default search locations for Spotlight to the current folder or most recent search location.

## System Preferences

- ◆ **Set Time Delay for Screen Locking  (p. 22)**   When you require a password to wake up from a sleep, you can add a time delay before the password is required.

- ◆ **Screen Save Shuffle  (p. 103)**   You can shuffle through screen saver photos just as you shuffle through songs in iTunes.

- ◆ **Automatic Time Zone Setting  (p. 104)**   You can automatically use Wi-Fi hotspots to set the time zone for the current location.

- ◆ **Language and Text Preferences (p. 106-107)** The Language and Text Preferences pane replaces the International preference pane. The Text tab allows you to substitute symbols and text in applications.

- ◆ **Multi-Touch Gesture (p. 452)** All Mac notebooks with a Multi-Touch trackpad supports three- or four-finder gestures.

## iCal

- ◆ **Automatic Setup (p. 366)** iCal can automatically setup up Gmail, Yahoo!, and Google calendars.

- ◆ **Show Inspector (p. 370-371)** The Inspector window is available at all time when you can view the details for multiple events.

## iChat

- ◆ **Different Statuses for Multiple Chat Accounts (p. 294)** If you log in to multiple account, you can have a different status for each one.

- ◆ **Select To or From Account (p. 300)** When you have multiple accounts, you can select a To or From account to use during a conversation.

- ◆ **Date and Time Stamp Conversations (p. 301)** You can mark your conversations with the current date and time.

- ◆ **Show Past Conversations (p. 301, 311)** If you save your conversations, you can have iChat automatically save the last 5, 25, 100, or 250 messages.

- ◆ **Search for a Buddy in Spotlight (p. 302)** You can search for a buddy's IM address in Spotlight.

- ◆ **Quick Look Capable (p. 303)** When you receive a file in iChat, you can instantly preview it with Quick Look.

- ◆ **High Resolution iChat Theater (p. 306)** iChat can display iChat Theater content at higher resolution, up to 640 x 480.

- ◆ **Lower Bandwidth (p. 306)** iChat requires just 300 Kbps bandwidth to deliver near DVD quality, 640 x 480 video chats.

- ◆ **Close Other Chats (p. 309)** When you have multiple chats open at the same time, you can Control-click the active chat, and then click Close Other Chats to exit the others.

## Mail

- ◆ **Support for Microsoft Exchange (p. 260-261)** Mail provides built-in support for Microsoft Exchange 2007. You can use your Mac to work with all your messages, contacts, and calendars in one place.

- **Reorderable Sidebar  (p. 278)**   You can rearrange items on the sidebar where you want them.

- **Flight Data Detector  (p. 268)**   Mail includes a data detector for airline flights. Mail can identify flight numbers and then take you directly to the Dashboard Flight Tracker widget to get up-to-date flight information.

## Preview

- **Smart Text Selection (p. 150-151)**   Preview uses artificial intelligence to identify the components of a PDF so it can select text more effectively.

- **Image Scaling  (p. 150-151)**   The Adjust Image Size command provides higher-quality image scaling.

- **Multiple Documents in a Window  (p. 150-151)**   You can open multiple PDFs in a single document window.

- **Import from Scanner  (p. 150-151)**   You can scan, view, and correct your files and images in Preview. the scanner detects the placement of images and documents on the scanner.

- **Annotation Toolbar  (p. 150-151)**   Provides tools to annotate a document.

- **Soft Proof with Profile  (p. 150-151)**   Allows you to see what your images will look like when printed, on the Web, or on a printing press.

- **Contact Sheet for Images  (p. 150-151)**   You can display multiple images in a document as a contact sheet of thumbnails.

- **Image Correction Histogram  (p. 150-151)**   You can adjust images using a live RGB histogram.

## QuickTime Player

- **Improved Player  (p. 334)**   QuickTime Player displays movies with a new interface and high-quality video.

- **Visual Chapters (p. 334)**   QuickTime Player displays frame-based thumbnail images for each chapter marker instead of text-only.

- **Live HTTP Streaming  (p. 334)**   QuickTime X uses HTTP live streaming technology to playback live video online using a Web server, such as Mac OS X Server and Apache.

- **Improved Color Accuracy  (p. 334)**   QuickTime X improves color management and capabilities of ColorSync.

- **Accelerated Video Decoding  (p. 334)**   QuickTime X uses GPU (Graphics Processing Unit) to decode video in order to provide a more fluid playback and free up CPU (Central Processing Unit) for other tasks.

- **Trim a Movie  (p. 336-337)**   You can trim unwanted portions from the beginning or end using frame-based thumbnails to make it easier.

◆ **Capture Live Audio or Video (p. 336-337)** You can capture live audio and video using your iSight camera, FireWire camcorder, or microphone.

◆ **Record your Screen (p. 336-337)** You can record the steps you take on your computer screen.

◆ **Save for the Web (p. 336-337)** You can save movies for use on the Web, which includes iPhone and Computer.

◆ **Share Media (p. 336-337)** You can share movies in a format for use on iTunes, MobileMe, and YouTube.

## Safari

◆ **Top Sites (p. 234-235)** Tracks and previews your favorite sites in a thumbnail view.

◆ **Full History Search with Cover Flow (p. 236, 238)** Search and browse history and bookmarks in Cover Flow.

◆ **Faster Browsing and More Resistant to Crashes** The browser displays JavaScript 50 percent faster. If a browser plug-in crashes, the content stops working, but Safari continues to run.

## TextEdit

◆ **Automatic Spelling Correction (p. 171-172)** You can automatically fix spelling errors as you type.

◆ **Support for Data Detectors (p. 171)** TextEdit detects text, like dates and addresses, in a document and allows you to create a new contact, map an address, or create an iCal event.

## Universal Access

◆ **VoiceOver Trackpad Control (p. 122-125)** You can control VoiceOver using your trackpad, which represents the active window.

◆ **Greater Braille Device Support (p. 122-125)** Snow Leopard adds greater support for braille displays, which includes wireless Bluetooth devices.

◆ **Browse Web Pages with Web Spots (p. 122-125)** Snow Leopard can identify important areas of a Web page, so you can jump from one important spot to another without having to view every element on the page.

◆ **Automatically Read Web Pages (p. 122-125)** VoiceOver can begin reading a Web page immediately when the page is loaded.

◆ **Web Table Support (p. 120-125)** VoiceOver provides full support for navigating Web tables.

# Index

Watch Me Do action, 502
window, parts of, 492-494
Workflow log and panes, 493, 494
Workflow variable list, 493, 494
working with workflows, 503
autosaving TextEdit preferences, 194

## B

Back button on toolbar, 17
backdrops in Photo Booth, 331
backgrounds
    desktop backgrounds, selecting, 102
    in e-mail message text, 269
    iChat window background, changing, 311
backing up, 477. *See also* archiving; disk
        image; Time Machine
    on CDs or DVDs, 490
    compressed files and folders, 435
    e-mail, 281
    formatting, backups prior to, 438
    iCal calendar, 371
    to iDisk, 479
    iTunes library, 327
    MobileMe, backing up files, 358-359
Back to My Mac, accessing computer with,
        420-421
baseline for characters, changing, 182
BBEdit, 436
BinHex format, 251
birthday calendars, 369
blocking
    e-mail, 284-285
    iChat buddies, 302
    pop-up windows, 255
Bluetooth. *See also* iSync
    Application Services with, 436
    desktop icon, 5
    with Mac for Windows, 465, 472-473
    making Internet connection with, 226
    moving items with, 414
    Passkey with, 413
    preferences, setting, 415
    printers, installing, 199
    setting up network, 412-413
    sharing, 405
boldfacing
    document text, 178

e-mail message text, 269
    fonts, 155
Bonjour, 289
    list of Web sites, viewing, 238
    printers
        installing, 198-199
        sharing, 202-203
    problems with, 308
    saving chats, 311
    starting messaging, 309
    turning on, 308
bookmarks. *See also* Safari
    with DVD Player, 333
Bookmarks Library. *See* Safari
Boolean operators with Spotlight search, 57
Boot Camp Assistant, 112, 465. *See also*
        Mac for Windows
    installing Windows on Mac, 468-469
    preparing Mac for Windows, 466-467
    removing Windows with, 474-475
    upgrading from beta, 467
BOOTP (boot protocol), 223
borders for table cells, 185
bouncing e-mail, 284-285
Braille, VoiceOver supporting, 122, 125
brightness on monitor, changing, 454
broadband connection. *See* cable modems
browsers. *See* Web browsers
buddies. *See* iChat
bulleted lists, 184
    in e-mail message text, 269
burning. *See* CDs; DVDs
Business, Dashboard displaying, 158-159
.bzip files, opening, 434

## C

cable modems, 220
    Ethernet with, 223
    firewalls for, 409
    sharing connection, 408
cache
    for e-mail, 260
    Safari cache, emptying, 236
calculations. *See also* Calculator
    Grapher, creating graphs with, 145
Calculator, 130
    conversions, performing, 146-147

VLAN (Virtual Local Area Network), 429